A New Star-Rating System & Other Exciting News from Frommer's!

In our continuing effort to publish the savviest, most up-to-date, and most appealing travel guides available, we've added some great new features.

Frommer's guides now include a new **star-rating system.** Every hotel, restaurant, and attraction is rated from 0 to 3 stars to help you set priorities and organize your time.

We've also added **seven brand-new features** that point you to the great deals, in-the-know advice, and unique experiences that separate travelers from tourists. Throughout the guide, look for:

Finds   Special finds—those places only insiders know about

Fun Fact   Fun facts—details that make travelers more informed and their trips more fun

Kids   Best bets for kids—advice for the whole family

Moments   Special moments—those experiences that memories are made of

Overrated   Places or experiences not worth your time or money

Tips   Insider tips—some great ways to save time and money

Value   Great values—where to get the best deals

Here's what the critics say about Frommer's:

"Amazingly easy to use. Very portable, very complete."

—*Booklist*

"Detailed, accurate, and easy-to-read information for all price ranges."
—*Glamour Magazine*

"Hotel information is close to encyclopedic."
—*Des Moines Sunday Register*

"Frommer's Guides have a way of giving you a real feel for a place."
—*Knight Ridder Newspapers*

Frommer's®

Chicago with Kids

1st Edition

by Laura Tiebert

Wiley Publishing, Inc.

About the Author

Laura Tiebert is a freelance writer whose travels have taken her from the frozen tundra of Dawson City in Yukon Territory to the wide beaches of Muscat, Oman. A native Midwesterner, she lived in New York City for years before returning to Chicago. Today, she stays a bit closer to home in Evanston, IL, where she lives with her husband, Andrew, and son, Joel, born just after the first draft of this book was completed.

Published by:

Wiley Publishing, Inc.

909 Third Ave.
New York, NY 10022

ISBN 0-7645-6724-1
ISSN 1541-6372

Editor: Myka Carroll
Production Editor: M. Faunette Johnston
Cartographer: Roberta Stockwell
Photo Editor: Richard Fox
Production by Wiley Indianapolis Composition Services

For information on our other products and services or to obtain technical support, please contact our Customer Care Department within the U.S. at 800-762-2974, outside the U.S. at 317-572-3993 or fax 317-572-4002.

Wiley also publishes its books in a variety of electronic formats. Some content that appears in print may not be available in electronic formats.

Manufactured in the United States of America

5 4 3 2 1

Contents

List of Maps

An Invitation to the Reader

In researching this book, we discovered many wonderful places—hotels, restaurants, shops, and more. We're sure you'll find others. Please tell us about them, so we can share the information with your fellow travelers in upcoming editions. If you were disappointed with a recommendation, we'd love to know that, too. Please write to:

Frommer's Chicago with Kids, 1st Edition
Wiley Publishing, Inc. • 909 Third Ave. • New York, NY 10022

An Additional Note

Please be advised that travel information is subject to change at any time—and this is especially true of prices. We therefore suggest that you write or call ahead for confirmation when making your travel plans. The authors, editors, and publisher cannot be held responsible for the experiences of readers while traveling. Your safety is important to us, however, so we encourage you to stay alert and be aware of your surroundings. Keep a close eye on cameras, purses, and wallets, all favorite targets of thieves and pickpockets.

New! Frommer's Star Ratings & Icons

Every hotel, restaurant, and attraction listing in this guide has been ranked for quality, value, service, amenities, and special features using a star-rating scale. In country, state, and regional guides, we also rate towns and regions to help you narrow down your choices and budget your time accordingly. Hotels and restaurants are rated on a scale of zero stars (recommended) to three stars (exceptional). Attractions, towns, and regions are rated according to the following scale: zero stars (recommended), one star (highly recommended), two stars (very highly recommended), and three stars (must-see).

In addition to the rating system, we also use seven icons to highlight insider information, useful tips, special bargains, hidden gems, memorable experiences, kid-friendly venues, places to avoid, and other useful information:

| Finds | Fun Fact | Kids | Moments | Overrated | Tips | Value |

The following abbreviations are used for credit cards:

AE American Express	DISC Discover	V Visa
DC Diners Club	MC MasterCard	

FROMMERS.COM

Now that you have the guidebook to a great trip, visit our website at **www.frommers.com** for travel information on nearly 2,500 destinations. With features updated regularly, we give you instant access to the most current trip-planning information available. At Frommers.com, you'll also find the best prices on airfares, accommodations, and car rentals—and you can even book travel online through our travel booking partners. At Frommers.com, you'll also find the following:

- Online updates to our most popular guidebooks
- Vacation sweepstakes and contest giveaways
- Newsletter highlighting the hottest travel trends
- Online travel message boards with featured travel discussions

How to Feel Like a Chicago Family

What's the best part about visiting Chicago with your kids? On the positive side, Chicago is a big city. You'll find a rich diversity in cultures and languages and the opportunity to expose your kids to many different sights, sounds, and people. Free activities abound: Parks, a zoo, and the beach are a few of Chicago kids' favorite things—and they won't cost you a penny. Transportation is easy: Kids love the "El", carriage rides, trolley cars, and buses. And most activities are located around a compact city center—a brief bus or train ride from hotels on the Magnificent Mile or in River North or the Loop will get you to any of the downtown museums or the Lincoln Park Zoo. You'll always find a coffee shop just around the corner, great restaurants and shopping, and miles of walkable terrain for you and your kids.

The negatives? Chicago is a big city. Streets, shops, and museums can get crowded in the summer. Panhandlers can be a problem in certain congested downtown areas. Traffic can be hazardous—you'll need to be extra careful around busy intersections. (***Warning:*** Cabs will not slow down for anyone— even families with kids). The "El" is not always stroller-friendly and getting through the station onto the train can be challenging. You may find yourself having to walk up flights of stairs carrying the diaper bag, stroller, and more.

Is it worth it? Millions of visitors who flock to our city every year can't be wrong.

As I wrote this book, I had a very special interest in exploring Chicago with kids: My husband and I were expecting our first child in fall 2002. With this impending parenthood not only came a curiosity about how life would change for us in the big city, but also a welcome by fellow parents into their ranks. They were very generous in sharing their stories about how best to experience Chicago with kids. I have them to thank for the wide variety of activities, advice, and opinions you'll find in this book.

In this book, I am working on three assumptions: One is that when you travel with kids, there has to be something in it for them. You can't expect kids to enjoy adult activities. (In fact, take a kid into a fancy department store or to a fine French restaurant, and the parents might not enjoy it either!) But while we want to keep the kids happy, the goal of this book is to find activities that offer something for parents and kids alike.

The second assumption is a preference for the simple over the complex. Take your 3-year-old to the zoo and she may wind up spending more time watching squirrels chase each other than the big cats emerging from their dens. And that's okay. Later on, she'll appreciate the larger animals! I emphasize some off-the-beaten track, simple (and often inexpensive) ideas for entertaining your kids. These ideas have been contributed and road-tested by a cadre of Chicago parents.

The third is that you will seek out activities that are unique to Chicago. Now, some people are comfortable going to Hard Rock Cafe or Six Flags because they have them in their own city—and their kids like that sort of predictability. More power to you—and those places are certainly listed in this guidebook. My focus, however, is on transportation, museums, and food that say "Chicago."

This city can be a magical place for families, filled with new discoveries and favorite places you'll want to visit again and again over the years. Many of my friends recall annual trips to Chicago with great fondness. Breakfast with Santa at the Walnut Room at Marshall Field's, Colleen Moore's Fairy Castle at the Museum of Science and Industry, and Buckingham Fountain's invigorating spray on a windy day will soon become part of your family lore, too.

1 Frommer's Favorite Chicago Family Experiences

Chicago has made vast strides in beautifying the city and developing visitor-friendly attractions. The best news for families is the creation of Museum Campus, now (in my humble opinion) the number-one collection of museums located on one walkable campus in the country. The campus brought together three great Chicago institutions—the Field Museum of Natural History, John G. Shedd Aquarium, and Adler Planetarium & Astronomy Museum—by actually rerouting major streets to make the area more pedestrian-friendly. In addition, Millennium Park, Chicago's overdue new park near Michigan Avenue and the Art Institute, is beginning to take shape. Navy Pier was rehabilitated and opened in the mid-1990s, quickly becoming the city's number-one tourist destination. The North Loop theater district has risen from a decades-long slumber. And, the retail expansion along the city's fabled Magnificent Mile has yet to slow down.

From the simple pleasures of summer baseball to the complexities of the world of science, here are my favorite Chicago experiences for families.

- **Encountering Jurassic Wonders:** Sue, the largest T-rex skeleton ever uncovered, has made the Field Museum her home. (Don't be taken aback by her intimidating presence in the museum's grand entry hall). But don't be surprised if your kids are just as much in awe of the Field's many classic kid

charmers: a life-size Egyptian tomb, rooms of glittering gemstones, the royal Cameroon palace from Africa, and hundreds of stuffed animals (not of the teddy bear variety) in their habitat. Beware of the Field's mesmerizing qualities on adults and kids alike: A friend of mine began meditating in an Indian tepee, only to open his eyes and find the museum closed! See p. 128.

- **Exploring Underwater Life:** Most kids have a fascination for life under the sea, and an afternoon watching dolphins frolic and colorful tropical fish swim circles around a mammoth tank is sure to enthrall. John G. Shedd Aquarium, with its all-time favorite dolphin show and precious Beluga whales, is a sure-fire winner with kids. See p. 131.

- **Marveling at the Innovations of Science and Industry:** You can't go wrong at the Museum of Science and Industry, Chicago's perennial kids' favorite. Watch chicks hatch in an incubator. Catch an IMAX movie at the Henry Crown space theater. Step aboard a captured World War II U-boat or a retired 727 United Airlines jetliner. Travel deep into a replica of a Southern Illinois coal mine. With so much to do, you might want to divide and conquer by spending a couple of afternoons here. See p. 134.

- **Taking to the Water from Navy Pier:** Chicago's number-one tourist attraction is home to another kids' favorite—the Chicago Children's Museum. Navy Pier is also the jumping-off point for many of the boat tours of Lake Michigan, so find a vessel that's your speed, from power-boats to tall-masted schooners, and take to the water! See p. 135.

- **Talking to the Animals:** Located within Chicago's famous lakefront park, the Lincoln Park Zoo is convenient, compact, and charming. And what's not to love about a place that's open 365 days a year, and never charges a cent for admission? This, the nation's oldest zoo, is famous for its major collection of gorillas. The adjoining Farm-in-the-Zoo allows urban kids to wander a working farm and meet cows, pigs, horses, chicks, and goats. See p. 162.

- **Riding the "El":** *L* is not just the 12th letter of the alphabet, but also the greatest, least expensive entertainment your kids will enjoy in Chicago. Hop a southbound Brown Line elevated train, and watch the city unfold as the train crosses the Chicago River and screeches through downtown canyons. See "Kid-Friendly Tours," in chapter 6.

- **Cruising Chicago's Waterways:** A Chicago River cruise should be one of your first stops in our fair city. I didn't step aboard until I'd lived in the city for 2 years—and boy, did I miss out! Older kids will love the Chicago Architecture Foundation's river cruise. Wee ones will get a kick out of the Buccaneer Pirate Adventure Cruises. Either way, the best way to see Chicago's world-renowned architecture is from the water. See "Kid-Friendly Tours," in chapter 6.

- **Ogling Our Inland Ocean:** Chicago's magnificent lakefront is an emerald strand of parks and sand beaches, linked by running, walking, rollerblading, and biking trails. Don't be surprised when our great lake looks more like the ocean to your kids. At 22,300 square miles in size and reaching depths of 900 feet, you can't see across Lake Michigan. And, it's the only Great Lake that lies wholly in U.S. Territory. Chicago is blessed with 29 miles of lakefront for biking, 'blading, or simply being, so get out there and enjoy the country's "third coast." See "Enjoying the 'Third Coast': Chicago's Beaches," in chapter 8.

- **Getting the Blues:** Even kids can get the blues, thanks to alcohol- and smoke-free nights at Blue Chicago, one of the city's many fabled blues venues (p. 230). The blues is the first original music of America and the basis for rock 'n' roll. It's an authentic piece of Chicago's heart and soul that you absolutely should not miss. If you want to learn more, read *Blues for Dummies,* written by the father-and-son team of Lonnie Brooks and Wayne Baker Brooks, two of Chicago's beloved blues musicians.

- **Rooting for the Home Team:** Win or lose (and sorry to say, historically speaking, it's usually lose) an afternoon at Wrigley Field is a thrill for kids and adults alike. Even if the Cubbies aren't hitting them out of the park, hot dogs, peanuts in the shell, and a rousing rendition of "Take Me Out to the Ballgame" are sure to please. This most charming of major league ballparks is a slice of Americana that you should not miss. One afternoon spent in the embrace of the Friendly Confines will have you hooked on the sheer magic of Wrigley Field. See p. 236.

Chicago & Vicinity

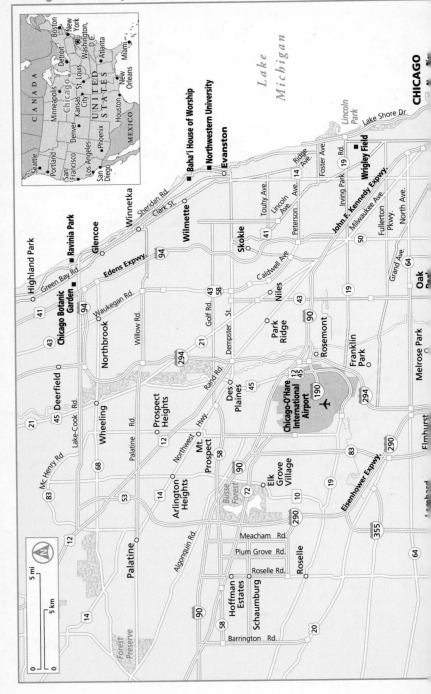

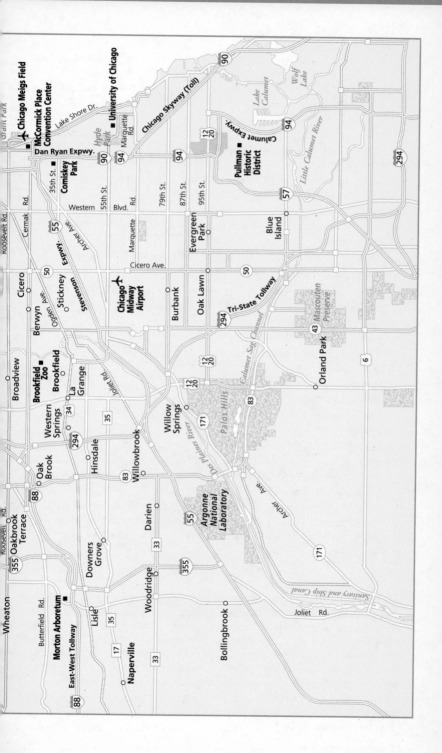

C Chicago Dateline

1673 French explorers Marquette and Joliet discover portage at Chicago linking the Great Lakes region with the Mississippi River valley.

1779 Afro-French-Canadian trapper Jean Baptiste Point du Sable establishes a trading post on the north bank of the Chicago River. A settlement follows 2 years later.

1794 General "Mad" Anthony Wayne defeats the British in the Battle of Fallen Timbers; disputed Illinois Territory is finally ceded to the young American Republic by treaty a year later.

1803 Garrison of Fort Dearborn is established in Chicago, commanded by the grandfather of artist James McNeill Whistler.

1818 Illinois is admitted to the Union as the 21st state.

1833 Town of Chicago is officially incorporated, with little more than 300 residents.

1837 Chicago is incorporated as a city, with about 4,000 residents.

1847 The *Chicago Tribune* begins publishing.

1848 The 96-mile Illinois and Michigan Canal is opened, linking the Great Lakes with the Mississippi River.

1850 Chicago's population is roughly 30,000.

1856 Chicago is chief railroad center in the United States.

1870 Chicago's population numbers almost 300,000, making it perhaps the fastest-growing metropolis in history.

1871 The Great Chicago Fire burns large sections of the city; rebuilding begins while the ashes are still warm.

1882 The 10-story Montauk Building, the world's first skyscraper, is erected.

1892 The city's first elevated train goes into operation.

1893 Completely recovered from the Great Fire, Chicago hosts its first World's Fair, the World's Columbian Exposition. The world's first Ferris wheel is a big draw.

1905 Robert S. Abbott founds the *Chicago Defender,* which becomes the nation's premier African-American newspaper and later plays a major role in encouraging Southern blacks to move north during the "Great Migration" years.

2 The Best Hotel Bets

You won't find them a bargain, but several years of expansion and new construction for Chicago hotels means the city offers a wide variety, from hip boutique hotels to huge facilities for convention-goers, and thankfully, a nice crop of family-friendly hotels. (The downside: Room rates keep rising, making budget lodgings harder to find). The recent Chicago debuts of the luxury Peninsula, Le Méridien, and Sofitel chains prove that the city's building boom shows no signs of slowing.

- **Most Family Friendly:** With cribs, laundry service, and every room a suite, the **Embassy Suites**

1908   The Chicago Cubs win their second World Series. They haven't won one since.

1917   The Chicago White Sox win the World Series—and they also haven't won one since.

1920–33   During Prohibition, Chicago becomes a "wide-open town"; rival mobs battle violently throughout the city for control of distribution and sale of illegal alcohol.

1931   Notorious Chicago gangster Al Capone finally goes to jail—for tax evasion.

1942   Scientists, led by Enrico Fermi, create the world's first nuclear chain reactions under Stagg Field at the University of Chicago.

1955   Richard J. Daley begins his term as mayor; he is widely regarded as the "last of the big-city bosses."

1960   John F. Kennedy and Richard Nixon hold the first televised presidential debate in WBBM-TV's studios.

1966   Civil rights leader Martin Luther King, Jr., moves to Chicago to lead a fair housing campaign.

1974   The 1,454-foot Sears Tower is completed, becoming the tallest building in the world.

1979   Jane Byrne becomes the first woman elected mayor of Chicago.

1983   Harold Washington becomes the first African-American mayor of Chicago.

1986   The Chicago Bears win their only Super Bowl.

1999   Michael Jordan, arguably the best basketball player ever, retires (for the second time) after leading the Chicago Bulls to six NBA championships in the previous 8 years.

2000   The Goodman Theatre opens its new $46 million theater complex in the Loop, completing the revitalization of the downtown theater district.

2002   Millennium Park, Chicago's largest public works project in decades, rises at the north end of Grant Park. The centerpiece—a steel-sheathed band shell—is designed by architect Frank Gehry.

Hotel Chicago–Downtown, 600 N. State St. (✆ **800/362-2779**), is ideal for families looking for a little more space than the typical hotel room provides. The in-room Nintendo, indoor pool, and location near a couple popular kid-friendly venues—ESPN Zone and the Hard Rock Cafe—should keep Junior happy, too. See p. 74.

- **Best Neighborhood Hotel:** Children 12 and under stay free at **Best Western Hawthorne Terrace Hotel,** 3434 N. Broadway (✆ **888/675-2378**). Small in size, with 59 rooms and junior suites, the rooms offer refrigerators, microwaves, and irons. Parking is a bargain at $16 a day. See p. 80.

- **Best Views:** This isn't an easy call. Peering over the elevated tracks, **The Silversmith,** 10 S. Wabash Ave. (© **800/2CROWNE**), in the Loop, offers a distinctly urban vista; see p. 56 for more details. But consider several other hotels for their mix of lake and city views: **Four Seasons Hotel Chicago** (p. 62), **The Drake** (p. 60), **The Ritz-Carlton Chicago** (p. 65), and **Park Hyatt Chicago** (p. 64).

- **When Hipness Is Important:** A hip hotel that's known for romance is using its small size—and sense of whimsy—to cater to kids. **Hotel Burnham,** 1 W. Washington at State St. (© **877/294-9712**) keeps wee ones entertained with special offers for tea at American Girl Place Cafe and deals at the museums and theaters. During holidays, you'll find special activities in the hotel lobby, including decorating gingerbread men at Christmas and hunting for eggs at Easter. Diaper bags, cribs, high chairs, changing tables, and more are available upon request. Rooms are clubby but glamorous, with plush beds, mahogany writing desks, and chaise lounges. See p. 57.

- **When Price Is No Object:** The attention to detail, regal pampering, and well-connected concierges you will find at both the ultra-luxe **Ritz-Carlton Chicago,** 160 E. Pearson St. (© **800/621-6906;** p. 65), and **Four Seasons Hotel Chicago,** 120 E. Delaware Place (© **800/332-3442;** p. 62), make them the hotels of choice for travelers who want to feel like royalty while in town.

- **When Price Is Your Main Object: Red Roof Inn Chicago Downtown,** 162 E. Ontario St. (© **800/733-7663**), offers a fabulous location for a bargain price (p. 72). But the **Hampton Inn & Suites Chicago–Downtown,** 33 W. Illinois St. (© **800/HAMPTON**) gets bonus points for being a bargain stay, plus having a pool. See p. 74.

- **Best Pool:** With its dazzling all-tile junior Olympic-size pool constructed in 1929, the **Hotel InterContinental Chicago,** 505 N. Michigan Ave. (© **800/327-0200**), takes this award easily. See p. 68.

- **Best Hotel Restaurant for Kids:** Go for **Café Atwood,** the stylish and funky restaurant fronting State Street at **Hotel Burnham,** 1 W. Washington (© **877/294-9712**). Amazingly, this eclectic restaurant welcomes kids and features a special kids' menu. See p. 57.

- **Tops for Teens:** For a theatrical hotel experience, the **House of Blues Hotel,** 333 N. Dearborn St. (© **877/569-3742**), can't be beat, with its riotous mix of colors and playful attitude. See p. 73.

- **Tops for Toddlers: Homewood Suites,** 40 E. Grand Ave. (© **800/CALL-HOME**) offers cribs, high chairs, and babysitting services in a great location in River North. See p. 70.

3 The Best Dining Bets

With pizza and hot dogs among the city's signature dishes, Chicago is food heaven for kids. Before you run out and buy a case of antacids, however, take heart: Wonderful cuisine to please adults abounds, too. And I'm going to send you in that direction, right after I grab a garlic- and pepper-laden hot dog.

- **Best Views:** A location right on the Magnificent Mile means the **Hancock Observatory,** 875 N. Michigan Ave., offers an up-close-and-personal view of the city from its observation deck. Visit the **Signature Room at the 95th** (© 312/787-9596), a sleek restaurant with adjoining lounge after a long day of touring. On a clear day, you can see 50 miles and part of three surrounding states—Michigan, Indiana, and Wisconsin. (Moms and daughters, make sure to visit the restroom—it's got the best views in the restaurant!) See p. 140.

- **Best Ice Cream:** Since the 1920s, **Margie's Candies,** 1960 N. Western Ave., at Armitage Ave. (© 773/384-1035), has been serving up mammoth sundaes in conch shell–shaped dishes. Margie is gone now, but her husband still mans the cash register. Don't miss the homemade hot fudge, real butterscotch, and caramel. The place is frozen in time—about 1940, to be exact—and is stuffed with kitschy dolls, boxes of homemade candy, stuffed animals, and news clippings through the years. See p. 214.

- **Best Outdoor Eating:** Long tables and family-style dining reign in **Greektown,** making it a comfortable and fun destination for families; see "The Randolph Street Market District & Greektown," in chapter 5. At **Pegasus,** 130 S. Halsted St. (© 312/226-3377), a rooftop garden allows diners a panoramic view of the Chicago skyline. See p. 93.

- **Most Kid-Friendly Service:** Scoozi, an Italian restaurant in River North at 410 W. Huron, (© 312/943-5900), is a family favorite for its Sunday afternoon pizza-making event that lets kids loose with tomato sauce and cheese to create their own pizzas (under the supervision of Scoozi chefs, who keep mess to a minimum and pop finished pizzas into the wood-burning oven). The evening is great for parents, too, who get a short break to enjoy their meal and some grown-up conversation. Make a reservation, because your window of opportunity is small: The restaurant runs the program on Sundays only, from 4 to 5 pm. See p. 103.

- **Best Kids' Menu:** How many times have you seen the big three on kids' menus? Burgers, chicken fingers, and buttered noodles are great, but when you want to expand your horizons (just a little), head for **Wishbone,** 1001 Washington St. at Morgan St. (© 312/850-2663), or 3300 N. Lincoln Ave. (© 773/549-2663). You'll find a little southern flair to the kids' menu, with sweet potatoes and mac 'n' cheese among the offerings. See p. 92.

- **Best Burgers:** The hamburger at **Iron Mike's Grille,** 100 E. Chestnut St. (© 312/587-8989), tastes more like chopped steak and can easily feed two. Sports fans will be entertained by football memorabilia and Bears fans can relive the glory days of former Coach Mike Ditka, who owns the place. Take your kids to the main dining room, though, because the bar vicinity tends to get a little foggy from cigar smoke. See p. 94.

- **Best Barbecue:** At longtime city favorite **Carson's,** 612 N. Wells St. (© 312/280-9200), $17.95 gets you a full slab of incredible baby-back ribs, accompanied by a bowl of Carson's almost-as-famous coleslaw and a choice of potatoes. See p. 101.

- **Best Breakfast:** Although the restaurant is located in the young professional haven of Lincoln

Park, parents report that the managers and staff at **Toast,** 746 W. Webster St. at Halsted St., (*② 773/ 935-5600*), are baby- and kid-crazy. The pancakes and waffles are pretty crazy, too: Stacks arrive covered in fruit, yogurt, powdered sugar, and more. See p. 113.

- **Best Family-Style Dining: Maggiano's,** 516 N. Clark St. (*② 312/ 644-7700*), is a mecca for Italian family-style dining. Heaping plates of pasta meant to be shared make Maggiano's a good choice for a budget-conscious family. In fact, everything on the menu is super-size. Steaks are all more than a pound, and most pasta dishes weigh in at over 25 ounces. You're expected to share dishes, pass things around, and try a little bit of everything. See p. 102.

- **Best Asian Food:** If you go to **Big Bowl,** 6 E. Cedar St. at Rush St., (*② 312/640-8888*), at the beginning of your visit to Chicago, I guarantee you will make a repeat visit before you leave. The food here is addictive. From noodle soups to pad Thai (try the tofu and veggie version), your kids will find tons to love here. The restaurant bustles and kids will blend right in with the other activity. Make sure to grab a handful of individually wrapped fortune cookies on your way out! See p. 97.

- **Best Hot Dog: Gold Coast Dogs,** 418 N. State St. (*② 312/ 527-1222*), serves up the authentic item, meaning a Vienna All-Beef Frank slathered with mustard, green relish, chopped onion, sliced tomato, hot peppers, and celery salt. Your kids might be brave enough to ask for and receive ketchup, but as an adult, I wouldn't risk the disapproving, raised-eyebrow look you'll get from the counter staff. You can

round out the meal with cheese fries, made from Idaho potatoes and topped with a generous glob of Wisconsin cheddar. See p. 118.

- **Best Pizza:** In the town where deep-dish pies were born, Chicagoans take their out-of-town relatives to either **Gino's East,** 633 N. Wells St (*② 312/943- 1124; p. 104*), or **Lou Malnati's,** 439 N. Wells St. (*② 312/828- 9800; p. 118*), to taste the real thing: mouthwatering slabs of pizza loaded with fresh ingredients atop delectably sweet crusts. Lou's fan base is so enamored that the restaurant has even instituted a popular overnight mail-order business to get expatriate Chicagoans with a deep-dish jones over the hump.

- **Best Fast Food:** Even though you're in the hometown of McDonald's, our vote goes to **foodlife** in Water Tower Place, 835 N. Michigan Ave. (*② 312/ 335-3663*), a food court exemplar with everything from Asian noodles to pizza to smoothies. See p. 99.

- **Best Brunch:** Cajun and southern cooking is in store for you at **Wishbone,** 1001 W. Washington Blvd. (*② 312/850-2663*). Primitive art, bright colors, and a bustling crowd make this a great place for kids. A diverse crowd, from Harpo Studios employees (Oprah is headquartered right around the corner) to business people in suits and ad agency types, frequent the place. For brunch, try the salmon cakes. See p. 92.

- **Best Girls' Day Out:** Can't help but notice those dark red bags that girls carry like badges of honor up and down Michigan Avenue? They come from **American Girl Place,** 111 E. Chicago Ave. (*② 877/247-5223*), which also features a cafe. Call well in advance for lunch reservations or to catch a performance of "The American Girls Revue" in their 150-seat theater. See p. 93.

- **Best Boys' Night Out:** What red-blooded American kid doesn't love baseball? **Harry Caray's,** 33 W. Kinzie St. (© **312/828-0966**), is one of Chicago's most flamboyant eateries, filled with uniforms, helmets, cards, and photographs. Ever hurled a baseball from a pitcher's mound to home plate? To get an idea of the distance, check out the bar—it measures 60 feet, 6 inches, the exact distance from hill to plate. See p. 101.

- **Best Neighborhood Hang-Out: Stanley's,** 1970 N. Lincoln Ave. (© **312/642-0007**), is a classic Lincoln Park restaurant with a family-friendly bent. When you walk in, there's a bar, but the adjacent dining room feels like you've entered someone's family room,

decorated with photos, quilts, bowling trophies, and children's drawings. This popular family spot has a special kids' menu. On Saturday and Sunday there's an all-you-can-eat brunch buffet, featuring make-your-own omelets, build-your-own-Belgian waffles, home-fried potatoes, fried chicken, and mashed potatoes. Daily specials are posted on the chalkboard out front. See p. 113.

- **Best Retro Diner:** Sure, it's a chain, but **Johnny Rocket's,** 901 N. Rush St. (© **312/337-3900**), is a great replica of a 1950s diner. Burgers wrapped in paper, fries (ketchup is poured for you by your friendly wait person), and flavored sodas from the fountain are sure to please kids. Kids' meals are available for $4.25, and ask for a menu to color. The location just behind the 900 N. Michigan mall makes the diner a perfect stop during a visit to the Magnificent Mile.

2

Planning a Family Trip to Chicago

Planning a trip is half the fun—and when kids are involved, planning is a chance to make them active participants in the upcoming family adventure. Ward off any potential kid meltdowns ("I didn't know we were going to do that!") by talking through the activities you all can enjoy. In this chapter, we'll look at how to find up-to-date information on those activities, when to go, and how to get here.

1 Visitor Information

SOURCES OF INFORMATION

The **Chicago Office of Tourism,** Chicago Cultural Center, 78 E. Washington St., Chicago, IL 60602 (© **312/744-2400** or TTY 312/744-2947; www.ci.chi.il.us/Tourism), will mail you a packet of materials with information on upcoming events and attractions. The **Illinois Bureau of Tourism** (© **800/2CONNECT** or TTY 800/406-6418; www.enjoy illinois.com) will also send you a packet of information about Chicago and other Illinois destinations.

The number-one publication for families in the Chicago area is *Chicago Parent* (© **708/386-5555;** fax 708/524-8360), a monthly magazine that has won many awards as best regional parenting publication in the nation. Contact the magazine to request a copy of its May issue, which is the annual "Going Places" guide, a comprehensive listing of what to do with kids in the six-county metro area.

HELPFUL WEBSITES

Check out *Chicago Parent* magazine's website, **www.chicagoparent.com**, prior to your visit, for a look at the calendar of events and excellent features on exploring Chicago with kids.

www.gocitykids.com provides a wealth of information, including current calendars of events for Chicago. You can search for activities, restaurants, and hotels, and see what's happening in specific neighborhoods. **http://chicago. urbanbaby.com** zeros in on such topics as baby gear, play spaces, and kid-friendly community events.

www.digitalcity.com/chicago gives general information about Chicago provided by the *Chicago Tribune;* **www. metromix.com** is the *Tribune*'s entertainment-oriented site. **www.chireader. com** is the site of the *Chicago Reader,* the city's alternative weekly paper.

Many of the city's performing arts groups sell tickets online through **www.ticketweb.com**, so you can reserve seats before leaving home.

2 Money

ATMS

ATMs in Chicago are linked to a national network that most likely includes your bank at home. **Cirrus** (© **800/424-7787;** www.mastercard. com) and **PLUS** (© **800/843-7587;**

www.visa.com) are the two most popular networks; check the back of your ATM card to see which networks your bank belongs to. Use the toll-free numbers to locate ATMs in Chicago. When you ask for directions to an ATM, Chicagoans may point you to the nearest "Cash Station," our local term (Cash Station is the biggest ATM network in the city); almost every machine labeled "Cash Station" is part of the Cirrus or PLUS network.

Be sure to check the daily withdrawal limit before you depart. And note that many banks have begun to impose a fee ranging from 50¢ to $3 every time you use an ATM in a different city. Your own bank may also charge you a fee for using ATMs from other banks. You can also withdraw cash advances from your credit cards at any bank (though you'll start paying hefty interest on the advance the moment you receive the cash, and you won't receive frequent-flier miles on an airline credit card).

CREDIT CARDS

Credit cards are invaluable when traveling. They are a safe way to carry money and provide a convenient record of all your expenses; you can withdraw cash advances from your credit cards at any bank (though you'll start paying hefty interest on the advance the moment you receive the cash), usually at the ATM if you know your personal identification number (PIN). If you've forgotten yours, call the number on the back of your credit card and ask the bank to send it to you, which usually takes 5 to 7 business days.

These days, everyone pays with plastic, even for the smallest purchase. So go ahead and use your card for a cup of coffee and a bagel—few merchants will bat an eye. You can use just about any credit card here; one that might be more popular around Chicago than in other parts of the

country is Discover, which is owned by Sears, the Chicago-based retailer.

TRAVELER'S CHECKS

These days, traveler's checks seem less necessary, but if you're withdrawing money every day, you might be better off with them—provided that you don't mind showing identification every time you want to cash a check. Most downtown restaurants, hotels, and shops in Chicago accept traveler's checks, and banks generally exchange them for cash (for a small fee). When you get away from downtown and the more affluent neighborhoods, however, smaller restaurants and shops may be reluctant to accept traveler's checks. American Express offices are open Monday through Saturday in Chicago. (See "Fast Facts: Chicago," in chapter 3 for office locations.) AAA members can obtain checks without a fee at most AAA offices.

WHAT TO DO IF YOUR WALLET IS LOST OR STOLEN

In case of loss or theft, almost every credit card company has an emergency toll-free number that you can call if your wallet or purse is lost or stolen. A representative may be able to wire you a cash advance off your credit card immediately and, in many places, can deliver an emergency credit card in a day or two. The **toll-free information directory** will provide the issuing bank's toll-free number if you dial ℂ 800/555-1212. **Citicorp Visa**'s U.S. emergency number is ℂ 800/336-8472. **American Express** cardholders and traveler's check holders should call ℂ 800/221-7282 for all money emergencies. **MasterCard** holders should call ℂ 800/307-7309. If you opt to carry traveler's checks, be sure to keep a record of their serial numbers, separate from the checks, of course, so that you're guaranteed a refund in just such an emergency.

3 When to Go

When should you go to Chicago? That depends on what kind of weather you like. Chicago has it all—heat and humidity, sub-zero temps, and wind, wind, wind. The city has a reputation for being really cold in the winter. In reality, it's about as cold as any other northern city. Maybe it's that wind that makes the cold seem more bitter. Still, most visitors prefer planning trips to Chicago in late spring through early fall. If you can't make it during prime time, err on the side of arriving later in fall rather than early in spring. Spring in Chicago can be notoriously late, while beautiful days can extend to Thanksgiving.

Don't be afraid to try the off-season: Museums are wide open, shops have sales (especially in Jan), and the streets aren't clogged with pedestrians. Chicago is definitely a four-season destination because its inhabitants are hardy enough to be out and about even in the depths of winter. As an added incentive to "off-season" travelers, hotel rates are rock bottom during the winter.

One thing is certain: Whenever you decide to go, you should be prepared for changeable weather. Chicagoans like to joke that if you don't like the weather, just wait an hour. One beautiful summer afternoon, I left my apartment in jeans and a t-shirt, only to have to buy a sweatshirt downtown when the wind shifted and the temperature plummeted 15 degrees in 15 minutes. Even in July, make sure that you bring a light jacket or sweater. In the winter, however fashionable you are trying to be, don't think you can get by without a hat.

For current conditions and forecasts, dial © **312/976-1212** or check www.ci.chi.il.us/Tourism/Weather.

Chicago's Average Temperatures & Precipitation

	Jan	Feb	Mar	Apr	May	June	July	Aug	Sept	Oct	Nov	Dec
High °F	20.2	33.9	44.3	58.8	70.0	79.4	85.3	82.1	75.5	64.1	48.2	35.0
°C	-6.5	1.0	6.8	14.9	21.1	26.3	29.6	27.8	24.4	17.8	8.99	1.67
Low °F	13.6	18.1	27.6	38.8	48.1	57.7	62.7	61.7	53.9	42.0	31.4	20.3
°C	-10.2	-7.7	-2.4	3.8	8.9	14.3	17	16.5	12.2	5.6	-0.3	-6.5
Rainfall (in.)	1.60	1.31	2.59	3.66	3.15	4.08	3.63	3.53	3.35	2.28	2.06	2.10

KIDS' FAVORITE CHICAGO EVENTS

Chicago is a festival city, with ethnic parades, food, music, art and flower fairs, and street celebrations packing the calendar. Particularly in the summer, it can be tough to choose among activities. In the winter, you'll have fewer choices, but some of the perennial favorites take place then.

To discover the latest and greatest special events in the city, ask the **Chicago Office of Tourism** (© **312/744-2400**) or the **Illinois Bureau of Tourism** (© **800/2CONNECT**) to mail you a copy of *Chicago Calendar of Events,* an excellent quarterly publication that surveys special events, including parades and street festivals, concerts and theatrical productions, and museum exhibitions. Also ask to be sent the latest materials produced by the **Mayor's Office of Special Events** (© **312/744-3315,** or the Special Events Hot Line 312/744-3370, TTY 312/744-2964), which keeps current with citywide and neighborhood festivals. You'll find food, music and flower fairs, plus garden walks and more.

Remember that new events might be added every year, and that occasionally special events are discontinued or rescheduled. So, to avoid disappointment, be sure to telephone in advance to the sponsoring organization, the Chicago Office of Tourism, or the Mayor's Office of Special Events to verify dates, times, and locations.

January

Chicago Cubs Convention. For kids who love baseball, even though

What Things Cost in Chicago	U.S.$
Cab from O'Hare Airport to downtown hotel	30.00
Cab from Midway Airport to downtown hotel	24.00
Shuttle from O'Hare to downtown hotel	19.00
Shuttle from Midway to downtown hotel	14.00
Subway or bus ride	1.50
Transfer (good for two additional rides)	.30
Ticket to John Hancock Center Observatory	9 adults, 6 kids
Ticket to Sears Tower Skydeck	9.50 adults, 6.75 kids
Hot dog at Gold Coast Dogs	2.00
Movie ticket	8.75 adults, 5.50 kids
20-oz. soft drink at drug or convenience store	1.29
16-oz. apple juice	1.39
Weekday Chicago Tribune	.50
Weekday Chicago Sun-Times	.35
Package of Pampers at drug store	12.99
1-quart can prepared Similac formula	4.99

April and Opening Day seem (and are) very far away, Cubs fans dream of next season at this convention, held at the Chicago Hilton and Towers. Players sign autographs and collectors buy, sell, and swap memorabilia. Call © 773/404-CUBS for more information. Mid-January.

Azalea and Camellia Flower Shows. Just when you and the kids are going crazy from cabin fever, the **Lincoln Park Conservatory** (© 312/742-7737) and **Garfield Park Conservatory** (© 312/746-5100) come alive with spring-blooming flowers such as azaleas, tulips, and hyacinths. Late January.

Chicago Boat, RV & Outdoor Show, McCormick Place, 23rd Street and Lake Shore Drive (© 312/946-6262). This extravaganza has been a Chicago tradition for nearly 70 years. All the latest boats and recreational vehicles are on display, plus trout fishing, a climbing wall, boating safety seminars, and big-time entertainment. Late January.

February

Chinese New Year Parade, Wentworth and Cermak streets (© 312/326-5320). The twisting dragon is sure to please kids as it winds down the street at this annual celebration. Call to verify the date, which varies from year to year, depending on the lunar calendar (usually between Jan 21 and Feb 19).

Chicago Auto Show, McCormick Place, 23rd Street and Lake Shore Drive (© 630/495-2282). A tradition since 1901, more than a thousand cars and trucks, domestic and foreign, are on display. Kids can get behind the wheel of the latest models at this event, which draws nearly a million car owners or wannabe owners. Mid-February.

International Cluster of Dog Shows, McCormick Place South, 23rd Street and South Lake Shore Drive (© 773/237-5100). See canines great and small strut their stuff. They're all adorable, but only one can win "best in show." More than 10,000 AKC (American Kennel Club) purebred dogs of all breeds heat up the competition. It's quite a scene, particularly in the poodle area, where you can see dogs getting their hair blow dried until they look like rock stars. Third week in February.

March

Spring Flower Shows. Spring is sprung a little earlier in the conservatories than it does outside in the real world, and thank goodness. See the lilies, daffodils, tulips, pansies, and other flowering perennials at **Lincoln Park Conservatory** (© 312/742-7737) and **Garfield Park Conservatory** (© 312/746-5100). Throughout March and April.

St. Patrick's Day Parade. Even the Chicago River puts on the green for St. Patrick's Day—in fact, the river is dyed Kelly green for the occasion. The parade runs along Dearborn Street from Wacker Drive to Van Buren; the best place to view it is around Wacker and Dearborn. Saturday closest to March 17.

April

Opening Day. Bundle up the kids and head for the ballpark to join the diehard fans (and bring your long underwear). Optimism reigns supreme and fans hope again that this will be their season. And even if it's not, hot dogs and peanuts will take some of the edge off. For the Cubs, call © 773/404-CUBS; for the White Sox, call © 312/674-1000. Early April.

May

Buckingham Fountain Color Light Show, in Grant Park, at Congress Parkway and Lake Shore Drive. The water and the ever-changing colored lights put on their show in the landmark fountain daily until 11pm nightly. May 1 through October 1.

The Ferris Wheel and **Pier Walk,** at Navy Pier, 600 E. Grand Ave.

(© **312/595-PIER**). Give your kids a bird's-eye view of Chicago from the Ferris wheel (those who are slightly less fond of heights should stick to the carousel). Another seasonal event along the water is Pier Walk, a temporary installation of more than 150 large-scale sculptures displayed along the pier's South Dock. May through October.

Art 2002 Chicago, at Navy Pier's Festival Hall, 600 E. Grand Ave. This is one of the country's largest international contemporary art fairs. More than 200 art galleries and 2,000 artists participate in the 5-day event. The event is usually preceded by a bus tour through the city's gallery districts in River North and Wicker Park. For information, call © **312/649-0065.** Mother's Day weekend.

Wright Plus Tour, at The Frank Lloyd Wright Home & Studio (© **708/848-1976**). Kids can glimpse inside the brilliant mind of Frank Lloyd Wright on this annual tour, which features 10 buildings in Oak Park, including Frank Lloyd Wright's home and studio, the Unity Temple, and several other notable Oak Park buildings in both Prairie and Victorian styles. Tickets go on sale March 1 and can sell out within 6 weeks. Third Saturday in May.

June

Ravinia Festival, Ravinia Park, in suburban Highland Park on the North Shore of Chicago (© **847/266-5100** for ticket reservations). Summer wouldn't be summer without this festival. Kids can enjoy a picnic on the lawn while parents revel in the music of the Chicago Symphony Orchestra. Pack a picnic, jump on the Metra, and join the crowds sitting under the stars on the lawn. *One warning:* Ravinia is so popular that many of the first-rate visiting orchestras, chamber ensembles, pop artists, and dance companies sell out in advance. June through September.

Chicago Blues Festival, Petrillo Music Shell, at Jackson Drive and Columbus Drive in Grant Park (© 312/744-3315). The line-up looks better every year at this festival. Admission is free, but get there in the afternoon to stake out a spot on the lawn for the evening shows. You'll discover young up-and-coming blues stars (including some who are the offspring of blues greats, such as Shamekia Copeland, daughter of Johnny Copeland). A shuttle bus will take you from the park to blues clubs. Call for information. First week in June.

57th Street Art Fair, at 57th and Kimbark streets in Hyde Park (© 773/493-3247; www.57th streetartfair.org). This is the oldest juried art fair in the Midwest—in 2002, it celebrated its 55th anniversary. Kids will especially enjoy the arts and crafts projects and the fun rides. First weekend in June.

Chicago Gospel Festival, Petrillo Music Shell, at Jackson Drive and Columbus Drive in Grant Park (© 312/744-3315). This is the largest outdoor, free-admission event of its kind. Blues may be the city's more famous musical export, but Chicago is also the birthplace of gospel music: Thomas Dorsey, the "father of gospel music," and the greatest gospel singer ever, Mahalia Jackson, were Southsiders. This 3-day festival offers music on 3 stages with more than 40 performances. Early June.

Printers Row Book Fair, on Dearborn Street from Congress to Polk (© 312/987-9896). One of the largest free outdoor book fairs in the country, this weekend-long event features readings by children's book authors, book signings, and panel discussions on everything from writing your first novel to finding an agent. Also on offer are more than 150 booksellers displaying new, used, and antiquarian books for sale; a poetry tent; and special activities for children. Early June.

Old Town Art Fair, historic Old Town neighborhood, at Lincoln Park West and Wisconsin Street (© 312/337-1938; www.oldtown triangle.com). Children's art activities are on offer at this fair; adults will appreciate the more than 200 painters, sculptors, and jewelry designers from the Midwest and around the country. The fair also features an art auction, a garden walk, and food and drink. Second weekend in June.

Wells Street Art Festival, Wells Street from North Avenue to Division Street (© 312/951-6106). Held on the same weekend as the Old Town Art Fair, this arts fest is still lots of fun, with 200 arts and crafts vendors, food, music, and carnival rides. Second weekend in June.

Andersonville Midsommarfest, along Clark Street from Foster to Balmoral avenues (© 773/728-2995). You can relive the Scandinavian heritage of Andersonville, once Chicago's principal Swedish community. Parents rave about the Swedish American Museum's kids' exhibits, and don't miss the Swedish Bakery across the street. Second weekend in June.

Boulevard Lakefront Bike Tour. This 10-mile leisurely tour especially for families lets you explore the city, from neighborhoods and the lakefront to Chicago's historic link of parks and boulevards. It starts and ends at the University of Chicago in Hyde Park, which also hosts the annual Bike Expo, with vendors and entertainment, on that day. Contact Chicagoland Bicycle Federation at ℂ **312/42-PEDAL.** A Sunday in mid-June.

Puerto Rican Fest, Humboldt Park, Division Street and Sacramento Boulevard (ℂ **773/276-0200).** One of Chicago's animated Latino street celebrations, this festival includes 5 days of live music, theater, games, food, and beverages. It peaks with a parade that wends its way from Wacker Drive and Dearborn Street to the West Side Puerto Rican enclave of Humboldt Park. Mid-June.

Summer Solstice Celebration, Museum of Contemporary Art, 220 E. Chicago Ave. (ℂ **312/280-2660).** Hip urbanites party for 24 hours straight, as the MCA transforms into a madcap festival of art, dance, music, and performance activities. General admission is $5; children 12 and under are admitted free. June 21 to 22.

Jammin' at the Zoo, Lincoln Park Zoo, 2200 N. Cannon Dr., at Fullerton Parkway (ℂ **773/742-2000).** Family fun is the emphasis at this concert; however, depending on the featured musical act, you might find that singles are more dominant at this perfect date venue. The lovely lawn south of the zoo's Park Place Café is certainly one of the more unusual outdoor venues for rock, zydeco, and reggae music. The first of three summer concerts is held in late June.

Grant Park Music Festival, Petrillo Music Shell, at Jackson Drive and Columbus Drive in Grant Park (ℂ **312/742-4763).** The free outdoor musical concerts in the park begin the last week in June and continue through August. If your kids are old enough to stay up past 10, call to find out about the movies in the park, shown outdoors on a large screen.

Taste of Chicago, Grant Park (ℂ **312/744-3315).** *Warning:* This food fest is hot, sweaty, and can get claustrophobic. If your kids are small or don't do well in crowds, avoid it. Going on a weekday morning will help you miss the heaviest crowds. Three-and-a-half million people eat their way through cheesecake, ribs, and pizza, while scores of Chicago restaurants cart their fare to food stands set up throughout the park. On the evening of July 3, things get pretty hairy when Chicago launches its Independence Day fireworks, and crowds are at their sweaty peak. Admission is free; you pay for the sampling, of course. Late June and the first week of July.

Chicago Country Music Festival, Petrillo Music Shell, at Jackson Drive and Columbus Drive in Grant Park (ℂ **312/744-3315),** is less claustrophobic than Taste of Chicago and therefore more kid-friendly. And it's free! You'll see big-name entertainers of the country-and-western genre. Late June (during the 1st weekend of Taste of Chicago).

Gay & Lesbian Pride Parade, on Halsted Street, from Belmont Avenue to Broadway, south to Diversey Parkway, and east to Lincoln Park (ℂ **773/348-8243).** This parade is flamboyant and colorful, the culmination of a month of activities by Chicago's gay and lesbian community. The floats, marching units, and colorful characters will keep you entertained, so pick a spot on Broadway for the best view. Last Sunday in June.

Farmers markets open at two dozen sites all over the city at the end of the month and continue weekly through October. Downtown sites are Daley Plaza (every other Thurs) and Federal Plaza (every Tues). For other locations and times, call © **312/744-9187.**

July

Independence Day Celebration (© **312/744-3315**). Celebrated in Chicago on July 3, concerts and fireworks are the highlights of the festivities in Grant Park. The sight of fireworks exploding over and reflecting off of Lake Michigan is well worth it. Take public transportation, or walk.

Irish–American Heritage Festival, Irish–American Heritage Center, 4626 N. Knox Ave. at Montrose Avenue (© **773/282-7035**). If your kids are into Irish dancing, made famous by the Broadway show *Riverdance,* make sure to check out this festival, featuring Irish music, dance, food, readings, and children's entertainment. Second weekend in July.

Sheffield Garden Walk, starting at Sheffield and Webster avenues (© **773/929-WALK**). One of Chicago's largest street parties, it sounds a bit more refined than it actually is—but here's your chance to snoop into the lush backyards of Lincoln Park homeowners. There are also live bands, children's activities, and food and drink vendors on tap. Mid-July.

Chicago Yacht Club's Race to Mackinac Island (© **312/861-7777**). Kids who love boats will get a kick out of watching the start of this 3-day competition. At Monroe Street Harbor, boats set sail on Saturday for the grandest of the inland water races. Mid-July.

Venetian Night, from Monroe Harbor to the Adler Planetarium (© **312/744-3315**). Whimsical decorations on a carnival of illuminated boats make this a great kids' event. Fireworks and synchronized music by the Grant Park Symphony Orchestra complete the scene. Watch from the shoreline, or, if you can swing it, get on board a friend's boat. End of July.

Newberry Library Book Fair and Bughouse Square Debates, 69 W. Walton St. and Washington Square Park (© **312/255-3501**). For teens with an interest in history, this fair will be a hit. Held over 4 days, Newberry Library sells tens of thousands of used books, most under $2. The highlight is soapbox orators re-creating the Bughouse Square Debates in Washington Square Park, just across the street. Pulitzer Prize–winning author Studs Terkel emcees the spirited chaos among left-wing agitators. Late July.

August

Oz Festival, Lincoln Park (© **773/929-8686**). "The magical spirit of Frank Baum's book *The Wizard of Oz*" is the focus here, with plenty for kids to enjoy. This popular event is held on a grassy area along Cannon Drive on the east side of the Lincoln Park Zoo. First weekend of August.

Chicago Air & Water Show, North Avenue Beach (© **312/744-3315**). Kids love this hugely popular show, held on the lake at North Avenue Beach, and overhead, features Stealth bombers, F-16s, and special appearances by U.S. Air Force Thunderbirds and Navy Seals. Because the crowds are intense at North Avenue Beach, try grabbing a portable radio and hanging at Oak Street Beach, along the Gold Coast. Admission is free. Mid-August.

Viva! Chicago Latin Music Festival, Petrillo Music Shell, at Jackson Drive and Columbus Drive in Grant Park (© **312/744-3370**). Salsa, mambo, and the latest Latin rock groups hit the stage for this free festival. Last weekend in August.

Chicago Jazz Festival, Petrillo Music Shell, Jackson Drive and Columbus Drive in Grant Park (© **312/744-3315**). Chicago-style jazz, plus several national headliners are always on hand. The event is free; kids are welcome. Late August to early September (Labor Day weekend).

September

Mexican Independence Day Parade, along Dearborn Street between Wacker Drive and Van Buren Street (**312/744-3315**). Chicago is home to the nation's second largest Mexican-American population, and that makes for a great parade. Another parade is held on the next day on 26th Street in the Little Village neighborhood (© **773/521-5387**). Saturday in mid-September.

World Music Festival Chicago, various locations around the city (© **312/744-6630**). Already enormously popular in its 4th year, the festival is a major undertaking by the city's Department of Cultural Affairs. Call ahead for tickets, as many events sell out. The festival is held at venues around town—notably, the Chicago Cultural Center, Museum of Contemporary Art, Old Town School of Folk Music, and Hot House. You'll see top performers from Zimbabwe to Hungary to Sri Lanka, performing traditional, contemporary, and fusion music. Shows are a mix of free and ticketed ($10 or less) events. Call for information and to receive updates on scheduled performances. Late September.

Celtic Fest Chicago, Petrillo Music Shell, Jackson Drive and Columbus Drive in Grant Park (© **312/744-3315**). The city's newest music festival celebrates the music and dance of Celtic traditions from around the world. Late September.

October

Chicago Marathon (© **312/527-2200**). Whether or not you or your kids are runners, cheering on the harriers is an uplifting experience. Sponsored by LaSalle Bank, Chicago's marathon is a major event on the international long-distance running circuit. Some of the world's top runners turn up for it. It begins and ends in Grant Park, but can be viewed from any number of vantage points along the race route. Late Sunday in October.

Spooky Zoo Spectacular, Lincoln Park Zoo, 2200 N. Cannon Dr. at Fullerton Parkway (© **312/742-2000**). Dress your tots in their Halloween finest for the free treats that are dispensed at various animal habitats. Bozo the Clown—himself a Chicago native—kicks things off with a parade through the zoo grounds.

November

The Big Top, United Center, 1901 W. Madison St. (© **312/455-4000**); and the Allstate Arena, 6920 N. Mannheim Rd., Rosemont (© **847/635-6601**). This is the month that Ringling Brothers, Barnum & Bailey comes to Chicago to set up its tent. Tickets are available from Ticketmaster (© **312/559-1212**). Throughout November.

Magnificent Mile Lights Festival (© **312/642-3570**). Beginning at dusk, a colorful parade of Disney characters makes its way south along Michigan Avenue, from Oak Street to the Chicago River, with holiday lights being illuminated block by block as the procession passes. Carolers, elves, and minstrels appear with Santa along the avenue throughout the day and into the evening, and many of the retailers offer hot chocolate and other treats. Saturday before Thanksgiving.

Christmas Tree Lighting, Daley Center Plaza, in the Loop (☎ 312/744-3315). Combine the tree lighting with another Chicago Christmas tradition—the windows at Marshall Field's, at Randolph and State streets, just a few blocks east of Daley Center Plaza. The day after Thanksgiving, around dusk.

Zoo Lights Festival, Lincoln Park Zoo, 2200 N. Cannon Dr. (☎ 312/742-2000). Colorful illuminated displays brighten long nights during the holidays. Another special tradition is the annual Caroling to the Animals, a daylong songfest on a Saturday early in the month. Late November through the first week in January.

December

A Christmas Carol, Goodman Theatre, 170 N. Dearborn St. (☎ 312/443-3800). This is both a seasonal favorite and a Chicago institution; it's been performed for more than 2 decades. The show runs from around Thanksgiving to the end of December.

The Nutcracker, Joffrey Ballet of Chicago, Auditorium Theatre, 50 E. Congress Pkwy. The esteemed company performs its Victorian–American twist on this holiday classic. For tickets, call ☎ 312/901-1500 (Ticketmaster) or 312/739-0120 (Joffrey office). The production runs for 3 weeks from late November to mid-December.

4 What to Pack

As you have heard too many times already, Chicago's weather is changeable. So while I can give you general guidelines for packing for various seasons, always check out **www.weather.com** or **www.chicagotribune.com** for the long-range forecast. (Granted, in Chicago, they seem to have it wrong at least half of the time, but it's better than a complete shot in the dark.) What would you wear in your own city in this weather? Pack it. Leave room in the suitcase—never stuff it to overflowing—because you will undoubtedly buy items while traveling. In fact, one seasoned traveler trick is to pack an empty nylon duffel bag in your suitcase. On the way home, you can stuff it with souvenirs and other Chicago loot.

Because you are apt to hit four seasons in just one Chicago day, here are some packing tips:

• **Pack a light sweater and jacket,** even for summer. The Windy City can get quite breezy, and that lake air has a chill at night. Theaters and restaurants can also overdo the air-conditioning, so a light sweater helps you ward off arctic chill.

• You are not too stylish to bring **practical headgear** to Chicago in the winter. Believe me, you will appreciate this advice later. When it gets cold in Chicago, no one goes without head covering.

• Pack **shorts** for a late spring or early fall trip as well as for summer. You can always pair them with a sweatshirt if it gets chilly.

• **Bring layers.** You can always stuff that jacket into your backpack, but if you skip it altogether, you may end up regretting it. This way, you'll be able to stay out all day without running back to your hotel for frequent wardrobe adjustments.

As far as dress codes go, unless you and your kids are planning a big night out at the Pump Room at the Omni Ambassador East Hotel, you will be just fine in "nice casual" attire. For men, that means a dress shirt, sports jacket, and tie for the fanciest places. For women, a long skirt with boots and a nice sweater goes just about anywhere in the winter. In the summer, you'll be comfortable in cool slacks and cotton tops with sandals. If you are planning a very special night out, check to see if the restaurant enforces a dress code. Otherwise, you might end up borrowing a less-than-attractive tie and jacket from the maitre d'.

You'll find that people dress more conservatively here than in New York or Los Angeles, and as a traveler, you can blend in easily with a suitcase full of the basics: khakis, jeans, shorts, sandals, boots, and sweaters.

5 Insurance & Health

TRAVEL INSURANCE AT A GLANCE

Check your existing insurance policies before you buy travel insurance to cover trip cancellation, lost luggage, medical expenses, or car rental insurance. You're likely to have partial or complete coverage. But if you need some, ask your travel agent about a comprehensive package. The cost of travel insurance varies widely, depending on the cost and length of your trip, your age and overall health, and the type of trip you're taking. Some insurers provide packages for specialty vacations, such as skiing or backpacking. More dangerous activities may be excluded from basic policies.

And keep in mind that in the aftermath of the September 11, 2001 terrorist attacks, a number of airlines, cruise lines, and tour operators are no longer covered by insurers. *The bottom line:* Always, always check the fine print before you sign on; more and more policies have built-in exclusions and restrictions that may leave you out in the cold if something does go awry.

For information, contact one of the following popular insurers:

- **Access America** (© **800/284-8300;** www.accessamerica.com)
- **Travel Guard International** (© **800/826-1300;** www.travelguard.com)
- **Travel Insured International** (© **800/243-3174;** www.travelinsured.com)
- **Travelex Insurance Services** (© **800/228-9792;** www.travelex-insurance.com)

STAYING HEALTHY

You won't need to take any unusual precautions when traveling to Chicago. The regular assortment of antacids, anti-diarrheals, and some acetaminophen or ibuprofen for headaches should suffice. Lake Michigan rarely gets rough enough to advise bringing motion sickness medication for boat tours; however, if you plan a long fishing excursion, you may want to add some to your bag.

Pack prescription medications in your carry-on luggage, and carry prescription medications in their original containers. Also bring along copies of your prescriptions in case you lose your pills or run out. And don't forget sunglasses and an extra pair of contact lenses or prescription glasses.

WHERE TO GO IF YOU GET SICK AWAY FROM HOME

In downtown Chicago, the most centrally located hospital is **Northwestern Memorial Hospital,** 251 E. Huron St. (© **312/926-2000**), just east of Michigan Avenue. Their physician referral service is © **312/926-8000.** The emergency department is at 250 E. Erie Street, near Fairbanks Court (© **312/926-5188**).

MEDICAL INSURANCE

If you worry about getting sick away from home, consider purchasing **medical travel insurance** and remember to carry your ID card in your purse or wallet. Most health insurance policies cover you if you get sick away from home—but check, particularly if you're insured by an HMO. Members of **Blue Cross/Blue Shield** can now use their cards at select hospitals in

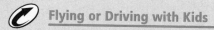

Flying or Driving with Kids

FOR A PLANE TRIP

When traveling with kids, consider packing the following in your carry-on bag:

- The number of diapers your child wears in a day, plus an extra three
- A changing pad in case the tiny restroom in the airplane has no pull-out changing table
- A minimal number of toys—one coloring book and a stuffed animal will suffice
- Bottles for infants, sippy cups and snacks for toddlers
- A goodie bag with surprises, like a Discman with a CD of music or stories, books, or small plastic toys

For more comprehensive advice on flying with children, see "Getting There," below, and pick up a copy of *Frommer's Fly Safe, Fly Smart* by Sascha Segan (Wiley, 2002).

FOR A CAR TRIP

If you will be renting a car in Chicago, inquire about reserving a child safety seat; most major rental car agencies have these available for a small fee. (Avis, for example, charges $5 per day or $25 per week.)

Driving to Chicago? Long-distance car travel with kids presents a completely different packing challenge. Pack the following to help your car trip go more smoothly:

- A cooler with drinks, snacks, fruits, and veggies.
- A flashlight to help locate items that have rolled under your seat for the 10th time in the last 5 minutes!
- Window shades for the sun.
- Audiotapes of stories or children's songs. Many parents put a TV/VCR in between the two front seats so kids can watch videos. Because a video lasts 30 minutes to an hour, it's a great help for long stretches with nothing to do.

Other items to consider bringing include a first-aid kit, a box of wipes for clean-ups, blankets, plastic bags for motion sickness, and a change of clothes. Always have a cellphone in case of emergencies.

---

most major cities worldwide (© **800/810-BLUE** or www.bluecares.com for a list of hospitals).

If you require additional insurance, try one of the following companies:

- **MEDEX International** (© **888/MEDEX-00** or 410/453-6300; www.medexassist.com)
- **Travel Assistance International** (© **800/821-2828;** www.travelassistance.com; for general information on services, call the company's Worldwide Assistance Services, Inc., at 800/777-8710).

The cost of travel medical insurance varies widely. Check your existing policies before you buy additional coverage. Also, check to see if your medical insurance covers you for emergency medical evacuation: If you have to buy a one-way same-day ticket home and forfeit your nonrefundable round-trip ticket, you may be out big bucks.

> **Tips Quick I.D.**
>
> Tie a colorful ribbon or piece of yarn around your luggage handle, or slap a distinctive sticker on the side of your bag. This makes it less likely that someone will mistakenly appropriate it. And if your luggage gets lost, it will be easier to find.

If you suffer from a chronic illness, consult your doctor before your departure. For conditions like epilepsy, diabetes, or heart problems, wear a **Medic Alert Identification Tag** (© 800/825-3785;   www.medicalert.org), which will immediately alert doctors to your condition and give them access to your records through Medic Alert's 24-hour hot line.

6 Words of Wisdom on Traveling Safely with Kids in Chicago

The easiest way to stay safe in Chicago is to **hold hands with your kids.** It's safe and fun, without being overly protective. Keep your kids close and within eyeshot, and be extra careful around busy intersections. Cabs will not slow down for anyone—even families with kids. Do not cross anywhere but at traffic lights (it sounds obvious, but I've seen parents with strollers crossing in the middle of busy streets). Again, drivers won't stop for you in the city just because you have a stroller. Stay on major streets and avoid construction sites.

Visitors should steer clear of situations where your kids could get lost in a crowd. At the ballpark, Chicago parents say they wait until most of the crowd files out so kids can go at their own pace. Remember, Michigan Avenue and major attractions can get crowded in the summer. **Make contingency plans for reuniting,** even in the most ordinary situations. Start at the information desk at whatever attraction you're visiting, and make a plan to meet there in case you and your kids get split up.

Another tip is to **use public transportation.** If you are driving in to the city, park in a central location and walk or take the El or bus. Don't plan on taking a cab with small children unless you want to carry a car seat with you. Some parents find trains to be easier with children than the buses because you can roll strollers right onto trains, and you don't have to stand on a busy street corner waiting for the bus.

Finally, **travel light** and avoid being overburdened or distracted by too much gear. Carry water, juice, and snacks (downtown, you will pay a ton to buy these items). Also, be prepared for a lack of chain fast-food outlets. When visiting major attractions, you may be able to avoid taking a stroller because most places rent them. If you do feel the need to bring a stroller, make sure it's light and narrow—some of the sturdy but wide strollers are hard to maneuver through city crowds and narrow store aisles.

Several books on the market offer additional tips to help you travel with kids. *How to Take Great Trips with Your Kids* (The Harvard Common Press; $9.95), is full of good general advice that can apply to travel anywhere. *Family Travel Times* (© 888/822-4FTT; www.familytraveltimes. com) is an excellent online newsletter updated twice monthly. Subscriptions are $39 a year, $49 for 2 years. Sample articles are available on the newsletter's website.

7 Getting There

BY PLANE
THE MAJOR AIRLINES

Domestic carriers that fly regularly to O'Hare include **American** (© 800/433-7300; www.aa.com), **Continental** (© 800/525-0280; www.continental.com), **Delta** (© 800/221-1212; www.delta.com), **Northwest** (© 800/225-2525; www.nwa.com), **United** (© 800/864-8331; www.united.com), and **US Airways** (© 800/428-4322; www.usairways.com). Commuter service is also provided by several regional airlines. Airlines that fly to Chicago's Midway Airport are **America West** (© 800/235-9292; www.americawest.com), **Air Tran Airways** (© 800/247-8726; www.airtran.com), **ATA** (© 800/435-9282; www.ata.com), **Continental** (© 800/525-0280; www.continental.com), **Frontier** (© 800/432-1359; www.frontierairlines.com), **Northwest** (© 800/225-2525; www.nwa.com), and **Southwest** (© 800/435-9792; www.iflyswa.com). The toll-free numbers listed are for use in the United States and Canada.

FLYING FOR LESS: TIPS FOR GETTING THE BEST AIRFARES

Airfares are a great example of capitalism at work: Passengers within the same airplane cabin rarely pay the same fare for their seats. Rather, each pays what the market will bear. Business travelers who need to purchase tickets at the last minute, change their itinerary at a moment's notice, or get home before the weekend pay the premium rate, known as the full fare. Passengers who can book their ticket long in advance, who don't mind staying over Saturday night, or who are willing to travel on a Tuesday, Wednesday, or Thursday after 7pm will pay a fraction of the full fare. On most flights, even the shortest hops, the full fare is close to $1,000 or more, but a 7-day or 14-day advance purchase ticket is closer to $200 to $300. Here are a few other easy ways to save:

- Periodically, airlines lower prices on their most popular routes. Check your newspaper for advertised discounts, or call the airlines directly and ask if any **promotional rates** or special fares are available. You'll almost never see a sale during the peak summer vacation months of July and August, or during the Thanksgiving or Christmas seasons; in periods of low-volume travel, however, you should pay no more than $400 for a cross-country flight. If your schedule is flexible, ask if you can secure a cheaper fare by staying an extra day or by flying midweek. (Many airlines won't volunteer this information.) If you already hold a ticket when a sale breaks, it may even pay to exchange your ticket, which usually incurs a charge, which now might be up to $100.

  Note: The lowest-priced fares often are nonrefundable, require advance purchase of 1 to 3 weeks and a certain length of stay, and carry penalties for changing dates of travel.

- **Consolidators,** also known as bucket shops, are a good place to find low fares. Consolidators buy seats in bulk from the airlines and then sell them back to the public at prices below even the airlines' discounted rates. Their small ads usually run in the Sunday travel section at the bottom of the page. Before you pay, however, ask for a confirmation number from the consolidator, and then call the airline itself to confirm your seat. Be prepared to book your ticket with a different consolidator if the airline can't confirm your reservation. Also be aware that bucket-shop tickets are usually nonrefundable or rigged with stiff cancellation penalties, often as high as 50% to 75% of the ticket price.

Council Travel (© 800/226-8624; www.counciltravel.com) and **STA Travel** (© 800/781-4040; www.statravel.com) cater especially to young travelers, but their bargain-basement prices are available to people of all ages. **Travel Bargains** (© 800/AIR-FARE; www.1800airfare.com) was formerly owned by TWA but now offers the deepest discounts on many other airlines, with a 4-day advance purchase. Other reliable consolidators include **1-800-FLYCHEAP**(www.1800flcheap. com); **TFI Tours International** (© 800-745-8000 or 212/736-1140), which serves as a clearinghouse for unused seats; or "rebators" such as **Travel Avenue** (© 800/333-3335 or 312/876-1116) and the **Smart Traveler** (© 800/448-3338 in the U.S. or 305/448-3338), which rebate part of their commissions to you.

- Search **the Internet** for cheap fares. Great last-minute deals are available through free weekly e-mail services provided directly by the airlines. Websites such as **Frommers.com** (www.frommers. com), **Travelocity** (www.travel ocity.com), **Expedia** (www.expedia. com), **Qixo** (www.qixo.com), and **Orbitz** (www.orbitz.com) allow consumers to comparison shop for airfares, access special bargains, book flights, and reserve hotel rooms and rental cars.

- Join a travel club such as **Moment's Notice** (© 718/234-6295; www.momentsnotice.com) or **Travelers Advantage** (© 877/259-2691; www.travelersadvan tage.com), which supply unsold tickets at discounted prices. You pay an annual membership fee to get the club's hot line number. Of course, you're limited to what's available, so you have to be flexible.

- Join **frequent-flier clubs.** It's best to accrue miles on one program, so you can rack up free flights and achieve elite status faster. But it makes sense to open as many accounts as possible, no matter how seldom you fly a particular airline. It's free, and you'll get the best choice of seats, faster response to phone inquiries, and prompter service if your luggage is stolen, your flight is canceled or delayed, or if you want to change your seat.

CHICAGO'S AIRPORTS

The one experience most Chicago visitors share is **O'Hare International Airport** (© 773/686-2200). O'Hare has long battled with Atlanta's Hartsfield for the title of the world's busiest airport. The airport reigns as a major hub for making connections

---

Tips   Kids with Colds

It's even more difficult for kids to make their ears pop during takeoff and landing. The eustachian tube is especially narrow in children; the passage is even tighter when mucous membranes are swollen. This can make ascent and descent especially painful—even dangerous—for a child with congested sinuses. If your little one is suffering from a cold or the flu, it's best to keep him grounded until he recuperates, if that's an option. (If you must travel with your child as scheduled, give them an oral child's decongestant an hour before ascent and descent or administer a spray decongestant before and during takeoff and landing.)

worldwide. O'Hare boasts its own police force, ZIP code, medical center, cemetery, and chapel.

O'Hare is located northwest of the city proper, about a 25- to 30-minute drive from downtown, depending, of course, on the traffic. A cab ride into the city will cost you about $30 to $35. You can also ask the taxi-stand attendant to arrange a shared ride for you, which will cost about $15 per person.

For $1.50, you can take the El (vernacular for the elevated train), which will efficiently get you downtown in about 40 minutes, regardless of traffic. Trains leave every 6 to 10 minutes during the day, and every half-hour in the evening and overnight. O'Hare also has outposts for every major car rental company (see "Getting Around," in chapter 3 for details).

O'Hare has information booths in all five terminals, most located on the baggage level. The multilingual personnel, who are outfitted in red jackets, can assist travelers with everything from arranging ground transportation to getting information about local hotels. The booths also offer a plethora of useful tourism brochures. The booths, labeled "Airport Information," are open daily 9am to 8pm.

On the opposite end of the city, the Southwest Side, is Chicago's other major airport, **Midway** (© 773/838-0600). A new terminal, which opened in 2001, has eased considerable crowding problems and expanded the selection of restaurants and shops. Although it's smaller than O'Hare and fewer airlines have routes here, Midway is closer to the Loop and you may be able to get a cheaper fare flying into here. (Always check fares flying into both airports if you want to find the best deal.) The El Orange Line extends to Midway, so you can make it downtown in about half an hour for $1.50. Please note that the Orange Line stops operating each night at

about 11:30pm and resumes service by 5am. Trains leave the station every 6 to 15 minutes. Most major car rental companies have counters at Midway as well.

You can find the latest information on both airports at the city's Department of Aviation website: **www.ohare.com**.

Continental Air Transport (© 800/654-7871 or 312/454-7800; www.airportexpress.com) services most first-class hotels in Chicago with its blue-and-white Airport Express vans; ticket counters are located at both airports near the baggage claim (outside Customs at the international terminal at O'Hare). For transportation to the airport, reserve a spot from one of the hotels (check with the bell captain). The cost is $19 one-way ($34 round-trip) to or from O'Hare and $14 one-way ($25 round-trip) to or from Midway. The shuttles operate from 6am to 11:30pm. For limo service from either O'Hare or Midway, call **Carey Limousine of Chicago** (© 312/663-1220), or **Chicago Limousine Services** (© 312/726-1035). Depending on the number of passengers and whether you opt for a sedan or stretch limo, the service will cost about $75 to $125, including gratuity and tax.

With 1 week's notice, CTA paratransit offers door-to-door lift services to and from O'Hare for travelers with disabilities. Visitors must be registered with a similar program in their home city. For information, call © 312/432-7025, 312/917-4357, or 312/917-1338 TTY.

ADDITIONAL TIPS TO EASE YOUR FLIGHT

If you plan carefully, you can make it fun to fly with your kids.

- You'll save yourself a good bit of aggravation by **reserving a seat in the bulkhead row.** You'll have more legroom, and your children

Air Travel Security Measures

In the wake of the terrorist attacks of September 11, 2001, the airline industry implemented sweeping security measures in airports. Although regulations vary from airline to airline, you can expedite the check-in process and alleviate airport stress by taking the following steps:

- **Arrive early.** Times vary from airport to airport, depending on their size. Figure on arriving for check-in anywhere from a minimum of an hour in advance to at least 2 hours before your scheduled flight.
- **Don't count on curbside check-in.** Some airlines and airports have stopped curbside check-in altogether, whereas others offer it on a limited basis. For up-to-date information, check with the individual airline.
- **Be sure to carry plenty of documentation.** An up-to-date, government-issued photo ID (federal, state, or local) is now required. You may need to show this at various checkpoints. With an E-ticket, you may be required to have with you printed confirmation of purchase, and perhaps even the credit card with which you bought your ticket. This varies from airline to airline, so call ahead to make sure you have the proper documentation.
- **Know what you can carry on—and what you can't.** Travelers in the United States are now limited to one carry-on bag, plus one personal bag (such as a purse or a briefcase). The **Transportation Security Administration (TSA)** has also issued a list of banned carry-on items; for more information, check the TSA website at www.tsa.gov. Your airline may have additional restrictions on carry-on items, so call ahead to avoid problems.
- **Prepare to be searched.** Expect spot-checks. Electronic items (such as a laptop or cellphone) should be readied for additional screening. Be prepared to shift your jewelry, loose change, and any other metallic items on your person to bins before you go through security.
- **It's no joke.** If anyone asks you security-related questions, don't be flip. The agents will not hesitate to call security.

will be able to spread out and play on the floor underfoot. You're also more likely to find sympathetic company in the bulkhead area, as families with children tend to be seated there.

- Be sure to **pack items for your kids in your carry-on luggage.** See the "Flying Or Driving With Kids" box on p. 23 for specific advice.
- **Have a long talk with your children** before you depart for your trip. If they've never flown before, explain to them what to expect. If they're old enough, you may even want to describe how flight works and how air travel is even safer than riding in a car. Explain to your kids the importance of good behavior in the air—how their own safety can depend upon their being quiet and staying in their seats during the trip.
- **Pay extra careful attention to the safety instructions** before

takeoff. Consult the safety chart behind the seat in front of you and show it to your children. Be sure you know how to operate the oxygen masks, as you will be expected to secure yours first and then help your children with theirs. Be especially mindful of the location of emergency exits. Before takeoff, plot out an evacuation strategy for you and your children in your mind's eye.

- Ask the flight attendant **if the plane has any special safety equipment for children.** Make a member of the crew aware of any medical problems your children have that could manifest during flight.

- **Be sure you've slept sufficiently** for your trip. If you fall asleep in the air and your child manages to break away, there are all sorts of sharp objects that could cause injury. Especially during mealtimes, it's dangerous for a child to be crawling or walking around the cabin unaccompanied by an adult.

- **Be sure your child's seatbelt remains fastened properly,** and try to reserve the seat closest to the aisle for yourself. This will make it harder for your children to wander off—in case, for instance, you're taking the redeye or a long flight and you do happen to nod off. You will also protect your child from jostling passersby and falling objects—in the rare but entirely possible instance that an overhead bin pops open.

In the event of an accident, unrestrained children often don't make it—even when the parent does. Experience has shown that it's impossible for a parent to hold onto a child in the event of a crash, and children often die of impact injuries.

For the same reason, sudden turbulence is also a danger to a child who is not buckled into his own seat belt or seat restraint. According to Consumer Reports Travel Letter, the most common flying injuries result when unanticipated turbulence strikes and hurtles passengers from their seats.

- **Try to sit near the lavatory,** though not so close that your children are jostled by the crowds that tend to gather there. Consolidate trips there as much as possible.

- Try to **accompany children to the lavatory.** They can be easily bumped and possibly injured as they make their way down tight aisles. It's especially dangerous for children to wander while flight attendants are blocking passage

---

(**Fun Fact** O'Hare, Oh My

Chicago's O'Hare International Airport handles more passengers and aircraft operations than any other airport in the world. Consider these tidbits:
- Approximately 200,000 travelers pass through O'Hare each day.
- O'Hare served more than 72 million passengers in 2000.
- The total airport complex covers nearly 7,700 acres, with 172 aircraft gates housed in 4 terminal buildings.
- O'Hare Airport has 75 commercial, commuter, and cargo airlines offering frequent service.
- Chicago's airports generate about 500,000 jobs for the region, representing personal income of $37 billion a year.
- O'Hare is completely self-supporting, requiring no local taxpayer dollars to keep it going.

In-Flight Fun for Kids

With one of these children's game books on board, even the longest plane ride will go faster.

Great Games for Kids on the Go: Over 240 Travel Games to Play on Trains, Planes, and Automobiles
by Penny Warner
Retail price: $12.95
Ages 4 to 8
This book is full of entertaining educational games to help your kids while away the miles. Each game is highly engaging and entertaining and requires few materials and very little space.

Brain Quest for the Car: 1100 Questions and Answers All About America
by Sharon Gold
Retail price: $10.95
Ages 7 to 12
This book features cards with questions about American geography, culture, and customs.

Vacation Fun Mad Libs: World's Greatest Party Game
by Roger Price
Retail price: $3.99
Ages 8 and up
As suggested by the title, this book is chock-full of Mad Libs. Your kids will want to keep playing even after you're touched down.

with their service carts. On crowded flights, the flight crew may need as much as an hour to serve dinner. It's wise to encourage your kids to use the rest room as you see the attendants preparing to serve.

- Be sure to **bring clean, self-containing compact toys.** Leave electronic games at home. They can interfere with the aircraft navigational system, and their noisiness, however lulling to children's ears, will surely not win the favor of your adult neighbors. Magnetic checker sets, on the other hand, are a perfect distraction, and small coloring books and crayons also work well, as do card games like Go Fish.

- Some airlines **serve children's meals first.** When you board, ask a flight attendant if this is possible, especially if your children are very young or seated toward the back of the plane. After all, if your kids have a happy flight experience, everyone else in the cabin is more likely to as well.

- You'll certainly be grateful to yourself for packing **tidy snacks** like rolled dried fruit, which are much less sticky and wet and more compact and packable than actual fruit. Blueberry or raisin bagels also make for a neat, healthy sweet and yield fewer crumbs than cookies or cakes. Ginger snaps, crisp and not as crumbly as softer cookies, will also help curb mild cases of motion sickness. And don't forget to stash a few resealable plastic bags in your purse. They'll prove invaluable for storing everything from half-eaten crackers and fruit to checker pieces and matchbox cars.

BY CAR

Chicago is serviced by interstate highways from all major points on the compass. I-80 and I-90 approach from the east, crossing the northern sector of Illinois, with I-90 splitting off and emptying into Chicago via the Skyway and the Dan Ryan Expressway. From here, I-90 runs through Wisconsin, following a northern route to Seattle. I-55 snakes up the Mississippi Valley from the vicinity of New Orleans and enters Chicago from the west along the Stevenson Expressway, and in the opposite direction it provides an outlet to the Southwest. I-57 originates in southern Illinois and forms part of the interstate linkage to Florida and the South, connecting within Chicago on the west leg of the Dan Ryan. I-94 links Detroit with Chicago, arriving on the Calumet Expressway and leaving the city via the Kennedy Expressway en route to the Northwest.

Here are a few approximate driving distances in miles to Chicago: from **Milwaukee,** 92; from **St. Louis,** 297; from **Detroit,** 286; from **Denver,** 1,011; from **Atlanta,** 716; from **Washington, D.C.,** 715; from **New York City,** 821; and from **Los Angeles,** 2,034.

BY TRAIN

Rail passenger service, although it may never approach the grandeur of its heyday, has made enormous advances in service, comfort, and efficiency since the creation of Amtrak in 1971. As in the past, but on a reduced scale, Chicago remains the hub of the national passenger rail system. Traveling great distances by train is certainly not the quickest way to go, nor always the most convenient. But many travelers still prefer it to flying or driving.

For tickets, consult your travel agent or call **Amtrak** (© **800/USA-RAIL;** www.amtrak.com). Ask the reservations agent to send you Amtrak's useful travel planner, with information on train accommodations and package tours.

When you arrive in Chicago, the train will pull into **Union Station** at 210 S. Canal between Adams and Jackson streets (© **312/655-2385**). Bus nos. 1, 60, 125, 151, and 156 all stop at the station, which is just west across the river from the Loop. The nearest El stop is at Clinton Street and Congress Parkway (on the Blue Line), which is a fair walk away, especially when you're carrying luggage.

BY BUS

The **Greyhound Bus Station** in Chicago is at 630 W. Harrison (© **800/231-2222** travel information, © 312/408-5980 bus station; www.greyhound.com), not far from Union Station. Several city buses (nos. 60, 125, 156, and 157) pass in front of the terminal building, and the nearest El stop is at Clinton Street and Congress Parkway on the Blue Line.

---

8 Show & Tell: Getting Kids Interested in Chicago

Kids will be most interested in your upcoming adventure when they have input into the activities you plan. Use this book to tell your kids about the great adventures awaiting them in Chicago—riding the El, climbing into a captured World War II U-boat at the Museum of Science and Industry, riding a high-speed elevator to see the sights from the John Hancock Center, or going to a McDonald's that's also a rock 'n' roll museum.

On television, you might point out shows set in Chicago. *ER* often shows outdoor scenes with the El. Currently, on Fox, *The Andy Richter Show* is set in downtown Chicago, among what will become familiar sights.

Movie-wise, you can rent *Blues Brothers* and show Jake and Elmo jumping the bridge across the river and careening down the street under the El tracks. *Ferris Bueller's Day Off* is a classic set in Chicago and the suburbs. In fact, most of the John Hughes movies (*Pretty in Pink, Sixteen Candles,* and *The Breakfast Club*) are set in the Chicago area.

Children's books set in Chicago that will be readily available at your local library or bookstore include *Fair Weather* by Richard Peck, in which a 19th-century farming family turned upside down by a visit to Chicago for the 1893 World's Columbian Exposition; *Playoff Dreams* by Fred Bowen, in which a boy attends a ball game with his uncle at Wrigley Field, and learns the story of the legendary Cubs player and Hall of Fame member Ernie Banks; and *The Dragon of Navy Pier* by Kate Noble, in which Charlie, a young dragon on a carousel, comes alive one night and sets out to explore Navy Pier.

Show your kids photos of landmarks—Wrigley Field is a familiar sight to most of us. You might also find photos of Soldier Field, United Center (with its statue to Michael Jordan), the soaring John Hancock Center (with its girded black "Xs" crisscrossing all the way up the building), the Chicago Water Tower (the only building to survive the fire of 1871, allegedly started by Mrs. O'Leary's cow), Sears Tower, and the lakefront. Discuss the El trains and show kids photos of the elevated tracks. Show them the Chicago bridges that raise and lower, stopping traffic so boats can make their way to the lake. Tell them that the Chicago River that these bridges span runs from the lake (rather than into it, as most rivers do)—and about the engineering marvel that reversed its flow.

3

Getting to Know Chicago

The best advice on orienting yourself on Chicago's streets? Look for our inland ocean. Whenever you spot Lake Michigan dead ahead, you are facing east. Another directional no-brainer? If you are on the Magnificent Mile, or in the Loop, look up. The tallest building around is that black glass behemoth, the Sears Tower, and it's to the south.

The orderly configuration of Chicago's streets and the excellent public transportation system make this city more accessible than most of the world's other large cities. This chapter provides an overview of the city's design, as well as some suggestions for how to maneuver within it. The chapter also lists some resources that traveling families frequently need, from babysitters to 24-hour pharmacies.

1 Orientation

VISITOR INFORMATION

The **Chicago Office of Tourism** runs a toll-free visitor hot line (© **877/CHICAGO** or 312/744-2400, TTY 312/744-2947) and operates three visitor information centers staffed with people who can answer questions and stocked with plenty of brochures on area attractions, including materials on everything from museums and city landmarks to lakefront biking maps and even fishing spots. The main visitor center, located in the Loop and convenient to many places that you'll likely be visiting, is on the first floor of the **Chicago Cultural Center,** 78 E. Washington St. (at Michigan Ave.). The center has a phone that you can use to make hotel reservations and several couches and a cafe where you can study maps and plan your itinerary. The center is open Monday through Wednesday 10am to 7pm, Thursday 10am to 9pm, Friday 10am to 6pm, Saturday 10am to 5pm, and Sunday 11am to 5pm; it's closed on holidays.

A second, smaller center is located in the heart of the city's shopping district, in the old pumping station at Michigan and Chicago avenues. Recently renamed the **Chicago Water Works Visitor Center,** its entrance is on the Pearson Street side of the building, across from the Water Tower Place mall. It's open daily 7:30am to 7pm. This location has the added draw of housing a location of Hot Tix, which offers both half-price day-of-performance and full-price tickets to many theater productions around the city, as well as a gift shop. Part of the building has been converted into a theater, including a small cabaret space for tourist-oriented shows and a larger playhouse for the acclaimed Lookingglass Theatre.

A third visitor outpost is located at **Navy Pier** in the Illinois Market Place gift shop; it's open Sunday through Thursday from 10am to 9pm, and Friday and Saturday from 10am to midnight.

The **Illinois Bureau of Tourism** (© **800/2CONNECT** or TTY 800/406-6418) can provide general and specific information 24 hours a day.

The agency also has staff at the information desk in the lobby of the **James R. Thompson Center,** 100 W. Randolph St., in the Helmut Jahn–designed building at LaSalle and Randolph streets in the Loop. The desk is open Monday through Friday from 8:30am to 4:30pm.

INFORMATION BY TELEPHONE   The **Mayor's Office of Special Events** operates a recorded hot line (© **312/744-3370**) listing current special events, festivals, and parades occurring throughout the city. The city of Chicago also maintains a 24-hour information line for those with hearing impairments; call © **312/744-8599.**

PUBLICATIONS   Pick up a free copy of *Chicago Parent* magazine at any bookstore, public library, park district buildings, or children's specialty shop. You will also find copies in newspaper vending boxes on Michigan Avenue. Each issue includes a daily calendar of events and a museum page that keeps readers abreast of new openings of interest to kids.

Chicago's major daily newspapers are the *Tribune* and the *Sun-Times.* Both have cultural listings, including movies, theaters, and live music, not to mention reviews of the very latest restaurants that are sure to have appeared in the city since this guidebook went to press. The Friday edition of both papers contains a special pullout section with more detailed, up-to-date information on special events happening over the weekend. *Chicago* magazine is an upscale monthly with good restaurant listings.

In a class by itself is the *Chicago Reader,* a free weekly that is an invaluable source of entertainment listings, classifieds, and well-written articles on contemporary issues of interest in Chicago. Published every Thursday (except the last week of Dec), the weekly has a wide distribution downtown and on the North Side; it is available in many retail stores, in building lobbies, and at the paper's offices, 11 E. Illinois St. (© **312/828-0350**), by about noon on Thursday.

Another free weekly, *New City* (© **312/243-8786**), also publishes excellent comprehensive listings of entertainment options. Appealing to a slightly younger audience than the *Reader,* its editorial tone tends toward the edgy and irreverent. Published every Wednesday, it's available in the same neighborhoods and locations as the *Reader.*

Most Chicago hotels stock their rooms or lobbies with at least one informational magazine, such as *Where Chicago,* that lists the city's entertainment, shopping, and dining locales.

CITY LAYOUT

The **Chicago River** forms a **Y** that divides the city into its three geographic zones: North Side, South Side, and West Side (Lake Michigan is where the East Side would be). The downtown financial district is called **the Loop.** The city's key shopping street is **North Michigan Avenue,** also known as the **Magnificent Mile.** In addition to department stores and vertical malls, this stretch of property north of the river houses many of the city's most elegant hotels. North and south of this downtown zone, Chicago stretches along 29 miles of Lake Michigan shoreline that is, by and large, free of commercial development, reserved for public use as green space and parkland from one end of town to the other.

Chicago proper today has about 3 million inhabitants living in an area about two-thirds the size of New York City; another 5 million make the suburbs their home. The villages north of Chicago now stretch in an unbroken mass nearly to the Wisconsin border; the city's western suburbs extend 30 miles to Naperville, one of the fastest-growing towns in the nation over the past 2 decades. The real

> **Fun Fact   A River Runs Through It**
>
> The Chicago River remains one of the most visible of the city's major physical features. It's spanned by more movable bridges (52 at last count) than any city in the world. An almost-mystical moment occurs downtown when all the bridges spanning the main and south branches—connecting the Loop to both the near–West Side and the near–North Side—are raised, allowing for the passage of some ship or barge or contingent of high-masted sailboats. The Chicago River has long outlived the critical commercial function that it once performed. Most of the remaining millworks that still occupy its banks no longer depend on the river alone for the transport of their materials, raw and finished. The river's main function today is to serve as a fluvial conduit for sewage, which, owing to an engineering feat that reversed its flow inland in 1900, no longer pollutes the waters of Lake Michigan. Recently, Chicagoans have begun to discover another role for the river, that of leisure resource, providing short cruises on its water, park areas, cafes, and public art installations on its banks, and the beginnings of a riverside bike path that connects to the lakefront route near Wacker Drive. Actually, today's developers aren't the first to wonder why the river couldn't be Chicago's Seine. A look at the early-20th-century beaux arts balustrades lining the river along Wacker Drive, complete with comfortably spaced benches—as well as Parisian-style bridge houses—shows that Daniel Burnham knew full well what a treasure the city had.

signature of Chicago, however, is found between the suburbs and the Loop, where a colorful patchwork quilt of residential neighborhoods gives the city a character all its own.

FINDING AN ADDRESS   Having been a part of the Northwest Territory, Chicago is laid out in a **grid system,** with the streets neatly lined up as if on a giant piece of graph paper. Because the city itself isn't rectangular (it's rather elongated), the shape is a bit irregular, but the perpendicular pattern remains. Easing movement through the city are a half-dozen or so major diagonal thoroughfares.

Point zero is located at the downtown intersection of State and Madison streets. **State Street** divides east and west addresses, and **Madison Street** divides north and south addresses. From here, Chicago's highly predictable addressing system begins. Making use of this grid, it is relatively easy to plot the distance in miles between any two points in the city.

Virtually all of Chicago's principal north-south and east-west arteries are spaced by increments of 400 in the addressing system—regardless of the number of smaller streets nestled between them. And each addition or subtraction of 400 numbers to an address is equivalent to a half mile. Thus, starting at point zero on Madison Street and traveling north along State Street for 1 mile, you will come to 800 N. State St., which intersects Chicago Avenue. Continue uptown for another half mile and you arrive at the 1200 block of North State Street at Division Street. And so it goes, right to the city line, with suburban Evanston located at the 7600 block north, 9½ miles from point zero.

The same rule applies when you're traveling south, or east to west. Thus, heading west from State Street along Madison Street, Halsted Street—at 800 W. Madison St.—is a mile's distance, while Racine Avenue, at the 1200 block of West Madison Street, is 1½ miles from the center. Madison Street then continues westward to Chicago's boundary with the near suburb of Oak Park along Austin Avenue, which, at 6000 W. Madison, is approximately 7½ miles from point zero.

The key to understanding the grid is that the side of any square formed by the principal avenues (noted in dark or red ink on most maps) represents a distance of half a mile in any direction. Understanding how Chicago's grid system works is of particular importance to those visitors who want to do a lot of walking in the city's many neighborhoods and who want to plot in advance the distances involved in trekking from one locale to another.

The other ingeniously convenient aspect of the grid is that every major road uses the same numerical system. In other words, the cross street (Division St.) at 1200 N. Lake Shore Dr. is the same as at 1200 N. Clark St., which is the same as at 1200 N. LaSalle St., and so on.

STREET MAPS   A suitably detailed map of Chicago is published by **Rand McNally,** available at many newsstands and bookstores for $2.95 to $3.95 (the smaller, more manageable laminated versions run about $5.95). Rand McNally operates a thoroughly stocked retail store at 444 N. Michigan Ave. (© **312/ 321-1751**), just north of the Wrigley Building.

NEIGHBORHOODS IN BRIEF

The Loop & Vicinity

Downtown   In the case of Chicago, downtown means the Loop. The Loop refers literally to a core of primarily commercial, governmental, and cultural buildings contained within a corral of elevated train tracks, but greater downtown Chicago overflows these confines and is bounded by the Chicago River to the north and west, by Michigan Avenue to the east, and by Roosevelt Avenue to the south. The main attractions for families in the Loop are the Art Institute, the Cultural Center, and the Harold Washington Library. If you are catching a show, you'll find the revitalized theater district in the North Loop. Marshall Field's on State Street, famous for its windows during the holidays, anchors a strip of retail shopping.

The North Side

Near North/Magnificent Mile North Michigan Avenue is known as the Magnificent Mile, from the bridge spanning the Chicago River to its northern tip at Oak Street. Many of the city's best hotels, shops, and restaurants are to be found on and around elegant North Michigan Avenue. Here you'll find the Terra Museum of American Art and the Museum of Contemporary Art— but the focus is not museums, but shopping. The area stretching east of Michigan Avenue to the lake is also sometimes referred to as "Streeterville"—the legacy of George Wellington "Cap" Streeter, an eccentric, bankrupt showman who staked out 200 acres of self-created landfill here about a century ago after his steamship had run aground on the shore, and then declared himself "governor" of the "District of Lake Michigan." True story.

River North   Just to the west of the Mag Mile's zone of high life and sophistication is an old warehouse district called River North. It's also

Chicago Neighborhoods

A Dining in Lincoln Park & Wrigleyville;
Lincoln Park & North Side Accommodations;
Entertainment in Lincoln Park & Wrigleyville

B Dining & Shopping in Wicker Park/Bucktown

C Central Chicago Accommodations;
Central Chicago Attractions;
Central Chicago Dining;
Entertainment in the Loop & Magnificent
Mile

D Near North & River North Accommodations;
Magnificent Mile Shopping

E The Loop Sculpture Tour

F South Michigan Avenue
& Grant Park Attractions

G Hyde Park Attractions

0 1 mi
0 1 km

LINCOLNWOOD

Touhy Ave.

Rogers

ROGERS PARK

Devon Ave.

Loyola University/
Mundelein College

Peterson Ave.

Northeastern
Illinois University

14

41

Foster Ave.

ANDERSONVILLE

Lawrence Ave.

LINCOLN SQUARE

UPTOWN

Broadway

Lake Shore Dr.

90
94

Irving Park Rd.

19

IRVING PARK

A

WRIGLEYVILLE

Addison St.

Wrigley
Field

Belmont Ave.

LAKEVIEW

*Lake
Michigan*

John F. Kennedy Expwy.

Milwaukee Ave.

41

LINCOLN
PARK

DePaul
University

*Lincoln
Park*

Fullerton Ave.

LOGAN
SQUARE

Pulaski

BUCKTOWN/
WICKER PARK

Halsted St.

C

OLD
TOWN

64

North Ave.

B

GOLD COAST

*Oak Street
Beach*

Humboldt
Park

NEAR NORTH

50

Grand Ave.

Chicago Ave.

RIVER
NORTH

D

STREETER-
VILLE

← To Oak Park

*Garfield
Park*

United
Center

NEAR
WEST

La Salle St.

Navy Pier

Magnificent Mile

Washington St.

Cicero Ave.

Eisenhower Expwy.

THE
LOOP

290

Chicago River

State St.

E

Michigan Ave.

*Grant
Park*

Roosevelt Rd.

*Douglas
Park*

Cermak Rd.

Museum Campus

F

✈ **Meigs Field**

Ogden Ave.

PILSEN

CHINATOWN

■ **McCormick
Place**

31st St.

31st St.

*31st Street
Beach*

Sanitary and Ship Canal

55

BRIDGEPORT

35th St.

*Burnham
Park*

Stevenson Expwy.

CANARYVILLE

**Comiskey
Park**

Pershing Rd.

Oakwood
Blvd.

Archer Ave.

Blvd.

Ave.

Ave.

47th St.

St.

Michigan Ave.

Dr. Martin Luther King Jr. Dr.

Lake Shore Dr.

Kedzie Ave.

Western

Damen

Ashland

Halsted

Garfield Blvd.

G

51st St.

*Washington
Park*

55th St.

✈
Midway Airport

55th St.

HYDE PARK
Midway
Plaisance

the site of most "chain" restaurants catering to the kid set. Over the past 15 to 20 years, the area has experienced a rebirth as one of the city's most vital commercial districts, and today it is filled with many of the city's hottest restaurants, nightspots, art galleries, and loft dwellings. Several large-scale residential loft-conversion developments have lately been sprouting on its western and southwestern fringes.

The Gold Coast Some of Chicago's most desirable real estate and historic architecture are found along Lake Shore Drive, between Oak Street and North Avenue and along the adjacent side streets. Despite trendy little pockets of real estate popping up elsewhere, the moneyed class still prefers to live by the lake. This residential area doesn't offer much for kids, but does have beautiful scenic streets for walking. On the neighborhood's western edge, the northern stretch of State Street just south of Division Street has, in recent years, developed into a thriving zone of restaurants, bars, and nightclubs.

Old Town West of LaSalle Street, principally on North Wells Street between Division Street and North Avenue, is the nightlife district of Old Town. On Wells Street, a few blocks east and a few blocks west of North Avenue, you'll find plenty of families and strollers during the day. This area was a hippie haven in the 1960s and '70s, but in recent years its residential areas have been rapidly gentrified as Cabrini Green, America's most notorious housing project, has finally fallen to the wrecking ball. Old Town's biggest claim to fame, the legendary Second City comedy club, has served up the lighter side of life to Chicagoans for more than 30 years.

Lincoln Park Chicago's most popular residential neighborhood is fashionable Lincoln Park. The neighborhood is notable for visiting families because it is bordered on the east by the huge park of the same name, which is home to two major museums and one of the nation's oldest zoos (established in 1868). The trapezoid formed by Clark Street, Armitage Avenue, Halsted Street, and Diversey Parkway also contains many of Chicago's most happening bars, restaurants, retail stores, music clubs, and off-Loop theaters—including the nationally acclaimed Steppenwolf Theatre Company.

Lakeview & Wrigleyville Wrigleyville is the name given to the neighborhood in the vicinity of Wrigley Field—home of the Chicago Cubs—at Sheffield Avenue and Addison Street. Many homesteaders have moved into these areas in recent years, and a slew of nightclubs and restaurants have followed in their wake. Midway up the city's North Side is a one-time blue-collar, now mainstream middle-class and Bohemian quarter called Lakeview. It has become the neighborhood of choice for many gays and lesbians, recent college graduates, and a growing number of residents priced out of Lincoln Park. The main thoroughfare is Belmont Avenue, between Broadway and Sheffield Avenue.

Uptown & Andersonville Uptown, along the lake and about as far north as Foster Avenue, is where the latest wave of immigrants—including internal migrants from Appalachia and the Native American reservations—has settled. Vietnamese and Chinese immigrants have transformed Argyle Street between Broadway and Sheridan Road into a teeming market for fresh meat, fish, and all kinds of exotic vegetables. Slightly to the north and west is the old Scandinavian neighborhood of Andersonville, whose main drag is Clark Street, between Foster and Bryn Mawr avenues. This neighborhood is friendly to families, with the feel of a small Midwestern village, albeit one with an eclectic mix of Middle Eastern restaurants, a distinct cluster of women-owned businesses, and a burgeoning gay and lesbian community. You'll find Ann Sather restaurant, the Swedish-American Museum, the Swedish Bakery, and Women and Children First, a great bookstore.

Lincoln Square Families flock to Old Town School of Folk Music's theater and education center, a beautiful restoration of a former library building, in this neighborhood located west of Andersonville and slightly to the south, where Lincoln, Western, and Lawrence avenues intersect. Lincoln Square was the home to Chicago's once-vast German–American community. Lincoln Square now also has a distinctly Greek flavor, with several restaurants of that nationality, to boot. The surrounding leafy residential streets are now experiencing an influx of white middle-class families.

Rogers Park Rogers Park, which begins at Devon Avenue, is located on the northern fringes of the city bordering suburban Evanston. Its western half has been a Jewish neighborhood for decades. The eastern half, dominated by Loyola University's lakefront campus, has become the most cosmopolitan enclave in the entire city: Asians, East Indians, Russian Jews, and German Americans live side by side with African Americans and the ethnically mixed student population drawn to the Catholic university. Much of Rogers Park has a neo-hippie ambience, but the western stretch of Devon Avenue is a Midwestern slice of Calcutta, settled by Indians who've transformed the street into a veritable restaurant row of tandoori chicken and curry-flavored dishes.

The West Side

Near West On the Near West Side, just across the Chicago River from the Loop, on Halsted Street between Adams and Monroe streets, is Chicago's old "Greek Town," still the Greek culinary center of the city. Much of the old Italian neighborhood in this vicinity was the victim of urban renewal, but remnants still survive on Taylor Street; the same is true for a few old delis and shops on Maxwell Street, dating from the turn of the 20th century when a large Jewish community lived in the area.

Bucktown/Wicker Park Centered near the confluence of North, Damen, and Milwaukee avenues, where the Art Deco Northwest Tower is the tallest thing for miles, this resurgent area is said to be home to the third-largest concentration of artists in the country. Over the past century, the area has hosted waves of German, Polish, and, most recently, Spanish-speaking immigrants (not to mention writer Nelson Algren). In recent years, it has morphed into a bastion of hot new restaurants, alternative culture, and loft-dwelling yuppies surfing the gentrification wave that's washing over this still-somewhat-gritty neighborhood.

The South Side

South Loop The generically rechristened South Loop area was Chicago's original "Gold Coast" in the late 19th century, with Prairie Avenue (now a historic district) as its most exclusive address. But in the wake of the 1893 World's Columbian Exposition in Hyde Park, and continuing through the

Prohibition era of the 1920s, the area was infamous for its Levee vice district, home to gambling and prostitution, some of the most corrupt politicians in Chicago history, and Al Capone's headquarters at the old Lexington Hotel. However, in recent years, its prospects have turned around. The South Loop—stretching from Harrison Street's historic Printers Row south to Cermak Road (where Chinatown begins), and from Lake Shore Drive west to the south branch of the Chicago River— is one of the fast-growing residential neighborhoods in the city.

Pilsen Originally home to the nation's largest settlement of Bohemian-Americans, Pilsen (which derives its name from a city in Bohemia) was for decades the principal entry point in Chicago for immigrants of every ethnic stripe. Centered at Halsted and 18th streets just southwest of the Loop, it is now the second-largest Mexican–American community in the United States. One of the city's most vibrant and colorful neighborhoods, Pilsen has been happily invaded by the outdoor mural movement launched years earlier in Mexico, and it boasts a profusion of authentic taquerias and bakeries. The neighborhood's annual Day of the Dead celebration, which begins in September, is an elaborate festival that runs for 8 weeks. The artistic spirit that permeates the community isn't confined to Latin American art. In recent years, artists of every stripe, drawn partly by the

availability of loft space in Pilsen, have nurtured a small but thriving artists' colony.

Bridgeport & Canaryville Bridgeport, whose main intersection is 35th and Halsted streets, has been the neighborhood of two Mayor Daleys, father and son (the son moved not too long ago to the new Central Station development in the South Loop area). After the old Comiskey Park was torn down, the Chicago White Sox stayed in Bridgeport, inaugurating their new stadium there. Nearby Canaryville, just south and west, is typical of the "back of the yard," blue-collar neighborhoods that once surrounded the Chicago Stockyards. Neither area offers much to the typical visitor; in fact, "outsiders" aren't all that welcome.

Hyde Park Hyde Park's main attraction for families is the world-famous Museum of Science and Industry. Hyde Park is like an independent village within the confines of Chicago, right off Lake Michigan and roughly a 30-minute train ride from the Loop. The main drag is 57th Street, and the University of Chicago—with all its attendant shops and restaurants—is the neighborhood's principal tenant. The most successful racially integrated community in the city, Hyde Park is an oasis of furious intellectual activity and liberalism that, ironically, is hemmed in on all sides by neighborhoods suffering some of the highest crime rates in Chicago.

2 Getting Around

The best way to savor Chicago is by walking its streets. Fortunately, it's also one of the easiest ways to get around with kids. But when walking is not practical— such as when moving between distant neighborhoods or getting around on cold winter days—Chicago's public train and bus systems are efficient modes of transportation. In fact, they may be the least expensive way of entertaining your child while visiting the city.

BY PUBLIC TRANSPORTATION

The **Chicago Transit Authority (CTA)** operates an extensive system of trains and buses throughout the city of Chicago. The sturdy system carries about 1.3 million passengers a day. Recently, the CTA has been trying to reverse declining ridership by sprucing up some of the grittier stations and introducing more efficient operating procedures, such as timetables and new fare cards. Subways and elevated trains (known as the El) are generally safe and reliable, although it's advisable to avoid long rides through unfamiliar neighborhoods late at night.

The bus and the El each has its pros and cons when traveling with kids. Parents with infants might prefer the El, since carrying a baby and a stroller up the bus steps (then paying the fare and finding a seat as the bus lurches into traffic) requires strength, coordination, and nerves of steel. Until your child can climb up steps, the easy-on, easy-off advantage of the El makes it the better choice (in spite of the fact that you might have to carry your stroller up and down stairs to reach the train platform).

Fares for the bus, subway, and El are $1.50, with an additional 30¢ for a transfer that allows CTA riders to make two transfers on the bus or El within 2 hours of receipt. Children under 7 ride free, and those between the ages of 7 and 11 pay 75¢ (15¢ for transfers). Senior citizens can also receive the reduced fare if they have the appropriate reduced-fare permit. (Call ✆ **312/836-7000** for details on how to obtain one, although this is probably not a realistic option for a short-term visitor.)

Adopting a system used by other urban transit agencies, the CTA uses credit card–size fare cards that automatically deduct the exact fare each time you take a ride. The reusable cards can be purchased with a preset value already stored ($13.50 for 10 rides, or $16.50 for 10 rides and 10 transfers), or riders can obtain cards at vending machines located at all CTA train stations and charge them with whatever amount they choose (a minimum of $3 and up to $100). If within 2 hours of your first ride you transfer to a bus or the El, the turnstiles at the El stations and the fare boxes on buses will automatically deduct from your card just the cost of a transfer (30¢). If you make a second transfer within 2 hours, it's free. The same card can be recharged continuously.

Fare cards can be used on buses, but you can't buy a card on the bus. If you get on the bus without a fare card, you'll have to pay $1.50 cash (either in coins or in dollar bills); the bus drivers cannot make change, so make sure that you've got the right amount before hopping on board.

CTA INFORMATION   The CTA operates a useful telephone information service (✆ **836-7000** or TTY 836-4949 from any area code in the city and suburbs) that functions daily from 5am to 1am. When you want to know how to get from where you are to where you want to go, call the CTA. Make sure that you specify any conditions you might require—the fastest route, for example, or the simplest (the route with the fewest transfers or the least amount of walking), and so forth. You can also check out the CTA's website at **www.transit chicago.com**. Excellent CTA comprehensive maps, which include both El and bus routes, are usually available at subway or El stations, or by calling the CTA. The CTA also has added a toll-free customer service hot line (✆ **888/YOUR-CTA** or TTY 888/CTA-TTY1 Mon–Fri 7am–8pm, with voice mail operating after hours) to field questions and feedback. While the new fare-box system has eliminated the need for ticket agents, agents are still available at some El stations to offer customer assistance.

Tips **The Visitor Pass**

Consider buying a **Visitor Pass,** which works like a fare card and allows individual users unlimited rides on the El and CTA buses over a 24-hour period. The cards cost $5 and are sold at airports, hotels, museums, Hot Tix outlets, transportation hubs, and Chicago Office of Tourism visitor information centers. Also available now are 2-, 3-, and 5-day passes. While the passes save you the trouble of feeding the fare machines yourself, remember that they're economical only if you plan to make at least three distinct trips at least 2 or more hours apart. (You get 2 additional transfers for an additional 30¢ on a regular fare.)

BY THE EL & THE SUBWAY   The rapid transit system operates five major lines, which the CTA recently began identifying by color (although Chicagoans often still refer to them by their points of origin): the **Red Line** (also known as the Howard/Dan Ryan Line) runs north-south; the **Green Line** (also known as the Lake Street Line) runs west-south; the **Blue Line** (also known as the O'Hare Line) runs west-northwest to O'Hare Airport; the **Brown Line** (also known as the Ravenswood Line) runs in a northern zigzag route; and the **Orange Line** runs southwest, serving Midway airport.

A separate express line, the **Purple Line,** services Evanston, while a smaller, local line in Skokie (the **Yellow Line,** also known as the Skokie Swift) is linked to the north-south Red Line. Skokie and Evanston are adjacent suburbs on Chicago's northern boundary.

Study your CTA map carefully (there's one printed on the inside back cover of this guide) before boarding any train. While most trains run every 5 to 20 minutes, decreasing in frequency in the off-peak and overnight hours, some stations close after work hours (as early as 8:30pm) and remain closed on Saturday, Sunday, and holidays. The Orange Line train does not operate from about 11:30pm to 5am, the Brown Line operates only north of Belmont after about 9:30pm, the Blue Line's Cermak branch has ceased operating overnight and on weekends, and the Purple Line no longer runs overnight as well.

The CTA recently posted timetables on the El platforms so that you can determine when the next train should arrive.

BY BUS   Add to Chicago's gridlike layout a comprehensive system of public buses and virtually every place in the city is within close walking distance of a bus stop. Other than on foot or bicycle, the best way to get around Chicago's warren of neighborhoods—the best way to actually see what's around you—is by riding a public bus. (The view from the elevated trains can be pretty dramatic too; the difference is that on the trains, you get the backyards, while on the bus, you see the buildings' facades and the street life.) Look for the **blue-and-white signs to locate bus stops,** which are spaced about 1 or 2 blocks apart.

A few buses that are particularly handy for many visitors are the **no. 146 Marine/Michigan,** an express bus from Belmont Avenue on the North Side that cruises down North Lake Shore Drive (and through Lincoln Park during non-peak times) to North Michigan Avenue, State Street, and the Grant Park museum campus; the **no. 151 Sheridan,** which passes through Lincoln Park en route to inner Lake Shore Drive and then travels along Michigan Avenue as far south as Adams Street, where it turns west into the Loop (and stops at Union

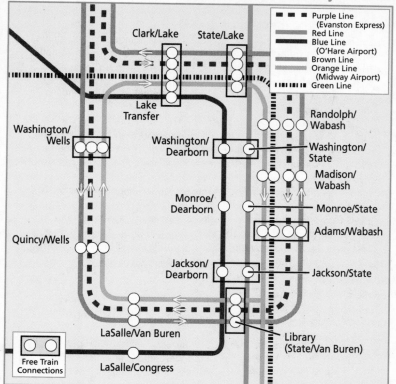

Station); and the **no. 156 LaSalle,** which goes through Lincoln Park and then into the Loop's financial district on LaSalle Street.

PACE buses (© **836-7000** from any Chicago area code, or 847/364-7223, Mon–Fri 8am–5pm; www.pacebus.com) cover the suburban zones that surround Chicago. They run every 20 to 30 minutes during rush hour, operating until mid-evening Monday through Friday and early evening on weekends. Suburban bus routes are marked no. 208 and above, and vehicles may be flagged down at intersections because few of the lines have bus stops that are marked.

BY COMMUTER TRAIN

If you plan to visit suburban destinations, your best public transportation bet is the **Metra** commuter railroad (© **312/322-6777** or TTY 312/322-6774 Mon–Fri 8am–5pm; at other times, call Regional Transportation Authority [RTA] at © 312/836-7000 or TTY 312/836-4949; www.metrarail.com). The Metra serves the six-county suburban area around Chicago with 12 train lines. Several terminals are located downtown, including **Union Station** at Adams and Canal streets, **LaSalle Street Station** at LaSalle and Van Buren streets, **North Western Station** at Madison and Canal streets, and **Randolph Street Station** at Randolph Street and Michigan Avenue.

To visit some of the most affluent suburbs in the country, take the **Union Pacific North Line** (previously known as the North Western train), which

Fun Fact **Sky Train: Chicago's El**

It's a rare Hollywood film or TV series set in the Windy City that doesn't frame its stars against that most archetypal of Chicago images: the city's elevated train system, more commonly known as the **"El."** But the origin of the El has nothing to do with its celebrated gritty, rumbling, rail-screeching urban aesthetic.

Chicago made a miraculous recovery after the Great Fire of 1871— within 20 years, a sea of neighborhoods appeared on former prairies and swamps, and the downtown district overflowed with people, streetcars, wagons, horses, and horse droppings. The boom created two problems: It was hard to get downtown quickly in the pre-automobile era, and, once you got downtown, it was impossible to actually move around.

So Chicago took to the sky, building a system of elevated trains 15 feet above all the madness. The South Side line (part of today's Green Line) was the first, opening in 1892 and running to 39th Street, about 5 miles south from downtown; the following year, the line was extended to Jackson Park, bringing commuters to the World's Fair. In 1893, the Lake Street line (also part of today's Green Line) began running to the West Side, and the Metropolitan West Side Elevated (part of today's Blue Line, serving the Northwest and West sides) opened in 1895.

The first El trains on the South Side and Lake Street lines were steam-powered, but the Metropolitan West Side Line debuted with a new-fangled electric style of train. The cleaner, quieter trains were a hit, and the other El lines followed the West Side's lead. In 1896, the Lake Street Line started using electricity, and the South Side Line got wired in 1898. These lines were run by competing companies, and each line had its own terminal on the outskirts of downtown, so commuters still had to negotiate the traffic and the filth of downtown streets once they got off the train.

In 1895, the three El companies collaborated to build a set of tracks into and around the central business district that all the lines would then share. By 1897, the "Loop" was up and running, but it would take almost 100 years before the "El" would connect the whole city.

Chicago's El wasn't the nation's first. That honor belongs to New York City, which started running its elevated trains in 1867, 25 years before Chicago. But the New York El has almost disappeared, moving underground and turning into a subway early this century. With 289 miles of track, Chicago has the biggest El in the country, and the second-largest public transportation system.

departs at the North Western Station, and select from among the following destinations: Kenilworth, Winnetka, Glencoe, Highland Park, and Lake Forest.

The **Metra Electric** (once known as the Illinois Central–Gulf Railroad, or the IC) runs close to Lake Michigan on a track that occupies some of the most valuable real estate in Chicago. It will take you to Hyde Park. You can catch the

Metra Electric in the Loop at the Randolph Street Station and at the Van Buren Street Station at Van Buren Street and Michigan Avenue.

Commuter trains have graduated fare schedules based on the distance you ride. On weekends and holidays and during the summer, Metra offers a family discount that allows up to three children under age 12 to ride free when accompanying a paid adult. The commuter railroad also offers a $5 weekend pass for unlimited rides on Saturday and Sunday.

BY TAXI

I don't recommend taking taxis with young children, because you will not be able to use a car seat in a taxi. With older children, however, taxis are a pretty affordable way to get around the Loop and to get to the dining, shopping, and entertainment options found beyond downtown, such as on the Near North Side, in Old Town and Lincoln Park, and on the Near West Side. But for longer distances, the fares will add up.

Taxis are easy to hail in the Loop, on the Magnificent Mile and the Gold Coast, in River North, and in Lincoln Park, but if you go much beyond these key areas, you might need to call. Cab companies include **Flash Cab** (© 773/ 561-1444), **Yellow Cab** (© 312/TAXI-CAB or 312/829-4222), and **Checker Cab** (© 312/CHECKER or 312/243-2537).

The meter in Chicago cabs currently starts at $1.60 and increases $1.40 for each mile, with a 50¢ surcharge for each additional rider age 12 to 65.

BY CAR

Chicago is laid out so logically that it's relatively easy for visitors to get around the city by car. Although rush-hour traffic jams are just as frustrating as they are in other large U.S. cities, traffic runs fairly smoothly at most times of the day. The combination of wide streets and strategically spaced expressways makes for generally easy riding. But Chicagoans have learned to be prepared for unexpected delays; it seems that at least one major highway and several downtown streets are under repair throughout the spring and summer months. (Some say we have 2 seasons here: winter and construction.)

Great diagonal corridors—such as Lincoln Avenue, Clark Street, and Milwaukee Avenue—slice through the grid pattern at key points in the city and shorten many a trip that would otherwise be tedious on the checkerboard surface of the Chicago streets. **Lake Shore Drive** (also known as the Outer Drive) has to be one of the most scenic and useful urban thoroughfares anywhere. You can travel the length of the city (and beyond), never far from the great lake that is Chicago's most awesome natural feature.

DRIVING RULES   One bizarre anomaly in the organization of Chicago's traffic is the occasional absence of signal lights off the principal avenues, notably in the River North and Streeterville neighborhoods. A block east or west of the Magnificent Mile (North Michigan Ave.)—one of the most traveled streets in the city—you will in some cases encounter only stop signs to control the flow of traffic. Once you've become accustomed to the system, it works very smoothly, with everyone—pedestrians and motorists alike—advancing in their proper turn.

Unless otherwise posted, a right turn on red is allowed after stopping and signaling.

PARKING   Parking regulations are vigorously enforced throughout the city. Read signs carefully: The streets around Michigan Avenue have no-parking restrictions during rush hour—and I know from firsthand experience that your car will be towed immediately. Many neighborhoods have adopted resident-only parking that prohibits others from parking on their streets, usually after 6pm each day (even all day in a few areas, such as Old Town). The neighborhood around Wrigley Field is off-limits during Cubs night games, so look for yellow sidewalk signs alerting drivers about the dozen-and-a-half times the Cubs play under lights. You can park in permit zones if you're visiting a friend, who can provide you with a pass to stick on your windshield. Beware of tow zones, and, if visiting in winter, make note of curbside warnings regarding snow plowing.

A safe bet is valet parking, which most restaurants provide for $6 to $9. Downtown you might also opt to park in a public garage, but you might have to pay the premium prices common in any metropolitan area. (Several garages connected with malls or other major attractions offer discounted parking with a validated ticket.)

The city runs convenient public parking underneath **Grant Park,** with entrances at Michigan Avenue at Van Buren Street (© 312/747-2519) and Michigan Avenue and Monroe Street (© 312/742-7530). You can get an "early-bird" daily rate of $13 if you're in by 10am; otherwise, you'll pay $10 for the first hour, $13 for up to 2 hours and $16 for 2 to 10 hours. You'll find similar (or slightly higher) prices at most other downtown lots, including **McCormick Place Parking,** 2301 S. Lake Shore Dr. (© 312/747-7194); **Midcontinental Plaza Garage,** 55 E. Monroe St. (© 312/986-6821); and **Navy Pier Parking,** 600 E. Grand Ave. (© 312/595-7437).

CAR RENTAL Hertz (© 800/654-3131), **Avis** (© 800/831-2847), **National** (© 800/227-7368), and **Budget** (© 800/527-0700) all have offices at O'Hare Airport and at Midway Airport. Each company also has at least one office downtown: Hertz at 401 N. State St., Avis at 214 N. Clark St., National at 203 N. LaSalle St., and Budget at 65 E. Lake St.

BY BOAT

Boat transport is a great way to get around with kids. And boat traffic in Chicago has been stirring up a bigger wake these days. **Shoreline Sightseeing** (© **312/222-9328**) has started ferrying passengers on the lake between Navy Pier and the Shedd Aquarium, and on the Chicago River between Navy Pier and the Sears Tower (Adams St. and the river). The **water taxis** operate daily Memorial Day to Labor Day every half-hour and cost $6 for adults, $5 for seniors, and $3 for children.

If you are staying in the suburbs and traveling to the Magnificent Mile, kids will love a ride on the Metra commuter train followed by a ride on a shuttle boat operated by **Wendella Commuter Boats** (© **312/337-1446**), which float daily April through October between a dock below North Western Station, the commuter train station across the river from the Loop, and the Wrigley Building (the boats dock on the northwest side of the Michigan Ave. bridge). The ride, which costs $1.50 each way (or 10 rides for $11) and takes about 8 minutes, is popular with both visitors and commuters. The service operates every 10 minutes from 7am to 7pm.

Wendella recently added a water taxi of its own, a 38-foot, 74-passenger river bus operating daily between the North Western and Union Station train stations and the River East pier (just east of the Michigan Avenue bridge) beginning at 9am. A one-way fare costs $2.

BY BICYCLE

I wouldn't recommend trying to ride bicycles on the city streets with kids. While the city of Chicago has earned kudos for its efforts to improve conditions for bicycling, it can still be a rough road trying to compete with cars and their drivers, who aren't always so willing to share the road. You might, however, want to take to the lakefront path or area parks.

Bike Chicago (© **800/915-BIKE**), located at Navy Pier, rents all sorts of bikes, including tandems and four-seater "quadcycles," as well as in-line skates. Bikes rent for $8 an hour or $30 a day ($20 an hour for quadcycles). Bike Chicago also offers free delivery to hotels for group daily rentals and leads a free lakefront bike tour from Navy Pier at 1:30pm daily. Helmets, pads, and locks are free. The shop is open daily from 8am to about 11pm, weather permitting.

The **Chicagoland Bicycle Federation** (© **312/42-PEDAL;** www.chibike fed.org), a nonprofit advocacy group, is a good resource for bicyclists. The group publishes several bicycling maps with tips on recommended on-street routes and parkland routes, and a guide to safe cycling in the city.

3 Planning Your Outings

Planning a day of touring a city with kids is a little like mapping out a military campaign: You should have a list of sights to hit, and a precise idea of how you will get from one activity to the next, leaving time in between for potty breaks and snack stops. If you plan carefully and center all your days' activities in close proximity, you can save yourself a lot of wasted transit time.

Prime areas for families include the **Magnificent Mile,** with the John Hancock Center, American Girl Place, FAO Schwarz, Niketown and other shopping destinations; **Streeterville,** home of Navy Pier and the Museum of Contemporary Art; **River North,** with lots of chain establishments, including ESPN Zone, Hard Rock Cafe, Rock 'n' Roll McDonald's, and Ed Debevic's; **Lincoln Park,** with the park, zoo, and botanical gardens; **Museum Campus,** with four museums within walking distance of each other; and **Hyde Park,** home to the Museum of Science and Industry.

FINDING A RESTROOM

The number-one tip for visitors from Chicago parents: Know where the nearest restroom is at all times! So, part of your daily battle plan must include knowing prime locations for restrooms. First order of business: Always use the bathroom at your hotel before you leave, and stop in the restroom before you leave any museum or restaurant. Failing that, key restrooms in prime locations include: **900 N. Michigan Avenue mall,** on the second and fifth floors; **John Hancock Center,** in the lower level; **Water Tower Place;** and **Nordstrom's,** located in the Shops at North Bridge. Most **Starbuck's** have restrooms—just ask the barista for the key. Major hotel lobbies are also good bets. Most restaurants will take pity on a distressed child, so just ask; some store owners may do the same.

NURSING MOMS & INFANTS

Chicago is slightly more conservative than other big cities: While most people will see a nursing mom and look the other way, some might stare rudely. If you need to breast-feed an infant, you'll feel most comfortable in women's lounges in major department stores. (**Nordstrom's** is best.)

FAST FACTS: Chicago

American Express Travel-service offices are located at the following locations: across from the Art Institute, at 122 S. Michigan Ave. (© 312/435-2595); across from the Virgin Megastore, at 605 N. Michigan Ave. (© 312/435-2570); and in Lincoln Park, at 2338 N. Clark St. (© 773/477-4000).

Area Codes Like many other urban areas, Chicago has been split into several different area codes. The **312** area code long held by the entire city proper now applies to the Loop and the neighborhoods closest to it, including River North, North Michigan Avenue, and the Gold Coast. The rest of the city now has **773** for an area code. Suburban area codes are **847** (northern), **708** (west and southwest), and **630** (far west). Prefixes that have been assigned the new area code are listed in the front of the telephone book.

Babysitters Check with the concierge or desk staff at your hotel, who are likely to maintain a list of reliable sitters with whom they have worked in the past. Many of the hotels work with the **American Registry for Nannies & Sitters, Inc.** (© **800/240-1820** or 773/248-8100; fax 773/248-8104), a state-licensed babysitting service that can match you with a sitter. The sitters are required to pass background checks, provide multiple child-care references, and be trained in infant and child CPR. It's best to make a reservation 24 hours in advance; the office is open from 9am to 5pm. Rates are about $12 per hour, with a 4-hour minimum.

Business Hours Shops generally keep normal business hours, Monday through Saturday from 10am to 6pm. Most stores generally stay open late at least 1 evening a week. And certain businesses, such as bookstores, are almost always open during the evening hours all week. Most shops (other than in the Loop) are now open on Sunday as well, usually from noon to 5pm. Malls, including Water Tower Place at 835 N. Michigan Ave., are generally open until 7pm (Marshall Field's and Lord & Taylor in Water Tower Place stay open until 9pm) and are open Sunday as well. Banking hours in Chicago are normally from 9am (8am, in some cases) to 3pm Monday through Friday, with select banks remaining open later on specified afternoons and evenings.

Car Rentals See "Getting Around," earlier in this chapter.

Dentists The 24-hour **Dental Referral Service** (© 630/978-5745) can refer you to an area dentist. You also might try your hotel concierge or desk staff, who often keep a list of dentists.

Doctors In the event of a medical emergency, your best bet—unless you have friends who can recommend a doctor—is to rely on your hotel physician or go to the nearest hospital emergency room. **Northwestern Memorial Hospital** also has a **Physician Referral Service** (© 877/926-4664). See also "Hospitals," below.

Driving Rules See "Getting Around," earlier in this chapter.

Drugstores **Walgreens,** 757 N. Michigan Ave. at E. Chicago Street (© 312/664-4000), is open 24 hours. Two other 24-hour locations are 641 N. Clark St. at W. Ontario Street (© 312/587-0904), and 1200 N. Dearborn at W. Division Street (© 312/943-0971). **Osco Drugs** has a toll-free number

(© 800/654-6726) that you can call to locate the 24-hour pharmacy nearest you.

Embassies & Consulates   See appendix A, "For International Visitors."

Emergencies   For fire or police emergencies, call © **911**. The nonemergency phone number for the Chicago Police Department is © **312/747-6000**. The city of Chicago proclaims the following policy: "In emergency, dial 911 and a city ambulance will respond free of charge to the patient. The ambulance will take the patient to the nearest emergency room according to geographic location." If you desire a specific, nonpublic ambulance, call **Chicago Ambulance** (© **773/521-7777**).

Hospitals   The best hospital emergency room in Chicago is, by consensus, at **Northwestern Memorial Hospital,** 251 E. Huron St. (© **312/926-2000;** www.nmh.org), which opened its new state-of-the-art medical center right off North Michigan Avenue in spring 1999. The emergency department (© **312/926-5188** or 312/944-2358 for TDD access) is located at 240 E. Erie St. near Fairbanks Court. For an ambulance, dial © **911**.

Maps   See "City Layout," in section 1, "Orientation," earlier in this chapter.

Newspapers & Magazines   The *Chicago Tribune* (© **312/222-3232;** www.chicagotribune.com) and the *Chicago Sun-Times* (© **312/321-3000;** www.suntimes.com) are the two major dailies. The *Chicago Reader* (© **312/828-0350;** www.chireader.com) is a free weekly that appears each Thursday, with all the current entertainment and cultural listings. *Chicago Magazine* (www.chicagomag.com) is a monthly that is widely read for its restaurant reviews. *CS* is a free lifestyle monthly that covers nightlife, dining, fashion, shopping, and other cultural pursuits. The *Chicago Defender* covers local and national news of interest to the African-American community. The Spanish-language *La Raza* (www.laraza.com) reports on stories from a Latino point of view. *Windy City Times* (www.outlineschicago.com) publishes both news and feature articles about gay and lesbian issues.

Police   For emergencies, call © **911**. For nonemergencies, call © **312/747-6000**.

Post Office   The new main post office is at 433 W. Harrison St. (© **312/654-3895**), with free parking; there are also convenient branches in the Sears Tower, the Federal Center Plaza at 211 S. Clark St. (designed by Mies van der Rohe, no less), the James R. Thompson Center at 100 W. Randolph St., and a couple of blocks off the Magnificent Mile at 227 E. Ontario St.

Radio   **WBEZ** (91.5 FM) is the local National Public Radio station, which plays jazz in the evenings. **WFMT** (98.7 FM) specializes in fine arts and classical music, and for years was the home of Studs Terkel's syndicated interview show. One of the more special stations anywhere recently celebrated its 25th anniversary: **WXRT** (93.1 FM), a progressive rock station whose DJs don't stick to corporate-sanctioned play lists but mix things up with shots of blues, jazz, and local music. On the AM side of the dial, you'll find talk radio on **WGN** (720) and **WLS** (890)—two longtime stations that got their names from their immodest owners (respectively, that would be the *Chicago Tribune,* the "World's Greatest Newspaper"; and Sears, the "World's Largest Store"). News junkies should tune to **WBBM** (780) for nonstop news, traffic, and weather reports, and sports fans will find company on the talk station **WSCR** (1160).

Safety Chicago has all the crime problems of any urban center, so use your common sense and stay cautious and alert. Everyone has a different comfort level in unfamiliar terrain, so you'll have to decide for yourself where and when you want to venture. At night you might want to stick to well-lighted streets along the Magnificent Mile, River North, Gold Coast, and Lincoln Park (stay out of the park proper after dark, though), which are all high-traffic areas late into the night. Don't walk alone at night, and avoid wandering down dark residential streets, even those that seem perfectly safe. Muggings can—and do—happen anywhere.

After dark, you might want to avoid the Loop's interior, which gets deserted after business hours, as well as neighborhoods such as Hyde Park, Wicker Park (beyond the busy intersection of Milwaukee, Damen, and North avenues), and Pilsen, which border areas with more troublesome reputations.

You can also ask the concierge at your hotel or an agent at the tourist visitor center for recommendations about visiting a particular area of the city.

If you're traveling alone, avoid riding the El after the rush-hour crowds thin out. Of course, it's always smarter to ride with a group. Many of the El stations can be eerily deserted at night, when you'll have to wait around for 15 minutes or longer for the next train. In that case, it's a good idea to spring for a taxi. Buses are a safe option, too, especially nos. 146 and 151, which pick up along North Michigan Avenue and State Street and connect to the North Side via Lincoln Park.

Blue-and-white police cars are a common sight, and officers also patrol by bicycle downtown and along the lakefront and by horseback at special events and parades. There are police stations in busy nightlife areas, such as the 18th District station at Chicago Avenue and LaSalle Street in the hopping restaurant and entertainment mecca of River North, and the 24th District station (known as Town Hall) at Addison and Halsted streets, located in the heart of the gay district and blocks from the busy strip of sports bars and nightclubs in Wrigleyville.

Taxes The local sales tax is 8.75%. Restaurants in the central part of the city, roughly the 312 area code, are taxed an additional 1%, for a total of 9.75%. The hotel room tax is 3%.

Time Zone All of Illinois, including Chicago, is located in the central time zone, so clocks are set 1 hour earlier than those on the East Coast and 2 hours later than those on the West Coast. Chicago switches to daylight saving time on the first Sunday in April, and back to standard time on the last Sunday in October.

Transit Info The **CTA** has a useful number to find out which bus or El train will get you to your destination: ⓒ **836-7000** (from any area code in the city or suburbs) or TTY 836-4949.

Weather For the **National Weather Service**'s current conditions and forecast, dial ⓒ **312/976-1212** (for a fee), or check the weather on the Web at www.ci.chi.il.us/Tourism/Weather.

Family-Friendly Accommodations

Hotels in Chicago traditionally rely on a robust convention trade and tourism market. During the week, Chicago's busy convention market, individual business travelers, and a small minority of tourists fill the city's hotels to capacity. The last few years have seen a building boom, mostly in the high-end market, bringing international players such as the Peninsula and Sofitel into the Midwestern market—wonderful hotels, but not the kind that cater to families. Thankfully, you'll find plenty of kid-friendly lodgings in the hot River North neighborhood. Budget lodgings, unfortunately, are becoming harder to find anywhere near downtown.

Because Chicago's hospitality industry caters first and foremost to the business traveler, the hotels tend to empty out by Friday. (Keep in mind, though, that rooms are sometimes available at rock-bottom rates during conventions if a hotel is unable to book to capacity.) Many hotels are sometimes willing to reduce prices on the weekends to push up their occupancy rates. And, many hotels known as "business hotels" have made efforts to add family-friendly amenities to entice families to stay the weekend. Still, the hotel industry has been so strong in Chicago in recent years that you won't find reservation agents as willing or able to wheel and deal as they once were. You never know, however, when some huge convention will gobble up all the desirable rooms in the city even on the weekends, so

you're wise to book a room well in advance whenever you plan to visit. To find out if an upcoming convention coincides with the dates you plan to visit Chicago, contact the **Chicago Convention & Visitors Bureau** (© 312/567-8500; www.choosechicago.com—click on "Convention Calendar").

If the city has a slow season, it's the depth of winter, when outsiders tend to shy away from the cold and the threat of being snowed in at O'Hare. Serious bargain hunters might choose to visit then. The Convention & Visitors Bureau usually offers a special promotion, "Winter Delights," from January to March. Call © 877/244-2246 for a brochure, or check out www.877chicago.com. The brochure includes discounts on many of Chicago's leading hotels and restaurants.

If you'd like to watch your pennies but the idea of sightseeing in a heavy down coat doesn't appeal to you, another option is to stay in a less-expensive hotel during the week and move into swell digs for the weekend finale.

A NOTE ABOUT PRICES I've divided hotels into four price categories: **Very Expensive** means double-occupancy rooms typically cost upwards of $300 per night; **Expensive** rooms cost around $200 to $300; **Moderate,** about $150 to $250; and **Inexpensive,** $85 to $150.

The rates given in this chapter are per night and do not include taxes. Prices are always subject to availability and vary seasonally. (The lower rates tend to be offered Jan–Mar and on nonholiday weekends.)

RESERVE IN ADVANCE Whatever hotel or hotels you choose, regardless of season, making reservations well in advance will help ensure that you get the best rate available. While toll-free phone numbers have been provided for the hotels reviewed, you might find better rates by calling the hotel's reservations office directly. Most hotels have check-in times somewhere between 3 and 6pm; if you are going to be delayed, call ahead and reconfirm your reservation to prevent cancellation.

RESERVATION SERVICES You can check on the latest rates and availability, as well as book a room, by calling the **Illinois Reservation Service** (© 800/491-1800). The 24-hour service is free. Another reservation service is **Hot Rooms** (© 800/468-3500 or 773/468-7666; www.hotrooms.com), which offers discounts at selected downtown hotels. The 24-hour service is free, but if you cancel a reservation after it has been booked, you're assessed a $25 fee. For a copy of the annual *Illinois Hotel-Motel Directory*, which also provides information about weekend packages, call the **Illinois Bureau of Tourism** at © 800/2CONNECT.

BED & BREAKFAST RESERVATIONS A centralized reservations service called **Bed & Breakfast/Chicago Inc.,** P.O. Box 14088, Chicago, IL 60614 (© 800/375-7084 or 773/394-2000; fax 773/394-2002; www.chicago-bed-breakfast.com), lists more than 70 accommodations in Chicago. If you're of an adventurous bent, you'll find options ranging from high-rise and loft apartments to guest rooms carved from a former private club on the 40th floor of a Loop office building. Most lie within 3 miles of downtown (many are located in the Gold Coast, Old Town, and Lincoln Park) and will run you $135 to $300 for apartments, and as low as $85 for guest rooms in private homes. *Note:* Most B&Bs require a minimum stay of 2 or 3 nights; also, many have restrictions on children. Some accept only children over age 10, for example, while others will not accept kids of any age. It's always wise to ask if children are welcome when making reservations.

ACCESSIBILITY Most hotels are prepared to accommodate travelers with physical disabilities, but you should always inquire when you make reservations to make sure that the hotel can meet your particular needs. Older properties, in particular, might not have been able to adapt their structures to meet current requirements or might have limited numbers of specially equipped rooms.

1 The Loop

Strictly speaking, "downtown" in Chicago means the Loop—the central business district, a 6-by-8-block rectangle enveloped by elevated tracks on all four sides. An outer circle beyond this literal loop of tracks is bounded on the north and west by the Chicago River and its south branch, forming an elbow on two sides; on the east by Michigan Avenue running along the edge of Grant Park; and on the south by the Congress Expressway. Within these confines are the city's financial institutions, trading markets, and municipal government buildings, making for, as you might expect, quite a lot of hustle and bustle Monday through Friday. Come Saturday and Sunday, however, the Loop is pretty dead, despite the fact that it is also home to major music and theater venues and is near the Art Institute.

The Loop has an interesting mix of grand old hotels, such as the Palmer House, and brash new upstarts, most notably the hip triad run by the West

> **Fun Fact   Did You Know?**
>
> Merriel Abbott, the dance choreographer who booked all the acts at the Palmer House's famed Empire Room—one of the nation's leading supper clubs from the 1930s to the 1950s—gave Liberace and Bob Fosse their first breaks. Liberace, a cocktail pianist at the club, was "discovered" in Milwaukee by Abbott, who is credited with dressing up the flamboyant entertainer's piano with a candelabra to lend his act some pizzazz. Fosse, a native Chicagoan, made his debut at age 18 as part of a dance team. He and his partner made $500 a month in 1947; Liberace was paid a miserly $1,100 for 5 weeks in 1946.

Coast–based Kimpton Group: the Hotel Burnham, Hotel Monaco, and Hotel Allegro. Despite their differences, all offer undeniable convenience for families who prefer to be at the center of the city.

EXPENSIVE

Palmer House Hilton ★ *Overrated*   Chicago's oldest hotel, the namesake of legendary State Street merchant prince Potter Palmer, is decidedly from another era (although this building is actually the 3rd Palmer House). All the rooms are in the process of being renovated, but upgrades at the palatial Palmer House take place, understandably, on a staggered basis, so be sure to ask for a refurbished room when making reservations. Bathrooms are on the smallish size, though some rooms come with two bathrooms, a plus for families. Kids might appreciate the sheer size of the place, with plenty of room to wander, and the location is good for access to the Museum Campus. Despite the room redos, the Palmer House feels somewhat lost in time. The elegance of the lobby isn't matched in the rooms (decorated in an anonymous midlevel hotel style) or the clientele (which tends heavily toward conventioneers). And don't expect grand views of surrounding skyscrapers (most rooms look out into offices across the street). The Palmer House's days as one of Chicago's top hotels are definitely past.

17 E. Monroe St. (at State St.), Chicago, IL 60603. © 800/HILTONS or 312/726-7500. Fax 312/917-1797. www.hilton.com. 1,640 units. $129–$420 double; $450–$1,500 suite. Kids 18 and under stay free in parent's room. Rollaways $25/night; no cribs. AE, DC, DISC, MC, V. Valet parking $33 with in/out privileges; self-parking across the street $23. Subway/El: Red Line to Monroe/State. **Amenities:** 4 restaurants (including the legendary but dated Trader Vic's, a Polynesian restaurant), 2 lounges; indoor pool; health club; Jacuzzi; sauna; concierge; business center; shopping arcade; 24-hr. room service; babysitting; laundry service; 24-hr. dry cleaning; executive rooms. *In room:* AC, TV w/ video games, dataport, minibar, coffeemaker, hair dryer, iron.

Renaissance Chicago Hotel ★★   Despite several name changes, the Renaissance is still one of the most upscale hotels in the city, located at the top of State Street, just across the bridge from the Magnificent Mile and steps from the Loop's attractions. Although business travelers are the hotel's bread and butter, I was happy to discover that the hotel has bent over backwards to accommodate families traveling with children. One huge plus: A pool on the fourth floor is open from 6:30am to 10pm, with no restrictions on children's use. The hotel's restaurants offer kids' menus for breakfast, lunch and dinner, offering everything from French toast to ravioli. Kids will appreciate the Sony PlayStation games on the television.

The hotel embraces its location with bay windows offering stunning views of the river and the towers of North Michigan Avenue. The rooms are tasteful and rather understated. Standard double rooms include a small sitting area with a

Central Chicago Accommodations

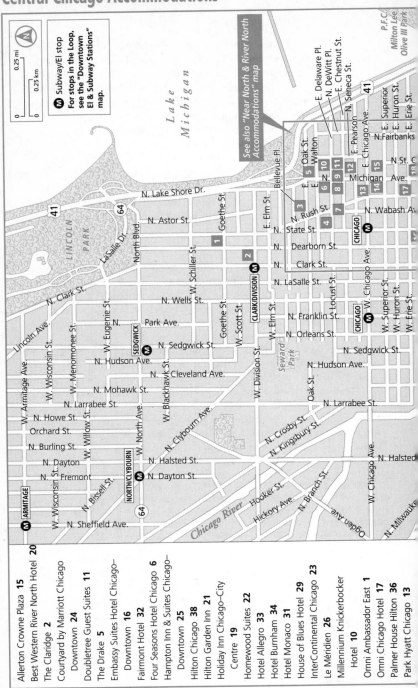

Allerton Crowne Plaza **15**
Best Western River North Hotel **20**
The Claridge **2**
Courtyard by Marriott Chicago Downtown **24**
Doubletree Guest Suites **11**
The Drake **5**
Embassy Suites Hotel Chicago–Downtown **16**
Fairmont Hotel **32**
Four Seasons Hotel Chicago **6**
Hampton Inn & Suites Chicago–Downtown **25**
Hilton Chicago **38**
Hilton Garden Inn **21**
Holiday Inn Chicago–City Centre **19**
Homewood Suites **22**
Hotel Allegro **33**
Hotel Burnham **34**
Hotel Monaco **31**
House of Blues Hotel **29**
InterContinental Chicago **23**
Le Méridien **26**
Millennium Knickerbocker Hotel **10**
Omni Ambassador East **1**
Omni Chicago Hotel **17**
Palmer House Hilton **36**
Park Hyatt Chicago **13**

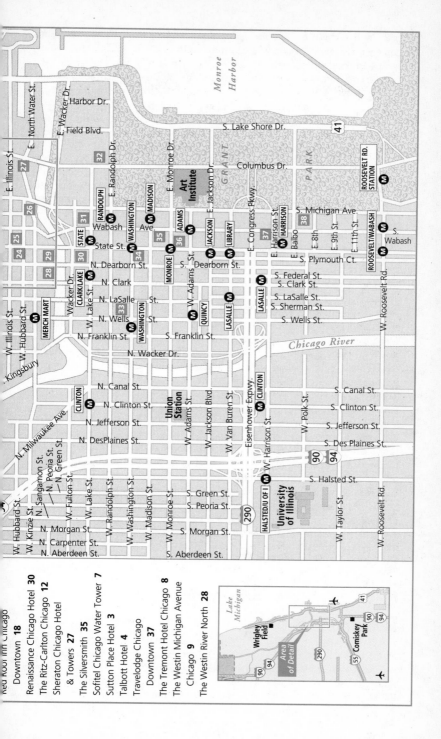

couch and smallish bathrooms; deluxe doubles have much bigger bathrooms (some with separate showers and bathtubs) and two couches. Club-level rooms, located on the top four floors, are half a room larger and have their own concierge in a private lounge, where complimentary continental breakfast and evening hors d'oeuvres and pastries are served. Families often request connecting rooms, one of which has a king bed and the other, two queen-size beds. I'd also recommend requesting a room on the 20th floor or higher on the east side for views of both the Chicago River and Lake Michigan. Another good bet is rooms on the hotel's north side, all of which have river views.

1 W. Wacker Dr. (at State St.), Chicago, IL 60601. © **800/HOTELS-1** or 312/372-7200. Fax 312/372-0093. www.renaissancehotels.com. 553 units. $199–$310 double; $240–$360 Club Level double; $500–$2,500 suite. Kids under 18 stay free in parent's room. No rollaways; cribs free. Weekend rates available. AE, DC, DISC, MC, V. Valet parking $32 with in/out privileges; self-parking $22 with in/out privileges. Subway/El: Brown Line to State/Lake, or Red Line to Washington/State. Small pets accepted. **Amenities:** 2 restaurants; lounge; indoor pool w/ skylights; health club w/ sauna and whirlpool; concierge; 24-hr. Kinko's business center; salon; 24-hr. room service; babysitting; laundry service; club-level rooms. *In room:* A/C, TV w/ pay movies and PlayStation, dataport, minibar, coffeemaker, hair dryer, iron.

The Silversmith ★ *Finds* You might call the Silversmith a hidden gem. The landmark building, designed by the celebrated firm of D. H. Burnham and Company, was built in 1897 to serve the jewelry and silver trade on Wabash Avenue, still known as Jeweler's Row. While the hotel isn't a traditional "family" hotel, it does provide cribs, babysitting service, and toys and games. Word about The Silversmith has been slow getting out (even many Loop office workers who pass by it every day don't know it's there), so it doesn't book up as quickly as other hotter spots. That's good news for families on vacation because it means that the hotel is more willing to make a deal on room rates. (The suites—perfect for families—often get discounted, I hear.) There is also more likely to be room at this inn during the busy convention season.

Rooms come in varying configurations, with 12-foot-high ceilings, 10-foot picture windows, handsome Frank Lloyd Wright–inspired wrought-iron fixtures, armoires, and homey bedding; bathrooms are generously sized. Most rooms along the hotel's main corridor tend to be dark (with windows looking into neighboring office buildings). For a better—and quintessentially Chicago—view, get a room at the front on the fifth floor or higher, overlooking Wabash Avenue and the El tracks.

10 S. Wabash Ave. (at Madison St.), Chicago, IL 60603. © **800/2CROWNE** or 312/372-7696. Fax 312/372-7320. www.sixcontinentshotels.com. 143 units. $149–$249 double; from $289 suite. Kids 16 and under stay free in parent's room. Rollaways $20/night; cribs free. Weekend rates available. AE, DC, DISC, MC, V. Valet parking $25 with in/out privileges. Subway/El: Brown, Green, or Orange lines to Madison/Wabash, or Red Line to Washington/State. **Amenities:** Deli; lounge; tiny fitness room (w/ access to nearby health club for a fee); concierge; business center and secretarial services; limited room service; babysitting; laundry service; dry cleaning; club-level rooms. *In room:* A/C, TV w/ pay movies, dataport, minibar, coffeemaker, hair dryer, iron, safe.

MODERATE

Hotel Allegro ★ *Value* While not quite in the same hip-o-sphere as the Hotel Monaco, its too-cool-for-school sibling (see below), the Kimpton Group's splashy Allegro is loads of fun and a good value. Guests enter a whimsical lobby that feels like a cartoon with its plush, eclectic, and boldly colorful furnishings, but the overarching theme here is musical entertainment. Adjoining the hotel is the historic Palace Theatre, a former vaudeville house reopened in 1999 as a venue for first-run Broadway shows. Kids will enjoy seeing the staff perform musical numbers in the lobby 5 to 6:30pm daily. The whimsy of the lobby segues into the rooms, which vary wildly in size and configuration. (For the smallest ones, however, guests can pay their rate in accordance with how tall they stand in inches.) Suites have robes, VCRs, and two-person Jacuzzi tubs. For a family of 3 or more, the hotel recommends a king suite with a two-person Jacuzzi tub; the room includes a living room and separate bedroom with a king bed.

Befitting a place where the concierge wears a stylish leather jacket and the doorman hums along to the tunes playing on speakers out front, the Allegro appeals to younger travelers. The hotel's restaurant, 312 Chicago, attracts nonguests in search of excellent Italian cuisine. There's no kids' menu, but the restaurant is accommodating to families.

171 W. Randolph St. (at LaSalle St.), Chicago, IL 60601. © **800/643-1500** or 312/236-0123. Fax 312/236-0917. www.hotelallegro.com. 483 units. $139–$259 double; $225–$399 suite. Kids 17 and under stay free in parent's room. Rollaways and cribs free. AE, DC, DISC, MC, V. Valet parking $26 with in/out privileges. Subway/El: All lines to Washington. **Amenities:** Restaurant; cocktail lounge; exercise room (and access to nearby health club w/ indoor pool); concierge; business services; salon; limited room service; same-day laundry service; dry cleaning. *In room:* A/C, TV w/ pay movies, fax, dataport, minibar, hair dryer, iron.

Hotel Burnham ★★★   Here's a hip hotel that's known for romance, but it's also using its small size—and sense of whimsy—to cater to kids. The Burnham is my top choice for families in this price category, provided you book a suite, which will offer you and the little ones plenty of space.

The result of a brilliant $30 million restoration in 1999 of the historic Reliance Building—one of the first skyscrapers ever built and a highly significant architectural treasure—this intimate boutique hotel (named for Daniel Burnham, whose firm designed it in 1895) is the work of the Kimpton Group, the trend-setting West Coast–based chain behind the Allegro and Monaco hotels. It occupies a prime spot in the heart of State Street, across from Marshall Field's and 1 block south of the suddenly hopping North Loop theater district. The Burnham is a must for architecture buffs: Wherever possible, the restoration retains period elements—most obviously in the hallways, which recall the original office corridors with terrazzo tile floors, white marble wainscoting, mahogany door and window frames, and room numbers painted on the translucent glass doors.

Rooms are clubby but glamorous, with plush beds, mahogany writing desks, and chaise lounges. The hotel's 19 suites feature a separate living-room area and CD stereo systems. To keep wee ones entertained, the hotel offers coloring books and crayons, games, and Super Nintendo. During holidays, you'll find special activities in the hotel lobby, including decorating gingerbread men around Christmas and hunting for eggs at Easter. Diaper bags, cribs, high chairs, changing tables, and more are available upon request. And, there's a turndown service with cookies and milk. The hotel's restaurant offers a children's menu. Ask the concierge for special offers for tea at American Girl Place Cafe, and deals at the museums and theaters.

1 W. Washington (at State St.), Chicago, IL 60602. © **877/294-9712** or 312/782-1111. Fax 312/782-0899. www.burnhamhotel.com. 122 units. $139–$279 double; $239–$429 suite. Kids 17 and under stay free in parent's room. Rollaways and cribs free, but available in suites only. AE, DC, DISC, MC, V. Valet parking $29 with in/out privileges. Subway: Red or Blue lines to Washington/State. **Amenities:** Restaurant; small fitness room and access to nearby health club; concierge; business services; 24-hr. room service; laundry service; dry cleaning. *In room:* A/C, TV, fax, dataport, minibar, hair dryer, iron.

Hotel Monaco ★★   More California-chic than French Riviera–suave, this playful 14-story boutique hotel greets guests with derby-hatted doormen, funky house music, and a goldfish for your room that comes with its own name.

(Naturally, the ability to acquire a personal goldfish tends to be kids' favorite aspect of this hotel.) Given the hotel's playful spirit, it attracts a younger clientele, with an overall vibe that is laid-back and friendly rather than so-hip-it-hurts. (This is Chicago, after all, not New York.)

The plush, jewel-toned 1930s French Deco decor at the Kimpton Group's most upscale Chicago property infuses sizable rooms resembling theatrical set pieces—eclectic furnishings include Deco armoires, mahogany writing desks, and marshmallow-soft beds. The lack of a pool is somewhat compensated for by the luxurious Jacuzzi bathtubs. Families enjoy the suites, some of which adjoin to rooms with two double beds. (For your wannabe Jimi Hendrix, there's a "Party Like a Rock Star" suite with a Sony 52-disc CD player, rock costume replicas, an electric guitar and amplifier, concert photographs of rock icons, and a 19-inch TV set that appears to have been thrown through the window.) Rooms on the top three floors give you a vista of the Chicago River and surrounding skyscrapers. The cozy lobby is the spot for free morning coffee and an evening wine reception. You'll find the concierge happy to help with a list of kid-friendly attractions.

225 N. Wabash Ave. (at Wacker Dr.), Chicago, IL 60601. © **800/397-7661** or 312/960-8500. Fax 312/960-8538. www.monaco-chicago.com. 192 units. $179–$299 double; $279–$429 suite. Kids 17 and under stay free in parent's room. Rollaways $20/night; cribs free. AE, DC, DISC, MC, V. Valet parking $28 with in/out privileges. Subway/El: Blue Line to State/Lake. Small pets accepted. **Amenities:** Restaurant; fitness room and access to nearby health club; concierge; business center; 24-hr. room service; in-room massage; babysitting; laundry service; dry cleaning. *In room:* A/C, TV w/ pay movies, fax, dataport, minibar, coffeemaker, hair dryer, iron.

2 South Loop

Unlike the area surrounding North Michigan Avenue—the "Mag Mile"—the South Loop is less about glamour and more about old Chicago. Running the length of Grant Park, South Michigan Avenue is ideal for a long city stroll, passing grand museums, imposing architecture, and the park's greenery and statuary. But although this stretch was once Chicago's most regal hotel row, it's certainly the worse for the wear today. The ancient Congress Hotel is dilapidated and best avoided, despite its prime location at Michigan Avenue and Congress Parkway. And the landmark Blackstone Hotel, a classic icon of old Chicago, has been closed since 1999—now, the building is being converted into luxury condominiums. It's all part of a trend in the neighborhood toward revitalization, with the conversion of industrial buildings into loft apartments. Old-timers might complain about gentrification, but it's good news for visitors, who now find more restaurant options and livelier street life. The proximity to Grant Park and State Street shopping makes the area attractive, particularly when summer music festivals or holiday shopping is on the agenda.

EXPENSIVE

Hilton Chicago ★★   When it erupted onto Michigan Avenue in 1927, this massive brick-and-stone edifice billed itself as the largest hotel in the world. It certainly owns one of the most colorful histories of any Chicago hotel. Guests have included Queen Elizabeth, Emperor Hirohito, and every president since FDR. The classical-rococo public spaces—including the Versailles-inspired Grand Ballroom and Grand Stair Lobby—are magnificent, but the rest of the hotel is firmly entrenched in the present. The hotel is a solid choice for families: There's plenty of space to wander, and it's close to all of the major museums and Grant Park (great for when the kids need to burn off some energy). Even better, there's a heated swimming pool and a fitness center with a whirlpool and sauna, all open to kids.

Some rooms are on the small side, but all are comfortable and warm, and many of the standard rooms have two bathrooms. Adjoining rooms are available; ask when you call for reservations. The views from those higher up facing Michigan Avenue offer a sweeping view of Grant Park and the lake. The hotel's Tower section offers a separate registration area, upgraded amenities (including robes, fax machines, and VCRs), and a lounge open 6am to 11pm, serving complimentary continental breakfast and evening hors d'oeuvres and cocktails.

720 S. Michigan Ave. (at Balbo Dr.), Chicago, IL 60605. (C) **800/HILTONS** or 312/922-4400. Fax 312/922-5240. www.hilton.com. 1,544 units. $179–$369 double; from $299 junior suite. Weekend rates $145–$219 main hotel; $195–$265 Tower. Kids 18 and under stay free in parent's room. Rollaways $25/night; cribs free. AE, DC, DISC, MC, V. Valet parking $24; self-parking $22. Subway/El: Red Line to Harrison/State. **Amenities:** 4 restaurants; 2 lounges; indoor pool; health club w/ indoor track, Jacuzzi, sauna, and steam room; concierge; business center; 24-hr. room service; massage; babysitting; laundry service; 24-hr. dry cleaning. *In room:* A/C, TV w/ pay movies, dataport, minibar, coffeemaker, hair dryer, iron.

INEXPENSIVE

Chicago Downtown Travelodge *Value*   You won't be reveling in luxury, but Travelodge promises and delivers neat, clean rooms at reasonable prices. The hotel's location near the Loop and Museum Campus is excellent: You are half a block from Grant Park and all the summer festivals, and only 4 blocks from the Field Museum. This 12-story hotel is one of few budget lodgings you'll find in the heart of the Loop. The hotel was built in 1925 as the Harrison Hotel, and for many years was one of the premier hotels in the city. Since Travelodge acquired the property 6 years ago, they've been promoting it as "a touch of old Chicago" and working to restore the property. To date, all guest rooms and the lobby have been renovated.

Families should request one of the "Sleepy Bear Den" rooms, which offer privacy for parents and for kids—but not too much privacy. The room is separated into two areas with an archway: On one side is a king bed for the parents, and on the other side is a double bed for the kids, specially decorated with whimsical curtains and bedding. Each side has its own television and VCR; the kids' side is stocked with children's movies. Also included is a microwave and refrigerator. Other rooms suitable for families offer two beds and two bathrooms. There's no pool, but two restaurants cater to families: Chicago Carry-Out offers full breakfasts and sandwiches, and Charming Wok offers inexpensive Chinese fare from 11am to 11pm.

65 E. Harrison St. (at S. Wabash Ave.), Chicago, IL 60605. (C) **888/515-6375** or 312/427-8000. Fax 312/427-8261. www.travelodge.com. 250 units. $105–$165 double. Kids 17 and under stay free in parent's room. Rollaways $10/night; cribs free. AE, DC, DISC, MC, V. Indoor garage parking $15/car or small van, includes one in/out per day at no charge. Subway/El: Red Line to State/Harrison. **Amenities:** 2 restaurants. *In room:* A/C, TV w/ pay movies, fax, dataport, minibar, coffeemaker, hair dryer, iron.

3 The East Side

The term "East Side" is a relatively new one and is used to describe the high-rise/high-rent district east of Michigan Avenue, south of the river, and north of Grant Park. Don't be surprised if Chicagoans look at you a little funny when you ask directions to the East Side; it has yet to find its way into the geographical lexicon of the city. Don't expect happening restaurants or great stores; the area is essentially one of elite hotels, residential towers, and office buildings. The East Side is definitely a luxury "privacy zone," and the hotels here make the most of that mandate. They're all located in Illinois Center, a huge Mies van der Rohe–inspired mixed-use development that, despite its cluttered density, can seem a bit isolated from the rest of downtown Chicago.

VERY EXPENSIVE

Fairmont Hotel ★★   The Fairmont is easily one of the city's most luxurious hotels, offering an array of deluxe amenities and services. This is the kind of place that regularly hosts high-level politicians and high-profile fund-raisers. The overall effect is chic but a bit impersonal. The entrance looks out on anonymous office towers, and you're likely to wander the circular lobby a bit before finding the check-in desk. Still, families rave about the huge rooms and bend-over-backwards service; although families aren't the hotel's primary market, you will be made to feel more than welcome.

The large rooms are decorated in a comfortable, upscale style. (Ask for one with a lake view, although even the cityview rooms offer some distance from neighboring offices.) The posh bathrooms feature extra-large tubs, separate vanity areas, and swivel TVs. The windows even open (a rarity in high-rise hotels), so you can enjoy the breeze drifting off Lake Michigan. Suites have one or two bedrooms, a living room, a dining area, and a built-in bar—and all come with lake views. You can access Lakeshore Athletic Club without walking outside. The club has a pool; unfortunately, the club is open to children only on Sundays. The hotel is connected to the city's underground pedway system (one of my favorite activities to do with kids), through which you can walk all the way to Marshall Field's on State Street on inclement days without stepping outside.

200 N. Columbus Dr. (at Lake St.), Chicago, IL 60601. © 800/527-4727 or 312/565-8000. Fax 312/856-1032. www.fairmont.com. 692 units. $279–$354 double. Weekend rates begin at $139. Kids under 18 stay free in parent's room. Rollaways $35/night; cribs free. AE, DC, DISC, MC, V. Valet parking $33 with in/out privileges. Subway/El: Brown, Orange, or Green line to Randolph. Pets accepted. **Amenities:** 2 restaurants; lounge; access to Lakeshore Athletic Club, one of the top health clubs in the city (w/ full-court basketball, climbing wall, pool, and spa); concierge; business center; salon; 24-hr. room service; babysitting; laundry service; 24-hr. dry cleaning. In room: A/C, TV w/ pay movies, CD player, fax, dataport, minibar, hair dryer, iron.

4 Near North & the Magnificent Mile

Along the Magnificent Mile—a stretch of Michigan Avenue running north of the Chicago River to Oak Street—you'll find most of the city's premium hotels. The location can't be beat.

VERY EXPENSIVE

The Drake ★★★   If ever the term "grande dame" fit a hotel, it's The Drake. Fronting East Lake Shore Drive with a prominent rooftop marquee that has a signature on the city's skyline, the landmark building opened in 1920 and soon became one of the city's finest hotels. Although it's now owned by Hilton, long-time Chicagoans still think of The Drake with possessive pride; it's our version of New York's Plaza or Paris's Ritz.

For all its old-time glamour, the hotel seems a bit of a dowager when compared to the glitzy Four Seasons (see below), but this, of course, is part of The Drake's charm. A recent $100 million renovation has streamlined its design. One of the nicer additions: coffee lounges on each floor with lake views. The Drake is not particularly family-oriented because of its lack of a pool, game room, and other kid-friendly amenities, but plenty of families have made it a tradition to stay here.

Parents will be happy to know that the typical room is generous in size and furnished comfortably with a separate sitting area; some have two bathrooms.

Near North & River North Accommodations

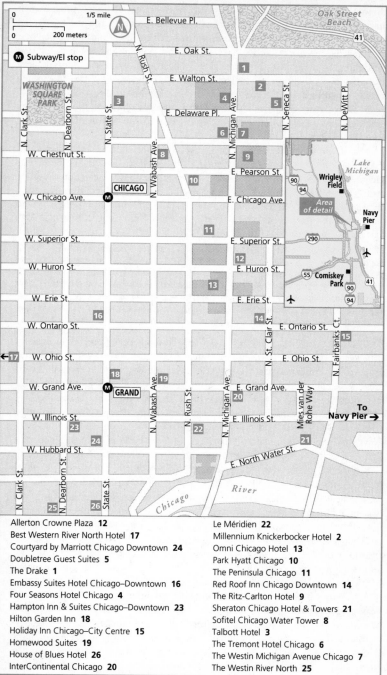

Allerton Crowne Plaza **12**
Best Western River North Hotel **17**
Courtyard by Marriott Chicago Downtown **24**
Doubletree Guest Suites **5**
The Drake **1**
Embassy Suites Hotel Chicago–Downtown **16**
Four Seasons Hotel Chicago **4**
Hampton Inn & Suites Chicago–Downtown **23**
Hilton Garden Inn **18**
Holiday Inn Chicago–City Centre **15**
Homewood Suites **19**
House of Blues Hotel **26**
InterContinental Chicago **20**

Le Méridien **22**
Millennium Knickerbocker Hotel **2**
Omni Chicago Hotel **13**
Park Hyatt Chicago **10**
The Peninsula Chicago **11**
Red Roof Inn Chicago Downtown **14**
The Ritz-Carlton Hotel **9**
Sheraton Chicago Hotel & Towers **21**
Sofitel Chicago Water Tower **8**
Talbott Hotel **3**
The Tremont Hotel Chicago **6**
The Westin Michigan Avenue Chicago **7**
The Westin River North **25**

Rooms and suites on the slightly more expensive "executive floors" provide such additional amenities as personalized stationery, disposable cameras, a generous continental breakfast in a private lounge, and free cocktails and hors d'oeuvres, plus a daily newspaper, and valet assistance for polishing shoes, packing and unpacking, and securing theater tickets. The fourth and fifth floors have a lounge open to all guests, where soft drinks and fresh-brewed coffee and tea are available without charge. The lakeview rooms are lovely, and—no surprise— you'll pay more for them. Be forewarned that cityview rooms on the lower floors look out onto a facing building on Walton Place, so you'll probably be keeping your drapes shut.

Even if you don't stay at the hotel, take your kids to the lavishly decorated Palm Court for afternoon tea, accompanied by a harpist. The hotel's restaurants include the Oak Terrace, a large dining room serving up American fare and some great views of the lake and Michigan Avenue; the Cape Cod Room, a local favorite for seafood; and Coq d'Or, one of Chicago's most atmospheric piano bars. All of the restaurants have kids' menus, but I'd recommend dining at Oak Terrace, the most casual of the three.

140 E. Walton Place (at Michigan Ave.), Chicago, IL 60611. ℂ 800/55-DRAKE or 312/787-2200. Fax 312/787-1431. www.thedrakehotel.com. 537 units. $255–$295 double; $335–$395 executive floor; from $600 suite. Weekend rates start at $289 with continental breakfast. Kids 18 and under stay free in parent's room. Rollaways and cribs free. AE, DC, DISC, MC, V. Valet parking $31 with in/out privileges. Subway/El: Red Line to Chicago/State. **Amenities:** 3 restaurants; 2 lounges; fitness center; concierge; business center; shopping arcade; barbershop; 24-hr. room service; babysitting; in-room massage; laundry service; 24-hr. dry cleaning; executive-level rooms. *In room:* A/C, TV w/ pay movies, dataport, minibar, coffeemaker, hair dryer, iron.

Four Seasons Hotel Chicago ★★★   A fabulous pool and indulgences for little people make this ultra-luxury hotel a thumbs-up for families. The city's reigning box-office megastar hotel has consistently been lauded by those in the know as one of the top hotels in the world. The city's tallest hotel, the Four Seasons occupies a rarefied aerie between the 30th and 46th floors above the Mag Mile's most upscale vertical mall. The beautiful rooms have English furnishings, custom-woven carpets and tapestries, and dark wood armoires. Each has windows that open to let in the fresh air. Bathrooms boast such indulgences as a lighted makeup mirror, oversize towels and robes, scales, and Bulgari toiletries.

Kid-friendly services include little robes, balloon animals, Nintendo, a special room-service menu, and milk and cookies. Ask about the "Kids for All Seasons" weekend package, available Friday through Sunday, which includes small gifts and discounts from kids' retailers, and a $50 credit toward food and beverage in the hotel. Most indulgent of all, however, are the twin beds—so soft that the hotel's gift shop sells about a hundred of them each year for $1,200 a piece. As a special treat for wee ones, the hotel has an ice cream man who will visit your room and let kids choose an ice cream and topping—including Oreo pieces, gummy bears, M&M's, sprinkles, freshly whipped cream, and chocolate sauce and caramel sauce.

An 18-foot-high white marble fountain marks the entrance to the opulent Seasons Restaurant, which, under the very talented Chef Mark Baker, has become one of the most respected gourmet dining destinations in Chicago. I'd recommend that families try Sunday brunch at this restaurant: A special Harry Potter castle is set up in a separate kids' dining area that's supervised. You can enjoy the best brunch in Chicago while your kids are within eyesight having a wonderful dining experience of their own. Bon appétit!

120 E. Delaware Place (at Michigan Ave.), Chicago, IL 60611. ℂ 800/332-3442 or 312/280-8800. Fax 312/280-1748. www.fourseasons.com. 343 units. $425–$575 double; $545–$3,500 suite. Weekend rates from $265. Kids under 18 stay free in parent's room. Rollaways and cribs free. AE, DC, DISC, MC, V. Valet parking

$32 with in/out privileges; self-parking $23. Subway/El: Red Line to Chicago/State. Pets accepted. **Amenities:** 2 restaurants (The Café offers a kids' menu); lounge; indoor pool (unrestricted access for kids); fitness center; concierge; business center; salon; 24-hr. room service; babysitting; laundry service; 24-hr. dry cleaning. *In room:* A/C, TV/VCR w/ pay movies and Nintendo, dataport, minibar, coffeemaker, hair dryer, iron.

Le Méridien ★★ Tucked into the back of The Shops at North Bridge mall, Le Méridien is another new addition to the competitive high-end Chicago hotel market. Opened last summer, this hidden gem brings the charm of a European hotel into a modern shopping mall. Families will like the convenience of having a whole mall just a few steps away, meaning you can get out without even putting on your coat. A quick elevator ride connects you with stores such as Nordstrom and Kenneth Cole or Chicago's Magnificent Meal food court, where you can grab everything from a Fluky's hot dog to Italian fare at Tuscany Cafe.

Le Méridien touts its design philosophy as "European with a French accent," which, in this case, means marble floors, vaguely 18th-century-inspired furniture, and some whimsical artwork (a large painting of a Napoleonic figure with the head of a dog hangs in the lobby). A terrace offers outdoor seating, and a casual bistro is hidden away in the back of the lobby (depending on your perspective, it's either pleasantly secluded or isolated). Rooms are on the small side (especially the least expensive ones on the north side). Amenities are top-of-the-line: Every room offers a Sony PlayStation, cordless phone, high-speed Internet access, and an in-room safe that allows you to plug in and charge your laptop or cellphone while it's locked away.

High rollers will want to book one of the suites overlooking Michigan Avenue; a few even come with private terraces, something few hotels in this city can offer. Some say the Grand Terrace Suite, at $1,700 a night, is the best hotel room in the city. The private terrace is twice the size of the room itself and, situated above Michigan Avenue, it offers a jaw-dropping, unobscured, picture-postcard view of the Magnificent Mile all the way to Oak Street Beach. And, even though you are outdoors and right in the hustle and bustle of a major city, on a busy weekday, you can hardly hear the people and traffic below.

Le Méridien can't quite compete with the Park Hyatt or the Peninsula (see below) in the glamour department, but its cozy style should appeal to travelers looking for some place a little more personal.

520 N. Michigan Ave. (pickup and drop-off location on Rush St.), Chicago, IL 60611. © **800/543-4300** or 312/645-1500. Fax 312/645-1550. www.lemeridien-hotels.com. 311 units. $425 double; $505–$575 suite. Kids 12 and under stay free in parent's room. Rollaways $20/night; cribs free. AE, DC, DISC, MC, V. Valet parking $33 with in/out privileges. Subway/El: Red Line to Chicago/State. Pets accepted. **Amenities:** Restaurant; bar; health club w/spa, Jacuzzi, and steam room; concierge; business center; 24-hr. room service; in-room massage; babysitting; laundry service; same-day dry cleaning. *In room:* A/C, TV w/ pay movies and PlayStation, CD player, dataport, minibar, fridge, coffeemaker, hair dryer, iron, safe.

Omni Chicago Hotel ★ No less a Chicago luminary than Oprah Winfrey has stamped the Omni Chicago with her coveted imprimatur, designating it the official crash pad for guests appearing on her show. While the hotel's hushed tones exude a feeling of business rather than pleasure, the Omni Kids Program makes younger guests feel welcome. All children receive a bag of games and ideas for Chicago activities, Nintendo in their rooms, and kids' menus.

All the units are suites with one king-size or two double beds. Each suite, tastefully decorated in deep greens and burgundies, has a living room with a sitting area, a dining table, a wet bar, and a refrigerator, all of which are divided from the bedroom by a set of French doors. About a third of the suites have pull-out sofas. You can request a corner suite with lots of light and views looking down Michigan Avenue, for $20 extra.

676 N. Michigan Ave. (at Huron St.), Chicago, IL 60611. © **800/843-6664** or 312/944-6664. Fax 312/266-3015. www.omnihotels.com. 347 units. $259–$329 suite. Weekend rates $179–$209. Kids 17 and under stay free in parent's room. Rollaways $20/night; cribs free. AE, DC, DISC, MC, V. Valet parking $32 with in/out privileges. Subway/El: Red Line to Grand/State. **Amenities:** Restaurant; lounge; lap pool; health club; Jacuzzi; courtesy car available for trips within the downtown area; business services; 24-hr. room service; babysitting; laundry service; 24-hr. dry cleaning; executive-level rooms. *In room:* A/C, TV w/ pay movies and Nintendo, fax, dataport, minibar, coffeemaker, hair dryer, iron, safe.

Park Hyatt Chicago ★★★   The international Hyatt hotel chain is based in Chicago, so there was quite a bit of pride on the line with the opening of the upscale Park Hyatt Chicago in spring 2000. Not only does the hotel occupy one of the most desirable spots on North Michigan Avenue, overlooking Water Tower Square, but it also is going head-to-head with the city's two reigning luxury kingpins, the nearby Four Seasons and Ritz-Carlton—and the new Peninsula Chicago as well. The Park Hyatt rates high for the "cool" factor, but still can't quite match the Four Seasons in terms of kid-friendly perks.

Luxury might be the watchword here, but the look is anything but stuffy: The lobby feels like a sleek modern art gallery. German painter Gerhard Richter's *Piazza del Duomo Milan* masterpiece is the visual centerpiece of the space, providing ample evidence of what visual treats lie in store for guests. Rooms feature Eames and Mies van der Rohe reproduction furniture, window banquettes with stunning city views (the windows actually open), and, for those facing east, the similarly modern Museum of Contemporary Art and lakefront. The bathrooms are especially wonderful: A sliding cherry-wood wall can be pulled back for a view of the city while you soak in the oversize tub.

Families often book connecting rooms, one with a king bed and one with two double beds. Every room has a CD and DVD player with a flat-screen TV, and the concierge will loan from their library of DVDs (including kids' movies) at no cost. The health club is only open to those over 16, but the pool welcomes kids—and it's a stunner, with city views looking south and bronze-colored tiles. If you plan to spend significant time at American Girl Place, ask about the hotel's special packages, which might include a welcome kit with a CD of the store, breakfast in the hotel's restaurant (to fortify you for a strenuous day of shopping), and bath products in a "scrub-a-dub" kit for girls.

The crown jewel of the Park Hyatt is NoMI, a restaurant nestled on the seventh floor overlooking Water Tower Square and the Museum of Contemporary Art. Serving French-inspired cuisine by Chef Sandro Gamba and featuring an *Architectural Digest*–worthy interior by New York–based designer Tony Chi, with an adjoining outdoor terrace, NoMI (an acronym for North Michigan) has been one of Chicago's most sought-after reservations since the hotel's opening. Parents will want to book a sitter for an evening out here—it's a bit too chic to be kid-friendly.

800 N. Michigan Ave., Chicago, IL 60611. © **800/233-1234** or 312/335-1234. Fax 312/239-4000. www.hyatt.com. 203 units. $320–$465 double; $695–$2,785 suite. Kids 18 and under stay free in parent's room. No rollaways; cribs free. AE, DC, DISC, MC, V. Valet parking $36 with in/out privileges. Subway/El: Red Line to Chicago/State. **Amenities:** Restaurant; lounge; indoor pool; health club w/ Jacuzzi and spa; concierge; business center w/ computer technical support; 24-hr. room service; massage; babysitting; laundry service; 24-hr. dry cleaning. *In room:* A/C, TV/DVD w/ pay movies, CD player, dataport, minibar, coffeemaker, hair dryer, iron.

The Peninsula Chicago ★★★   Do believe the hype. The first Midwest location from the luxury Peninsula hotel group promised to wow us, and it does not disappoint. Taking design cues from the chain's flagship Hong Kong hotel, the Peninsula Chicago mixes an Art Deco sensibility with modern, top-of-the-line amenities.

Rooms are average in size (the "junior suites" are especially small, with living rooms that can comfortably seat only about 4 people). Rooms that are popular with families include suites with two double beds, or adjoining rooms that offer one room with a king bed and one with two double beds. The hotel's in-room technology is cutting-edge: A small silver "command station" by every bed allows guests to control all the lights, curtains, and room temperature without getting out from under the covers. The marble-filled bathrooms are wonderful, with separate shower stalls and tubs, vanities with plenty of room to sit, and another "command station" by the bathtub. Add in the flat-screen TVs and DVD players, and you've got a classic hotel that's very much attuned to the present.

Kids' amenities include a treat upon arrival: milk and cookies (or popcorn and soda, if they're beyond the cookies-and-milk age). Rooms can be equipped with PlayStation 2s, DVDs, and a library of kids' movies—make sure to request them when you make your reservation. The bright, airy spa and fitness center fill the top two floors—check out the view from the outdoor deck. The spa has an Olympic-size pool, and one lane is always reserved for family swim. The 20th-floor health club is also open to children, with no restrictions. You can obtain childcare services through the concierge.

The sultry hotel bar—hidden from the lobby behind curved, leather-covered walls—is a top spot for a romantic evening with your mate. The Lobby is the best bet for families, with a kids' menu. Don't miss breakfast at Pierre Gourmet, located just outside the hotel at the corner of Superior and Rush streets for some of the best baked goods on the Magnificent Mile. The hotel's other restaurants, including The Avenue and Shanghai Terrace, are best left to the adults.

730 N. Michigan Ave., Chicago, IL 60611. ℂ 866/288-8889 or 312/337-2888. Fax 312/932-9529. www.peninsula.com. 339 units. $425–$495 double; $485–$4,500 suite. Kids 17 and under stay free in parent's room. Rollaways and cribs free. AE, DC, DISC, MC, V. Valet parking $32 with in/out privileges. Subway/El: Red Line to Chicago/State. **Amenities:** 4 restaurants; bar; indoor pool with outdoor deck; fitness center; spa; Jacuzzi; sauna; concierge; business center; 24-hr. room service; in-room massage; babysitting; laundry service; same-day dry cleaning. *In room:* A/C, TV/DVD w/ pay movies, fax, dataport, minibar, fridge upon request, hair dryer, safe.

The Ritz-Carlton Chicago ★★★

Perched high atop Water Tower Place, the Ritz-Carlton casts a soothing presence on guests as they're deposited into the airy 12-floor lobby. Not surprisingly, the quality of the accommodations is of the highest caliber. The standard rooms have traditional furnishings; suites have an additional living area furnished with a sofa and chair, a writing desk, a second TV and VCR, and a stereo. Lake views cost more but are spectacular. Families will find this luxury crash pad quite welcoming: Every child receives a gift and can borrow toys and games from a stash kept by the concierge. PlayStation and Nintendo are available, and kids' food is available from room service 24 hours a day. Teenagers receive a special gift pack upon arrival.

Guests staying in Premier Suites are treated to a gratis wardrobe pressing upon arrival, personalized stationery, Bulgari toiletries, and fresh flowers. Service is the Ritz-Carlton's selling point, whether it's the "compcierge" who helps guests with computer problems or the "allergy-sensitive" rooms that are cleaned with special nonirritating products and come stocked with nonfeather duvets and pillows, and hypoallergenic bath products on request.

Whether or not you stay here, the Ritz-Carlton is an elegant place for afternoon tea, served at 2:30 and 4:30pm in the lobby. At one end of the lobby is the Greenhouse restaurant, designed with a glass roof and wall that seems to jut out over the city. The hotel's gastronomic claim to fame is The Dining Room, one of Chicago's finest, serving French cuisine under the direction of acclaimed chef Sarah Stegner. The hotel's excellent Sunday brunch includes a special buffet for children replete with M&Ms, macaroni and cheese, and pizza.

160 E. Pearson St., Chicago, IL 60611. *C* 800/621-6906 or 312/266-1000. Fax 312/266-1194. www.four seasons.com. 430 units. $375–$455 double; $545–$3,500 suite. Weekend rates from $265. Kids under 18 stay free in parent's room. Rollaways and cribs free. AE, DC, DISC, MC, V. Valet parking $32 with in/out privileges; self-parking $23.50 with no in/out privileges. Subway/El: Red Line to Chicago/State. Pets accepted. **Ameni-ties:** 4 restaurants; 2 lounges; indoor pool; health club w/ spa, Jacuzzi, and sauna; children's programs; concierge; business center; 24-hr. room service; in-room massage; babysitting; laundry service; same-day dry cleaning; Premier Suites. *In room:* A/C, TV/VCR w/ pay movies, fax, dataport, minibar, hair dryer.

Sheraton Chicago Hotel & Towers ⭐
Here's a beautifully located hotel, sitting on the riverfront with a view of the lake. Families will appreciate being a short walk to Navy Pier or the Art Institute and steps from Michigan Avenue, with shopping, entertainment, and buses that take you to Museum Campus. You'll also be close to walking paths along the river and lake.

You can request a room with views of the Chicago River, Lake Michigan, or the city skyline, and suites are available. The indoor pool and sun deck on the seventh floor has wraparound views; in fact, they renovated the pool in 2002, the hotel's 10th year of operation. There's a charge for using the fully equipped health club, with treadmills, lifecycles, elliptical cross trainers, life steps, and weight training; a sauna; and massage therapy. If parents want to spend time on their own, babysitting services are available through the concierge.

The hotel boasts six restaurants and lounges, including Shula's Steakhouse. For families wanting a quick bite, there's also a snack bar and cafe.

301 E. North Water St., Chicago, IL 60611. *C* 877/242-2558 or 312/464-1000. Fax 312/464-9140. www.sheratonchicago.com. 1,209 units. $99–$469 double; from $450 suite. Weekend rates around $199. Kids 17 and under stay free in parent's room. Rollaways $25/night; cribs free. AE, DC, DISC, MC, V. Valet park-ing $35 with in/out privileges. Bus: 151 to Michigan Ave. Bridge; walk east. **Amenities:** 3 restaurants and lounges; indoor pool; health club; sauna; business center; 24-hr. room service; massage. *In room:* A/C, TV w/ PlayStation, dataport, minibar, coffeemaker, hair dryer, iron, safe.

Sofitel Chicago Water Tower ⭐⭐⭐
Chicago's latest and greatest hotel opened in June 2002 to rave architectural reviews for its striking white stone and glass facade and geometric shape: A narrow prism tower rises from a square base. Located 1 block west of the Magnificent Mile, the Sofitel doesn't cater specifi-cally to families, but service is so accommodating that you and your kids will be made to feel right at home. Of the 415 rooms, there are 55 suites that offer pull-out sofas, with striking views of the lake and city. (To comfortably fit a crib in the room, you'll want a suite.)

All of the employees seem to hail from exotic French-speaking locales such as Morocco, giving the hotel an international flair that you won't find in most of Chicago's hotels. The interior is stylish, with a funky, modern flair and color combos that stray far from the traditional, with deep purples and reds combin-ing with black and white graphics. The beds are outfitted with fabulously fluffy and inviting duvets. Babysitting services are available upon request, and little guests receive their own Sofitel teddy bear.

20 E. Chestnut St. (at Wabash St.), Chicago, IL 60611. *C* 312/324-4000. Fax 312/324-4026. www.sofitel.com. 415 units. $429–$499 double; $599–$1,500 suite. Kids under 12 stay free in parent's room. No rollaways; cribs free. AE, DC, DISC, MC, V. Self-parking $33 with in/out privileges. Subway/El: Red Line to Chicago/State. Pets accepted. **Amenities:** Restaurant; lounge; fitness center; concierge; 24-hr. room service; babysitting; laundry service. *In room:* A/C, TV/VCR w/ pay movies, fax, dataport, minibar, hair dryer.

EXPENSIVE

Allerton Crowne Plaza ⭐   The resurrection of the historic Allerton a few years ago was a highly significant event in Chicago. Built in 1924 as a "club hotel" providing permanent residences for single men and women, it was converted into the luxury flagship hotel of the upscale Crowne Plaza chain. It's a wonderful sight to most Chicagoans, for whom the Allerton is a beloved landmark on the Magnificent Mile.

The Italian Renaissance–inspired exterior has been painstakingly restored to its original dark-red brickwork and stone carvings and limestone base. Too bad the distinctive exterior style wasn't replicated inside. However, visitors who want to stay in a place that feels new—without being too trendy—should be satisfied with the reinvented Allerton. Because it was built for single men and women, even the suites aren't that big; families should also ask about adjoining rooms. The Allerton is an old-time Chicago hotel, so don't expect to find loads of family-friendly amenities such as a pool or game room. There's a fitness center, but kids aren't allowed. Rooms, however, might make up for the lack of amenities with their warm and homey feel. Snag one overlooking Michigan Avenue to get the best views (or at least stop by the hotel's Renaissance Ballroom for a peek at the Mag Mile).

701 N. Michigan Ave. (at Huron St.), Chicago, IL 60611. ✆ 800/227-6963 outside Illinois, or 312/440-1500. Fax 312/440-1819. www.crowneplaza.com. 443 units. $189–$329 double; $289–$399 suite. Kids 19 and under stay free in parent's room. Rollaways $25/night; cribs free. AE, DC, DISC, MC, V. Valet parking $32 with in/out privileges. Subway/El: Red Line to Chicago/State. **Amenities:** Restaurant; lounge; fitness center (w/ excellent city views); Jacuzzi; sauna; concierge; business center; 24-hr. room service; babysitting; laundry service; same-day dry cleaning. *In room:* A/C, TV w/ pay movies, dataport, minibar, coffeemaker, hair dryer, iron.

Doubletree Guest Suites ⭐   This full-service all-suites hotel is a very good choice for families seeking something with a little less starch. Best of all is its location: just off the Mag Mile and next door to the Hancock Building and Water Tower Place.

Suites might not be huge, but they're warm, inviting, and immaculate to boot. All feature a separate living room (with pullout sofa) and bedroom. The price depends on bed size, floor (some have spectacular lake views for $10 extra), and furnishings. The hotel doesn't feel that different from other Doubletree properties, but that consistency might be just what some people are looking for.

The homespun service and little touches are what count here: fresh flowers in the lobby and two freshly baked chocolate-chip cookies presented to guests on check-in. The hotel's high spot—literally—is the fitness center on the 30th floor, and the pool is surrounded by stunning views of Navy Pier and the Magnificent Mile; kids are welcome at both. The hotel also is home to Chicago's excellent incarnation of New York's Park Avenue Café, a great choice if you want to get a babysitter one evening. A better choice for families is Mrs. Park's Tavern, featuring creative American fare. The restaurant has a kids' menu and sidewalk seating that offers prime people-watching in the shadow of the John Hancock building.

198 E. Delaware Place, Chicago, IL 60611. ✆ 800/222-TREE or 312/664-1100. Fax 312/664-9881. www.doubletreehotels.com. 345 units. $329–$379 double. Children under 18 stay free in parent's room. No rollaways (sofa beds in every suite); cribs free. AE, DC, DISC, MC, V. Valet parking $30 with in/out privileges. Subway/El: Red Line to Chicago/State. **Amenities:** 2 restaurants; lounge; indoor pool; health club w/ spa, Jacuzzi, and sauna; concierge; business center; 24-hr. room service; babysitting; laundry room; dry cleaning. *In room:* A/C, TV w/ pay movies, dataport, minibar, fridge, coffeemaker, hair dryer, iron.

Hilton Garden Inn ⭐   Although it might seem out of place in these urban climes, this Hilton Garden Inn—opened in fall 1999 and occupying a prime perch between North Michigan Avenue and the River North neighborhood—is every inch a big-city player. The hotel caters to business types, but families certainly won't feel out of place here: The building is adjacent to ESPN Zone, a Virgin Megastore, and the new Shops at North Bridge mall. The hotel features weekend packages for families, so ask for current deals when you call. The hotel doesn't have much personality—the lobby is strictly business and feels cold. What the place does have going for it—besides location—is a high-rise sensibility that should appeal to families looking for an urban experience. The ample rooms are located between the 13th and the 23rd floors. Views higher up, especially on the east side and from corner suites facing north and south, afford dramatic vistas of the cityscape and skyline. The hotel's six suites include a parlor area, wet bar, and dining table, with possible connections to adjacent rooms.

10 E. Grand Ave. (at State St.), Chicago, IL 60611. © **800/HILTONS** or 312/595-0000. Fax 312/595-0955. www.hilton.com. 357 units. $169–$309 double; $400–$700 suite. Kids 18 and under stay free in parent's room. Rollaways $15/night; cribs free. AE, DC, DISC, MC, V. Valet parking $32.50 with in/out privileges; self-parking $23 with no in/out privileges. Subway/El: Red Line to Grand/State. **Amenities:** Restaurant; lounge; indoor pool; fitness center w/ Jacuzzi and sauna; concierge; business center; limited room service; babysitting; laundry service; same-day dry cleaning. *In room:* A/C, TV w/ pay movies, dataport, fridge, coffeemaker, hair dryer, iron.

Hotel InterContinental Chicago ★★   The newer hotels might be getting all the attention, but the Hotel InterContinental remains a sentimental favorite for many Chicagoans (ranking right up there with The Drake in our affections). Originally built as an athletic club in 1929, the building's original lobby features truly grand details: marble columns, hand-stenciled ceilings, and historic tapestries. The addition of a drab, impersonal modern tower in the 1960s added more rooms but gave the InterContinental a somewhat schizophrenic quality. So the hotel's recent renovation came as welcome news; finally, the two sides have been integrated into a cohesive whole.

A soaring, four-story rotunda, topped by a 50-foot-wide dome, serves as the new entry point to the hotel, offering a suitably dramatic welcome. All rooms have been completely renovated to make them consistent throughout the property. You'll find classic mahogany furnishings, subdued but elegant decor, and smallish bathrooms (this is an older property, after all). Request a room in the South Tower for the best views. Families might want to request an executive suite in the North Tower, which provides one room with a king bed, connecting by French doors to a second room with a couch that pulls out into a bed.

While you're here, take your kids to the best pool in the city: The InterContinental's main claim to fame is the junior Olympic-size pool on the top floor. One of the first aboveground swimming pools ever built, it's decorated in a lavish "Venetian" style, with mosaics, marble columns, and painted tiles. Also be sure to ask about special family packages when making your reservation. Upon check-in, kids are presented with a tote bag containing crayons, coloring books, a kids' guide to Chicago, a coupon for a free video, and other goodies. Milk and cookies are provided at turndown.

The hotel's restaurant, Zest, is the only street-level restaurant on Michigan Avenue and offers a kids' menu. (Try to grab a table by the front windows to enjoy the never-ending street scene.)

505 N. Michigan Ave. (at Grand Ave.), Chicago, IL 60611. © **800/327-0200** or 312/944-4100. Fax 312/944-1320. www.chicago.interconti.com. 814 units. $248–$409 double; $500–$3,000 suite. Kids under 18 stay free in parent's room. Rollaways $25/night in historic North Tower only; cribs free. AE, DC, DISC, MC, V. Valet parking $27–$34 with in/out privileges. Subway/El: Red Line to Grand/State. **Amenities:** Restaurant; 2 lounges; indoor pool; fitness center w/ sauna; concierge; business center; 24-hr. room service; massage;

babysitting; laundry service; same-day dry cleaning; executive rooms. *In room:* A/C, TV w/ pay movies, data-port, minibar, coffeemaker, hair dryer, iron.

MODERATE

Courtyard by Marriott Chicago Downtown   Marriott's lower-budget chain offers families good value in the heart of River North. You're a short walk from Michigan Avenue, the Loop, and the many theme restaurants of River North, including the ESPN Zone. The trolley to Navy Pier stops a block from the hotel (on State St.). Plus, you'll get access to an indoor pool, fitness center (kids 12 and under must be supervised by an adult), whirlpool, sauna, and sun deck. Guest rooms are newly renovated and feature granite vanities, high-speed Internet access, and sofas, some with pull-out beds. Rooms especially good for families include connecting rooms (both double-bedded and king), and suites that offer a bedroom plus a sitting room with a sofa bed. The 30 East Café and Lounge offers breakfast buffet (with a special price of $6.95 for kids), lunch and dinner, and room service. There's no kids' menu, but the sandwich-and-soup fare is kid-friendly and most can order from the regular menu.

30 E. Hubbard St. (at State St.), Chicago, IL 60611. ℂ 800/321-2211 or 312/329-2500. Fax 312/329-0293. www.marriott.com. 337 units. $159–$199 double. Kids 18 and under stay free in parent's room. Rollaways and cribs free. AE, DC, DISC, MC, V. Valet parking $29 with in/out privileges; self-parking $20.50. Subway/El: Red Line to Grand/State. **Amenities:** Restaurant; lounge; exercise room; indoor pool; concierge; room service; laundry service and self-service laundry. *In room:* A/C, TV w/ pay movies, dataport, coffeemaker, hair dryer, iron.

Holiday Inn Chicago–City Centre ★★ *(Value)*   Enter the soaring modern atrium, with its vases of blooming fresh flowers, and you won't believe that this place is kin to Holiday Inn's assembly-line roadside staples. Its location is a nice surprise as well: east of the Magnificent Mile and close to the Ohio Street Beach and Navy Pier.

The Holiday Inn is a good bet for the budget-conscious family: Not only do kids under 18 stay free in their parents' room, but those 12 and under also eat free in the hotel's restaurants. There's a large outdoor pool, and you're located very near to Ohio Street and Oak Street beaches. Leave the pay-per-view movies one night and head to the McClurg Court cinemas next door. (Make sure you catch a flick in Theater 1, one of the largest in the city, for the full cinematic experience.)

Fitness devotees will rejoice because the Holiday Inn is located next door to the Lakeshore Athletic Club, where guests may enjoy the extensive facilities free of charge. (Family hours for the pool are Mon–Fri 8–10am, 2–5pm, and 7–9:30pm; Sat 8–11am and 2–8:30pm; and all day Sun.) The gym is only available to adults over 18. The hotel also has its own spacious outdoor pool and sun deck. The views are excellent, especially looking north toward the Hancock Building and Monroe Harbor. Rooms are clean and up-to-date, although pretty basic. Even the standard room should fit a family of 3 or 4 comfortably. You might want to splurge on one of the "master suites," which boast large living-room areas with wet bars, along with a Jacuzzi-style tub and sauna in the bathroom.

300 E. Ohio St. (at Fairbanks Court), Chicago, IL 60611. ℂ 800/HOLIDAY or 312/787-6100. Fax 312/787-6259. www.sixcontinentshotels.com. 500 units. $175–$230 double. Weekend and promotional rates $109–$159. Kids under 18 stay free in parent's room. Rollaways $20/night; cribs free. AE, DC, DISC, MC, V. Valet parking $19. Subway/El: Red Line to Grand/State. **Amenities:** 2 restaurants; bar; outdoor and indoor pools; access to nearby health club; Jacuzzi; sauna; children's programs; concierge; business services; limited room service; babysitting; laundry room; dry cleaning. *In room:* A/C, TV w/ pay movies, dataport, coffeemaker, hair dryer, iron.

Homewood Suites ⭐   Housed just off the Mag Mile in a sleek tower above retail shops, offices, and a health club—and adjacent to ESPN Zone—the hotel is "Italian Renaissance meets Crate & Barrel." Distressed-leather sofas, Mediterranean stone tile, wrought-iron chandeliers, and beaded lampshades adorn its sixth-floor lobby. The Homewood Suites makes an excellent choice for families; there's room in the suites for everyone to spread out, and preparing your own meals in the kitchen can be a real money-saver.

Rooms—one- and two-bedroom suites and a handful of double-double suites, which can connect to king suites—feature velvet sofas that are all sleepers, and the beds have big, thick mattresses. Each comes with a full kitchen, a dining-room table that doubles as a workspace, and decent-size bathrooms. The hotel provides a complimentary buffet breakfast and beverages and hors d'oeuvres every evening; there is also a free grocery-shopping service.

40 E. Grand Ave. (at Wabash St.), Chicago, IL 60611. ☏ **800/CALL-HOME** or 312/644-2222. Fax 312/644-7777. www.homewood-suites.com. $259 double suite. Kids under 18 stay free in parent's room. Rollaways and cribs free. AE, DC, DISC, MC, V. Valet parking $26 with in/out privileges. Subway/El: Red Line to Grand/State. **Amenities:** Fitness room w/ small pool and nice views of the city; concierge; business services; babysitting; laundry machines on all floors; dry cleaning. *In room:* A/C, TV w/ pay movies, fully equipped kitchen, coffeemaker, hair dryer, iron.

Millennium Knickerbocker Hotel ⭐   The epitome of Jazz Age indulgence when built in 1927 as the Davis, the Knickerbocker has since undergone more transformations than Madonna. During the Capone era, it was rumored to have shady underworld connections. In the 1970s, Hugh Hefner turned it into the gaudy Playboy Towers and invited the leisure-suit set to a perpetual disco inferno on the hotel's famed illuminated ballroom floor. By the time the 1980s rolled around, the Knickerbocker had been through the ringer.

Since becoming a Millennium Hotel about 2 years ago, the Knickerbocker has undergone a $10 million renovation and once more exudes vintage charm. Weekends are popular with families, thanks to the hotel's superb location a block from Oak Street Beach and across the street from The Drake. You'll be in the heart of Magnificent Mile shopping, and walking distance from the American Girl Place.

While the rooms aren't especially spacious, they are warm and comfortable. Bathrooms are small but nicely done. One caveat: Views are often rather dismal, but you can catch a glimpse of the lake in all rooms ending in 18, and corner rooms (ending in 17, 28, or 35) look onto Michigan Avenue. Families might consider staying on the Club level, which features upgraded rooms and a private lounge with complimentary breakfast, coffee, munchies, and board games. Kids get milk and cookies at turndown, and the hotel provides cribs and rollaways. The pay-per-view movies feature a children's program, and guests receive a 10% off coupon for Bloomingdale's, which has a children's department.

The hotel's restaurant, Nix, serves up regional American cuisine (including a kids' menu) in hip vertical presentations, but its passé decor recalls the slick mid-1980s. The lobby bar specializes in 40 blends of martinis. A pianist performs live in the bar Wednesday through Saturday.

163 E. Walton Place (½ block east of Michigan Ave.), Chicago, IL 60611. ☏ **800/621-8140** or 312/751-8100. Fax 312/751-9663. www.knickerbockerchicago.com. 305 units. $164–$274 double; $194–$294 club rooms; $284–$1,000 suite. Kids under 18 stay free in parent's room. Rollaways $20/night; cribs free. AE, DC, DISC, MC, V. Valet parking $30 with in/out privileges; self-parking $24. Subway/El: Red Line to Chicago/State. **Amenities:** Restaurant; bar; exercise room; concierge; business center; 24-hr. room service; babysitting; laundry service; dry cleaning; club-level rooms. *In room:* A/C, TV w/ pay movies, fax, dataport, minibar, coffeemaker, hair dryer, iron.

Talbott Hotel ★★ *(Finds*   The family-owned Talbott is a small, European-style gem. Constructed in the 1920s as an apartment building, the Talbott was converted to a hotel in 1989. That's great news for families, because the hotel has many suites with two bedrooms and two bathrooms, plus kitchen facilities. The location just off the Magnificent Mile is superb, and close to family-friendly restaurants such as Johnny Rocket's and Zoom Kitchen. Proprietors Basil and Laurie Ann Kromelow take a keen personal interest in the hotel's decor: Most of the gorgeous antiques strewn throughout are purchases from Basil's European shopping trips. The wood-paneled lobby, decorated with leather sofas and velvety armchairs, two working fireplaces, tapestries, and numerous French horns used for fox hunts, is intimate and inviting—all the better in which to enjoy your complimentary continental breakfast. Kids' amenities are sparser here than at some larger hotels, but the homey, non-chain hotel atmosphere, large suites, availability of kitchens, and prime location make this one of my favorites for families.

Rooms aren't quite as distinctive, although they are decorated in a perfectly comfortable midrange hotel style; they vary in size, so ask when making reservations. Suites and the hotel's "executive king" rooms entice with Jacuzzi tubs; suites have separate sitting areas with sofa beds and dining tables. The Talbott is not for families in need of extensive hotel facilities, but the cozy atmosphere and personal level of service appeals to visitors looking for the feeling of a small inn rather than a sprawling, corporate hotel.

20 E. Delaware Place (between Rush and State sts.), Chicago, IL 60611. ☎ **800/TALBOTT** or 312/944-4970. Fax 312/944-7241. www.talbotthotel.com. 149 units. $139–$429 double; $199–$429 suite. Kids under 18 stay free in parent's room. Rollaways $20/night; cribs free. AE, DC, DISC, MC, V. Self-parking $21. Subway/El: Red Line to Chicago/State. **Amenities:** Lounge; access to nearby health club; concierge; business services; 24-hr. room service; laundry service; dry cleaning; executive rooms. *In room:* A/C; TV, minibar, hair dryer, iron, safe.

The Tremont Hotel Chicago   Slightly more upscale than The Talbott, but with the same small, European-style feel, the Tremont has great appeal. The hotel is in the process of becoming more family-friendly, with plans for offering cribs and more, so ask about family amenities when you call. Suites are highly recommended for families, as some of the guest rooms tend to be on the small (or shall we say, "intimate") side. The cozy lobby with a fireplace sets the mood from the start. The furnishings are tasteful without being somber. Families will appreciate that rooms in the Tremont House—a separate building next door—have kitchenettes. Suites are designed so one room includes a king bed with its own television, minibar, and bathroom. The adjoining living room offers a couch that folds out into a bed, plus its own television, minibar, and bathroom.

The steak-and-chops restaurant off the lobby, the memorabilia-filled Iron Mike's Grille, is co-owned by legendary former Chicago Bears football coach Mike Ditka (see p. 94 for a full review).

100 E. Chestnut St. (1 block west of Michigan Ave.), Chicago, IL 60611. ☎ **800/621-8133** or 312/751-1900. Fax 312/751-8650. www.tremontchicago.com. 130 units. $199–$259 double; from $650 suite. Kids under 18 stay free in parent's room. Rollaways $20/night; cribs free. AE, DC, DISC, MC, V. Valet parking $30. Subway/El: Red Line to Chicago/State. **Amenities:** Restaurant; small exercise room (and access to nearby health club); concierge; business services; 24-hr. room service; massage; babysitting; laundry service; dry cleaning. *In room:* A/C, TV/VCR, CD player, minibar, coffeemaker, hair dryer, iron, safe.

The Westin Michigan Avenue Chicago ★★   Located across the street from the John Hancock Center, this hotel is right on the Magnificent Mile, steps from Bloomingdale's and Water Tower Place. In past years, The Westin was looking a bit shabby, but renovations have spruced up the lobby, fitness center, and guest rooms. Newly renovated rooms feature a marble foyer, expanded bathroom, and new furnishings and carpeting.

This hotel offers the Westin Kids Club for kids 12 and under. Other notable family amenities are the many baby and toddler accessories available to guests, from bottle warmers and cribs to night lights, jogging strollers, and electrical outlet covers. Kids are greeted with Westin Kids Club sports bottles or sippy cups, which are filled with complimentary beverages at meals. Also available are coloring books, bath toys, and a story line on the hotel phone that plays age-appropriate bedtime stories by dialing a four-digit number. The hotel restaurant will make sure kids' meals are ready when you arrive if you call in advance and special menus are available through room service, too. Older kids can while away the hours with in-room Sony PlayStation.

The Grill on The Alley has been winning great reviews and offers American cuisine in a contemporary atmosphere. You'll be comfortable bringing the kids here, and the kids' menu features pastas and burgers. A lobby cafe is a good stop for breakfast. The small fitness center is open to kids and includes free weights, treadmills, lifecycles and Stairmasters, and men's and women's locker rooms with saunas.

909 N. Michigan Ave., Chicago, IL 60611. (C) **800/228-3000** or 312/943-7200. Fax 312/397-5580. www.westinmichiganave.com. 751 units. $179–$250 double; from $600 suite. Kids 18 and under stay free in parent's room. Rollaways and cribs free. AE, DC, DISC, MC, V. Valet parking with in/out privileges $33. Bus: No. 151 to Delaware St. Pets accepted with $25 fee. **Amenities:** Restaurant; cafe; health club; sauna; children's programs; 24-hr. room service. *In room:* AC; TV w/ PlayStation, dataport, minibar, coffeemaker, hair dryer, iron.

INEXPENSIVE

Red Roof Inn Chicago Downtown ⭐ *Value*   In its previous incarnation as a Motel 6, this was one of the few budget finds in downtown Chicago. Now the hotel's corporate owners have taken the property up a notch, converting it into a slightly more upscale Red Roof Inn last summer. Although the rates have risen along with the name change, you're paying for a completely refurbished hotel. The lobby is small but cheery; all rooms have been upgraded, with new linens and carpeting and bigger TVs. For a family of 3 or 4, go for the king suite, which has a sofa bed, microwave, and refrigerator, all for a price that's only about $6 more than a double room. You're not going to find much in the way of amenities here, but the Red Roof Inn delivers a good value for its excellent location.

Room service is available through Coco Pazzo Café (p. 96), an excellent Northern Italian restaurant around the corner from the hotel's front door.

162 E. Ontario St. (½ block east of Michigan Ave.), Chicago, IL 60611. (C) **800/733-7663** or 312/787-3580. Fax 312/787-1299. www.redroof.com. 195 units. $87–$159 double; $99 suite. Kids 17 and under stay free in parent's room. No rollaways; cribs free. AE, DC, DISC, MC, V. Valet parking $24 with no in/out privileges; self-parking $22. Subway/El: Red Line to Grand/State. **Amenities:** Business services. *In room:* A/C, TV w/ pay movies, dataport, hair dryer, iron.

5 River North

The name "River North" designates a vast area parallel to the Magnificent Mile. The zone is bounded by the river to the west and south, and roughly by Clark Street to the east and by Chicago Avenue to the north. The earthy red-brick buildings that characterize the area were once warehouses of various kinds and today form the core of Chicago's art-gallery district. The neighborhood also has spawned many of the city's trendiest restaurants. You'll find many of the city's family-friendly hotels here. That, coupled with the proximity of tourist draws such as the Hard Rock Cafe, Rainforest Cafe and ESPN Zone, means River North is an area families should consider when booking a hotel.

VERY EXPENSIVE

House of Blues Hotel ★★★   The funky vibe makes this a great hotel for teenagers and anyone who wants a hotel to be an experience—not just a place to sleep. Blending Gothic, Moroccan, East Indian, and New Orleans influences, the House of Blues lobby is a riot of crimsons and deep blues (stop by to check it out even if you're not staying here).

You can catch your breath in the lighter, whimsical rooms, which feature some of the most exciting Southern folk art you'll ever come across. The casually dressed, friendly staff invents creative nightly turndowns for guests—such as fragrant mood crystals or a written thought for the day left on your pillow. One of the hotel's biggest selling points is its location in the entertainment-packed Marina Towers complex. Within steps of the hotel you've got the AMF Bowling Center (with billiards), a marina with boat rentals, the riverside Smith & Wollensky steakhouse (an outpost of the New York restaurant), the innovative Bin 36 wine bar and restaurant, and, of course, the House of Blues Music Hall and Restaurant. (Don't miss the Sun brunch at which gospel choirs perform—kids can order off the menu at a reduced rate.)

333 N. Dearborn St. (at the river), Chicago, IL 60610. © 877/569-3742 or 312/245-0333. Fax 312/923-2458. www.loewshotels.com. 367 units. $329–$364 double; $500–$750 suite. Weekend and promotional rates available. Kids 18 and under stay free in parent's room. Rollaways and cribs free. AE, DC, DISC, MC, V. Valet parking $28 with in/out privileges. Subway/El: Brown Line to Clark/Lake, or Red Line to Grand/State. Pets accepted. **Amenities:** Lounge; access to the very hip Crunch Health & Fitness Club; children's programs; concierge; business center; 24-hr. room service; babysitting; laundry service; same-day dry cleaning. *In room:* A/C, TV/VCR w/ pay movies and Nintendo, CD player, fax, dataport, minibar, coffeemaker, hair dryer, iron.

The Westin River North ★★★   On the northern bank of the Chicago River, the Westin River North has continued to evolve since it ceased being the Hotel Nikko a couple of years ago. Although the hotel has the personality of a business hotel, it has made an effort to be family-friendly. Especially notable are the many baby and toddler accessories available to guests, from bottle warmers and cribs to night lights, jogging strollers, and electrical outlet covers. Older kids can while away the hours with in-room Sony PlayStation. Like the Westin Michigan Avenue (p. 71), this hotel offers the Westin Kids Club for kids 12 and under. Kids are greeted with Westin Kids Club sports bottles or sippy cups, which are filled with complimentary beverages at meals. Other perks include coloring books, bath toys, and a story line on the hotel phone that plays age-appropriate bedtime stories by dialing a four-digit number. Kids' meals are available at the hotel restaurant with advance notice, and special menus are available through room service.

Changes have de-emphasized the hotel's unique aesthetic in the guest rooms, but traces of the hotel's Japanese sensibility linger in the small rock garden at the rear of the lobby and the bamboo growing beside one of the lobby's staircases. Rooms are similarly handsome, with furniture and artwork that give them a residential feel. King-bedded rooms will accommodate three; double-bedded rooms will accommodate five. For those who feel like splurging, a suite on the 19th floor more than satisfies, with three enormous rooms, including a huge bathroom and a large window offering a side view of the river.

320 N. Dearborn St. (on the river), Chicago, IL 60610. © 800/WESTIN1 or 312/744-1900. Fax 312/527-9761. www.westinrivernorth.com. 424 units. $239–$429 double; $329–$2,800 suite. Weekend rates $169–$229. Kids 18 and under stay free in parent's room. Rollaways $25/night; cribs free. AE, DC, DISC, MC, V. Valet parking $32 with in/out privileges; self-parking $16. Subway/El: Brown, Orange, or Green Line to State/Lake. Pets

under 25 lbs. accepted. **Amenities:** Restaurant; lounge; fitness center; concierge; business center; 24-hr. room service; babysitting; laundry service, same-day dry cleaning. *In room:* A/C, TV w/ pay movies and Nintendo, fax, dataport, minibar, coffeemaker, hair dryer, iron.

EXPENSIVE

Embassy Suites Hotel Chicago–Downtown ★★   A gushing waterfall and palm- and fern-lined landscaped ponds lie at the bottom of the huge central atrium. But its vaguely Floridian ambience is also part of what makes the Embassy Suites a very family-friendly hotel—even though it bills itself as a business hotel and does a healthy convention business. The other part is the mode of accommodations: All suites have two rooms, consisting of a living room with a sleeper sofa, a round table, and four chairs; and a bedroom with either a king-size bed or two double beds. For an extra $30, guests staying on the refurbished VIP floor get nightly turndown service and in-room fax machines and robes. At one end of the atrium, the hotel serves a complimentary cooked-to-order breakfast in the morning and, at the other end, supplies complimentary cocktails and snacks in the evening. And yes, there's a pool. On the weekends, step into the elevator and you'll find plenty of families with kids wrapped in towels making good use of the hotel as a weekend getaway.

Off the lobby is an excellent restaurant, Papagus Greek Taverna, and next door is a Starbucks with outdoor seating.

600 N. State St. (at W. Ontario St.), Chicago, IL 60610. © **800/362-2779** or 312/943-3800. Fax 312/943-7629. www.embassy-suites.com. 358 units. $159–$359 king suite; $169–$459 double suite. Kids 17 and under stay free in parent's room. No rollaways (sofa beds in every suite); cribs free. AE, DC, DISC, MC, V. Valet parking $30 with in/out privileges. Subway/El: Red Line to Grand/State. **Amenities:** Restaurant; coffee bar; indoor pool; exercise room w/ whirlpool and sauna; concierge; business center; limited room service; babysitting; laundry machines; dry cleaning; VIP rooms. *In room:* A/C, TV w/ pay movies and PlayStation, dataport, minibar, kitchenette, coffeemaker, hair dryer, iron.

INEXPENSIVE

Best Western River North Hotel *Value*   This former motor lodge and cold storage structure conceals a very attractive, sharply designed interior that scarcely resembles any Best Western in which you're likely to have spent the night. One of the few hotels located right in the midst of one of the busiest nightlife and restaurant zones in the city, it lies within easy walking distance of interesting boutiques and Chicago's art-gallery district. Rooms are spacious, and the bathrooms are spotless (though no-frills). One-room suites have a sitting area, while other suites have a separate bedroom; all suites come with a sleeper sofa. The Best Western's reasonable rates and rooftop pool (with sweeping views) will appeal to families on a budget—and the almost unheard-of free parking can add up to significant savings for anyone planning to stay a week or more.

125 W. Ohio St. (at LaSalle St.), Chicago, IL 60610. © **800/528-1234** or 312/467-0800. Fax 312/467-1665. www.bestwestern.com. 150 units. $109–$167 double; $173–$295 suite. Kids under 18 stay free in parent's room. Rollaways $10/night; cribs free. AE, DC, DISC, MC, V. Free parking for guests (1 car per room). Subway/El: Red Line to Grand/State. **Amenities:** Pizzeria; lounge; indoor pool; exercise room; business services; limited room service; babysitting; laundry service; VIP rooms. *In room:* AC, TV w/ pay movies and Nintendo, dataport, minibar, coffeemaker, hair dryer, iron, safe.

Hampton Inn & Suites Chicago–Downtown ★ *Value*   A welcome addition to the increasingly pricey hotel market in Chicago, the Hampton, which opened 2 years ago, has a combination of rooms, two-room suites, and studios. Families will appreciate the indoor pool and in-room Nintendo games and VCRs when the little ones need to chill out after a busy day of sightseeing. You won't have far to go to find dinner: the Hard Rock Cafe and Rainforest Café are both a few blocks' walk away.

Rooms are residential and warm, with framed collages of vintage Chicago postcards on the walls. The apartment-style suites feature galley kitchens with fridges, microwaves, dishwashers, and cooking utensils. Off the lobby is the Dearborn Diner, and a second-floor skywalk connects to Ruth's Chris Steakhouse next door. While the Hampton Inn does attract some business travelers on a budget, it is mainly a family hotel.

33 W. Illinois St. (at Dearborn St.), Chicago, IL 60610. © 800/HAMPTON or 312/832-0330. Fax 312/832-0333. www.hamptoninn-suites.com. 230 units. $139–$149 double; $159–$239 suite. Rates include buffet breakfast. Kids under 18 stay free in parent's room. Rollaways and cribs free. AE, DC, DISC, MC, V. Valet parking $28 with in/out privileges; self-parking $13 with no in/out privileges. Subway/El: Red Line to Grand/State. **Amenities:** Restaurant; indoor pool; exercise room w/ sauna; business services; limited room service; babysitting; laundry machines. *In room:* A/C, TV/VCR, dataport, coffeemaker, hair dryer, iron, safe.

6 The Gold Coast

The Gold Coast begins approximately at Division Street and extends north to North Avenue, bounded on the west by Clark Street and on the east by the lake. The area encompasses a short strip of some of the city's priciest real estate along Lake Shore Drive. From the standpoint of social status, the streets clustered here are among the finest addresses in Chicago. It's a lovely neighborhood for a stroll among the graceful town houses and the several lavish mansions that remain, relics from a glitzier past. The hotels here tend to be upscale without hitting the peak that some of the nearby Michigan Avenue hotels reach.

To locate these hotels, see the "Central Chicago Accommodations" map on p. 54.

EXPENSIVE

Omni Ambassador East ✦   The ring-a-ding glory days of the Ambassador East, when stars including Frank Sinatra, Humphrey Bogart, and Liza Minnelli shacked up here during layovers or touring stops in Chicago, are ancient history. But even though big-name celebs tend to ensconce themselves at the Ritz-Carlton or Four Seasons these days, the Ambassador name still evokes images of high glamour in these parts. For the past 50 years, celebrities who have come to town to mingle with Chicago's Gold Coast society have done so most publicly from the revered Booth One in the ritzy Pump Room restaurant. Less pricey than the Ritz-Carlton or Four Seasons, and located on a beautiful, tree-lined street in the Gold Coast, the Omni East is a good choice for families looking for accommodations near, but not on, the Magnificent Mile.

The Ambassador suffered a slow decline in the 1960s and '70s, which didn't turn around until 1986, when Omni bought and renovated the property. Today, after a recent second face-lift, the Ambassador East has reclaimed its strut and splendor. Rooms have been spruced up; bathrooms feature the usual higher-end amenities. Executive suites have separate sitting areas; Celebrity Suites (named for the stars who've crashed in them) come with a separate bedroom, two bathrooms, a small kitchen, and a dining room. Most extravagant is the Presidential Suite, which boasts a canopied terrace and marble fireplace. If money's no object, families will want to go for the Celebrity Suite, with its separate bedrooms and bathrooms, and kitchen. The Ambassador East has the same Kids' Program as the Omni Chicago (p. 63), and both Omnis make an extra effort for guests with disabilities, offering equipment such as TDD telephones and strobe fire alarms for deaf guests.

1301 N. State Pkwy. (1 block north of Division St.), Chicago, IL 60610. © **800/843-6664** or 312/787-7200. Fax 312/787-4760. www.omnihotels.com. 285 units. $209–269 double; $299–$759 suite. Kids 18 and under stay free in parent's room. Rollaways $25/stay; cribs free. AE, DC, DISC, MC, V. Valet parking $32.50 with in/out privileges. Subway/El: Red Line to Clark/Division. **Amenities:** Restaurant; small fitness room (and access to nearby health club); concierge; business services; 24-hr. room service; babysitting; 24-hr. laundry service; dry cleaning. *In room:* A/C, TV w/ pay movies, dataport, minibar, coffeemaker, hair dryer, iron.

Sutton Place Hotel ✰ The Sutton Place, a sleek granite-and-glass-skinned tower, lies at the confluence of chi-chi Oak Street, the revitalized scene on North State and Rush streets, and the posh Gold Coast residential district. Depending on your perspective, the Sutton Place will feel like either the apartment of a cool urban friend or a somewhat dated example of 1980s-era glitz. The modern rooms feature original Robert Mapplethorpe floral still-life photographs (collected by the hotel's owners) on the walls. Suites have separate sitting rooms and a wet bar. Some rooms have floor-to-ceiling windows with city and lake views, and a few of the priciest loft suites offer balconies and terraces. All the windows open to let in some fresh air.

Befitting its ritzy location, the Sutton Place caters to a demanding clientele with niceties such as robes and slippers and car service to the Loop on weekday mornings. Kids also get special treatment: cookies and milk at turndown, kid-size robes, and Johnson's bath amenities.

After you've left the kids with a babysitter, you might want to head downstairs to the Whiskey Bar & Grill, owned by L.A. nightclub impresario Rande Gerber (better known as Mr. Cindy Crawford). While the Windy City version of the Whiskey might not attract the same A-list celebrity crowd as the New York location, it's ideal for people-watching on frenetic Rush Street. (The dining area is quite small, so reserve in advance for prime viewing.)

21 E. Bellevue Place (at Rush St.), Chicago, IL 60611. © **800/606-8188** or 312/266-2100. Fax 312/266-2141. www.suttonplace.com. 246 units. $189–$335 double; $250–$395 suite. Kids under 18 stay free in parent's room. Rollaways $25/night; cribs free. AE, DC, DISC, MC, V. Valet parking $32. Subway/El: Red Line to Clark/Division. Small pets are accepted. **Amenities:** Restaurant/bar; exercise room (and access to nearby health club); concierge; courtesy car; business center; 24-hr. room service; babysitting; laundry service; same-day dry cleaning. *In room:* A/C, TV w/ pay movies, CD player, dataport, minibar, coffeemaker, hair dryer, iron.

MODERATE

The Claridge ✰ *(Finds)* If a modest, cost-effective option in a lovely setting within walking distance of Michigan Avenue, Division Street, and Old Town's nightlife, and Lincoln Park's many attractions sounds pretty good to you, don't dismiss the Claridge. Ask for a room above the eighth floor that overlooks the tree-lined street (kings and double-doubles are spacious and sunny); avoid at all cost the dark "king superior" rooms, which look onto the fire escape. Some deluxe accommodations have sitting areas, and three executive suites on the 14th floor have working fireplaces.

The Claridge won't overwhelm you with facilities; the hotel's restaurant and bar are both quite small. Where this small hotel really wins its Brownie points is for the very pleasant staff and nice touches. Kids will love the freshly baked cookies at turndown and the courtesy stretch limo that transports guests anywhere within a 2-mile radius of the hotel in the mornings. In the lobby, there's a small sitting area where your family can enjoy a complimentary hot breakfast buffet. The surrounding neighborhood of elegant town houses makes a great place for a stroll—without the traffic and noise of other downtown neighborhoods.

1244 N. Dearborn Pkwy. (1 block north of Division St.), Chicago, IL 60610. ℂ **800/245-1258** or 312/787-4980. Fax 312/266-0978. www.claridgehotel.com. 163 units. $165–$250 double; $475–$750 suite. Kids under 12 stay free in parent's room. Rollaways and cribs free. AE, DC, DISC, MC, V. Valet parking $31 with in/out privileges. Subway/El: Red Line to Clark/Division. Pets accepted. **Amenities:** Restaurant; lounge; exercise room; concierge; courtesy limo; business services; limited room service; laundry service; same-day dry cleaning. *In room:* A/C, TV w/ pay movies, dataport, minibar, coffeemaker, hair dryer, iron.

7 Lincoln Park & the North Side

If you prefer the feel of living amid real Chicagoans in a residential neighborhood, several options await you in Lincoln Park and farther north. Not only do these hotels tend to be more affordable than those closer to downtown, but they also provide a different vantage point from which to view Chicago. If you stay at the Majestic Hotel or the City Suites Hotel, for example, you can join the locals on a pedestrian pilgrimage to Wrigley Field for a Cubs game. The area is flush with restaurants, and public transportation via the El or buses is a snap.

MODERATE

The Belden-Stratford ★ *Finds*   This North Side hotel is a great option for families who want to do as the natives do in a neighborhood atmosphere. Actually a condominium building that offers 25 hotel rooms, the two-story lobby feels grandly European, and paneled entry doors lead the way to airy rooms with nine-foot ceilings, crown moldings, and plush carpeting. Rooms are large, the doorman greets you as if you were a resident, and Lincoln Park, where kids can run free, is across the street. You are right across from the Lincoln Park Zoo and the Conservatory, and steps from the lake and buses that will take you downtown in a matter of minutes.

Be sure to ask for a room with a park view, so you can watch runners pass and couples stroll. (Some rooms feature wrap-around views with south, west, and east exposures.) Even though it's a condominium building, there's maid and valet service and a rooftop sun deck. One downside: Because the Belden-Stratford is not a full-service hotel, there's no room service or concierge.

2300 N. Lincoln Park West, Chicago, IL 60614. ℂ **800/800-6261** or 773/281-2900. Fax 773/880-2039. www.beldenstratford.com. 25 units. $199–$289 double. Kids under 18 stay free in parent's room. Rollaways and cribs $20/night. AE, DC, DISC, MC, V. Valet parking $25 with in/out privileges. Subway/El: Red Line to Fullerton. **Amenities:** Fitness center; spa; salon; coin-op laundry. *In room:* A/C, TV; hair dryer and iron upon request.

Windy City Urban Inn ★★ *Finds*   Children over the age of 10 are welcome at this grand 1886 home, located on a tranquil side street just blocks away from busy Clark Street and Lincoln Avenue—both chock-full of shops, restaurants, and bars. While the inn is charming enough, the true selling point of the Windy City Inn is hosts Andy and Mary Shaw. He's a well-known political reporter, while she has 20 years of experience in the Chicago bed-and-breakfast business. Together, they not only have some great only-in-Chicago stories, but they also are excellent resources for anyone who wants to get beyond the usual tourist sites. Subtle Chicago touches give guests a distinctive experience: Blues and jazz play during the buffet breakfast, and local food favorites offered to guests include the famous cinnamon buns from Ann Sather's restaurant and beer from Goose Island Brewery.

The remodeled building is more open than the typical Victorian home. There are five rooms in the main house and three apartments in a coachhouse; all are named after Chicago writers. Two of the coachhouse apartments can sleep four:

Lincoln Park & North Side Accommodations

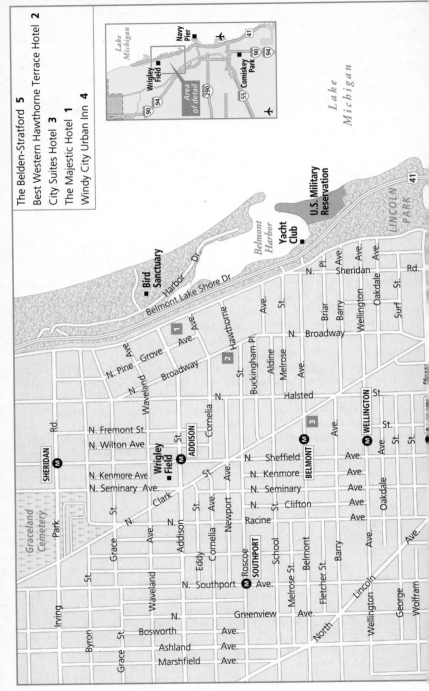

The Belden-Stratford **5**
Best Western Hawthorne Terrace Hotel **2**
City Suites Hotel **3**
The Majestic Hotel **1**
Windy City Urban Inn **4**

Lake Michigan

Fullerton Beach

LINCOLN PARK

Lincoln Park Zoo

North Pond

South Pond

Jersey Harbor

ke Shore Dr.

John Cannon Dr.

Chicago Historical Society

41

N. Burton Pl.
N. State St.
N. Dearborn St.
N. Clark St.
N. La Salle St.

Stockton

N. Lincoln Park West

Clark Ave.

Schiller

St.

5

N. Park Ave.

Eugenie Ave.

64

SEDGWICK

N. Sedgwick St.

Wisconsin St.

Menomonee St.

N. Cleveland Ave.
N. Mohawk St.
N. Larrabee St.

Deming Pl.

Arlington Pl.

4

Orchard St.
N. Burling St.

Lincoln Ave.

OZ PARK

Armitage Ave.

N. Orchard St.
N. Burling St.
N. Halsted St.

Freemont

Avenue

NORTH/CLYBOURN

St.

DePaul University

N. Dayton St.
N. Freemont St.
N. Bissell St.
N. Sheffield Ave.

Wisconsin St.

Willow St.

North Ave.

Weed St.

FULLERTON

Montana St.

Belden

Webster

Dickens

ARMITAGE

TREBES PARK

Clybourn

North

Kingsbury

Turning Basin

64

Wrightwood

N. Racine Ave.

Lakewood

Wayne

N. Southport Ave.

Fullerton

Ave.

Elston Ave.

Noble

Greenview

Altgeld

N. Ashland

North Ave.

Kennedy

Cortland St.

North Branch

Expressway

90 94

N. Wood St.

West St.

N. Greenview
N. Bosworth
N. Ashland

Subway/El stop M

N

0.25 mi
0.25 km

two in an upstairs bedroom and two on a bed that folds up against the wall. (Custom-made for the Shaws, these feature top-quality mattresses, making them much more comfortable than the Murphy beds of old.) Families should stay in one of these apartments, which are wonderfully cozy with their fireplaces and Jacuzzi tubs.

In good weather, guests are invited to eat breakfast on the back porch or in the garden between the main house and the coachhouse. There, you can sit back and imagine that you're living in your very own Chicago mansion—the type of home that many Chicagoans wish they could live in themselves.

607 W. Deming Place, Chicago, IL 60614. ✆ **877/897-7091** or 773/248-7091. Fax 773/248-7090. www.windycityinn.com. 8 units. $125–$285 double. Kids age 10 to 18 usually stay free in parent's room, although this depends on the room you book; ask when you make a reservation. No rollaways or cribs. Rates include buffet breakfast. AE, DC, DISC, MC, V. Parking $6 in nearby lot with in/out privileges. Subway/El: Red Line to Fullerton. *In room:* A/C, TV; hair dryer and iron available upon request.

INEXPENSIVE

Best Western Hawthorne Terrace Hotel ⭐ *Value*   A fantastic bargain for families who don't mind staying a bit north of the beaten track, this hotel offers plenty of space for a great price. The Hawthorne Terrace, located near Wrigley Field on the Near North side, was remodeled 5 years ago. The junior suites provide a room with two double beds, and an adjoining living room with a pullout couch; families of four will fit comfortably in one of these suites, which can also accommodate a crib. Amazingly, for the price, you also have access to a fitness center with a sauna and Jacuzzi. (Young children should be supervised by an adult.) A continental breakfast is offered in the lobby every morning. Parking is a bargain at $16 a day.

3434 N. Broadway, Chicago, IL 60657. ✆ **888/675-2378** or 773/244-3434. Fax 773/244-3435. www.best western.com. 59 units. $159–$179 double; $169 suite. Children 12 and under stay free in parent's room. No rollaways (sofa beds in junior suites); cribs free. AE, DC, DISC, MC, V. Parking $16 in nearby lot with in/out privileges. Subway/El: Red Line to Belmont. **Amenities:** Exercise room; laundry service and laundry room. *In room:* A/C, TV, fridge, coffeemaker, hair dryer, iron.

City Suites Hotel *Value*   A few doors down from the elevated train stop on Belmont Avenue, not far from the corner of Sheffield, an enterprising team called Neighborhood Inns of Chicago has turned a former transient dive into a charming small hotel, something along the lines of an urban bed-and-breakfast. Most rooms are suites, with separate sitting rooms and bedrooms, all furnished with first-rate pieces and decorated in a homey and comfortable style. Families should ask about the king suite, with a king bed and sitting area with sofa bed; they can also accommodate a crib. Fridges and microwaves are available upon request in suites.

A bonus—or drawback, depending on your point of view—is the hotel's neighborhood setting. Area locals include everybody from young professional families to gay couples to punks in full regalia. Blues bars, nightclubs, and restaurants abound hereabouts, making the City Suites a find for the bargain-minded and adventuresome. Room service is available from Ann Sather, a Swedish diner and neighborhood institution (see p. 115 for a full review).

933 W. Belmont Ave. (between Sheffield Ave. and Halstead St.), Chicago, IL 60657. ✆ **800/248-9108** or 773/404-3400. Fax 773/404-3405. www.cityinns.com. 45 units. $139–$179 double. Rates include continental breakfast. Kids 12 and under stay free in parent's room. No rollaways (sofa beds in suites); cribs free. AE, DC, DISC, MC, V. Parking $17 in nearby lot with in/out privileges. Subway/El: Red Line to Belmont. **Amenities:** Exercise room; business services; limited room service; laundry service; same-day dry cleaning. *In room:* A/C, TV w/ pay movies, dataport, minibar, coffeemaker, hair dryer, iron.

The Majestic Hotel ★★ *Finds*   Owned by the same group as the City Suites Hotel, the Majestic blends seamlessly into its residential neighborhood. Located on a charming tree-lined street (but convenient to the many restaurants and shops of Lincoln Park), the hotel welcomes kids with open arms. Some of the larger suites—the most appealing are those with sun porches—offer butler's pantries with a fridge, microwave, and wet bar. Families should ask about the two-room king suite, which features a bedroom with king bed, a living room with a sofa bed, and a kitchenette with refrigerator and microwave. The hotel is ideally suited for enjoying the North Side and is only a short walk from both Wrigley Field and the lake.

528 W. Brompton St. (at Lake Shore Dr.), Chicago, IL 60657. © **800/727-5108** or 773/404-3499. Fax 773/404-3495. www.cityinns.com. 52 units. $139–$179 double. Rates include continental breakfast. Kids under 12 stay free in parent's room; over age 12, $10 per person. No rollaways (sofa beds in suites); cribs free. AE, DC, DISC, MC, V. Self-parking $18 in nearby garage with no in/out privileges. Subway/El: Red Line to Addison; walk several blocks east to Lake Shore Dr. and then 1 block south. **Amenities:** Exercise room; business services; limited room service; laundry service; same-day dry cleaning. *In room:* A/C, TV w/ pay movies, dataport, minibar, coffeemaker, hair dryer, iron.

Family-Friendly Dining

Chicago has come into its own as a major dining destination, and that's not limited to the chic, see-and-be-seen spots. Plenty of options await families, too. Besides those stylish restaurants, you'll find an amazing array of steakhouses, family-style Italian restaurants, and every kind of ethnic cuisine you could possibly crave. You'll be surprised at the number and range of restaurants that welcome kids in Chicago. Even restaurants that don't offer a specialized kids' menu often will provide half-sized portions for children. Whether you're looking for a restaurant for your family's big night out or simply a no-frills spot to dig in, in this chapter you'll find places the locals go when they want to eat well.

Chicagoans have a passion for two foods your kids are probably passionate about too: hot dogs and pizza. Don't run out to buy a case of antacids just yet—options for adult stomachs also exist. And while anyone can tell you that Rainforest Cafe or Ed Debevic's is great for kids, what we've highlighted here are some unique dining ideas that are Chicago's own.

A NOTE ON PRICES Unfortunately, Chicago is no longer the budget-dining destination it once was. (Hipness doesn't come cheap.) I've divided restaurants into three price categories: "Expensive" means that dinner for a family of four will cost $75 and up; "Moderate," $40 to $75; and, at an "Inexpensive" place, you'll pay about $40 or less. But just because the prices have risen doesn't mean that the attitude has. Restaurants in Chicago might have gotten trendy, but we're still friendly.

To find out more about restaurants that opened since this book went to press, check out the *Chicago Tribune*'s entertainment website (**www.metromix.com**), the website for Chicago magazine (**www.chicagomag.com**), and the entertainment/nightlife website **www.chicago.citysearch.com**.

1 Restaurants by Cuisine

ALSATIAN

Brasserie Jo ⭐ (River North, $$$, p. 100)

AMERICAN

American Girl Place Cafe ⭐⭐⭐ (Magnificent Mile & the Gold Coast, $$$, p. 93)

Ann Sather ⭐⭐ (Wrigleyville & the North Side, $, p. 115)

Café Brauer ⭐ (Lincoln Park, $, p. 112)

Carson's ⭐ (River North, $$, p. 101)

Charlie's Ale House on Navy Pier ⭐ (Magnificent Mile & the Gold Coast, Lincoln Park, $, p. 98)

Cheesecake Factory (Magnificent Mile & the Gold Coast, $$, p. 95)

Dave & Buster's (River North, $, p. 104)

Key to Abbreviations: $$$ = Expensive $$ = Moderate $ = Inexpensive

ESPN Zone (Magnificent Mile &
the Gold Coast, $$, p. 96)

Goose Island Brewing Company
(Lincoln Park, $$, p. 110)

Hard Rock Cafe (River North, $,
p. 105)

Harry Caray's ★★ (River North,
$$$, p. 101)

Houston's (River North, $$,
p. 101)

Jack Melnick's Corner Tap (Magnificent Mile & the Gold Coast,
$$, p. 96)

John Barleycorn (Lincoln Park, $,
p. 112)

Mr. Beef ★ (River North, $,
p. 105)

Northside Café ★ (Wicker
Park/Bucktown, $, p. 117)

O'Brien's (Lincoln Park, $$$,
p. 110)

O'Donovan's (Wrigleyville & the
North Side, $, p. 116)

Oak Street Beachstro ★ (Magnificent Mile & the Gold Coast,
$$$, p. 94)

Rainforest Cafe (River North, $,
p. 106)

Stanley's ★★ (Lincoln Park, $,
p. 113)

Toast ★ (Lincoln Park, $, p. 113)

ASIAN

Big Bowl ★ (Magnificent Mile &
the Gold Coast, $, p. 97)

Flat Top Grill (Lincoln Park,
Wrigleyville & the North Side,
Randolph Street Market Dis-
trict, $, p. 112)

Hi Ricky Asia Noodle Shop &
Satay Bar ★ (Wrigleyville & the
North Side, $, p. 115)

Penny's Noodle Shop ★
(Wrigleyville & the North Side,
$, p. 116)

BARBECUE

Carson's ★ (River North, $$,
p. 101)

Twin Anchors ★ (Lincoln Park, $,
p. 114)

BISTRO

Bistro 110 ★★ (Magnificent Mile
& the Gold Coast, $$, p. 95)

BREAKFAST

Ann Sather ★★ (Wrigleyville &
the North Side, $, p. 115)

Billy Goat Tavern ★ (Magnificent
Mile & the Gold Coast, $,
p. 97)

Bourgeois Pig ★ (Lincoln Park, $,
p. 111)

Corner Bakery (Magnificent Mile
& the Gold Coast and citywide,
$, p. 98)

House of Blues (River North, $$,
105)

Lou Mitchell's ★★ (the Loop, $,
p. 91)

Toast ★ (Lincoln Park, $, p. 113)

Uncommon Grounds ★
(Wrigleyville & the North Side,
$, p. 116)

Wishbone ★★★ (Randolph Street
Market District, $, p. 92)

BURGERS

Billy Goat Tavern ★ (Magnificent
Mile & the Gold Coast, $,
p. 97)

Ed Debevic's ★ (River North, $,
p. 104)

Flapjaw Café (Magnificent Mile &
the Gold Coast, $, p. 98)

Green Door Tavern (River North,
$, p. 105)

John Barleycorn (Lincoln Park, $,
p. 112)

Northside Café ★ (Wicker
Park/Bucktown, $, p. 117)

CAJUN/CREOLE

Heaven on Seven ★★ (the Loop,
$, p. 90)

House of Blues (River North, $$,
p. 105)

Wishbone ★★★ (Randolph Street
Market District, $, p. 92)

CONTINENTAL

Bistro 110 ★★ (Magnificent Mile
& the Gold Coast, $$, p. 95)

DINER

Ed Debevic's ✿ (River North, $, p. 104)

Heaven on Seven ✿✿ (the Loop, $, p. 90)

Lou Mitchell's ✿✿ (the Loop, $, p. 91)

Manny's Coffee Shop & Deli ✿ (near the Loop, $, p. 91)

Nookies (Lincoln Park, $, p. 113)

Silver Cloud Bar & Grill ✿ (Bucktown/Wicker Park, $, p. 117)

Twisted Spoke ✿ (River North, $, p. 107)

ECLECTIC

foodlife ✿✿ (Magnificent Mile & the Gold Coast, $, p. 99)

Oak Street Beachstro ✿ (Magnificent Mile & the Gold Coast, $$$, p. 94)

FONDUE

Geja's Café ✿ (Lincoln Park, $$$, p. 110)

FRENCH

Brasserie Jo ✿ (River North, $$$, p. 100)

La Creperie ✿✿ (Lincoln Park, $, p. 113)

GERMAN

The Berghoff ✿ (the Loop, $$, p. 88)

GREEK

Artopolis (Greektown, $, p. 93)

Athena (Greektown, $$, p. 93)

Costas (Greektown, $$, p. 93)

Greek Islands (Greektown, $$, p. 93)

Parthenon (Greektown, $$, p. 93)

Pegasus (Greektown, $$, p. 93)

Santorini (Greektown, $$, p. 93)

HOT DOGS

Byron's Hot Dog Haus (Far North Side, $, p. 118)

Gold Coast Dogs (Magnificent Mile & the Gold Coast, $, p. 118)

Murphy's Red Hots (Wrigleyville, $, p. 119)

Superdawg Drive-In (Far North Side, $, p. 119)

The Wieners Circle (Lincoln Park, $, p. 118)

ITALIAN

Buca di Beppo (Wrigleyville & the North Side, $$, p. 114)

Coco Pazzo Café ✿ (Magnificent Mile & the Gold Coast, $$, p. 96)

Harry Caray's ✿✿ (River North, $$$, p. 101)

La Cantina Enoteca (the Loop, $$, p. 88)

Leona's (River North, $$, p. 102)

Maggiano's ✿ (River North, $$, p. 102)

Ranalli's Pizzeria, Libations & Collectibles (Lincoln Park, $, p. 118)

Rosebud on Taylor ✿✿ (near the Loop, $$, p. 89)

Scoozi ✿ (River North, $$, p. 103)

Tufano's Vernon Park Tap (near the Loop, $, p. 92)

Tuscany ✿ (near the Loop, $$$, p. 85)

The Village ✿ (the Loop, $$, p. 89)

Vivere ✿ (the Loop, $$, p. 90)

JAPANESE

Kabuki (Lincoln Park, $$, p. 111)

Ron of Japan (Magnificent Mile & the Gold Coast, $$$, p. 95)

Sai Café ✿ (Lincoln Park, $$, p. 111)

MEXICAN

Don Juan on Halsted ✿✿ (Lincoln Park, $$$, p. 107)

El Jardin (Lincoln Park, $, p. 112)

MIDDLE EASTERN

Reza's ✿✿ (River North, $$, p. 102)

NOODLES

Hi Ricky Asia Noodle Shop & Satay Bar ✦ (Wrigleyville & the North Side, $, p. 115)

Penny's Noodle Shop ✦ (Wrigleyville & the North Side, $, p. 116)

PIZZA

California Pizza Kitchen (Magnificent Mile & the Gold Coast, $, p. 98)

Edwardo's (Magnificent Mile & the Gold Coast, South Loop, and Lincoln Park; $; p. 118)

Gino's East ✦✦ (River North, $, p. 104)

Leona's (River North, $$, p. 102)

Lou Malnati's Pizzeria ✦ (River North, $, p. 118)

Pat's Pizzeria (Wrigleyville, $, p. 118)

Pizzeria Due (River North, $, p. 106)

Pizzeria Uno ✦ (River North, $, p. 106)

Ranalli's Pizzeria, Libations & Collectibles (Lincoln Park, $, p. 118)

SANDWICHES

Bourgeois Pig ✦ (Lincoln Park, $, p. 111)

Corner Bakery (Magnificent Mile, the Gold Coast, and citywide; $; p. 98)

Mrs. Levy's Delicatessan (Loop, $, p. 91)

Potbelly Sandwich Works (the Loop, $, p. 91)

Uncommon Grounds ✦ (Wrigleyville & the North Side, $, p. 116)

Zoom Kitchen ✦ (Magnificent Mile & the Gold Coast, Bucktown/Wicker Park, and Wrigleyville; $; p. 100)

SEAFOOD

La Cantina Enoteca (the Loop, $$, p. 88)

SOUTHERN

House of Blues (River North, $$, p. 105)

Wishbone ✦✦✦ (Randolph Street Market District, $, p. 92)

SOUTHWESTERN

Bandera (Magnificent Mile & the Gold Coast, $$$, p. 94)

SPANISH/TAPAS

Cafe Iberico ✦✦ (River North, $, p. 103)

STEAKHOUSE

Houston's (River North, $$, p. 101)

Iron Mike's Grille ✦✦ (Magnificent Mile & the Gold Coast, $$$, p. 94)

SWEDISH

Ann Sather ✦✦ (Wrigleyville & the North Side, $, p. 115)

2 The Loop

Chicago's business power center isn't exactly attuned to family dining—what you'll find here are corporate types on expense accounts. (Because of the area's business orientation, keep in mind that some of the downtown eateries are closed on Sun.) But, if you are spending the day touring the Loop's many attractions, we've pegged some great sandwich stops and reasonable dining options. The good news: Just west of the Loop, Little Italy offers inexpensive ethnic dining.

EXPENSIVE

Tuscany ✦ NORTHERN ITALIAN   Convenient to most downtown locations, a few blocks' stretch of Taylor Street is home to a host of time-honored, traditional, hearty Italian restaurants. Tuscany is one of the most reliable Italian restaurants on Taylor Street. In contrast to the city's more fashionable Italian

Central Chicago Dining

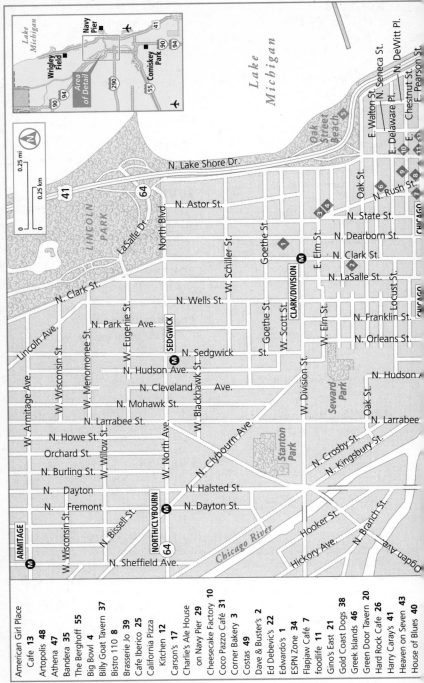

American Girl Place
  Cafe **13**
Artopolis **48**
Athena **47**
Bandera **35**
The Berghoff **55**
Big Bowl **4**
Billy Goat Tavern **37**
Bistro 110 **8**
Brasserie Jo **39**
Cafe Iberico **25**
California Pizza
  Kitchen **12**
Carson's **17**
Charlie's Ale House
  on Navy Pier **29**
Cheesecake Factory **10**
Coco Pazzo Café **31**
Corner Bakery **3**
Costas **49**
Dave & Buster's **2**
Ed Debevic's **22**
Edwardo's **1**
ESPN Zone **34**
Flapjaw Café **7**
foodlife **11**
Gino's East **21**
Gold Coast Dogs **38**
Greek Islands **46**
Green Door Tavern **20**
Hard Rock Cafe **26**
Harry Caray's **41**
Heaven on Seven **43**
House of Blues **40**

Iron Mike's Grille **5**
Jack Melnick's Corner Tap **28**
La Cantina Enoteca **54**
Leona's **19**
Lou Malnati's Pizzeria **23**
Lou Mitchell's **52**
Maggiano's **23**
Manny's Coffee Shop & Deli **51**
Mr. Beef **18**
Mrs. Levy's Delicatessen **53**
Oak Street Beachstro **5**
Parthenon **49**
Pegasus **45**
Pizzeria Due **32**
Pizzeria Uno **33**
Potbelly Sandwich Works **42**
Rainforest Café **27**
Reza's **15**
Ron of Japan **30**
Rosebud on Taylor **50**
Santorini **46**
Scoozi **16**
Tufano's Vernon Park Tap **50**
Tuscany **50**
Twisted Spoke **14**
The Village **54**
Vivere **54**
Wishbone **44**
Zoom Kitchen **6**

M Subway/El stop
For stops in the Loop, see the "Downtown El & Subway Stations" map.

> *Tips* **Chilling Out with an Italian Ice**
>
> When in Little Italy, do as the Italians do: Cool off with an Italian ice. In a heat wave, **Mario's Italian Lemonade**, at 1070 W. Taylor St., is popular—but it doesn't hold a plastic spoon to the lesser-known **Papa's Grand Stand,** 1407 W. Grand Ave. in River West (© **312/226-0321**).

---

spots, family-owned Tuscany has the comfortable feel of a neighborhood gathering place. Although the food is of enough quality to draw a fine-dining crowd, the unpretentious atmosphere means you'll find big tables of families, so don't worry about disturbing the peace. As you might expect, the extensive menu features the culinary fare of the Tuscany region, including pastas, pizzas, veal, chicken, and a risotto of the day, and the portions are large. There's no kids' menu, but half-orders are available. There's a second location in Wrigleyville across from Wrigley Field at 3700 N. Clark St. (© 773/404-7700).

1014 W. Taylor St. (between Racine Ave. and Halsted St.). © 312/829-1990. www.stefanirestaurants.com. High chairs, boosters. Reservations recommended. Main courses $9.25–$27. AE, DC, DISC, MC, V. Mon–Fri 11am–3:30pm; Mon–Thurs 5–11pm; Fri–Sat 5pm–midnight; Sun 2–9:30pm. Subway/El: Blue Line to Polk.

MODERATE

The Berghoff ✿ GERMAN   Spaetzle and sauerbraten are hot sellers at this long-time German landmark in Chicago's Loop. Having celebrated its centennial in 1998, the immense, 700-seat restaurant is housed in one of the first buildings constructed in the Loop after the Chicago Fire, and one of only two remaining buildings in the city with a cast-iron facade. The Berghoff holds Chicago liquor license no. 1, issued at the close of Prohibition, and it still serves its own brand of beer at $3 a stein. (*Good news for kids:* The Berghoff also serves its own root beer.) If you decide to belly up at the stand-up bar, you might notice that the bar clientele is still overwhelmingly male; the stand-up bar at The Berghoff didn't even admit women until 1969.

While the menu rotates seasonally, the German standard-bearers are always available. The Berghoff serves hundreds of orders of Wiener schnitzel every day, plus bratwurst, sauerbraten, corned beef, and the like. Sides of choice include spaetzle, creamed spinach, and red cabbage. Because some of us have arteries to worry about, the third and fourth generations of family management have added some lighter fare in the form of salads, broiled fish, and vegetarian dishes. There's a children's menu with smaller portions of dishes on the regular menu. The Berghoff also holds a popular Oktoberfest celebration each year in mid-September, serving brats, chicken, and pretzels, and hosting live music in the street.

17 W. Adams St. (between State and Dearborn sts.). © 312/427-3170. www.berghoff.com. Kids' menu, high chairs, boosters. Reservations recommended. Main courses $5.95–$11 lunch, $8.95–$18 dinner; kids' menu items under $5. AE, MC, V. Mon–Thurs 11am–9pm; Fri 11am–9:30pm; Sat 11am–10pm. Subway/El: Red or Blue lines to Jackson or Monroe.

La Cantina Enoteca *Value* ITALIAN/SEAFOOD   La Cantina is the most moderately priced of the three restaurants in the Italian Village. It makes the most of its basement location by creating the feel of a wine cellar. During the day, the restaurant attracts a daily regular clientele of lawyers, judges, and the like, many of whom eat at the bar. During pre-theater dining hours, you'll find plenty of other families eating here. Specializing in seafood, La Cantina offers at least five fresh varieties every day. The dinner menu offers a big-time bargain: A la carte dishes (most of which are under $20) include a salad, and for $2 more you also get soup, dessert, and coffee. As for the cuisine, there are no surprises where the pasta is concerned—all the reliable standards are here.

71 W. Monroe St. (between Clark and Dearborn sts.). © 312/332-7005. Sassy seats. Reservations recommended. Main courses (including soup, salad, dessert, and coffee) $12–$26; salads $9.95–$12; sandwiches $7.50–$7.95. Lunch prices slightly lower. AE, DC, DISC, MC, V. Mon–Thurs 11:30am–11pm; Fri 11:30am–midnight; Sat 5pm–midnight; Sun 4:30–8pm (seasonally). Subway/El: Red or Blue lines to Monroe.

Rosebud on Taylor ★★ *Value* ITALIAN   If you want a real Chicago dining experience, this is it: At Rosebud, you'll be surrounded by locals, not tourists. The old-style, dark rooms are filled with families celebrating birthdays and older couples who have been coming here for years. If your kids are on the verge of a hunger meltdown, make sure to ask for breadsticks to tide them over: You can expect to wait well beyond the time of your reservation. Rosebud is known for its enormous helpings of pasta, served up in massive white bowls. Expect to walk out with a doggy bag, or—even better—have your whole table share a few dishes. But the portions aren't just large; they're delicious. Most pastas lean toward heavy Italian-American favorites: deep-dish lasagna and fettuccine alfredo that defines the word *rich*. But the menu has been hipped up with more modern takes on Italian cooking. Rosebud also offers five different cavatelli dishes, a house specialty, and a tempting selection of "secondi"—meat, fish, and poultry dishes.

If you don't feel like trekking to the original, Rosebud offers another, trendier version just off the Mag Mile at 720 N. Rush St., at Superior Street (© 312/266-6444).

1500 W. Taylor St. (1 block east of Ashland Ave.). © 312/942-1117. High chairs, boosters. Reservations recommended, especially on weekends. Main courses $5.95–$13 lunch, $11–$30 dinner. AE, DC, DISC, MC, V. Mon–Thurs 11am–10pm, Fri 11am–11pm, Sat 5–11pm, Sun 4–10pm. Subway/El: Blue Line to Polk.

The Village ★ SOUTHERN ITALIAN   Upstairs in the Italian Village is The Village, with its charming interpretation of alfresco dining in a small Italian town, complete with a midnight-blue ceiling, twinkling "stars," and banquettes tucked into private, cavelike little rooms. It's the kind of pan-Chicago place where you might see one man in a tux and another in shorts. With 200 items, the menu is so big and broad that it's sure to satisfy. Those old-time, hearty southern Italian standards are all here, and at a great value. We're talking veal Marsala, eggplant parmigiana, tortellini alla bolognese, and, yes, even pizza. The lunch menu is somewhat abbreviated but still offers an enormous selection of salads, pasta, meats, and sandwiches.

Finds **The Italian Village**

The building at 71 W. Monroe St. houses three separate Italian restaurants, collectively known as the Italian Village. Each restaurant has a unique take on Italian ambience and cooking; they also share an exemplary wine cellar and fresh produce grown in a family garden. Each of the three restaurants in the Italian Village is detailed in this section. Families with young children will be most comfortable at moderately priced La Cantina Enoteca; if you have older kids, they might enjoy the atmospheric The Village, designed to recreate a dining experience in the Italian countryside.

Moments   Watching the World Float by from Chicago's Riverwalk

The outdoor cafes along the banks of the Chicago River's main branch, between Wabash Avenue and Wells Street, are run by restaurants that change from year to year, so we can't recommend specific dishes. But food is almost an afterthought: Kids will thrill to the parade of schooners and speedboats cruising along the Chicago River on their way to Lake Michigan. Open seasonally.

71 W. Monroe St. (between Clark and Dearborn sts.). © 312/332-7005. Sassy seats. Reservations recommended (accepted for parties of 3 or more). Main courses (including salad) $11–$24; salads $5.50–$10; pizza $11–$14; sandwiches $7.95–$15. Lunch prices slightly lower. AE, DISC, MC, V. Mon–Thurs 11am–1am; Fri–Sat 11am–2am; Sun noon–midnight. Subway/El: Red or Blue lines to Monroe.

Vivere ⊛ REGIONAL ITALIAN   On the main floor of the Italian Village is Vivere, the Italian Village's take on gourmet cooking. Teenagers might enjoy this upscale—but not snobbish—take on Italian fare. Created by Chicago designer Jordan Moser, the chic interior, with rich burgundies, textured walls, spiraling bronze sculptures, and fragmented mosaic floors, complements the modern cuisine. In addition to excellent daily risotto and fresh fish dishes served three ways, Vivere presents interesting preparations of game and a particularly good *petto d'anatra*, a duck breast with escarole sautéed in red wine and balsamic vinegar. Pastas, which at lunch are available either in "primi" appetizer size or as the main course, range from the basic linguine alla bolognese to the slightly daring *agnolottini di fagiano* (pheasant-filled pasta with butter, sage, and Parmesan).

71 W. Monroe St. (between Clark and Dearborn sts.). © 312/332-4040. Sassy seats. Reservations recommended. Main courses $13–$25. AE, DC, DISC, MC, V. Mon–Thurs 11:30am–2:30pm and 5–10pm; Fri 11:30am–2:30pm and 5–11pm; Sat 5–11pm. Subway/El: Red or Blue lines to Monroe.

INEXPENSIVE

Heaven on Seven ⊛⊛ *Finds* CAJUN/DINER   Kids will love the "every day is Mardi-Gras" feel of this highly popular spot, a favorite of local workers. Just check out the lunchtime crowd that packs the restaurant, located on the seventh floor of the Garland Building, across from Marshall Field's. What's not to like about a bowl of gumbo for only $3.95? Chef/owner Jimmy Bannos's Cajun and Creole specialties, most of which run about $9 or $10 and come with a cup of soup, include such Louisiana staples as red beans and rice, a catfish po' boy sandwich, and jambalaya. If your kids don't have a taste for Tabasco, the enormous coffee-shop-style menu covers all the traditional essentials: grilled-cheese sandwiches, omelets, tuna, the works. Indulge in chocolate pecan pie or chicory coffee crème brûlée for dessert. On the first and third Fridays of the month, Heaven on Seven hosts special dinners from 5:30 to 9pm. Although the Loop original has the most character, in the past couple of years more Mardi Gras–infused locations have opened along the Mag Mile at 600 N. Michigan Ave. (© 312/280-7774), adjacent to a cineplex, and in Wrigleyville at 3478 N. Clark St. (© 773/477-7818); unlike the original location, both accept reservations and credit cards.

111 N. Wabash Ave. (at Washington St.), 7th floor. © 312/263-6443. Kids' menu, high chairs, boosters. Reservations not accepted. Menu items $2.75–$9.95; kids' menu $4.95 (incl. soda and ice-cream sandwich). No credit cards. Mon–Fri 8:30am–5pm, Sat 10am–3pm; 1st and 3rd Fri of month 5:30–9pm. Subway/El: Red Line to Washington/State.

Lou Mitchell's ★★ *Finds* BREAKFAST/DINER   The genuine article, Lou Mitchell's is a Loop dining institution, located across the south branch of the Chicago River from the Loop, a block farther west than Union Station. A French food critic passing through Chicago rated Lou Mitchell's the number-one breakfast spot in America, home of the "five-star breakfast." Quirky touches bound to amuse kids are everywhere: If the waiter discovers you're from out of town, don't be surprised if a table flag of your home state or country is plopped down on your table.

Don't worry about the line to get in; female patrons get boxes of Milk Duds, and everyone gets free donut holes while they wait. Turnover is continuous and service efficiently attentive. If your kids are old enough, you might shorten the wait for a table by grabbing a counter seat. One specialty here is the airy omelets served in sizzling skillets; you'll double your pleasure (and cholesterol) with Mitchell's use of double-yolk eggs. Orders arrive with thick slabs of toasted Greek bread and homemade marmalade. You might also have the best bowl of oatmeal you've ever eaten—deliciously creamy. Orange juice and grapefruit juice are freshly squeezed. At the end of your meal, a small paper cup of vanilla soft serve ice cream will be offered up, gratis. If you eat breakfast here, you'll likely be filled enough to make it practically to dinner without even noticing that you missed a meal.

565 W. Jackson Blvd. (at Jefferson St.). © 312/939-3111. High chairs, boosters. Reservations accepted for groups of 8 or more. Breakfast items $1.95–$6.95. No credit cards. Mon–Sat 5:30am–3pm; Sun 7am–3pm. Subway/El: Blue Line to Clinton.

Manny's Coffee Shop & Deli ★ *Value* DINER   If your itinerary includes a trip back in time, make sure you visit Manny's, a Chicago institution since 1942. Kid highlights include spaghetti, beef stew, rice pudding, German chocolate cake, and the occasional special, from franks and beans to chop suey. Adults can grab a tray and navigate the fast-moving line. Even if they go for more standard fare, kids will be awed by the carving station known for its enormous corned-beef sandwiches (about half a lb.), Reubens, world-class hot pastrami, and steamship rounds the size of VW Beetles. Gruff yet friendly staff in paper hats take their métier seriously, and the effect—and the food—is absolutely reassuring. Seat yourself and snarf down knishes, borscht, liver and onions, meat loaf, tongue, and stewed prunes. Introduce your kids to the old-fashioned joys of cream soda and Green River.

1141 S. Jefferson St. © 312/939-2855. www.mannysdeli.com. High chairs, boosters. Reservations not accepted. Main courses $4.95–$8.95. Cash only. Mon–Sat 5am–4pm. Subway/El: Red Line to Roosevelt.

Mrs. Levy's Delicatessen SANDWICHES   Should you be planning a trip up the Sears Tower, here's the perfect place to stop and fortify your family first. This retro deli displays signed photos of famous patrons and offers up deli staples such as knishes, blintzes, and homemade soups. Sandwiches are piled high and include corned beef, beef brisket, and pastrami; soup of the day might include sweet-and-sour cabbage, chicken matzo ball, and mushroom barley.

233 S. Wacker Dr. (Sears Tower), mezzanine level. © 312/993-0530. High chairs. Reservations not accepted. All main courses under $8. AE, DC, DISC, MC, V. Mon–Sat 11am–5pm. Subway/El: Brown Line to Wells/Franklin.

Potbelly Sandwich Works *Value* SANDWICHES   Ask a Chicagoan where to go for a great sandwich, and he'll invariably point the way to Potbelly. Yes, there's a potbelly stove inside, as well as a player piano and other Old West saloon-type memorabilia, but go here for the mouthwatering made-to-order namesake comestibles. (That's all they serve.) Prepared on homemade sub rolls stuffed with turkey, Italian meats, veggies, pizza ingredients, and more, and layered with lettuce, tomato, onion, pickles, and Italian seasonings, they're warmed in a countertop toaster oven. Even with all the fixin's, each is under $5. Tempting milkshakes keep the blender mighty busy. Potbelly has other locations throughout the city, including ones at 2264 N. Lincoln Ave. between Belden Avenue and Webster Street (© 773/528-1405), and in The Shops at North Bridge, 520 N. Michigan Ave. (© 312/527-5550), that are convenient to Loop and Magnificent Mile sightseers and shoppers.

190 State St. (at Lake St.) © **312/683-1234.** High chairs, boosters. Reservations not accepted. Main courses $3.50–$5.50. Cash only. Mon–Sun 11am–11pm. Subway/El: Red Line to State.

Tufano's Vernon Park Tap ITALIAN   Taking the family to the United Center to suffer along with the Chicago Bulls? Here's a great spot to fortify your family for the long evening ahead. Located on the eastern edge of Little Italy, Tufano's has been family-owned for 60 years and has attracted neighborhood regulars as well as celebrities and politicians. (Check out the wall of photos that includes everyone from Tommy LaSorda to Dolly Parton.) The bar is a Chicago classic, and the cuisine is Italian. Traditional pasta dishes are a forte here, as is Tufano's lemon chicken with potatoes. On the weekends, go for the homemade ravioli and cavatelli. On Friday, regulars choose the seafood salad.

1073 W. Vernon Park Pl. © **312/733-3393.** High chairs, boosters. Reservations not accepted. Menu items $7–$13. Cash only. Tues–Thurs 11am–10pm; Fri 11am–11pm; Sat 4–11pm; Sun 3–9pm. Subway/El: Blue Line to UIC/Halsted.

3 The Randolph Street Market District & Greektown

Much of the Market District is about the "scene"—and when traveling with kids, making the scene ranks pretty low. But you might want to make a trip to the district just to dine at **Wishbone,** or to experience adjacent **Greektown,** filled with cheap eats and noisy, boisterous restaurants where kids blend right in. Greektown sits on the district's eastern border. There's nothing much to do here besides eat—but if you have a few days in Chicago, try to make it here for at least one meal.

Transportation to Greektown and the Market District is easy, by the way—it's about a $5 cab ride from Michigan Avenue or a slightly longer trek by bus (no. 8 or 9) or El, with stops at Halsted and Lake, a block from the restaurants. The walk from the Loop is very pleasant and totally secure in the daytime, but at night, save your stroll for Michigan Avenue.

MARKET DISTRICT

Wishbone ★★★ SOUTHERN/CAJUN/BREAKFAST   This Southern-style restaurant has much to recommend it. First, it's a homegrown restaurant, not a chain. Second, children can be kept busy looking at the large and surrealistic farm-life paintings on the walls or reading a picture book, *Floop the Fly,* loaned to diners (written and illustrated by the parents of the owners). The food is diverse enough that both adults and kids can find something to their liking, but there's also a new menu geared just to children. The sprawling, loft-style space is quirky enough to be fun (plenty of folk art), but still relaxed and attitude-free.

Known for Southern food and big-appetite breakfasts, Wishbone's extensive, reasonably priced menu blends hearty, home-style choices with healthful and vegetarian items. Brunch is the 'Bone's claim to fame, when an eclectic crowd of bedheads packs in for the plump and tasty salmon cakes, omelets, and red eggs (a lovely mess of tortillas, black beans, cheese, scallions, ancho chile sauce, salsa, and sour cream). Brunch can be a mob scene, though, so try lunch or dinner; offerings run from "yardbird" (charbroiled chicken with sweet red-pepper sauce) and blackened catfish to hoppin' John or Jack (vegetarian variations on the black-eyed pea classic). Variety is Wishbone's strong point: Every entree comes with a choice of sides, so everyone can mix and match to their hearts' content. The restaurant provides outdoor seating in nice weather.

There's a newer location at 3300 N. Lincoln Ave. (📞 773/549-2663), but the original location has more character.

1001 Washington St. (at Morgan St.). 📞 312/850-2663. Kids' menu, high chairs, boosters. Reservations accepted for parties of 6 or more (no reservations on Sun). Main courses $3.25–$8.75 breakfast and lunch, $5.75–$14 dinner; kids' menu $4–$8. AE, DC, DISC, MC, V. Mon 7am–3pm; Tues–Fri 7am–3pm and 5–10pm; Sat–Sun 8am–3pm and 5–11pm. Reachable by $5 taxi ride from the Loop.

GREEKTOWN

A short cab ride from the Loop across the south branch of the Chicago River will take you to the city's Greektown, a row of moderately priced and inexpensive Greek restaurants clustered on Halsted Street between Van Buren and Washington streets. The neighborhood was spruced up for the 1996 Democratic convention and has only gotten better. Many restaurants have wonderful outdoor seating and spectacular views of the city—plus, long tables of families and shouts of "Opa!" make quite a ruckus that will keep your kids entertained. **Greek Islands,** 200 S. Halsted St. (📞 **312/782-9855**); **Santorini,** 800 W. Adams St., at Halsted Street (📞 **312/829-8820**); **Parthenon,** 314 S. Halsted St. (📞 **312/726-2407**); and **Costas,** 340 S. Halsted St. (📞 **312/263-0767**), are all good bets for gyros, Greek salads, shish kebabs, and the classic moussaka. My top pick for families is **Athena,** 212 S. Halsted St. (📞 **312/655-0000**), which has a stunning three-level outdoor seating area, a fantastic choice for a warm summer evening. It's paved with brick and landscaped with 30-foot trees, flower gardens, and even a waterfall. Best of all: an incredible view of the downtown skyline with the Sears Tower right in the middle. **Pegasus,** 130 S. Halsted St. (📞 **312/226-3377**), has a rooftop patio serving drinks, appetizers, and desserts. **Artopolis,** 306 S. Halsted St. (📞 **312/559-9000**), a recent addition to the neighborhood, is a casual option offering up tasty Greek and Mediterranean specialties, wood-oven pizzas, and wonderful breads and French pastries.

4 The Magnificent Mile & the Gold Coast

Yes, the Mag Mile is all about designer shopping—and designer eating—and you'll pleasantly surprised to discover that plenty of those eateries welcome kids. In fact, a great many families who visit Chicago never stray far from the Magnificent Mile and the adjoining Gold Coast area. From the array of restaurants, shops, and pretty streets in the area, it's not hard to see why.

EXPENSIVE

American Girl Place Cafe ⭐⭐⭐ AMERICAN   Dining with dolly has never been done in a more appealing manner than at the cafe located inside the American Girl Place store. Not to be sexist, but most boys will be less than thrilled about spending time here surrounded by girls, dolls, and dresses: It's really best for a girls' day out. With an eye-popping black, white, and red polka-dot-and-stripe decor, the cafe has loads of kid appeal. The view of the water tower and surrounding street life from the third-floor cafe is wonderful. Parents and daughters can bond over lunch, dinner, or tea, and dolly (only of the American

Girl species, of course) can join in, settled on a special booster seat. Treats on the menu include fresh cinnamon buns, frittata quiche, chicken fingers, macaroni and cheese, and tic-tac-toe pizza. Top your meal off with a sugar cookie, carrot cake, or chocolate pudding flowerpot, and wash everything down with a pink lemonade or hot chocolate. American Girl Place is a destination for many families visiting Chicago, so plan well in advance to avoid disappointing the American girl in your life. The cafe recommends booking 8 to 12 weeks in advance.

111 E. Chicago Ave. ℂ 877/247-5223. High chairs, boosters. Reservations required. Prix-fixe menu (includes gratuity) breakfast $16, brunch $17, lunch $17, dinner $18. AE, DC, DISC, MC, V. Mon–Thurs 11:30am–3pm and 5–10pm; Fri 11:30am–3pm and 5–11pm; Sat 5–11pm; Sun 11am–3pm and 5–10pm. Subway/El: Red Line to Chicago/State.

Bandera SOUTHWESTERN   The open-range ambience here is created by the chicken roasting over a hickory-burning fire. (The fake pony-skin that covers the bar stool seats also adds to the charm.) While some complain that the room even gets a bit too smoky from that open fire, in the wintertime, Bandera's got a cozy rustic Western feel. If your kids will eat cornbread and roasted chicken with mashed potatoes, they'll do fine here. Menu offerings include roasted prime rib, pork tenderloin with barbecue sauce, Western beef back ribs, and wood-roasted salmon. This is a national chain, so the restaurant might look awfully familiar, but a location on Michigan Avenue that affords views of the street life below make this branch particularly well situated.

535 N. Michigan Ave. ℂ 312/644-3524. Kids' menu, high chairs, boosters. Main courses $15–$25; kids' menu $5–$10. AE, DC, MC, V. Mon–Thurs 11:30am–10pm; Fri–Sat 11:30am–11pm. Subway/El: Red Line to Grand. Bus: 151 and 157.

Iron Mike's Grille ★★ STEAKHOUSE   For many Chicago football diehards, the glory days of former Coach "Iron" Mike Ditka, who led the Bears to victory in Super Bowl XX in 1985, are still alive and well. Football memorabilia lines the walls of this restaurant, filled with amber light and dark wood. Kids who are at all into the game might inadvertently get a little history lesson—even the Bears' 1985 victory, seemingly still fresh in the minds of Bears' fans who love to relive the glory days, probably qualifies as ancient history to your kids. Televisions in the posh bar allow patrons to sip Scotch and pray for "da Coach" to return, simultaneously. Upstairs, there's a cigar lounge that gets pretty pungent: Families would be best off in the downstairs dining room. The hamburger here (really, a chopped steak burger) is one of the best in the city and easily feeds two. Appetizers here are called "Kickoffs" and include a "Duck Cigar," a hand-rolled pastry with a hearty duck-and-mushroom filling, and a "Souper Bowl" of bayou-influenced black-bean soup. There are lots of salads, pastas, and seafood dishes to choose from, but why be a wimp? Go for the "Fullback Size" filet mignon, with spinach and homemade onion rings, or "Da Pork Chop," surrounded by warm cinnamon apples and a green peppercorn sauce.

100 E. Chestnut St. (in the Tremont Hotel, between Michigan Ave. and Rush St.). ℂ 312/587-8989. Kids' menu, high chairs, boosters. Main courses $12–$33 (less at breakfast, lunch, and brunch); kids' menu $5–$8. AE, DC, DISC, MC, V. Mon–Thurs 7am–11pm; Fri–Sat 7am–midnight; Sun 7am–10pm. Valet parking $7. Subway/El: Red Line to Chicago Ave., walk 2 blocks north to Chestnut St.

Oak Street Beachstro ★ AMERICAN/ECLECTIC   Could a location be more prime? Settled on the curve of Oak Street Beach, this bistro offers tables on the sand. (The cafe is open in warm weather only and opens in early May.) Take a dip in the lake with your family, then head up the beach for specialties such as the grilled salmon sandwich, Cobb salad, and salmon filet. Less exotic offerings such as salads, sandwiches, and pasta should please kids. For the grown-ups, beer and wine is available, and frozen drinks can be made sans alcohol for the kids. Outdoor seating provides some of the best people-watching around. Saturdays and Sundays, you'll find a breakfast buffet from 8 to 11:30 a.m. Come at twilight and you'll be treated to a beautiful violet sky.

1000 N. Lake Shore Dr. at Oak Street Beach. © 312/915-4100. High chairs, boosters. Reservations accepted for parties of 6 or more only. Main courses $15–$25. AE, DC, DISC, MC, V. May–Oct (weather permitting) Mon–Thurs 11am–8:30pm; Fri 11am–9:30pm; Sat 8am–9:30pm; Sun 8am–8:30pm. Subway/El: Red Line to Chicago. Bus: 145, 146, 147 and 151.

Ron of Japan JAPANESE   The heyday of teppanyaki dining (you know, Japanese chefs chopping and grilling at your table, with the accompanying flashing knives and flying shrimp tails) passed decades ago, but the show is still a kid-pleaser. Specialties include shrimp with egg yolk sauce, filet mignon, prime rib served on a samurai sword, and Shogun dinner (lobster and steak). Grilled on an iron plate set into each table, the food is cut, seasoned, and served by chefs who dish up amazing flair as well as flavor. The restaurant has 14 such tables—larger ones accommodate up to 10 diners, the smaller ones, six or so. As knives and peppershakers fly through the air, meats sizzle on the hot iron plate. Above each grill/table is a retractable hood that keeps smoke out of everyone's eyes.

230 E. Ontario St. © 312/644-6500. Kids' menu, high chairs, boosters. Reservations accepted for parties of 8 or more. Main courses $15–$25; kids' menu $13–$15. AE, DC, DISC, MC, V. Mon–Thurs 5–9:30pm; Fri 5–10:30pm; Sat 5–10pm; Sun 4:30–9pm. Subway/El: Red Line to Chicago/State. Bus: 151 and 157.

MODERATE

Bistro 110 ★★ BISTRO/CONTINENTAL   Bistro 110 enjoys a prime location just a half block west of North Michigan Avenue. A neighborhood crowd gathers here for the bistro's changing weekly specials, posted on a chalkboard, where you can also check out the weather forecast and other local news. This popular spot opened in 1987, putting it on the cutting edge of the bistro-style dining trend. The restaurant is much larger than an authentic bistro would be, with plenty of hustle and bustle that helps families fit right in.

The menu does cover a broad price range and several bistro classics, such as escargots in puff pastry, mussels in white wine sauce, French onion soup, cassoulet, and steak au poivre. More ambitious items include a spice-rubbed lamb (roasted and braised for 20 hr.), and wood-roasted Maine sea scallops over spinach and basmati rice. Chicago holds Bistro 110 dear for the roasted heads of garlic served with crusty bread, and an early commitment to wood roasting of meats and vegetables. (The wood-roasted items, including a delicious, savory half chicken and a bountiful roast vegetable plate, are among your best bets here—some of the other items can be inconsistent.) The kids' menu ranges from beef tenderloin to grilled cheese. Sunday brunch, complete with a jazz trio from New Orleans, is a good time to bring your kids. (Yes, the trio will visit your table and "serenade" you—rather loudly.) Brunch is extremely popular, so get there early to avoid a long wait.

110 E. Pearson St. (just west of Michigan Ave.). © 312/266-3110. www.bistro110restaurant.com. Kids' menu, high chairs, boosters. Main courses $13–$28; kids' menu $6–$14. AE, DC, DISC, MC, V. Mon–Thurs 11:30am–10pm; Fri–Sat 11:30am–11pm; Sun 11am–10pm. Subway/El: Red Line to Chicago/State.

Cheesecake Factory AMERICAN   It really must take a factory to produce the 34 flavors of cheesecake offered here. While this restaurant is one of the usual "kid-friendly" suspects, a handy location on Michigan Avenue and the prospect of outdoor dining on the John Hancock Center Plaza makes this better than your average chain dining experience. The restaurant is big and noisy, and be prepared for your name to be added to a long list when you arrive. (You'll be given a pager for the wait.) The odd decor, with copper-colored metal sculpted into aerodynamic shapes that overhang the entryways, gives kids plenty to gawk at while you wait.

Even picky eaters will find something to order on the enormous menu. There's no kids' menu, but the regular menu features chicken strips and mini cheeseburgers, among other tot treats. Baja chicken tacos, barbecue ranch chicken salad, and avocado egg rolls are a few of the items on the wide-ranging menu. And the cheesecake! Save room for white chocolate raspberry truffle, chocolate peanut butter cookie dough, or seasonally, pumpkin cheesecake. Why they also serve fudge cake, carrot cake, and ice cream sundaes, I'll never know—apparently some misguided diners don't opt for cheesecake!

875 N. Michigan Ave. (in the plaza of the John Hancock Center). ✆ **312/337-1101**. High chairs, boosters. Main courses $8.95–$16. AE, DC, DISC, MC, V. Mon–Thurs 11:30am–11pm; Fri–Sat 11:30am–12:30am; Sun 10am–10pm. Subway/El: Red Line to Chicago/State.

Coco Pazzo Café ⭐ NORTHERN ITALIAN   Here's the perfect combination for families: food sophisticated enough for grownups, simple enough for kids. An added plus is a scenic sidewalk cafe for that rare perfect-weather day in Chicago. The cafe is the more casual version of Coco Pazzo restaurant. The decor is colorful, with ceramic tile, wall murals, and a copper-topped bar. Cuisine is rustic Tuscan and Northern Italian. The menu includes focaccia, thin-crust pizza, seafood, veal, chicken dishes, and pasta. For adults, specialties include fish cartoccio (fresh fish in parchment paper), gnocchi with tomato and basil, and tagliolini with wild mushrooms. Sunday brunch features a fixed-price menu that varies every week.

636 N. St. Clair St. ✆ **312/664-2777**. High chairs, boosters. Reservations recommended. Main courses $8–$15. AE, DISC, V. Sun–Thurs 11:30am–10:30pm; Fri–Sat 11:30am–11:30pm. Subway/El: Red Line to Chicago. Bus: 3, 157, 151, 145, 146 and 147.

ESPN Zone AMERICAN   Grown-ups prone to indigestion should tread carefully here. (Maybe you'll want to skip dining here and just hit the arcade?) The frenetic activity inside this temple of televised athletics will likely please your kids (and please you too, if you have trouble keeping them entertained), but can be a bit overwhelming. Every wall is covered with television screens or sports art, with a full-on visual and audio assault on your senses. This massive 35,000-square-foot sports-themed dining and entertainment complex features three components: the Studio Grill, designed with replicas of studio sets from the cable networks' shows (including *SportsCenter*); the Screening Room, a sports pub featuring a 16-foot screen and an armada of TV monitors and radio sets carrying live broadcasts of games; and the Sports Arena, a gaming area with interactive and competitive attractions. Good news for adults: The food here is better-than-average tavern fare, including quite a few salads and upscale items such as a salmon filet baked on cedar and served with steamed rice and grilled vegetables.

43 E. Ohio St. (at Wabash Ave.). ✆ **312/644-3776**. Kids' menu, high chairs, boosters. Main courses $7.25–$20; kids' menu $5–$8. AE, DISC, MC, V. Sun–Thurs 11:30am–11:30pm; Fri–Sat 11:30am–midnight. Subway/El: Red Line to Grand.

Jack Melnick's Corner Tap AMERICAN   This casual neighborhood pub is housed in the former Blackhawk Lodge. In a turnaround from the more formal dining atmosphere at Blackhawk Lodge, the new restaurant is aiming for a comfortable, welcoming, and fun environment—a local hangout where folks can "come as they are." Specialties include burgers done seven ways, chopped salads, and home-style specials such as barbecued ribs and chicken. A 50-foot old-fashioned bar is the epicenter of Jack's, featuring an extensive bottle and tap beer selection from around the world "from Old Style to Newcastle." The dining room has always been one of my favorite spots on the Magnificent Mile, with a screened-in porch area that lets in the lake breeze in the summer, and a stone fireplace and deep booths that make for cozy dining in the wintertime. Desserts include apple pie, banana cream pie, and a chocolate chip cookie skillet sundae.

41 E. Superior St. (at Wabash Ave.). ℂ 312/266-0400. Kids' menu, high chairs, boosters. Reservations only accepted for parties of 10 or more. Main courses $8–$15; kids' menu $4. AE, DC, DISC, MC, V. Mon–Sun 11:30am–midnight. Subway/El: Red Line to Chicago/State.

INEXPENSIVE

Big Bowl ★ *Value* ASIAN   You know you're in a kid-friendly Asian restaurant when you sit down and crayons and a bowl of white rice are brought to the table. Big Bowl also has a great kid's menu—no cheeseburgers, just smaller portions of the same Asian food the adults eat. Okay, so the restaurant is yet another creation of Rich Melman's Lettuce Entertain You empire. But it's friendly, affordable and the kind of place that's got dishes so addictive, I dare you to only go once during your visit. Start with a glass of the signature fresh ginger ale or a fresh-brewed fruit-flavored iced tea; either will wake up your taste buds. The menu covers a range of Asian specialties: Chinese pot stickers, Thai curries, Vietnamese spring rolls. The indecisive can go with one of several combinations, each offering a mix of soup, salad, appetizers, or noodles. The straightforward crunchy sesame chicken is a reliable standby, mixing crispy chicken pieces with fresh Asian vegetables in a light soy sauce. Other good bets are the teriyaki beef and spicy flat noodles with tofu and veggies. You can also put together your own mix of flavors at the large stir-fry bar. If you're looking for delivery, Big Bowl will rush pot stickers to your hotel, no problem. Big Bowl has two other Chicago locations, both of which re-create the same upscale diner decor: 159 W. Erie St. in River North (ℂ 312/787-8297) and 60 E. Ohio St., just off the Magnificent Mile (ℂ 312/951-1888).

6 E. Cedar St. (at Rush St.) ℂ **312/640-8888.** Kids' menu, high chairs, boosters. Reservations not accepted. Main courses $8–$13; kids' menu $5–$8. AE, DC, DISC, MC, V. Sun–Thurs 11:30am–10pm, Fri–Sat 11:30am–11pm. Subway/El: Red Line to Clark/Division.

Billy Goat Tavern ★ *Value* BURGERS/BREAKFAST   "Cheezeborger, Cheezeborger—No Coke . . . Pepsi." Viewers of the original *Saturday Night Live* will certainly remember the classic John Belushi routine, a moment in the life of a crabby Greek short-order cook. The comic got his material from the Billy Goat Tavern, located under North Michigan Avenue near the bridge that crosses to the Loop. Just BUTT IN ANYTIME says the sign on the red door with the picture of the billy goat on it. The tavern has traditionally been a hangout for the newspaper workers and writers who occupy the nearby Tribune Tower and Sun-Times Building, but its *Saturday Night Live* fame attracts droves of tourists, a la the "Cheers" bar in Boston. Offering beer and greasy food (of course, "cheezeborgers"), families will feel most at home during lunchtime, when tourists and office workers pop in for a quick burger.

430 N. Michigan Ave. ℂ **312/222-1525.** Kids' menu. Reservations not accepted. Menu items $4–$8; kids' menu $2–$4. No credit cards. Mon–Fri 7am–2am; Sat 10am–2am; Sun 11am–2am. Subway/El: Red Line to Chicago/State.

California Pizza Kitchen PIZZA   Way, way back in the early 1990s, "CPK" was plying its new concept of exotic toppings made on individual-sized pies. The concept is a bit stale, but kids still get a kick out of creating and swapping pieces of their individual pizzas. Names like Tandoori Chicken, Hawaiian, B.L.T., Peking Duck, and Grilled Burrito might cause an "Ewwwww!" reaction from your kids, but you'll likely be safe with tamer options such as barbecued chicken. Traditional meat-and-cheese pizzas are also available, as are soups, salads, pasta dishes, and desserts. If all else fails, there's a children's menu with pepperoni pizza; Caesar salad topped with cheddar goldfish crackers; buttered noodles; and brownies. A second location is at 52 E. Ohio St. (℃ 312/787-6075).

835 N. Michigan Ave. (Water Tower Place, 7th floor). ℃ **312/787-7300.** Kids' menu, high chairs, boosters. Reservations not accepted. Menu items $7–$10; kids' menu items $5. AE, DC, DISC, MC, V. Mon–Sat 11am–10pm; Sun noon–9pm. Subway/El: Red Line to Chicago/State.

Charlie's Ale House on Navy Pier ⭐AMERICAN   One of several outdoor dining options along Navy Pier, this outpost of the Lincoln Park restaurant wins for lip-smacking pub fare and a great location on the southern promenade overlooking the lakefront and Loop skyline. It's a great vantage point for Wednesday- and Friday-night fireworks, too. The Navy Pier location is handy for sightseers; kids will like the burgers and, maybe, the chicken potpie. The original location in Lincoln Park triumphs with a wonderful beer garden, which is welcoming to families. (The restaurant says everyone is welcome—except dogs!) It's spacious, surrounded by tall ivy-covered brick walls, and buzzing with activity and good vibes. The Lincoln Park restaurant is at 1224 W. Webster Ave. (℃ 773/871-1440); take the Red Line to Sheffield.

700 E. Grand Ave. ℃ **312/595-1440.** Kids' menu, high chairs, boosters. Reservations accepted only for parties of 15 or more. Main courses $11–$17; kids' menu $5. AE, DC, DISC, MC, V. Mon–Fri 11am–8pm; Sat–Sun 11am–10pm. Subway/El: Red Line to Grand/State; transfer to Navy Pier's free trolley.

Corner Bakery BREAKFAST/SANDWICHES   In case of emergency hunger meltdown, it's a good idea to have located the nearest Corner Bakery ahead of time. A very popular (and justifiably so) destination, there are about a dozen cafes around town. It's easy to get addicted to the coffee and sweets here: In fact, when my former office mates and I counted up our visits each week, we decided to dub our local branch "Corner Bankruptcy." Sandwiches, salads, fruit, and amazing baked-good desserts are highlights. (Try the lemon bars dusted with powdered sugar, or the peanut butter brownie, or the mini caramel Bundt cake—try anything!) The homemade chips sprinkled with Parmesan are impossible to resist. Grilled panini with turkey, bacon, and cheese, or homemade mac and cheese will appeal to kids. Some of the main locations include one in River North at 516 N. Clark St. (℃ 312/644-8100), attached to Melman's Maggiano's Italian restaurant; and locations east of Michigan Avenue at 676 N. St. Clair St., at Erie Street (℃ 312/266-2570).

1121 N. State St. (at Cedar St.). ℃ **312/787-1969.** High chairs, boosters. Reservations not accepted. Menu items $6–$9. AE, DC, DISC, MC, V. Mon–Thurs 7am–8:30pm; Fri–Sat 7am–9pm; Sun 7am–8pm. Subway/El: Red Line to Clark/Division.

Flapjaw Café BURGERS   This down-home bar and grill is quite a find just off the Mag Mile: a low-key place serving burgers and grilled turkey sandwiches in baskets with fries. The bar-in-the-round with outlying tables and stools has a comfortable atmosphere. Although many young professionals come here for lunch and for a drink after work, it's a bustling, friendly place where kids are welcome. However, because tables are high—most seats are bar stool height—

Indulging Your Interest in Baking

While it's not exactly "baking," **Eli's Cheesecake World** does enable dessert fanatics to see the process of baking a Chicago favorite. A visit to the 62,000 square foot state-of-the-art bakery starts with a sneak peek at Eli's bakers busy at work, and ends with a slice of cheesecake. The bakery also offers a cafe and cheesecake bar, where over 30 different flavors are on sale by the slice each day. The cheesecake you'll see being made is served up at Eli's, the Place for Steak, 215 E. Chicago Ave. at Fairbanks Court (© **312/642-1393**), a Chicago institution founded 50 years ago by the late Eli Schulman, who opened a neighborhood delicatessen serving Central European comfort foods like potato pancakes and liver and onions.

Eli's Cheesecake World, located in the Irving Park area at 6701 W. Forest Preserve (© **773/736-3417**), holds workshops for kids and offers five different tour packages. If you have 10 people or fewer in your group, the "Sneak Peek" tour is available to walk-ins Monday through Friday at noon. By reservation, tours are available Monday through Friday between 10am and 3pm; call for Saturday and Sunday availability. Saturday and Sunday tours are "quiet tours"—there is no production on the weekends, but you will still get a peek into Eli's Bakery. For more information, check out www.elischeesecake.com.

this restaurant is better suited for kids over age 3, who can comfortably sit in a booster. The menu is very simple and straightforward: California-style pizza, grilled sandwiches, salads, soups, and appetizers—all fairly cheap. Sit outside for a nice view of street life around the Loyola University campus.

22 E. Pearson St. © 312/642-4848. High chairs, boosters. Reservations not accepted. All menu items under $8. AE, DC, DISC, MC, V. Mon–Thurs 11am–10pm; Fri and Sat 11am–11pm; Sun 12:30–8pm. Subway/El: Red Line to Chicago/State.

foodlife ★★ *Finds* ECLECTIC   Yes, another successful concept courtesy of Lettuce Entertain You's Rich Melman: a food court with a healthy twist. Located on the mezzanine of Water Tower Place, just outside the entrance of the Mity Nice Grill, foodlife consists of a dozen or so kiosks offering both ordinary and exotic specialties. Four hundred seats are spread out cafe-style in a very pleasant environment under realistic boughs of artificial trees festooned with strings of lights in the shapes of grapes and other fruits.

The beauty of a food court, of course, is that it tries to offer something for everybody. At foodlife, the burger-and-pizza crowd will be satisfied, but so will vegetarians and diners looking for, say, a low-fat Caesar salad. Diners here can also choose south-of-the-border dishes, an assortment of Asian fare, and veggie-oriented, low-fat fare. Special treats include the Miracle Juice Bar's fresh orange juice and raspberry fruit smoothie, as well as a host of healthy or gooey desserts, and, at a booth called Sacred Grounds, various espresso-based beverages. A lunch or a snack at foodlife is basically inexpensive, but the payment method (each diner receives an electronic card that records each purchase for a total payment upon exit) makes it easy to build up a big tab while holding a personal taste-testing session at each kiosk.

In Water Tower Place, 835 N. Michigan Ave. © **312/335-3663.** High chairs, boosters. Reservations not accepted. Most items $5–$10. AE, DC, DISC, MC, V. Juice, espresso, and corner bakery Sun–Thurs 7:30am–9pm; Fri–Sat 7:30am–10pm. All other kiosks Sun–Thurs 11am–9pm; Fri–Sat 11am–10pm. Subway/El: Red Line to Chicago/State.

Zoom Kitchen ⭐ SANDWICHES Zoom Kitchen offers budget-friendly dining in a hip cafeteria setting. One of three locations (the original is in Bucktown; a 2nd in Lakeview), the Gold Coast version features a funky, bright dining room (conveniently attached to the adjacent Diesel clothing store—yes, you can enter the restaurant through the store) and a mezzanine dining level. Long windows let you gaze upon Rush Street's hustle and bustle. Staffers man food stations along a counter, serving up salads, sandwiches, carved meats, and soups. Most items are made to order, a plus for fussy eaters: You can instruct the staff person on which ingredients to add to your salad—as it's being made. Turkey is carved and your sandwich is assembled before your eyes. There are 11 side dishes, and a weekly assortment of fresh pies and coffee tops off the meal. In warm weather, sidewalk seating puts you in a prime location for watching the daily fashion parade on Rush Street. An all-you-can eat brunch features a variety of salads, omelets, breakfast burritos, eggs Benedict, carved ham and roast beef, pancakes, biscuits and gravy, and desserts; it costs $12 ($6 for kids). Other locations are at 1646 N. Damen Ave. (© 773/278-7000) and 620 W. Belmont (© 773/325-1400).

923 N. Rush St. © **312/440-3500.** High chairs. Reservations not accepted. All main courses under $8. AE, MC, V. Mon–Sat 11am–10pm; Sun 11am–8pm. Subway/El: Red Line to Chicago/State.

5 River North

Most families visiting Chicago will find themselves heading for dinner in River North at least once during their stay. The city's hot spot for family dining, River North offers an ever-growing, something-for-everyone array of restaurants— from fast food to theme and chain restaurants (plus some of the most fashionable dining destinations, so parents might want to hire a sitter one night and return for "date night"). Whether you seek a quick dog or burger, a casual French meal, or contemporary American fine dining, River North has got it all.

EXPENSIVE

Brasserie Jo ⭐ ALSATIAN/FRENCH Brasserie Jo, the casual dining destination from partnership Jean Joho (Everest) and Lettuce Entertain You Enterprises, is a popular spot for convivial meals of robust fare in a Parisian, retro-chic setting. It's big and bustling enough to welcome kids, and once you explain that a croque-monsieur is really a toasted ham and cheese, your kids will find something wonderful on the menu. For the adults, following in the tradition of the classic Alsatian brasserie (translation: brewery), Brasserie Jo makes a malty house brew, and diners are welcome for a quick stop-in snack with a glass of wine or a full five-course meal.

Joho has toned down the Alsatian influences in the menu here since opening (although you can still get a hearty Alsatian *choucroute*), focusing more on casual French classics such as fruits de mer, onion soup, mussels marinière, salade niçoise, croque-monsieur, and steak frites. Other house specialties include the herb-roasted chicken, coq au vin, lobster bouillabaisse, braised lamb shank, and the "famous shrimp bag," phyllo pastry filled with shrimp, mushrooms, and leeks garnished with lobster sauce. Save room for the delightfully decadent crepes magnifique, which live up to their name with an amazing alchemy of thin crepes, bananas, and chocolate. Or bypass the dessert menu and take your cue from the bountiful "cheese chariot."

59 W. Hubbard St. (between Dearborn and Clark sts.). © 312/595-0800. www.leye.com. Kids' menu, high chairs, boosters. Reservations recommended. Main courses $12–$26; kids' menu $7–$9. AE, DC, DISC, MC, V. Mon–Thurs 11:30am–3pm and 5–10pm; Fri 11:30am–3pm and 5–11pm; Sat 5–11pm; Sun 5–10pm. Subway/El: Red Line to Grand, or Brown Line to Merchandise Mart.

Harry Caray's ★★ AMERICAN/ITALIAN   A shrine to the legendary Cubs play-by-play announcer, this landmark building near the Chicago River is a repository for the staggering collection of baseball memorabilia that Harry amassed, and it covers almost every square inch of the place. But you don't have to be a baseball lover to appreciate Harry's.

The dining rooms have an old-Chicago feel that is comfortable and familiar, with high tin ceilings, exposed brick walls, and red-checked tablecloths. It would be easy to lump Harry's with other celebrity restaurants, but as one reviewer pointed out, the food is better than it has to be. The portions are enormous; unless you want leftovers for days, plan to share. Main-course offerings run from traditional items such as pastas with red sauce to chicken Vesuvio, veal, and a variety of seafood choices. Harry's is also a good place to order big plates of meat: dry-aged steaks, lamb, veal, and pork chops. And from the list of side dishes, be sure to order the signature Vesuvio potatoes. The desserts are rich and decadent.

33 W. Kinzie St. (at Dearborn St.). © 312/828-0966. Kids' menu, high chairs. Main courses $7.95–$33; kids' menu $5–$7. AE, DC, DISC, MC, V. Mon–Thurs 11:30am–3pm and 5–10:30pm; Fri–Sat 11:30am–3pm and 5–11pm Sun noon–4pm (lunch bar only) and 4–10pm. Subway/El: Brown Line to Merchandise Mart, or Red Line to Grand.

MODERATE

Carson's ★ AMERICAN/BARBECUE   A true Chicago institution, Carson's calls itself "The Place for Ribs," and, boy, is it ever. The barbecue sauce is sweet and tangy, and the ribs are meaty. Included in the $18 price for a full slab of baby backs are coleslaw and one of four types of potatoes (the most decadent are au gratin), plus right-out-of-the-oven rolls.

For dinner there's often a wait, but don't despair. In the bar area you'll find a heaping mound of some of the best chopped liver around and plenty of cocktail rye to go with it. (Kids who turn up their noses at chopped liver should start with a kiddie cocktail instead.) When you're seated at your table, tie on your plastic bib—and indulge. In case you don't eat ribs, Carson's also barbecues chicken and pork chops, and the restaurant's steaks aren't bad. But ribs are the house specialty, so make sure that at least someone in your group orders them. (The waitstaff will be shocked if you don't.) If by some remarkable feat you have room left after dinner, the candy-bar sundaes are a scrumptious finale to the meal. Carson's popularity has led to something of a factory mentality among management, which evidently feels the need to herd 'em in and out, but the servers are responsive to requests not to be hurried through the meal.

612 N. Wells St. (at Ontario St.). © 312/280-9200. Kids' menu, high chairs, boosters. Reservations not accepted. Main courses $8.95–$30; kids' menu $6–$14. AE, DC, DISC, MC, V. Mon–Thurs 11am–11pm; Fri 11am–12:30am; Sat noon–12:30am; Sun noon–11pm. Closed Thanksgiving. Subway/El: Red Line to Grand.

Houston's AMERICAN/STEAKHOUSE   Here's a casual steakhouse that's always packed with families. Located next to the Lenox Hotel and Suites, Houston's is cavernous and dark, filled with deep booths lit by overhead fixtures that barely illuminate the tables. The place has a dark-wood-and-brass, 1980s feel to it. (Fittingly so, since it opened here in 1987—today there are 40 Houston's nationwide.) Houston's attracts a mix of tourists, conventioneers, and locals. It's a comfy space, and the booths have the advantage of giving everyone a feeling of privacy. Toasted cheese bread will be a hit with kids, and they'll make chicken fingers and hamburgers to keep the kids happy. For adults, the restaurant offers an extensive list of more than 40 wines collected mostly from California. At dinnertime, there's live piano music in the bar.

616 N. Rush St. ℂ 312/649-1121. High chairs, boosters. Reservations not accepted. Main courses $13–$25. AE, DC, DISC, MC, V. Mon–Thurs 11am–10pm; Fri 11am–11pm; Sat 11:30am–11pm; Sun 11:30am–10pm. Subway/El: Red Line to Grand. Bus: 145, 146, 147, 151.

Leona's ITALIAN/PIZZA   This Chicago-based home-style Italian food chain has a vast menu, good pizza, and budget-friendly prices. With 16 locations and still family-owned and operated after 52 years, Leona's is a real Chicago restaurant success story. All food is fresh and made from scratch. The River North location features a large, open, dining room. Be prepared for huge portions and unusually warm and hospitable service in a very family-friendly setting. The menu (actually, it reads more like a book) runs the gamut and includes ribs, chicken wings, steak sandwiches, burgers, pasta, pizza (deep dish or thin crust), and salads. If that's not enough, Leona's also has a children's menu featuring spaghetti marinara, chicken strips (fried, grilled, or barbecued), 6-inch pizzas, lasagna, fettuccine alfredo, and more.

646 N. Franklin St. ℂ 312/867-0101. Kids' menu. Main courses $9–$25; kids' menu $5–$8. AE, DC, DISC, MC, V. Mon–Thurs 11:30am–10:30pm; Fri 11am–midnight; Sat noon–midnight; Sun noon–10pm. Subway/El: Brown Line to Merchandise Mart; Red Line to Grand. Bus: 65, 22.

Maggiano's ⭐ ITALIAN   A great pick for large groups, Maggiano's is a shrine to family-style Italian dining. Like many of its fellow Lettuce Entertain You restaurants, Maggiano's feels a bit contrived, with traditional Italian red-checkered tablecloths and old family portraits (which family, we'll never know), designed to create the feel of Little Italy throughout the nine separate dining rooms. Still, heaping plates of pasta meant to be shared make Maggiano's a good choice for a large and budget-conscious family. In fact, everything on the menu is super-sized. Steaks are all more than a pound, and most pasta dishes weigh in over 25 ounces. You're expected to share dishes, pass things around and try a little bit of everything. The menu is vast and features Italian pasta classics such as chicken and spinach manicotti, eggplant parmesan and meat or marinara lasagna, plus chicken, veal, steaks and chops (try the Prime New York Steak al Forno, Gorgonzola, a strip steak served with caramelized onions and melted gorgonzola cheese), and seafood. Downstairs, there's a banquet room that accommodates parties of 20 to 200. On holidays, Maggiano's has live music.

516 N. Clark St. ℂ 312/644-7700. High chairs, boosters. Main courses $11–$33. AE, DC, DISC, MC, V. Mon–Thurs 11:30am–10pm; Fri–Sat 11:30am–11pm; Sun noon–10pm. Subway/El: Brown Line to Merchandise Mart; Red Line to Grand. Bus: 65, 22.

Reza's ⭐⭐ *(Value)* MIDDLE EASTERN   Whether your kids are avid eaters of Middle Eastern food, or you want to start exposing them to it, Reza's is a good option. With high ceilings and exposed brick, this warm and family-friendly restaurant is housed in a former microbrewery. Specialties include a deliciously rich chicken in pomegranate sauce. Kids might go for one of a variety of kebabs. Despite the menu's meat-heavy emphasis, there's a full selection of vegetarian options, too. The appetizer combo is a nice option for families, including hummus, stuffed grape leaves, tabbouleh, and other standbys. Reza's has another location in Andersonville, at 5255 N. Clark St. (☎ 773/561-1898), but the River North spot is the most convenient for visitors staying downtown.

432 W. Ontario St. (at Orleans St.). ☎ 312/664-4500. High chairs, boosters. Main courses $9.95–$17. AE, DC, DISC, MC, V. Daily 11am–midnight. Subway/El: Red Line to Grand.

Scoozi ✯ REGIONAL ITALIAN Families should plan to visit Scoozi on Sunday evening, when the restaurant gives kids "make your own pizza" time from 4 to 5pm. Chefs show kids how to make a pizza, then pop them in the wood-burning oven. Kids dine on their culinary masterworks, and you get a nice stretch of "adult time" at the table while your little chefs are at work.

Scoozi's sprawling loft space has been its home since 1986, the year it opened and began serving up authentic Italian cooking—a real pioneering effort at the time, complete with focaccia in its breadbaskets. Scoozi's menu is no longer unique, but Chicagoans return for its reliable lineup of Italian flavors. Appetizers include an antipasti bar (favorites are orzo with shrimp and wood-roasted mushrooms); deep-fried calamari with basil, aioli, and arrabbiata sauce; or small pizzas, such as one smothered with garlic spinach, oven-roasted tomatoes, and goat cheese. Main courses include *petto di pollo* (grilled chicken breast with baby artichokes, red potatoes, and warm coriander-seed vinaigrette); ravioli baked in a wood oven (smoked chicken, Taleggio cheese with smoked bacon, or artichoke); and *gnocchi con salsa rossa* (homemade potato dumplings in a tomato-basil cream). For dessert, head directly for the tiramisu.

410 W. Huron St. (at Orleans St.). ☎ 312/943-5900. Kids' menu, high chairs, boosters. Reservations recommended. Pasta $7.50–$11 lunch and dinner; main courses $8.95–$15 lunch, $9.95–$25 dinner; kids' menu $3.25. AE, DC, DISC, MC, V. Mon–Thurs 11:30am–2pm and 5–9:30pm; Fri 11:30am–2pm and 5–10:30pm; Sat 5–10:30pm; Sun 4–9pm. Subway/El: Red Line to Chicago.

INEXPENSIVE

Cafe Iberico ✯✯ SPANISH/TAPAS Families should arrive early to ensure getting a table at this wildly popular tapas joint with a festive atmosphere. I'd recommend this place for older kids and teens with adventurous palates. (Get them to try *pulpo a la gallega* for the best fried octopus around!) Crowds begin pouring in at the end of the workday, so if you arrive around dinnertime, expect a wait. Put a dent in your appetite with a plate of *queso de cabra* (baked goat cheese with fresh tomato-basil sauce). When your waiter returns with the first dish, put in a second order for a round of both hot and cold tapas. Then continue to order as your hunger demands. The waiters are pleasant yet can get a little harried, so it sometimes takes some effort to flag them down. A few standout dishes are the vegetarian Spanish omelet, *patatas bravas* (spicy potatoes with tomato sauce), *pincho de pollo* (chicken brochette with caramelized onions and rice), *pulpo y la plancha* (grilled octopus with potatoes and olive oil), and *salmon y la pimienta* (fresh grilled salmon with green peppercorn sauce). There are a handful of entrees on the menu, and a few desserts if you're still not sated. The caramel flan and the *plantano al caramelo* (sautéed banana with caramel sauce served with vanilla ice cream) are both excellent. There's also a gift shop and gourmet food shop. Cafe Iberico gets very loud, especially on weekends, so it makes for a fun group destination but is not the place for a romantic tête-à-tête.

739 N. LaSalle St. (between Chicago Ave. and Superior St.). ☎ 312/573-1510. High chairs. Reservations accepted during the week for parties of 6 or more. Tapas $3.50–$4.95; main courses $7.95–$13. DC, DISC, MC, V. Mon–Thurs 11am–11pm; Fri 11am–1:30am; Sat noon–1:30am; Sun noon–11pm. Subway/El: Red Line to Chicago/State, or Brown Line to Chicago.

Dave & Buster's AMERICAN   Good old-fashioned fun of the coin-operated variety means that you may have to tear your kids away from the games to get them to sit down for dinner. At the Chicago outpost of the Dallas-based mega entertainment and dining chain, you can combine casual dining and an evening's entertainment. (Don't send teens by themselves: Kids must be accompanied by an adult 25 years old or older.) The menu is expansive and features bar food, including pasta, burgers, steak, and ribs. Before you sit down to eat, let your kids burn off energy by getting lost in this neon-lit games emporium. You'll find 1950s-era carnival games, Vegas-style casino games, video games, and virtual reality tests. The main attraction is the glitzy Million Dollar Midway on the second level. Do your kids dream of being an Alpine ski racer or driving the Grand Prix? Video games on the Midway let them simulate the experience. Grownups might try a computerized version of blackjack or swing away at the indoor golf simulator, a "virtual" golf driving range that uses laser beams to calculate the ball's flight.

1024 N. Clark St. © **312/943-5151.** Kids' menu. Main courses $8–$18; kids' menu $5–$8. AE, DC, DISC, MC, V. Mon–Thurs 11am–1am; Fri–Sat 11:30am–2am; Sun 11:30am–midnight. Subway/El: Red Line to Clark/Division. Bus: 22, 70, 36.

Ed Debevic's 🎯 BURGERS/DINER   "Eat at Ed's" is the call to action at this temple to America's hometown lunch-counter culture. Wherever you sit, in an upholstered banquette or booth, or the lunch counter stools, you'll be surrounded by 1950s nostalgia. Tunes such as "Duke of Earl" and other vintage oldies fill the air. Food specialties include pot roast, fountain drinks—and meatloaf. Ed Debevic's calls itself the place "where meatloaf is king." There's no kids' menu, but with the entire menu based on burgers and fries, who needs one? The 50s-costumed wait staff cracks gum at you and dishes out rude comments along with the food. And, when the jukebox strikes up a song, don't be surprised if your waiter leaps onto the counter (or onto your table, if that's where he happens to be), to dance along. It's all a performance, but it works. One nice bonus is a good view of River North and the skyscrapers of the Loop to the south.

640 N. Wells St. © **312/664-1707.** High chairs, boosters. Reservations accepted only for parties of 15 or more. All main courses under $8. AE, DC, DISC, V. Summer hours: Sun–Thurs 11am–10pm; Fri–Sat 11am–midnight. Winter hours: Sun–Thurs 11am–10pm; Fri–Sat 11am–11pm. Subway/El: Brown Line to Franklin.

Gino's East ⭐⭐ PIZZA   This famous Chicago pizzeria invites patrons to scrawl all over the graffiti-strewn walls and furniture. Getting into the former location just west of the Magnificent Mile was a Chicago tourist rite of passage: waiting in the frigid cold (or sweltering heat) to get into Gino's. Now that the restaurant has moved into the vast space formerly occupied by Planet Hollywood, there are no more lines out front.

Many Chicagoans consider Gino's the quintessential deep-dish Chicago-style pizza. True to its reputation, the pizza is heavy (a small cheese pizza is enough for two), so work up an appetite before chowing down here. Specialty pizzas include the supreme, with layers of cheese, sausage, onions, green pepper, and mushrooms; and the vegetarian, with cheese, onions, peppers, asparagus, summer squash, zucchini, and eggplant. Next to the restaurant is Gino's carryout (© 312/988-4200); pizzas take 30 to 40 minutes' cooking time. If you want to take one home on the plane, call a day in advance and Gino's will pack a special frozen pizza for the trip.

633 N. Wells St. (at Ontario St.). © **312/943-1124.** Kids' menu, high chairs, boosters. Reservations not accepted. Pizza $6.95–$17; kids' menu $3.50. AE, DC, DISC, MC, V. Mon–Thurs 11am–11pm; Fri–Sat 11am–midnight; Sun noon–10pm. Subway/El: Red Line to Chicago/State.

Green Door Tavern BURGERS   The Green Door is a neighborhood refuge and a well-needed respite from the many trendy restaurants in River North. At lunch, you'll find the advertising and graphic-design types who work in the neighborhood chowing on burgers in the unpretentious atmosphere. The restaurant's wood-frame building was put up temporarily after the 1871 fire, presumably just before the city ordinance that banned such construction inside the newly designated "fire zone." The place began as a grocery store with living quarters on the second floor, and evolved into a restaurant in 1921. Later a speakeasy was

Finds **Soulful Brunch**

Head to **House of Blues,** 329 N. Dearborn St., at Kinzie Street (© **312/527-2583**), for its popular Sunday gospel brunch. To guarantee seating, it's a good idea to reserve 2 weeks in advance.

established in a downstairs room no longer open to the public. Apparently the original framing crew went light on the bracing timbers in a few places because the whole building leans to the right. About a decade ago, a newly constructed building across from The Green Door was consumed with fire and burned to the ground. Firefighters sprayed The Green Door, earning undying gratitude and an annual honorarium called the Golden Helmet Awards from the management.

There's no kids' menu, but regular menu items should please, including the hickory burger, the triple-decker grilled cheese, and the Texas chili. There are even a veggie burger and a turkey burger, and the menu includes some Cajun fare and pasta. Specials, including the Wednesday meat loaf offering, are posted daily.

678 N. Orleans St. (at Huron St.). © **312/664-5496**. High chairs, boosters. Reservations accepted only for parties of 7 or more. Main courses $6.95–$12. MC, V. Mon–Sat 11:30am–midnight. Subway/El: Brown Line to Chicago.

Hard Rock Cafe AMERICAN   Not just an eatery, Hard Rock Cafe is also one of Chicago's main tourist attractions. (Don't expect to find many locals or members of the over-30 age group here.) A regular rock 'n' roll museum, you could easily spend hours here pouring over the hundreds of drumsticks, concert photos, gold records, or autographed guitars of your favorite artists, including the likes of Mick Fleetwood and George Harrison. (The most popular pieces are a guitar autographed by the members of Nirvana and a motor scooter used in the 1979 movie *Quadrophenia,* which was based on The Who's album.) The food is pretty standard fare, with fajitas and burgers as specialties, plus a children's menu. But who comes here for the food? The round building has a circular bar decorated in a sports motif, with some nice touches: autographed bats by Ryne Sandberg, Mark Grace, Shawn Dunston, and Frank Thomas, among other ballplayers. Interesting restaurant fact: The original Hard Rock Cafe was founded June 14, 1971, in London by Isaac Tigrett and Peter Morton, the son of Chicago restaurateur Arnold Morton of Morton's steakhouse fame. The Chicago location was opened 12 years later.

63 W. Ontario St. © **312/943-2252**. Kids' menu, high chairs, boosters. Main courses $8–$15; kids' menu $6. AE, DISC, V. Mon–Thurs 11:30am–11pm; Fri 11:30am–11:30pm; Sat 11am–midnight; Sun 11am–10pm. Subway/El: Red Line to State/Grand.

Mr. Beef ★ *Finds* AMERICAN   Mr. Beef doesn't have much atmosphere or seating room, but it's a much-loved Chicago institution. Squeeze in alongside the lunchtime regulars and enjoy the atmosphere (or lack thereof). Families with small children will be happier getting their sandwiches to go, as lack of space

---

Tips **Rocking and Rolling at the Golden Arches**

The reality of traveling with kids means the occasional fast-food meal can be a real lifesaver. In McDonald's hometown (corporate headquarters is located in west suburban Oak Brook), I would be remiss in not mentioning the second-busiest franchise in the world. Only McDonald's in Moscow claims to be more trafficked than Chicago's **Rock N Roll McDonald's,** located at 600 N. Clark St. at Ohio St. (✆ **312/664-7940**). Along with Big Macs, shakes, and fries, you'll find a storehouse of memorabilia and other 1950s and 1960s tchotchkes, including a restored Corvette parked in the dining room and a collection of Beatles mementos.

---

means Mr. Beef is not a high chair–friendly place. Its claim to fame is the classic Italian beef sandwich, the Chicago version of a Philly cheese steak. The Mr. Beef variety is made of sliced beef dipped in jus, piled high on a chewy bun, and topped with sweet or hot peppers. Heavy, filling, and *very* Chicago. Mr. Beef really hops during lunchtime, when dusty construction workers and suit-wearing businessmen crowd in for their meaty fix. While you're chowing, check out the celebrity photos and newspaper clippings covering the walls, and you'll see why this place is considered a local monument.

666 N. Orleans St. (at Erie St.). ✆ 312/337-8500. Reservations not accepted. Sandwiches $5.95–$8.50. No credit cards. Mon–Fri 7am–4:45pm; Sat 10am–2pm. Subway/El: Red Line to Grand.

Pizzeria Uno ★ *Value* PIZZA   In 1943, Pizzeria Uno invented Chicago-style pizza, and many deep-dish aficionados still refuse to accept any imitations. You may eat in the restaurant itself on the basement level or, weather permitting, on the outdoor patio right off the sidewalk. Salads, sandwiches, and a house minestrone are also available, but, hey—the only reason to come here is for the pizza. (And in fact, 90% of the menu is dedicated to deep-dish pizza.)

Uno was so successful that the owners opened **Pizzeria Due** in 1955 in a lovely gray-brick Victorian town house nearby at 619 N. Wabash Ave. at Ontario Street (✆ **312/943-2400**). The menu is identical at both restaurants, although the space at Pizzeria Due is much larger. Be forewarned: This pizzeria serves no pizza before it's time. Pizza takes a minimum of 45 minutes to prepare. Thus, one popular feature at both places is the express lunch: a choice of soup or salad and a personal-size pizza, all for $5.

29 E. Ohio St. (at Wabash Ave.). ✆ 312/321-1000. High chairs. Lunch reservations accepted Mon–Fri. Pizza $5–$18. AE, DC, DISC, MC, V. Mon–Fri 11:30am–1am; Sat 11:30am–2am; Sun 11:30am–11pm. Subway/El: Red Line to Grand.

Rainforest Cafe AMERICAN   This Minnesota-based chain bills itself as "a wild place to shop and eat." The restaurant strives to create the feel of a rainforest with the sounds of waterfalls, thunder and lightning, and wild animals echoing throughout the place. Check out the floor-to-ceiling aquarium tanks, and duck to avoid the swinging orangutans. The menu features salads, sandwiches, and a range of entrees that will please a family of picky eaters. "Edge of the forest" fried chicken is a bestseller, as is the "mojo bones" rib appetizer. The kids' menu features standard burgers, hot dogs, and mac and cheese. The restaurant also sponsors educational programs designed to bring awareness of the planet's dwindling rainforests.

605 N. Clark St. (at Ohio St.) ✆ **312/787-1501.** www.rainforestcafe.com. Kids' menu, high chairs, boosters. Reservations recommended. Main courses $8–$10; kids' menu $5–$8. AE, DC, DISC, V. Mon–Thurs 11am–9:30pm; Fri 11am–10:30pm; Sat 11am–11pm; Sun 11am–9pm. Subway/El: Red Line to State/Grand.

Twisted Spoke ✮ _Finds_ DINER   Don't be scared off by the Easy Rider skeleton slowly rotating on a motorcycle atop a tall pole outside the Twisted Spoke: They feed everybody at this laid-back, off-the-beaten-path cafe that caters to the biker crowd but welcomes suburbanites and button-down businessfolk as well. Co-owners and brothers Cliff and Mitch Einhorn started the Spoke as a "family biker bar" in 1995. The place is filled with antique bike parts and accessories. The food is hearty and well prepared, from the cheese quesadillas to more than a dozen sandwiches, including curry chicken salad, twisted tuna salad, and barbecue chicken. But the Twisted Spoke's mouthwatering burgers are what draw most people here. The "Biker Brunch" features fare that swings wildly from "Real Oats for Real Men" to fruit salad to steak and eggs. It's served Saturday and Sunday from 11am to 3pm, as well as Saturday from midnight to 2:30am. Specials include meatloaf on Monday night, pasta on Wednesday, and fish fry on Friday. Enjoy the view from the great rooftop patio, but clear out while the night is still young, before the bar crowd heads up for bargain-priced beers. The patio overlooks the blue-collar corner of Ogden and Grand avenues and offers a unique cityscape view with the Sears Tower in the distance.

501 N. Ogden Ave. (at Grand Ave.). ✆ **312/666-1500.** High chairs, boosters. Reservations recommended for large parties. Main courses $5.25–$8.50. AE, MC, V. Sun–Fri 11am–1am; Sat 11am–2am. Bar open later. Bus: 65.

6 Lincoln Park

Singles and upwardly mobile young families inhabit Lincoln Park, the neighborhood roughly defined by North Avenue on the south, Diversey Parkway on the north, the park on the east, and Clybourn Avenue on the west. No surprise, then, that the neighborhood has spawned a dense concentration of some of the city's best restaurants.

EXPENSIVE

Don Juan on Halsted ✮✮ MEXICAN   Chef Patrick Concannon has the right culinary pedigree—he's done time at Charlie Trotter's and other top Chicago restaurants—but this time he's drawing on his family ties: The original Don Juan was opened by his mother in the suburb of Edison Park almost 20 years ago. In 2000, Concannon brought the family's dining concept to Lincoln Park. The space is inviting, with pale yellow and orange walls and terra-cotta floor tiles, and the outdoor courtyard fills up early in nice weather.

The menu mixes traditional Mexican flavors with unexpected ingredients. There's a new take on buffalo wings: chicken wings dipped in chipotle pepper sauce and covered with sesame seeds, served with bleu cheese sauce. The tuna tartare—now a staple of many high-end restaurants—is served here with tortilla chips, avocado, jicama, and mango sauce. Entrees include lamb shank, duck confit, and garlic-roasted chicken breast. A kids' menu with enchiladas, nachos, hamburgers, and hot dogs will appeal to kids with less adventurous palates.

1729 N. Halsted St. (between North Ave. and Willow St.) ✆ **312/981-4000.** Kids' menu, high chairs, boosters. Reservations accepted. Main courses $12–$20; kids' menu $3–$5. AE, DC, DISC, MC, V. Mon–Thurs 5pm–midnight; Fri–Sat 5pm–1am; Sun 5–10pm. Subway/El: Red Line to North/Clybourn.

Lincoln Park & Wrigleyville Dining

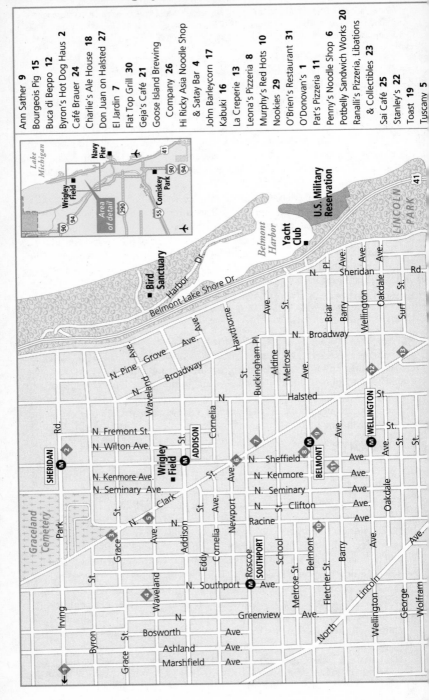

Lake
Michigan

Fullerton
Beach

Chicago
Historical
Society ■

N. State St.
N. Dearborn St.
N. Clark St.
N. La Salle St.

Shore Dr.

John Cannon Dr.

rsey Harbor

Lincoln Park
Zoo ■

Stockton
N. Lincoln Park West

South
Pond

North
Pond

Clark

Deming
Arlington Pl.

Orchard St.
N. Burling St.

ton Ave.

DePaul
University

Wrightwood
St.

Montana

N. Racine Ave.

Lakewood

Wayne

N. Southport Ave.

Greenview

N. Ashland

Altgeld

Lincoln

OZ
PARK

Ave.

North

Ave.

TREBES
PARK

Fullerton

Belden

Webster

Dickens

Clybourn

North

Ave.

North

Kennedy

Cortland

N. Wood

West St.

LINCOLN
PARK

Dr.

N. Park

N. Sedgwick

Wisconsin St.

Menomonee St.

Armitage

N. Orchard St.
N. Burling St.

N. Halsted

Freemont

N. Dayton St.
N. Freemont St.
N. Bissell St.
N. Sheffield Ave.

ARMITAGE

Wisconsin St.

Willow

North Ave.

Weed

Kingsbury

North

Branch

Elston Ave.

Expressway

N. Greenview
N. Bosworth
N. Ashland

Eugenie St.

N. Park Ave.

SEDGWICK

N. Cleveland Ave.
N. Mohawk St.
N. Larrabee St.

NORTH/CLYBOURN

St.

Avenue

Turning
Basin

Noble

Schiller

41

Geja's Café ✹ FONDUE   Are your kids over age 10? Can they sit through a 2-hour meal? If so, they will love Geja's (pronounced Gay-*haz*), an all-fondue restaurant. For some diners, the dark rathskeller decor will be a welcome change from the slick, commercial trattorias and bistros common all over the city. The owner, John Davis, has single-handedly preserved the fondue experience in Chicago, providing a fun and welcome break from the ordinary mode of dining.

Choose the connoisseur fondue dinner, the best Geja's has to offer. The meal begins with a Gruyère fondue appetizer, into which you dip apple wedges and chunks of dark bread. Next, a huge platter arrives, brimming with squares of beef tenderloin, lobster tails, and jumbo shrimp—all raw—and a caldron of boiling oil to cook them in—the reason why only kids 10 and up are allowed! These delicacies are accompanied by a variety of raw vegetables, and eight different dipping sauces. When the flaming chocolate fondue arrives for dessert, with fresh fruit and pound cake for dipping and marshmallows for roasting, you want to beg for mercy. As an added incentive, Geja's usually has a flamenco or classical Spanish guitarist to provide the background music. *One word of caution:* You have to work for your fondue—keeping track of how long each piece of meat has been cooking, and taking it out before it burns—so Geja's is not the best choice if you just want to sit back and be pampered.

340 W. Armitage Ave. (between Lincoln Ave. and Clark St.). (✆ 773/281-9101. Reservations accepted every day except late Fri–Sat. Main courses $20–$37. AE, DC, DISC, MC, V. Mon–Thurs 5–10:30pm; Fri 5pm–midnight; Sat 5pm–12:30am; Sun 4:30–10pm. Subway/El: Brown Line to Armitage. Bus: 22.

O'Brien's Restaurant AMERICAN   From the looks of the interior, you'd expect O'Brien's to be a rather ordinary restaurant with that standard "Irish pub" feel—dark wood, brass and hunter green feature prominently. But outdoors, you'll make an amazing discovery: the best alfresco dining in Old Town. And that's saying something, as you'll find multiple options up and down Wells Street. In good weather, the chance to kick back outdoors with your kids can make for a much less stressful dinner—who cares if a few fries wind up on the patio bricks? The birds will thank you for it. The outdoor patio has teakwood furniture, a gazebo bar in the center, and a mural of the owners' country club on a brick wall. Order the dressed-up chips, a house specialty. Rib-eye steak, Dover sole, and whitefish are specialties. The bar has a nice assortment of microbrews. Every night from 7pm until midnight, O'Brien's features piano music.

1528 N. Wells St. (2 blocks south of North Ave.). (✆ 312/787-3131. Kids' menu, high chairs, boosters. Reservations recommended. Main courses $15–$25; kids' menu $5–$8. AE, DC, DISC, MC, V. Daily 11am–2am. Subway/El: Brown Line to Sedgwick.

MODERATE

Goose Island Brewing Company AMERICAN   Some of the best beer in Chicago is manufactured at this comfy, award-winning microbrewery in the Clybourn corridor. (An impressive cast of professional beer critics agrees.) In the course of a year, Goose Island brewmeister Greg Hall (whose dad, John, is the pub/brewery's owner) produces about 100 varieties of lagers, ales, stouts, pilsners, and porters that change with the seasons. But why include a beer-oriented joint in a book for kids? Dining at the Goose is almost as good as the beer on tap.

The cut-above bar food includes burgers (including a killer, dragon-breath-inducing Stilton burger with roasted garlic), sandwiches (pulled pork, catfish po' boy, chicken Caesar), and some serious salads. Other specialties include blonde ale cheese fondue; a charcuterie plate featuring the fine dried, smoked, and cured meats of the local Paulina Market; and better-than-Mom's pot roast.

Goose Island is also known for its addictive homemade potato chips, fresh-brewed root beer, and orange cream soda. The zero-attitude, come-as-you-are ambience is very refreshing for a lazy afternoon pit stop or a casual lunch or dinner. A second location at 3535 N. Clark St. in Wrigleyville (© 773/832-9040) has an enclosed beer garden that welcomes kids.

1800 N. Clybourn Ave. (at Sheffield Ave.). © 312/915-0071. www.gooseisland.com. Kids' menu, high chairs, boosters. Reservations recommended on weekends. Sandwiches $7.50–$9.95; main courses $11–$19; kids' menu items under $5. AE, DC, DISC, MC, V. Mon–Fri 11:30am–1am; Sat 11am–2am; Sun 11am–midnight. Kitchen closes 2 hr. before the bar. Subway/El: Red Line to North/Clybourn.

Kabuki JAPANESE   Parents appreciate the laid-back atmosphere at this no-frills sushi restaurant located just off of the busy intersection of Clark and Fuller-ton. The clientele is mostly Lincoln Park's young professionals, but the atmosphere is welcoming to all. The menu runs the gamut of Japanese foods—sushi, sashimi, tempura, teriyaki, and noodles—in an intimate, 55-seat dining room. Bonsai trees, brush paintings, and window screens decorate a dining room that is dominated by two highly-trained sushi chefs from behind their 10-seat sushi bar. Those who want to sample sushi and try a little bit of everything should go for the 11-piece Kabuki combination. Timid beginners may also find a six-piece, cooked sushi platter a low-risk entree into the world of raw fish. For an appetizer, Kabuki recommends the *goma-ae*, a boiled spinach appetizer served cold in a sesame and peanut butter sauce, although your kids might also get a kick out of peeling and eating a pile of salty *edamame*, or soybeans cooked in the pod. When Kabuki overflows, you can head to Kabuki II, just a few doors down at 2473 N. Clark. In Wrigleyville, visit Kabuki III at 3647 N. Southport (© 773/281-9155).

2407 N. Clark. © 773/281-3131. High chairs, boosters. Reservations recommended. Main courses $8–$15. AE, MC, V. Mon and Wed–Thurs noon–3pm and 4:30–10pm; Fri noon–3pm and 4:30–11pm; Sat noon–11pm; Sun noon–10pm. Bus: 22 to Clark or 36 to Broadway.

Sai Café ★ JAPANESE   Here's another good spot to start exposing your kids to the wonders of Japanese cuisine. Despite some upscale sushi bars surfacing in high-profile restaurant districts in the past few years, Lincoln Park's modest Sai Café remains the people's choice. More than 30 varieties of sushi are lovingly pre-pared and served with élan in this neighborhood setting just off chic Armitage Avenue. And of course, white rice, chicken teriyaki, and shrimp and vegetable tempura are always on the menu, should all this be too much for your kids. A la carte selections come by the piece or maki-mono style, which pairs anything from tuna and avocado to flying-fish eggs and scallions, and then wraps it all up in rice and a thin sheet of dried seaweed. Main courses feature different meat, fish, and vegetables that can be dressed in tempura or teriyaki, or served sashimi style. Sai Café also offers a large selection of noodle and rice dishes.

2010 N. Sheffield Ave. (at Armitage Ave.). © 773/472-8080. High chairs, boosters. Main courses $7.25–$23 (a la carte sushi $1.50–$6.25 per piece). AE, DC, MC, V. Mon–Thurs 4:30–11pm; Fri–Sat 4:30pm–midnight; Sun 4:30–10pm. Subway: Brown Line to Armitage.

INEXPENSIVE

Bourgeois Pig ★ *Finds* BREAKFAST/SANDWICHES   Eclectic antiques fill this brownstone that's become a mecca for DePaul University students and neighborhood families. Bookshelves are packed with literature, and the atmos-phere is cluttered and comfy. The menu makes it clear that The Bourgeois Pig caters to an intellectual crowd: "The Sun Also Rises," "Pilgrim's Progress" and "The Old Man and the Sea" are among the menu's 25 gourmet sandwiches. Kids will enjoy the "build your own sandwich" menu, and staff will accommodate kids' tastes with less-than-gourmet fare such as American cheese. Baked goods, including ginger molasses cookies, are homemade. The Pig always ranks high in surveys for best cup of coffee in Chicago, so don't miss one of the four varieties brewed daily, or one of a mind-bending array of espresso drinks. Juices, shakes, and root beer made here are also great bets. You'll feel comfortable bringing kids in, as there are often a couple sets of parents with strollers parked inside. Treat the kids to an ice cream for dessert.

738 W. Fullerton Pkwy. (at Burling). ☎ 773/883-5282. High chairs, boosters. Main courses under $10. AE, DISC, MC, V. Mon–Thurs 6:30am–11pm; Fri 6:30am–midnight; Sat 8:30am–midnight; Sun 9am–11pm. Subway/El: Red or Brown line to Fullerton. Bus: 8, 11, 74.

Café Brauer ★ AMERICAN   A postcard-perfect view of the skyscrapers on North Michigan Avenue, plus Lake Michigan and the greenery of Lincoln Park, makes this a step above the average microbrewery. Stop here for lunch during a tour of the park, and grab a sandwich, kabob, or flatbread. (Brats and shrimp kabobs are among my favorites.) This pond-side cafe is conveniently near the Lincoln Park Zoo and reopened its doors to the public in 1990 after a major restoration. The beer garden, full of flowers and greenery, is perfectly family-friendly.

2021 Stockton Dr. ☎ 312/742-2480. Main courses under $8. AE, DC, DISC, MC, V. Mon–Sat 11am–8pm; Sun noon–8pm. Bus: 151 or 156.

El Jardin MEXICAN   The staff at this sometimes raucous and always fun restaurant loves to cater to kids. Because it's just 3 blocks south of Wrigley Field (that's where the "raucous" comes in), don't show up after a game unless you're prepared for a long wait. At other times, you'll be able to walk right in and grab a table in the two main dining rooms, sidewalk cafe, or backyard garden. The solid Mexican fare should keep both kids and grown-ups happy. Kids might try tacos, enchiladas, burritos, grilled chicken, or carne asada. Little ones can try *sopa de fideo,* a simple noodle soup. Should you have a special occasion to celebrate, the staff will happily trot out a flan decorated with candles.

3335 N. Clark St. ☎ 773/528-6775. High chairs, boosters. Main courses $8–$15. AE, DC, DISC, V. Sun–Thurs 11:30am–11pm; Fri and Sat 11:30am–midnight. Subway/El: Red, Brown or Purple Line to Belmont.

Flat Top Grill ASIAN   This create-your-own stir-fry restaurant often has lines, but never fear, they move quickly. Kids love creating their own dishes, and if you've never been here before, you might want to follow the suggested recipes on the giant blackboards. Choose from over 70 ingredients including rice, noodles, seafood, chicken, beef, veggies, and sauces—all for one low price. Best yet, the price includes multiple visits to the food line (a lifesaver if your brilliant culinary combination has gone awry). Other locations are at 1000 W. Washington Blvd. (☎ 312/829-4800) in the Randolph Street Market District and at 3200 N. Southport Ave. (☎ 773/665-8100) in Wrigleyville.

319 W. North Ave. ☎ 312/787-7676. www.flattopgrill.com. Kids' menu, high chairs, boosters. Main courses lunch $8, dinner $11; kids' stir-fry (under age 11) $5. AE, DC, DISC, MC, V. Mon–Thurs 5–10pm; Fri 11:30am–3pm and 5–11pm; Sat 11:30am–11pm; Sun 11:30am–10pm. Bus: 76.

John Barleycorn AMERICAN/BURGERS   Want to get a feel of what it's like to live in a Chicago neighborhood? Stop in to John Barleycorn, which has been a popular neighborhood pub and restaurant since the 1960s. There's a heavy emphasis on food here, so you won't feel like you're taking your kids to a bar. Located in a 19th-century building, the restaurant has that well-worn feel that makes you feel immediately at home. You won't find any pretensions here: Relax with a cold drink and a thick, juicy burger in the outdoor patio. The pub has a storied history, and reputedly served John Dillinger frequently when operating as a speakeasy in the 1920s. A collection of handmade ship models or a quick game of darts should entertain your kids while you're waiting for your food.

658 W. Belden Ave. Ⓒ 773/348-8899. High chairs, boosters. Reservations not accepted. All main courses under $8. AE, DISC, V. Mon–Fri 3pm–2am; Sat 9am–3am; Sun 9am–2am. Subway/El: Red Line to Fullerton.

La Creperie ★★ *Finds* FRENCH   Germain and Sara Roignant have run this intimate gem of a cafe since 1972, never straying from the reasonably priced crepes that draw repeat customers aplenty. (Hey, a crepe is just a pancake rolled up, right kids?) Onion soup, paté, and escargots are all good starters, but the highlights here are the whole-wheat crepes—each prepared on a special grill that Germain imported from his native Brittany. Single-choice fillings include cheese, tomato, egg, or ham; tasty duets feature chicken and mushroom or broccoli and cheese. Beef bourguignon, coq au vin, or curried chicken are the more adventurous crepe combinations. Non-crepe offerings are few: orange roughy and steak frites. Don't leave without at least sharing one of the dessert crepes, which tuck anything from apples to ice cream within their warm folds. La Creperie is a great option especially if you're taking in a show at one of the nearby off-Loop theaters, such as Briar Street, where the popular Blue Man Group is in residence.

2845 N. Clark St. (½ block north of Diversey Pkwy.). Ⓒ 773/528-9050. High chairs, boosters. Reservations accepted. Main courses $3.25–$15. AE, DC, DISC, MC, V. Tues–Fri 11:30am–3:30pm and 5–11pm; Sat 11am–11pm; Sun 11am–9:30pm. Subway/El: Brown Line to Diversey.

Nookies DINER   This "chain" of three restaurants is a Chicago favorite for standard breakfast fare. On weekends, you'll find Nookies packed with young professionals grabbing pancakes or an omelet after a long night out and families. This family-owned chain offers breakfast all day, plus soups, salads, and sandwiches. Tables and a lunch counter are available. Nookies has additional branches in Lincoln Park at 2114 N. Halsted St. (Ⓒ 773/327-1400), and in Lakeview at 3334 N. Halsted St. (Ⓒ 773/248-9888).

1748 N. Wells St. Ⓒ 312/337-2454. High chairs, boosters. Reservations not accepted. All main courses under $8. Cash only. Mon–Sat 6:30am–10pm; Sun 6:30am–9pm. Subway/El: Brown Line to Sedgwick.

Stanley's ★★ AMERICAN   Here's another great neighborhood bar and restaurant that stands in the heart of Lincoln Park, normally the epicenter of the young and the restless, but instead, caters to families. Stanley's front room is a bar with several booths, tall tables with old chrome and leather bar stools, satellite- and cable-fed TVs, and a jukebox. The adjacent dining room is an abrupt leap into the family den, decorated with photos, quilts, bowling trophies, and children's drawings. This popular family spot has a special kids' menu with corn dogs and PB&J. On Saturday and Sunday there's an all-you-can-eat brunch buffet, featuring make-your-own omelets, build-your-own-Belgian waffles, home-fried potatoes, fried chicken, and mashed potatoes for $11. Daily specials are posted on the chalkboard out front.

1970 N. Lincoln Ave. Ⓒ 312/642-0007. Kids' menu, high chairs, boosters. Main courses $8–$15; kids' menu $4. Mon and Tues 5pm–2am; Wed–Fri 11:30am–2am; Sat 11am–3am; Sun 11am–2am. Bus: 11 or 73 to Armitage.

Toast ★ AMERICAN/BREAKFAST   Located in Lincoln Park, Toast is homey yet slightly funky—note the shelf of vintage toasters. Kids are welcome here: The crayons and butcher-block table coverings will keep them busy, and the staff has a reputation for being baby and kid crazy. Breakfast is served all day and includes a twist on the usual diner fare. Pancakes come in all sorts of tempting varieties, from lemon/poppy seed drizzled with honey to the "pancake orgy" of a strawberry, mango, and banana-pecan pancake topped with granola, yogurt, and honey. (Try it: It tastes even better than it looks!) If pancakes equal dessert for you, try one of the omelets or the breakfast burrito. On the side, you can order grilled chicken sausage, applewood smoked bacon, or, of course, a stack of toast. Fresh-squeezed orange juice and grapefruit juice are also available. The lunch menu includes a range of creative sandwiches, salads, and wraps. Toast also has a second location in River North at 228 W. Chicago Ave. (✆ 312/944-7023).

746 W. Webster St. (at Halsted St.). ✆ 773/935-5600. High chairs, boosters. Reservations not accepted. Breakfast $3.95–$7.95. AE, DC, DISC, MC, V. Mon–Fri 7am–3pm; Sat–Sun 8am–4pm. Subway/El: Red Line to Fullerton.

Twin Anchors ✪ BARBECUE   Come early (around 5pm—later on, there's more of a bar scene) and experience this Old Town landmark; a fixture since the end of Prohibition, Twin Anchors manages to maintain the flavor of old Chicago. Actually, it also has a flavor of a supper club in northern Wisconsin, which is perhaps why so many transplanted small-town Midwesterners feel comfortable here. It's a friendly, family-owned pub with Frank Sinatra on the jukebox and on the walls. (He apparently hung out here on swings through town in the 1960s.) This totally unpretentious place has a long mahogany bar up front and a modest dining room in back with red Formica-topped tables crowded close. Of course, you don't need anything fancy when the ribs—the fall-off-the-bone variety—come this good. Even non-meat eaters may be swayed if they allow themselves one bite of the enormous slabs of tender baby-back pork ribs. (Go for the zesty sauce.) Hamburgers will keep kids happy. Ribs and other entrees come with coleslaw and dark rye bread, plus your choice of baked potato, tasty fries, and the even-better crisp onion rings. For dessert, there's a daily cheesecake selection.

1655 N. Sedgwick St. (1 block north of North Ave.). ✆ 312/266-1616. Kids' menu, high chairs, boosters. Reservations not accepted. Main courses $7.95–$18; sandwiches $3.50–$7.50; kids' menu $2.95. AE, DC, DISC, MC, V. Mon–Thurs 5–11:30pm; Fri 5pm–12:30am; Sat noon–12:30am; Sun noon–10:30pm. Subway/El: Brown Line to Sedgwick.

7 Wrigleyville & the North Side

Families visiting the area surrounding Wrigley Field will probably be in the neighborhood for that very reason—Wrigley Field. The area, however, has a long history of being a neighborhood of working-class families. Lately, it's gentrified as developers have built new town houses and apartments, and with that affluence has come a group of new, very popular restaurants spanning a range of culinary offerings and price ranges. Throughout the North Side, you'll find a wealth of ethnic restaurants that allow diners to embark on further gastronomic globetrotting.

MODERATE

Buca di Beppo ITALIAN   Always fantasized about being part of a wacky, extended Italian family? You'll feel you've found your home at this Italian-American restaurant (part of a national chain). The restaurant serves humongous family-style dishes in a catacomb-like setting of six cozy rooms. (The decor is eclectic, covered with garage-sale-type mementos gathered by the owners in

Italy.) The restaurant is a loud, high-energy place with large groups of diners. Request the "Pope Room," which features pontiff memorabilia and one special thronelike chair at its round table that has room for a pope and his thirteen bishops. Portions are huge—one order of chicken cacciatore serves up to five people, pizzas are measured in feet not inches, and meatballs weigh a half-pound each. Even the smaller portions of pasta serve up to 3 people.

2941 N. Clark St. (C) 773/348-7673. High chairs, boosters. Reservations not accepted, but you can call ahead to put your name on the list before you arrive at the restaurant. Main courses $7.95–$21. AE, DC, DISC, MC, V. Mon–Thurs 5–10pm; Fri 4–11pm; Sat 2–11pm; Sun noon–10pm. Subway/El: Brown Line to Wellington. Bus: 8.

INEXPENSIVE

Ann Sather ★★ SWEDISH/AMERICAN/BREAKFAST   A sign hanging by Ann Sather's door bears the following inscription: ONCE ONE OF MANY NEIGHBORHOOD SWEDISH RESTAURANTS, ANN SATHER'S IS THE ONLY ONE THAT REMAINS. That's somewhat true, although Svea's in Andersonville might dispute the claim. Ann Sather is a real Chicago institution, where you can enjoy Swedish meatballs with buttered noodles and brown gravy, or the Swedish sampler of duck breast with lingonberry glaze, meatball, potato-sausage dumpling, sauerkraut, and brown beans. All meals are full dinners, including appetizer, main course, vegetable, potato, and dessert. It's the sticky cinnamon rolls, though, that make addicts out of diners. Weekend brunch here can get frenzied, but the people-watching is priceless: a cross section of gay and straight, young and old, kids to seniors.

There are several other branches that serve only breakfast and lunch: a restaurant in Andersonville, at 5207 N. Clark St. ((C) 773/271-6677), and smaller cafes in Lincoln Park, at 2665 N. Clark St. ((C) 773/327-9522), and Lakeview, at 3416 N. Southport Ave. ((C) 773/404-4475).

929 W. Belmont Ave. (between Clark St. and Sheffield Ave.). (C) 773/348-2378. High chairs, boosters. Reservations accepted for parties of 6 or more. Main courses $7–$12. AE, DC, MC, V. Sun–Thurs 7am–10pm; Fri–Sat 7am–11pm. Free parking with validation. Subway/El: Red Line to Belmont.

Hi Ricky Asia Noodle Shop & Satay Bar ★ (Value) ASIAN/NOODLES   If your kids really like noodles, they'll be in nirvana at Hi Ricky, which offers dishes from Burma, Malaysia, Thailand, Japan, Indonesia, China, and Vietnam. The setting is simple and contemporary, with a big, airy feel and hardwood floors. The wide-open space makes it easy to maneuver a stroller or high chair into place. (Note the upside-down woks used as light fixtures along the open grill.) The dishes feature fresh ingredients, generous portions, and reasonable prices. Given the restaurant's name, you'll want to begin with an order or two of satay: You've got seven to choose from, or you can go for a sampler and try all of them (chicken, lamb, shrimp, tofu, and more). Main courses include spicy drunken noodles (broad noodles stir-fried with basil, greens, tomato, sprouts, and hot pepper—and a choice of tofu or a variety of meats) and the Malaysian Hokkien noodles (spicy curry fried egg and rice noodles with a choice of meats). The kids' menu includes egg rolls, chicken satay, and pot stickers. If there's a wait, never fear: Short turnover time for tables usually means you'll move right along. Other locations are in Wicker Park, at 1852 North Ave. ((C) 312/276-8300) and near downtown, at 941 W. Randolph St. ((C) 312/491-9100).

3730 N. Southport Ave. (between Irving Park Rd. and Addison St.). (C) 773/388-0000. Kids' menu, high chairs, boosters. Reservations not accepted. Main courses $5.95–$9.95; kids' menu $5. AE, DISC, MC, V. Mon–Thurs 11:30am–10pm; Fri 11:30am–11pm; Sat noon–11pm; Sun noon–10pm. Subway/El: Brown Line to Southport.

O'Donovan's (Finds) AMERICAN   This century-old neighborhood restaurant and jovial pub was sold by the Schulien family in 1999, but thankfully the new owners have kept up the tradition that has thrilled kids for decades: Magicians perform tableside tricks on Saturday evenings. (To avoid the bar-oriented rush, come early, at 5 or 6pm.) Although there's no kids' menu, ordering appetizers for the kids works just as well. For adults, burgers are the thing, although options also include steaks, chops, and seafood. As the night progresses, O'Donovan's draws a good mix of late-20-something blue- and white-collar patrons with a healthy selection of microbrews. On Sundays, the expansive buffet features all-you-can-eat scrambled eggs, bacon, sausage, carved ham, roast beef, waffles, and omelets made to order and biscuits and gravy; it costs $7.95.

2100 W. Irving Park Rd. © 773/478-2100. High chairs. Reservations not accepted. Main courses $6–$16. AE, MC, V. Tues–Thurs 4–10pm; Fri–Sat 4–11pm; Sun 10am–3pm. Subway/El: Brown Line to Irving Park. Bus: 11, 80.

Penny's Noodle Shop ★ (Value) ASIAN/NOODLES   Predating many of Chicago's pan-Asian noodle shops, Penny's has kept its loyal following even as others have joined the fray. Some of its success is in the unique location tucked beneath the El tracks: a tiny, pie-shaped space brightened with sunny yellow walls. With room for only a dozen tables and stools wrapping around the grill, Penny's is packed nightly with scrub-faced young people from the neighborhood. But the overall cuteness of the place doesn't detract from what happens in the open kitchen. Penny Chiamopoulous, a Thai native, has assembled a concise menu of delectable dishes, all of them fresh and made to order. Of course, noodles unite everything on the menu, so your main decision is choosing among noodles (crispy wide rice, rice vermicelli, Japanese udon, and so on) in a heaping bowl of soup and noodles spread out on a plate. There are several barbecued pork and beef entrees, and plenty of options for vegetarians. There's often a long wait, so you might want to try the second, larger location directly south on Sheffield Avenue at 960 W. Diversey Pkwy. (© 773/281-8448).

3400 N. Sheffield Ave. (at Roscoe and Clark sts.). © 773/281-8222. High chairs, boosters. Reservations not accepted. Main courses $4.50–$7.95. No credit cards. Tues–Thurs 11am–10pm; Fri–Sat 11am–10:30pm. Subway/El: Red Line to Belmont.

Uncommon Grounds ★ (Finds) BREAKFAST/SANDWICHES   A living-room atmosphere created by a wood-burning stove and artwork on the walls that rotates frequently (and is always available for purchase), Uncommon Grounds is home to local artists, musicians, and writers. (Five nights a week, you can check out a performance in the back room by a local trying to make the big time—highly recommended for families with teens.) Thankfully for families, the atmosphere is 100% smoke-free. Its menu is heartier and more extensive than most Chicago coffeehouses. Steaming bowls of latte and hot chocolate, plus yummy baked goods and a menu heavy on breakfast foods (nutty oatmeal with bananas; the "uncommon" breakfast burrito, a croissant with ham, egg, and cheese; and granola piled with fresh fruit and yogurt) are all favorites. One can't-miss choice is the apple-pecan whole-wheat pancakes with cranberry-honey butter. Lunchtime means sandwiches, hummus platter, and offerings of wine and beer. Pick a prime spot on the window seats, piled with cozy cushions. Teens will get a kick out of the Midwest's alternative press on hand here, from *The Reader* to *The Onion,* for your reading pleasure.

1214 W. Grace St. (at Clark St.). © 773/929-3680. Kids' menu, high chairs, boosters. Main courses $3–$10; kids' menu $2–$5. AE, DC, DISC, MC, V. Sat–Wed 8am–11pm; Thurs–Fri 8am–midnight. Subway/El: Red Line to Addison. Bus: 22.

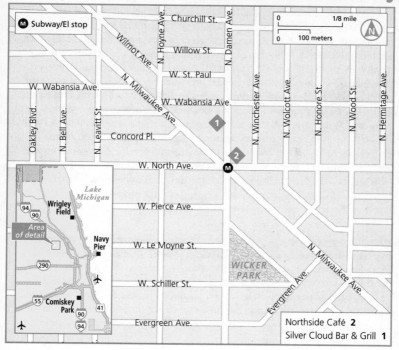

M Subway/El stop

Churchill St.
N. Hoyne Ave.
N. Damen Ave.
Wilmot Ave.
N. Milwaukee Ave.
Willow St.
W. St. Paul
W. Wabansia Ave.
N. Winchester Ave.
N. Wolcott Ave.
N. Honore St.
N. Wood St.
N. Hermitage Ave.
W. Wabansia Ave.
Oakley Blvd.
N. Bell Ave.
N. Leavitt St.
Concord Pl.
1
2
W. North Ave.
M

Lake Michigan
Wrigley Field
94
90
Area of detail
Navy Pier
290
55 Comiskey Park
90
41
94

W. Pierce Ave.
W. Le Moyne St.
WICKER PARK
N. Milwaukee Ave.
W. Schiller St.
Evergreen Ave.
Evergreen Ave.

0   1/8 mile
0   100 meters

Northside Café **2**
Silver Cloud Bar & Grill **1**

The booming Wicker Park/Bucktown area followed closely in the race to gentrification on the heels of Lincoln Park and Wrigleyville. First came the artists, photographers, and musicians, followed by armies of yuppies and young families, originally following the cheap rents and real estate, and later chasing the cachet that became attached to the neighborhood. Happily, what's now one of the city's hippest restaurant scenes includes a number of fun options for families. Get yourself to the nexus of activity at the intersection of North, Damen, and Milwaukee avenues, and you won't have to walk more than a couple of blocks in any direction to find a hot spot. (***Note to parents of teens:*** The house featured on MTV's *Real World Chicago* is just south of this intersection, on North Ave., the north side of the street.) Cab fare is within reason from downtown, or you can take the El's Blue Line to Damen.

INEXPENSIVE

Northside Café ★ *Value* AMERICAN/BURGERS   I highly recommend this spot for high-quality cheap eats. Burgers and sandwiches are all above average and ring in at a very reasonable $6 or $7. There's no pretense here: The back dining room looks like a rec room circa 1973, complete with a fireplace, pinball machines, and a pool table. In nice weather, Northside opens up its large patio for dining, and a skylit cover keeps it in use during the winter. It's a prime people-watching spot that can't be beat in good weather.

1635 N. Damen Ave. (at North and Milwaukee aves.). ☎ 773/384-3555. High chairs, boosters. Reservations not accepted. Menu items $5.95–$11. AE, DC, DISC, MC, V. Sun–Fri 11:30am–2am; Sat 11am–3am. Subway/El: Blue Line to Damen.

Silver Cloud Bar & Grill ⚸ DINER   How can kids not feel at home here? Silver Cloud is one of few Chicago restaurants I know that has tater tots on the menu (and naturally, every time I eat here, I work my entire meal selection around this "side"). This Bucktown restaurant's motto is FOOD LIKE MOM WOULD MAKE IF SHE WAS GETTING PAID. Here the grilled cheese is made with mozzarella, Monterey Jack, and cheddar on Italian bread and served with a bowl of Campbell's tomato soup. Roomy red leather booths are a hit with families. In good weather, sit outside. (The seating area is on the side street, so you avoid the noise of Damen Ave.) A sign at the bar asks WHY NOT ENJOY A NICE, RIPE CIGAR?—but never fear, families, there's no lighting up until after 10pm. This place is not a tourist hot spot, so enjoy the people-watching—most customers are neighborhood folks. On the weekends, Silver Cloud is a favorite of Chicagoans who flock to Bucktown for the dining and nightlife.

1700 N. Damen Ave. ✆ **773/489-6212.** High chairs, boosters. Main courses $8–$15. AE, DC, DISC, V. Mon–Thurs 11:30am–midnight; Fri 10am–2am; Sat 10am–3am; Sun 10am–midnight. Subway/El: Blue Line to Damen.

9 Only in Chicago

Pizza-loving and hot dog–inhaling kids have it made in Chicago: We've turned them from fast food into art forms. Of course, Chicagoans have their own take on these all-American staples, so to have an authentic taste of Chicago, shun the thin-crust pizza and ketchup as condiment of choice for hot dogs. Try them our way, and I guarantee you'll understand why Chicagoans are passionate about their dogs and pizza.

PIZZA

To the uninitiated: Chicago-style pizza, also known as deep-dish, is thick-crusted and often demands a knife and fork. The thin-crust variety favored in New York is also widely available; a third type, called stuffed, is similar to a pie, with a crust on both top and bottom. Many pizzerias serve both thick and thin, and some make all three kinds. Three of Chicago's best gourmet deep-dish restaurants are **Pizzeria Uno** (p. 106), **Pizzeria Due** (p. 106), and **Gino's East** (p. 104).

In River North, **Lou Malnati's Pizzeria** ⚸, at 439 N. Wells St. (✆ **312/828-9800**), bakes both deep-dish and thin-crust pizza and even has a low-fat cheese option. **Edwardo's** is a local pizza chain that serves all three varieties, but with a wheat crust and all-natural ingredients. (Spinach pizza is the specialty here, and deservedly so.) It has several Chicago locations, including one in the Gold Coast, at 1212 N. Dearborn St. at Division Street (✆ **312/337-4490**); one in Printers Row in the South Loop, at 521 S. Dearborn St. (✆ **312/939-3366**); and one in Lincoln Park, at 2662 N. Halsted St. (✆ **773/871-3400**). Yards from the farm in the Lincoln Park Zoo is **Ranalli's Pizzeria, Libations & Collectibles,** 1925 N. Lincoln Ave. (✆ **312/642-4700**), with its terrific open-air patio.

In Wrigleyville, just off Belmont Avenue, are **Leona's Pizzeria,** 3215 N. Sheffield Ave. (✆ **773/327-8861**), and **Pat's Pizzeria,** 3114 N. Sheffield Ave. (✆ **773/248-0168**), both of which serve all three kinds of pizza. Leona's also has a location in Little Italy, at 1419 W. Taylor St. (✆ **312/850-2222**), and Pat's has one downtown in the Athletic Club Illinois Center, at 211 N. Stetson Ave. (✆ **312/946-0220**).

HOT DOGS

Chicagoans like to think that they stand head and skewers above the rest of the world when it comes to hot dogs. The facades of Chicago's hot dog stands, as if by some unwritten convention, are all very colorful, with bright signs of red and yellow, exaggerated lettering, and comic illustrations of the wieners and fries. The classic Chicago hot dog includes a frankfurter by Vienna Beef (a local food processor and hallowed institution), heaps of chopped onions and relish so green it could be Pop Art, a slather of yellow mustard, pickle spears and fresh tomato wedges, a dash of celery salt, and, for good measure, two or three "sport" peppers, those thumb-shaped holy terrors that turn your mouth into its own bonfire. As Byron Kouris, the owner of **Byron's Hot Dog Haus,** at 1017 W. Irving Park Rd. (© 773/281-7474), so aptly summed up years ago, it's a veritable "garden on a bun."

Chicago is home to many standout hot dog stands and shops, such as **Gold Coast Dogs,** 418 N. State St., at Hubbard Street (© 312/527-1222). Two blocks off North Michigan Avenue, just across the river from the Loop, Gold Coast Dogs is a place where you can grab your food and run, or join the crowd at the stools around the counter. Hot dogs start at $1.90; burgers (beef, turkey, and veggie) start at $3.10. You can also have melted cheddar cheese on your french fries, and have some homemade brownies for dessert. It's open Monday through Friday from 7am to 10pm and Saturday and Sunday from 11am to 8pm.

Another local institution is **The Wieners Circle,** 2622 N. Clark St. (© 773/477-7444), as much for the hot dogs as for the picnic tables out front, the perfect vantage point for surveying the Lincoln Park scene. The order-taker will berate you and tell you to pay attention, but don't cringe or take offense: It's part of the well-honed shtick here. There's also **Murphy's Red Hots,** 1211 W. Belmont Ave. (© 773/935-2882), a neighborhoody spot not too far from Wrigley Field. Besides hot dogs, Murphy's serves charbroiled Polish sausages, burgers, and tasty hand-cut fries. A Japanese conglomerate even deemed Murphy's sufficiently authentic to select it as a model for a chain of hot dog stands in Japan.

But if you ask the locals for their sentimental favorite, we'll most likely steer you to the legendary **Superdawg Drive-In** (© 773/763-0660), at the intersection of Milwaukee, Devon, and Nagle avenues. It's impossible to miss: Mr. and Mrs. Superdawg, in Tarzan and Jane tableaux, beckon the masses from the rooftop, their beady eyes pulsing an electric red. Maurie and Florrie Berman haven't changed a thing about their place—the city's last real drive-in, with its Order-Matic ordering system and female carhops on roller skates—since they opened for business in 1948. Their main attraction still arrives in a red 1950s-design enclosed box that declares on one side, YOUR SUPERDAWG LOUNGES INSIDE, CONTENTEDLY CUSHIONED IN SUPERFRIES.

6

Exploring Chicago with Your Kids

While Chicago has sights that top any world traveler's list (although fewer than New York or London), Chicago offers big, friendly attractions for kids, too. Part of Chicago's kid-friendliness comes from the location of our major museums, which sit within walking distance of beaches and miles of parks. Kids can learn in the morning and run free in the afternoon. Compared to some major cities, outdoor space is easy to find, thanks to miles of unimpeded lakefront. And as every parent knows, being outdoors is a welcome relief when kids need to let off steam.

While crowds do pack the major museums on weekends and holidays, the crowdedness is not on the level of New York City on a similar day.

Summer is prime time here: Families flock *to* Chicago on the weekends—unlike other urban areas, where families *escape from* the city. When the weather is warm, you'll find that suburbanites, Wisconsinites, Iowans, and families from other surrounding states head to our city to enjoy the cool lake breeze.

Chicago's a no-nonsense Midwestern city, and most establishments are laid-back and open-minded. You won't get the kind of urban snobbery you might experience in other big cities. Though I hate to say it, Chicagoans are "nice"—another Midwestern quality—meaning you are more likely to get a sympathetic smile than the evil eye when trying to calm a crying child.

SIGHTSEEING SUGGESTIONS

If You Have 1 Day

If you have only 1 day (and if that day happens to be a Sat), you can get much of the flavor of the city from an **"El" tour of the Loop.** On Saturday afternoons, these free, 40-minute tours will take you through the heart of downtown on our century-old El train. (On any other day of the week, you can hop the El yourself for the same views, without the guided tour.) A Chicago Architecture Foundation tour guide will point out buildings of historic and architectural interest and discuss the history of the El.

After your tour, head south to the **Museum of Science and Industry,** the classic Chicago kids' attraction that never fails to enthrall. Afterward, head back to the city to dine at a restaurant near Michigan Avenue and the **Magnificent Mile.** Finish off the day with a stroll along the boulevard and up the **lakefront.** While you won't see the sun set over the lake (remember, the lake is always to the east), the colors can be spectacular anyway. (Interestingly, on the other side of the lake, those in Michigan and Indiana have the opposite view:

They never see the sun rise over the lake, only set.)

If You Have 2 Days

Get thee on the water: Take a boat tour of the Chicago River and Lake Michigan. Even if your kids are small, they'll enjoy being on the water, while adults will enjoy learning about our spectacular architecture. (Chicago is the home of modern architecture; for more on our best buildings, pick up *Frommer's Chicago.*) Some tours take you up and down the Chicago River, then through locks that release the boat into Lake Michigan. You'll see first-hand that the Chicago River is one of the engineering marvels of our nation, because its flow was reversed to move backwards from the lake, not into it, in order to prevent river water from polluting Lake Michigan.

Back on land, walk around **the Loop** to see the buildings and the city's extensive sculpture collection. Finish off the day with a shopping trip up the **Magnificent Mile,** and maybe a trip to the top of the **John Hancock Center.**

In the evening, if the Cubs are in town, catch a night game at **Wrigley Field.** Dine on hot dogs or bratwurst while you sip a beer and the kids polish off cotton candy and licorice whips.

If You Have 3 Days

If you can add a third day to your stay, explore the Near North Side. Stroll north along Michigan Avenue, starting from the Chicago River. You might want to stop to admire the gothic **Tribune Tower,** just north of the river on the east side of Michigan Avenue. The tower is home to one of the country's media giants, which owns WGN television and radio and the *Chicago Tribune* newspaper.

If your kids are old enough and mobile enough, continue walking north all the way up the Magnificent Mile, until you reach **Lake Shore Drive.** (If you're not in the mood to stroll, catch a 151 bus.) Here, you can cross under a pedestrian tunnel to **Oak Street Beach.** Keep walking north until you reach Fullerton Avenue, where you can wander around **Lincoln Park Zoo** and visit the **Farm-in-the-Zoo,** see the famed gorilla house, and check out Chicago's newest addition to its museum roster, the **Peggy Notebaert Nature Museum,** with its spectacular butterfly house.

In the evening, catch a show. You might find a musical playing in one of the **North Loop theater district**'s many venues, or you can check out the kid-pleasing **Blue Man Group** at Briar Street Theater in Lincoln Park.

If You Have 4 Days or More

On your fourth day, head to an outlying neighborhood or suburb. If your kids are 6 years or older, they might enjoy west suburban **Oak Park,** where special guided Youth Architectural Tours of **The Frank Lloyd Wright Home & Studio** cater to kids 6 to 14.

Many homes in the area were built or influenced by Wright, so if it's a nice day, make sure to take a stroll around the neighborhood. While in Oak Park, you should also visit the area's newest children's museum, **Wonder Works,** which opened in fall 2002. If you have a car, top off the day with a stop at **Peterson's Sweet Shop,** for their house specialty turtle sundae. See chapter 11 for more information.

If the Weather's Hot

During steamy Midwestern summer days, the best place to be is on the lake. Head for **Navy Pier,** where you can board **Seadog speedboat.** This sleek, bright yellow boat seats 149 passengers and jets across the

Central Chicago Attractions

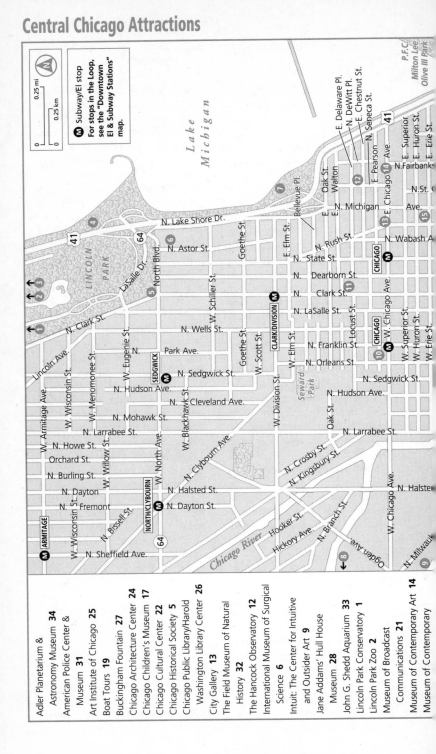

Monroe Harbor

E. Wacker Dr.

E. North Water St.

E. Illinois St.

E. Harbor Dr.

E. Field Blvd.

S. Lake Shore Dr. 41

E. Randolph Dr.

E. Monroe Dr.

Columbus Dr.

G R A N T   P A R K

ROOSEVELT RD. STATION

RANDOLPH

E. Randolph Dr.

WASHINGTON

MADISON

Art Institute

E. Jackson Dr.

ADAMS

Wabash   Ave.

JACKSON

LIBRARY

S. Michigan Ave.

E. Congress Pkwy.

S. Wabash

State St.

MONROE

S. Dearborn St.

E. Harrison St.

E. Balbo

E. 8th St.

E. 9th St.

E. 11th St.

ROOSEVELT/WABASH

STATE

N. Dearborn St.

N. Clark

N. LaSalle   St.

WASHINGTON

W. Adams   St.

QUINCY

HARRISON

S. Plymouth Ct.

S. Federal St.

S. Clark St.

LASALLE

ROOSEVELT

W. Roosevelt Rd.

Wacker Dr.

CLARK/LAKE

W. Lake St.

N. Wells   St.

N. Franklin St.

S. Franklin St.

S. LaSalle St.

S. Sherman St.

S. Wells St.

Chicago River

MERCH MART

N. Wacker Dr.

W. Illinois St.

W. Hubbard St.

Kingsbury

CLINTON

N. Canal St.

N. Clinton St.

N. Jefferson St.

N. DesPlaines St.

Union Station

W. Adams St.

W. Jackson Blvd.

W. Van Buren St.

Eisenhower Expwy.

CLINTON

W. Harrison St.

S. Canal St.

S. Clinton St.

S. Jefferson St.

S. Des Plaines St.

W. Polk St.

N. Milwaukee Ave.

W. Hubbard St.

W. Kinzie St.

N. Sangamon St.

N. Peoria St.

N. Green St.

W. Fulton St.

W. Lake St.

N. Morgan St.

N. Carpenter St.

N. Aberdeen St.

W. Randolph St.

W. Washington St.

W. Madison St.

W. Monroe St.

S. Green St.

S. Peoria St.

S. Morgan St.

S. Aberdeen St.

90 94

S. Halsted St.

290

HALSTED/U OF I

University of Illinois

W. Taylor St.

W. Roosevelt Rd.

S. Des Plaines St.

Lake Michigan

Wrigley Field

Area of detail

Comiskey Park

90 94

290

55

90 94

41

123

lake while guides give a narrated tour of facts and tales about Navy Pier, the lakefront, and the skyline.

When you're safely docked again at Navy Pier, you might want to head indoors to the air-conditioned comfort of the **Omnimax Theater** at the Museum of Science and Industry, or simply stroll the pier. (Your reward for going all the way to the end of the ¾-mile-long pier is one of the best views of the city.) For those not afraid of heights, take a ride on the 15-story Ferris wheel, and enjoy the spectacular view of Chicago's skyline. The pier is always packed with musicians, and inside you'll find shops and restaurants.

If the Weather's Cold

Parents rave about **Garfield Park Conservatory.** While the location is slightly off the beaten path in a run-down neighborhood, there is secure parking in a lot with security guards. Attendance went up 400% here in the past year with the glass sculpture exhibit by artist Dave Chihuly, so chances are, you won't be alone. Inside, check out the Elizabeth Morse Genius Children's Garden, where exhibits show a giant bee pollinating an enormous flower and demonstrate how the sun's rays spark photosynthesis in a plant leaf. A digging area (consisting of a huge pile of dirt and digging toys), waterfall, and slide from the second story mezzanine (along with the fact that the plants here can be touched) make this a great hands-on adventure for kids.

If You Have a Sitter

If you're a couple, book yourself a romantic table for two at one of Chicago's great grown-up restaurants. One of the hot spots is **Café des Architectes,** located in the Sofitel, 20 E. Chestnut St. at Rush Street (© 312/324-4000). The modern and elegant decor combines shades of purple with white leather banquettes. The food is modern French, and the service is solicitous. Specialties include a starter of grilled shrimp over bright purple, beet-infused couscous. One wonderfully unique entree is the melt-in-your-mouth butterfish, caught off the coasts of Portugal and France and flown in daily from Europe. If you're single, head to the **Art Institute** and linger over the impressionists, then head outdoors to the cafe for a leisurely glass of wine and a sandwich while you watch the world go by on Michigan Avenue.

It wouldn't be Chicago if you didn't get a taste of the blues: In fact, you just might decide that getting the blues is a good thing when you top off your evening at **Buddy Guy's Legends,** 754 S. Wabash Ave., between Balbo and 8th streets in the South Loop (© 312/427-0333). Everyone from Eric Clapton to Muddy Waters has stopped in to jam and listen to the best in blues at this club, owned and operated by Chicago blues legend Buddy Guy. Every January, Guy himself plays a series of shows—if you're in town, don't miss it. Those shows always sell out early, so call in advance. The cover charge ranges from $6 to $15.

1 Sights by Neighborhood

THE LOOP & VICINITY
DOWNTOWN

South Michigan Avenue & Grant Park Attractions

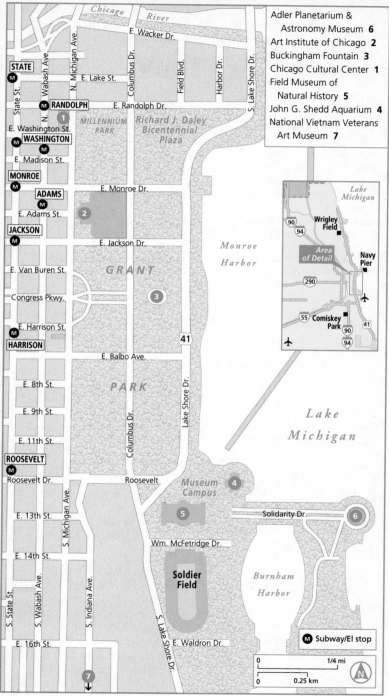

Adler Planetarium &
  Astronomy Museum **6**
Art Institute of Chicago **2**
Buckingham Fountain **3**
Chicago Cultural Center **1**
Field Museum of
  Natural History **5**
John G. Shedd Aquarium **4**
National Vietnam Veterans
  Art Museum **7**

Lake Michigan

Wrigley Field

Area of Detail

Navy Pier

Comiskey Park

Chicago River

E. Wacker Dr.

E. Lake St.

STATE
State St.
Wabash Ave.
N. Michigan Ave.

RANDOLPH
N. Michigan Ave.
E. Randolph Dr.

MILLENNIUM PARK

Richard J. Daley Bicentennial Plaza

E. Washington St.
WASHINGTON

E. Madison St.

MONROE

ADAMS
E. Adams St.

E. Monroe Dr.

JACKSON

E. Jackson Dr.

GRANT

E. Van Buren St.

Congress Pkwy.

E. Harrison St.
HARRISON

Monroe Harbor

Columbus Dr.
Field Blvd.
Harbor Dr.
S. Lake Shore Dr.

41

E. Balbo Ave.

PARK

E. 8th St.

E. 9th St.

E. 11th St.

ROOSEVELT
Roosevelt Dr.

Roosevelt

Museum Campus

Columbus Dr.

Lake Shore Dr.

Lake Michigan

E. 13th St.

S. Michigan Ave.

Solidarity Dr.

E. 14th St.

S. State St.
S. Wabash Ave.
S. Indiana Ave.

Wm. McFetridge Dr.

Soldier Field

Burnham Harbor

E. 16th St.

S. Lake Shore Dr.
E. Waldron Dr.

M Subway/El stop

0   1/4 mi
0   0.25 km

N

125

DuSable Museum of African-American History **2**
Museum of Science and Industry **5**
Oriental Institute Museum **4**
Robie House **3**
The Smart Museum of Art **1**

2 Kids' Top 10 Attractions

Adler Planetarium & Astronomy Museum   **All ages.** Kids can ride into outer space at the world's first StarRider virtual reality theater, which propels passengers on an exhilarating voyage of discovery into the infinity of space. You participate in the journey by operating controls on the armrests. The mind-blowing theater is part of the planetarium's $40 million facelift, completed in 1999. The new, 60,000 square-foot Sky Pavilion wraps itself around the 1920-built planetarium like a high-tech glass visor. Four exhibition galleries, Galileo's cafe, and a new gift shop round out the new addition. Of special interest are *From the Night Sky to the Big Bang,* which traces changing views of the cosmos over 1,000 years and features artifacts from the planetarium's extensive collection of historical astronomical instruments; and a **Solar Observatory,** which provides images of the sun taken by the SOHO satellite. The new cafe offers stunning views of Chicago's skyline.

The planetarium is located on Northerly Island, which is also occupied by Meigs Field, the landing strip for small, private aircraft. You'd never know it's an island, though, because it's connected to the museum campus by a causeway called Solidarity Drive, just up the road from the aquarium. The zodiacal 12-sided structure was founded by Sears, Roebuck and Co. executive Max Adler, who imported a Zeiss projector, invented in Germany in 1923, to Chicago in 1930. He wanted to bring the sky closer to people, hoping the novelty of the artificial sky would redirect attention to the real experience of watching a night sky. The result was the first planetarium built in the Western Hemisphere. For years, it has offered multimedia "sky shows" that re-create the nighttime skies and explore current topics in space exploration, and it has allowed visitors to view dramatic close-ups of the moon, the planets, and distant galaxies through a closed-circuit monitor connected to the planetarium's Doane Observatory telescope. (The latter is offered only on Fri after the 8pm sky show.) To find out what to look for in this month's sky, call the Nightwatch 24-Hour Hot Line (© **312/922-STAR**), or check out the planetarium's website.

Families might want to make a point of visiting during **"Far Out Fridays,"** from 5 to 10pm, which feature special activities suited to kids, including telescope viewings and sky shows.

1300 S. Lake Shore Dr. © **312/322-STAR**. Fax 312/322-2257. www.adlerplanetarium.org. Admission $5 adults, $4 seniors and children 4–17, free for children under 4. Free admission Tues. StarRider Theater and sky shows an additional $5 per person. Mon–Fri 9am–5pm, first Fri of every month until 10pm. StarRider Theater and sky shows at numerous times throughout the day; call © 312/922-STAR for current times. Bus: 12, 127, or 146.

Chicago Children's Museum ★★   **All ages.** Parents rave about the Chicago Children's Museum, now in its 20th year. Since it moved to Navy Pier in 1996, the museum has become one of the most popular cultural attractions in the city. The three-story museum has areas especially for preschoolers as well as for older children, and several permanent exhibits allow kids a maximum of hands-on fun. There are always creative temporary exhibitions on tap as well: Recent favorites included shows on Dr. Seuss and *Sesame Street.*

Dinosaur Expedition re-creates an expedition to the Sahara, allowing kids to experience camp life, conduct scientific research, and dig for the bones of *Suchomimus,* a Saharan dinosaur recently discovered by Chicago paleontologist Paul Sereno. (A full-scale model stands nearby.) A new permanent exhibit, *Play It Safe,* addresses possible safety issues in an interactive house and backyard. *WaterWays* allows visitors to learn about the uses and benefits of water resources by constructing dams to direct the flow of water, constructing fountains, and teaming up with others to blast a stream of water 50 feet in the air. *Face to Face: Dealing with Prejudice and Discrimination* is a multimedia display that helps kids identify prejudice and find ways to deal with it. There's also a three-level schooner that children can board for a little climbing, from the crow's nest to the gangplank; *PlayMaze,* a toddler-scale cityscape with everything from a gas station to a city bus that children under 5 can touch and explore; and an arts-and-crafts area where visitors can create original artwork to take home. The museum store is filled with educational and multicultural books, science toys, videos, music, and art supplies.

700 E. Grand Ave. © **312/527-1000**. www.chichildrensmuseum.org. Admission $6.50 adults and children, $5.50 seniors. Free admission Thurs 5–8pm. Summer daily 10am–5pm (Thurs until 8pm); fall–spring Tues–Sun 10am–5pm (Thurs until 8pm). Subway/El: Red Line to Grand/State; transfer to city bus or Navy Pier's free trolley bus. Bus: 29, 56, 65, or 66.

The Field Museum of Natural History ★★★   **All ages.** Kids love the Field Museum for its wide-open spaces, giant dinos, and hands-on exhibits. Little ones can indulge their inner Indiana Jones by exploring the shadowy tunnels of an Egyptian tomb or feeling the thrill of a passage across the Pacific Ocean in an

The Field Museum of Natural History

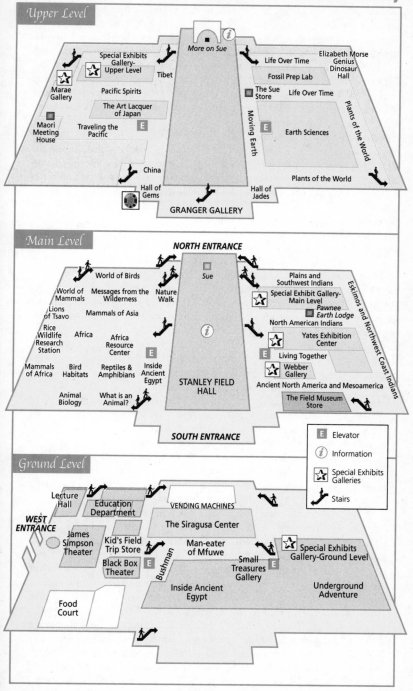

outrigger canoe. Or, explore the African continent by visiting a royal Cameroon palace, witnessing savanna wildlife, and traveling across the Sahara and back to Nigeria. Gleaming gems, giant stuffed elephants, mummies, and Native American artifacts will have your kids enthralled. Spread over the museum's 9 acres of floor space are scores of permanent and temporary exhibitions—some interactive, but most requiring the old-fashioned skills of observation and imagination. Some of the diorama-type exhibits have gotten musty over time, but many others have been completely overhauled, with plenty of activities to keep kids interested. Allow about 3 hours to see it all.

Start with the grand **Stanley Field Hall** (where you enter from either the north or south end). Standing proudly at the north side is the largest, most complete *Tyrannosaurus rex* fossil ever unearthed. Named **"Sue"** ★★ for the paleontologist who found the dinosaur in 1990 in South Dakota, the specimen was acquired by the museum for a cool $8.4 million following a high-stakes bidding war. The real skull is so heavy that a lighter copy had to be mounted on the skeleton; the actual one is displayed upstairs.

Families should head downstairs for two of the most popular kid-friendly exhibits. The pieces on display in ***Inside Ancient Egypt*** ★ were brought to the museum in the early 1900s, after researchers in Saqqara, Egypt, excavated two of the original chambers from the tomb of Unis-ankh, son of the Fifth Dynasty ruler Pharaoh Unis. This *mastaba* (tomb) of Unis-ankh now forms the core of a spellbinding exhibit that realistically depicts scenes from Egyptian funeral, religious, and other social practices. Visitors can explore aspects of the day-to-day world of ancient Egypt, viewing 23 actual mummies and realistic burial scenes, a living marsh environment and canal works, the ancient royal barge, a religious shrine, and a reproduction of a typical marketplace of the period. Many of the exhibits allow hands-on interaction, and there are special activities for kids, such as making parchment from living papyrus plants.

Next to the Egypt exhibit you'll find ***Underground Adventure,*** a "total immersion environment" populated by giant robotic earwigs, centipedes, wolf spiders, and other subterranean critters. The Disneyesque exhibit is a big hit with kids, but—annoyingly—requires an extra admission charge ($5 on top of regular admission for adults, $2 for kids). While you're downstairs, plug a dollar bill into one of the old-fashioned wax-molding machines and watch as your very own red T-Rex or green brontosaurus is shaped in front of your eyes. Kids get a thrill out of taking home their very own Field Museum dino.

The "peoples of the world" exhibits are not only mind-opening, but they're also great fun. ***Traveling the Pacific*** is hidden up on the second floor, but it's definitely worth a stop. Hundreds of artifacts from the museum's oceanic collection re-create scenes of island life in the South Pacific. (There's even a full-scale model of a Maori meeting house.) ***Africa,*** an assemblage of African artifacts and provocative, interactive multimedia presentations, takes viewers to Senegal, to a Cameroon palace, to the savanna and its wildlife, and on a "virtual" journey aboard a slave ship to the Americas. Native Chicagoans will quickly name two more signature highlights: the taxidermied bodies of **Bushman** (a legendary lowland gorilla who made international headlines while at the city's Lincoln Park Zoo) and the **Man-Eating Lions of Tsavo.** (The pair of male lions who munched nearly 140 British railway workers constructing a bridge in East Africa in 1898; their story is featured in the film *The Ghost and the Darkness.*)

The museum hosts special traveling exhibits, as well as numerous lectures, book signings, multiethnic musical and dance performances, storytelling events, and family activity days throughout the year. The Corner Bakery cafe, located just off the main hall, is a cut above the usual museum victuals. (To skip the lunchtime lines, pick up one of the pre-made salads or sandwiches and head for the cash register.) Families also flock to the McDonald's on the lower level.

Roosevelt Rd. and Lake Shore Dr. Ⓒ **312/922-9410** or 312/341-9299 TDD (for hearing-impaired callers). www.fmnh.org. Admission $8 adults; $4 seniors, children 3–17, and students with ID; free for teachers, armed-forces personnel in uniform, and children 2 and under. Free admission Wed. Daily 9am–5pm (except June 17–Aug 26 Thurs till 8pm). Closed Dec 25 and Jan 1. Bus: 6, 10, 12, 130, or 146.

Hamill Family Play Zoo ★★★   All ages.

Located within Chicago's largest zoo, the Brookfield Zoo (located in west suburban Brookfield), the Hamill Family Play Zoo lets kids talk to the animals in an up-close and personal way. In fact, the kids' zoo was designed to help kids, from infants to age 10, develop feelings of kinship with the natural world. Children can touch domesticated animals, help care for animals, search for insects under logs, watch zoo keepers prepare animal food, pretend to be a veterinarian, plant seeds, build feeders, and more. You'll find 300 individual animals from 58 species here, and specially trained staff is on hand to help make the most of your visit.

Other Brookfield Zoo exhibits let kids encounter bathing hippos and laugh at the antics of the orangutans. In total, the Brookfield Zoo is spread over 216 acres with 2,700 animals in residence. Kid favorites are Siberian tigers, snow leopards, giraffes, green sea turtles, and baboons. All the animals live in naturalistic environments that allow them to live side-by-side with other inhabitants of their regions (see Brookfield Zoo on p. 161 for more information).

8400 W. 31st St., Brookfield. Ⓒ **708/485-2200.** www.brookfieldzoo.org. Admission $3 adults, $2 seniors and children 3–11 (in addition to Brookfield Zoo admission $7 adults, $3.50 seniors and children 3–11). Memorial Day to Labor Day daily 9:30am–6pm; Labor Day to Memorial Day daily 10am–5pm. Hours extended for special events. Parking $6.75 per car. To reach the zoo from downtown, take I-290 West and exit at First Avenue. Turn left onto First Avenue and drive 2 miles to the zoo entrance. Subway/El: Blue Line to North Riverside; transfer to bus # 304.

John G. Shedd Aquarium ★★★   All ages.

What do kids love best about The Shedd? The dolphin show! But there's plenty more to see and do at this, the world's largest indoor aquarium. The Shedd is a marble octagon whose interior galleries are populated by thousands of denizens of river, lake, and sea. Opened in 1930, the Shedd debuted in auspicious fashion: It boasted the greatest variety of sea life ever exhibited at one institution and was the first inland aquarium to maintain permanent exhibits of both saltwater and freshwater animals. You'll need about 2 hours to take it all in.

Its star attraction—and the first thing you'll see as you enter—is the *Caribbean Coral Reef* exhibit. This 90,000-gallon circular tank occupies the beaux arts–style central rotunda, entertaining spectators who press up against the glass to ogle divers feeding nurse sharks, barracudas, stingrays, and a hawksbill sea turtle. More than 40 species have been added to the more than 200 already on display. New technology includes an enhanced sound system and a roving camera connected to video monitors mounted on the tank's periphery, which gives visitors close-ups of the animals inside. The most recent addition is *Amazon Rising: Seasons of the River,* a 10,000-square-foot exhibit that opened in summer 2000. More than 250 species of animals—including piranhas, birds, sloths, insects, spiders, snakes, caiman lizards, and monkeys—are on display in this re-creation of the Amazon basin.

The Shedd nearly doubled its size in 1991 with the opening of the 3-million-gallon saltwater **Oceanarium** ★★, an indoor marine mammal pavilion that re-creates a Pacific Northwest coastal environment and also happens to be the largest of its kind in the world. With its wall of windows revealing the lake outside, the Oceanarium creates a stunning optical illusion of one uninterrupted expanse of sea. As you follow a winding nature trail, you encounter beluga whales, white-sided dolphins, Alaskan sea otters, and harbor seals. A colony of penguins in a separate exhibit area inhabits a naturalistic environment meant to resemble the Falkland Islands in the southern sea off Argentina. You can observe all these sea mammals at play through large underwater viewing windows. On a fixed performance schedule in a large pool flanked by an amphitheater, a crew of friendly trainers puts the dolphins through their paces of leaping dives, breaches, and tail-walking. Check out the Oceanarium schedule as soon as you get to the Shedd; seating space fills up quickly for the shows, so you'll want to get there early.

If you want a quality sit-down meal in a restaurant with a spectacular view of Lake Michigan, check out Soundings, right there inside the aquarium.

1200 S. Lake Shore Dr. ℂ **312/939-2438.** www.sheddaquarium.org. Admission to both Aquarium and Ocean-arium $15 adults, $11 seniors and children 3–11, free for children under 3. Free admission to Aquarium Mon (Sept–Feb only), when Oceanarium admission is $6 adults, $5 children 3–11 and seniors. Oceanarium tickets available on a limited, first-come, first-served basis, so it's recommended you purchase tickets in advance at any Ticketmaster outlet, or call ℂ 312/559-0200. Summer Fri–Wed 9am–6pm, Thurs 9am–9pm; fall–spring Mon–Fri 9am–5pm, Sat–Sun 9am–6pm. Last entry into Oceanarium 4:45pm (5:45pm in summer). Bus: 6, 10, 12, 130, or 146.

The Lakefront ★★★ **All ages.** Chicago was blessed with forefathers with foresight. Thanks to them, the lakefront was declared in 1836 to be public ground "to remain forever open, clear, and free" from construction—that's why you won't find warehouses, docks, and private businesses along our beautiful lakeshore, as you do in many other cities. Instead, join Chicagoans in reveling in 30 miles of sand beaches, green lawns, flower beds, and bicycle paths. More than half of the 2,800 acres of lakefront were created by filling in the lake and building a string of splendid lakeshore parks (from north to south, Lincoln, Grant, Burnham, Jackson, Rainbow, and Calumet). Chicagoans take full advantage of the lakefront to walk, rollerblade, bike, run, swim, picnic, and play volleyball. Most activity takes place around **Oak Street Beach** (just north of the Magnificent Mile) and **North Avenue Beach** (several blocks north of Oak St.). One Chicago mom told me that a favorite activity of her kids is to sit on a bench at the beach and count the dogs as they go by. It's just that simple—kids' entertainment doesn't always have to come at a price.

The Loop Sculpture Tour ★★ **Ages 5 & up.** In the spirit of emphasizing free, flexible, and outdoor activities for kids, I can't fail to note the self-guided tour that lets you navigate through Grant Park and much of the Loop to view some 100 examples of Chicago's monumental public art. With the help of a very comprehensive booklet, *Loop Sculpture Guide* ($3.95 at the gift shop in the Chicago Cultural Center, 78 E. Washington St.), you'll get detailed descriptions of 37 major works, including photographs, plus about 60 other sites located nearby, identified on a foldout map of the Loop. You also can conduct a self-guided tour of the city's public sculpture by following "The Loop Sculpture Tour" map on p. 133.

The single-most-famous sculpture is **Pablo Picasso's** *Untitled,* located in Daley Plaza and constructed out of Cor-Ten steel, the same gracefully rusting material used on the exterior of the Daley Center behind it. Perhaps because it was the button-down Loop's first monumental modern sculpture, its installation

1 Untitled ("The Picasso"), Pablo Picasso (1967)
2 Chicago, Joan Miro (1981)
3 Monument with Standing Beast,
   Jean Dubuffet (1984)
4 Freeform, Richard Hunt (1993)
5 Flight of Daedalus and Icarus,
   120 N. LaSalle St., Roger Brown (1990)
6 Dawn Shadows, Louise Nevelson (1983)
7 Loomings and Knights and Squires,
   Frank Stella
8 Batcolumn, Claes Oldenburg (1977)
9 The Universe, Alexander Calder (1974)
10 Gem of the Lakes, Raymond Kaskey (1990)
11 San Marco II, Ludovico de Luigi (1986)

12 The Town-Ho's Story, Frank Stella (1993)
13 Ruins III, Nita K. Sutherland (1978)
14 Flamingo, Alexander Calder (1974)
15 Lines in Four Directions, Sol Lewitt (1985)
16 The Four Seasons, Marc Chagall (1974)
17 Untitled Sounding Sculpture,
   Harry Bertoia (1975)
18 Alexander Hamilton, Bela Lyon Pratt (1918)
19 Large Interior Form, Henry Moore (1983)
20 Celebration of the 200th Anniversary
   of the Founding of the Republic,
   Isamu Noguchi (1976)
21 The Fountain of the Great Lakes,
   Lorado Taft (1913)

in 1967 was met with hoots and heckles, but today "The Picasso" enjoys semi-official status as the logo of modern Chicago. It is by far the city's most popular photo opportunity among visiting tourists. Kids can view the Picasso from various perspectives and try to decide: Does its mysterious shape look like a woman, a bird, or a dog? At noon on weekdays during warm-weather months, you'll likely find a dance troupe, musical group, or visual-arts exhibition there as part of the city's long-running "Under the Picasso" multicultural program. Call ☎ **312/346-3278** for weekly updates of events.

Museum Campus ✹✹✹ **All ages.** The most beautiful collection of museums in any city in the United States lies southeast of Grant Park on Chicago's glistening lakefront. OK, so I am cheating a little by making "Museum Campus" one single kids' favorite. But the city has connected its great trio of museums on a landscaped 57-acre campus—thus, "Museum Campus"—so that they feel like one destination. Previously, busy Lake Shore Drive cut off the Field Museum of Natural History from the John G. Shedd Aquarium and the Adler Planetarium & Astronomy Museum. Thanks to an ambitious construction project that was the dream of city leaders for a decade, the northbound lanes of Lake Shore Drive were relocated to the west side of the area. With terraced gardens and broad walkways, the reclaimed parkland makes it easier for pedestrians to visit the museums and has provided new space for picnicking, theater, and museum education activities. Transportation improvements include a trolley from parking lots and the Roosevelt Road El and Metra stops.

To get to the Museum Campus from the Loop, head east across Grant Park from Balbo St. and S. Michigan Ave., trekking along the lakeshore route to the Field Museum, the aquarium, and the planetarium. Or, you can make your approach on the path that begins at 11th St. and Michigan Ave. Follow it to the walkway that spans the Metra tracks. Cross Columbus Dr. and then pick up the path that will take you under Lake Shore Dr. and into the Museum Campus. Bus 146 will take you to all 3 of these attractions. Call ☎ **836-7000** (any city or suburban area code) for the stop locations and schedule.

Museum of Science and Industry ✹✹✹ **All ages.** Generations of children recount fond memories of this world-famous museum, the granddaddy of every interactive museum. Good news: The museum is still thrilling kids today. Ask anyone who grew up around Chicago, and they will reminisce about school field trips to the museum, bringing their cans of soda wrapped in tin foil, and seeing their favorite exhibit—the *U-505* ✹✹ and *Coal Mine* ✹ inevitably top the list. The *U-505* is a German submarine that was captured in 1944 and brought to the museum 10 years later. Kids today are still fascinated by the claustrophobic reality of underwater naval life. The full-scale Coal Mine, which dates back to 1934, now incorporates modern mining techniques into the exhibit. Get to these exhibits quickly after the museum opens because they attract amusement-park-length lines during the day.

Visitors arriving by car get their first glimpse of the museum's exhibit, *All Aboard the Silver Streak!*, practically before they exit their vehicle: After a major refurbishing, the museum's Burlington Pioneer Zephyr, the world's first streamlined, diesel-electric, articulated train, was moved indoors and installed in the museum's three-story underground parking garage. A simulated train station has been installed along the 197-foot-long Zephyr, and visitors can explore the train and its on-board interactive exhibits.

At the end of 2002, the museum opened a new permanent exhibit, *The Great Train Story*, which replaces the museum's 60-year-old model railroad exhibit. The new exhibit takes 3,500 square feet and depicts the railroads winding journey between Chicago and Seattle. Kids can drive a Metra Train (our commuter line to the suburbs), open a drawbridge over the Chicago River, harvest timber in the Cascade Range, and boar a tunnel through the Rocky Mountains.

Younger children up to age 10 love to spend time at the **Idea Factory,** a "learning through play" environment that allows kids to explore scientific principles themselves. Another permanent exhibit, *Enterprise,* lets visitors take on the role of CEO for a day as they immerse themselves in the goings-on of a virtual company. *Reusable City* teaches children ecological tips with implements that they might find in their own backyard. *AIDS: The War Within,* is also geared to kids and when it opened a few years ago, it was the first permanent exhibit on the immune system and HIV, the virus that causes AIDS. And, not to be sexist, but girls (myself included) love **Colleen Moore's Fairy Castle,** a lavishly decorated miniature palace filled with priceless treasures. (Yes, those are real diamonds and pearls in the chandeliers.) The Castle is hidden away on the lower level.

A major attraction at the museum is the **Henry Crown Space Center,** where the story of space exploration, still in its infancy, is documented in copious detail, highlighted by a simulated space-shuttle experience through sight and sound at the center's five-story **Omnimax Theater.** But whatever your particular techno-fetish—from submarines to space capsules, from special effects to the mysteries of the human organism—you will find the object of your curiosity somewhere in this amazing museum. There's even a 133-foot United Airlines 727 attached to the balcony.

The Omnimax Theater offers double features on the weekends; call for show times. When you've worked up an appetite, you can visit one of the museum's five restaurants, including a Pizza Hut and an ice cream parlor, and there are also two gift shops. Allow about 3 hours for your visit.

57th St. and Lake Shore Dr. © 800/468-6674 outside the Chicago area, 773/684-1414, or TTY 773/684-3323. www.msichicago.org. Admission to museum only, $7 adults, $6 seniors, $3.50 children 3–11, free for children under 3. Free admission Thurs. Combination museum and Omnimax Theater $13 adults, $11 seniors, $8.50 children 3–11, free for children under 3 on an adult's lap. Omnimax Theater only, evening shows $10 adults, $8 seniors, $6 children, free for children under 3 on an adult's lap; Thurs $7 adults, $6 seniors, $5 children 3–11. Memorial Day to Labor Day daily 9:30am–5:30pm; rest of the year Mon–Fri 9:30am–4pm, Sat–Sun and holidays 9:30am–5:30pm. Closed Dec 25. Bus: 6, 10, 55, 151, or 156.

Navy Pier ⭐ **All ages.** After you've spent a couple of fun-filled hours at the Chicago Children's Museum, check out Navy Pier—Chicago's top tourist attraction, with more than 5 million visitors each year. Built during World War I, Navy Pier has been a ballroom, a training center for Navy pilots during World War II, and a satellite campus of the University of Illinois. In 1995, it underwent yet one more long-anticipated transformation, one that has returned it— at least in spirit—to its original intended purpose, a place for Chicagoans to come to relax and to be entertained.

Developers have resurrected the Grand Ballroom and have installed Crystal Gardens, with 70 full-size palm trees, dancing fountains, and other flora in a glass-enclosed atrium; a white-canopied open-air Skyline Stage that hosts concerts, dance performances, and film screenings; a carousel; and a 15-story Ferris wheel that's a replica of the original that debuted at Chicago's 1893 World's Fair. The 50 acres of pier and lakefront property also are home to a 3D **IMAX theater** (© **312/595-0090**), a small ice-skating rink, and the Chicago Shakespeare Theatre. Naturally, there are a handful of rather bland shops and pushcart vendors (except Barbara's Bookstore), and several restaurants, from a "high-tech" McDonald's replete with laser light shows to an outpost of Lincoln Park's

Museum of Science and Industry

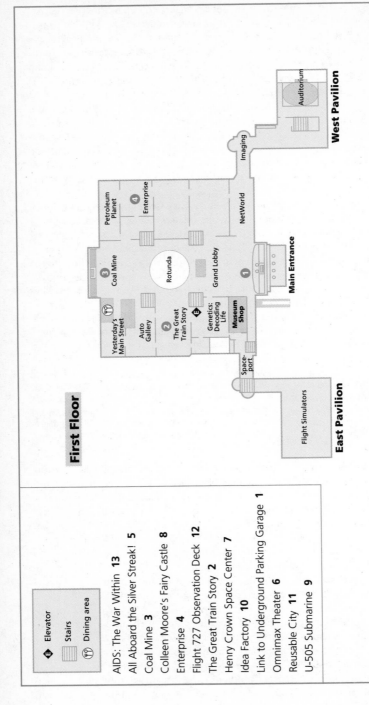

First Floor

Elevator

Stairs

Dining area

AIDS: The War Within **13**

All Aboard the Silver Streak! **5**

Coal Mine **3**

Colleen Moore's Fairy Castle **8**

Enterprise **4**

Flight 727 Observation Deck **12**

The Great Train Story **2**

Henry Crown Space Center **7**

Idea Factory **10**

Link to Underground Parking Garage **1**

Omnimax Theater **6**

Reusable City **11**

U-505 Submarine **9**

West Pavilion

East Pavilion

Main Entrance

Auditorium

Imaging

Petroleum Planet

Enterprise

NetWorld

Coal Mine

Rotunda

Grand Lobby

Yesterday's Main Street

Auto Gallery

The Great Train Story

Genetics: Decoding Life

Museum Shop

Space-port

Flight Simulators

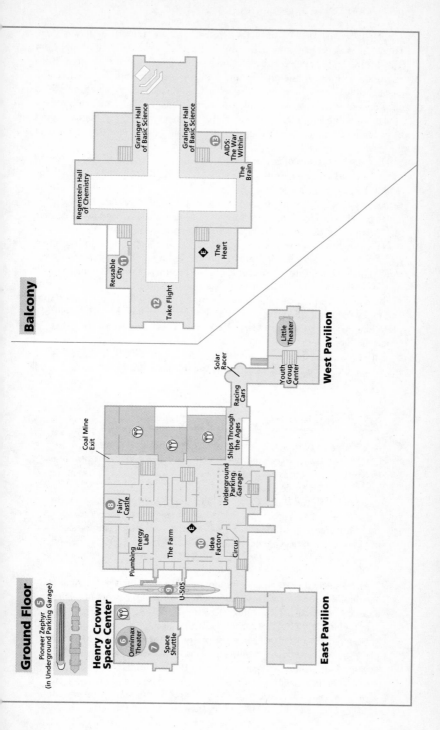

Ground Floor

Pioneer Zephyr 5
(in Underground Parking Garage)

Balcony

Regenstein Hall of Chemistry

Grainger Hall of Basic Science

Grainger Hall of Basic Science

13 AIDS: The War Within

The Brain

11 Reusable City

12 Take Flight

The Heart

Henry Crown Space Center

Coal Mine Exit

8 Fairy Castle

Plumbing

Energy Lab

The Farm

10 Idea Factory

Circus

Ships Through the Ages

Underground Parking Garage

Racing Cars

Solar Racer

U-505

9

6 Omnimax Theater

7 Space Shuttle

Little Theater

Youth Group Center

West Pavilion

East Pavilion

popular Charlie's Ale House to the white-tablecloth seafood restaurant Riva. There is also a beer garden with live music; Joe's Be-Bop Cafe & Jazz Emporium (run by Joe and Wayne Segal of Jazz Showcase fame), a Southern-style BBQ restaurant with live music nightly; and Bubba Gump Shrimp Co. & Market, a casual family seafood joint. Summer is one long party at the pier, with fireworks on Wednesday and Saturday evenings, street performers daily, and, for aspiring Freds and Gingers, "Dancing Under the Stars," a free dance-concert series featuring local orchestras playing a variety of music on Wednesday evenings at the east end of Navy Pier.

The **Smith Museum of Stained Glass Windows** is a remarkable installation of more than 150 stained-glass windows set in illuminated display cases. Occupying an 800-foot-long expanse on the ground floor of Navy Pier, the museum features works by Frank Lloyd Wright, Louis Sullivan, John LaFarge, and Louis Comfort Tiffany, and is divided into four themes: Victorian religious windows, Victorian secular windows, designs of the Prairie School, and contemporary designs.

Navy Pier hosts a variety of conventions and trade shows, including an international art exposition in May, pro-tennis exhibitions, and a flower and garden show. There's something for everyone, but the commercialism of the place might be too much for some people. If that's the case for you, take the half-mile stroll to the end of the pier, east of the ballroom, where you can find a little respite and enjoy the wind, the waves, and the city view, which is the real delight of a place like this. Or unwind in **Olive Park,** a small sylvan haven with a sliver of beach that lies just to the north of Navy Pier.

You'll find, moored along the south dock, more than half a dozen different sailing vessels, including a couple of dinner cruise ships, the pristine white-masted tall

---

C Slumbering at Chicago's Museums

A trend has swept our museums, and that trend is . . . sleeping. Three Chicago museums scheduled sleepovers in 2002, a trend that promises to continue. Whether or not you will actually get any sleep is up in the air, but it's sure to be a memorable experience.

Dozin' with the Dinos at the Field Museum allows kids to roam the halls, take part in workshops and tours, or explore a mummy's tomb by flashlight. With an adult in tow, children ages 6 to 12 can bring a sleeping bag and bed down with the dinos. The event costs $45 per person, including a snack and breakfast. Call *C* **312/665-7400** for reservations for the next sleepover.

The slightly threatening sounding **Sleeping with the Fish** evening at the **Shedd Aquarium** is an annual event that takes place on a Friday in September, usually from 6:30pm to 9am. The event costs $45 per person. Call *C* **312/939-2438** for more information.

Science Snoozeum at the Museum of Science and Industry takes place annually on one evening in November. Science activities are designed for groups of 10 kids, ages 7 to 12. One adult must accompany every 5 children. During the evening, students become detectives and solve a mystery using scientific techniques. Call the Snoozeum Hotline at *C* **773/684-9844**, ext. 2687, for more information and to register.

> **Tips Museum Free Days**
>
> Plan your time in Chicago carefully and you can save yourself admission fees to all of the city's major museums. Admission to special exhibitions and films are often extra on free days.
>
> **Sunday:** DuSable Museum of African-American History, Museum of Science and Industry, Chicago Children's Museum (5–8pm only)
>
> **Monday:** John G. Shedd Aquarium (Sept–Feb; oceanarium admission extra)
>
> **Tuesday:** Adler Planetarium & Astronomy Museum, Art Institute of Chicago, Museum of Contemporary Art, Peggy Notebaert Nature Museum, Terra Museum of American Art
>
> **Wednesday:** The Field Museum of Natural History
>
> **Friday:** Spertus Museum
>
> **Always Free:** Chicago Cultural Center, International Museum of Surgical Science, Jane Addams' Hull-House Museum, Garfield Park Conservatory, Intuit: The Center for Intuitive and Outsider Art, Lincoln Park Conservatory, Lincoln Park Zoo, Martin D'Arcy Gallery of Art, Mexican Fine Arts Center Museum, Museum of Broadcast Communications, Museum of Contemporary Photography, Newberry Library, Oriental Institute Museum, The Smart Museum of Art

ship *Windy*, and the 70-foot speedboats *Seadog I, II,* and *III.* In the summer months, water taxis operated by **Shoreline Sightseeing** (© **312/222-9328**) speed between Navy Pier and other Chicago sights. The River Taxi cruises between Navy Pier and downtown near the Sears Tower, and the Harbor Taxi cruises between Navy Pier and the Shedd Aquarium and the Field Museum. The boats run frequently daily from 10am to 6pm. One-way fare is $6 for adults, $5 for seniors, and $3 for children under 12; round-trip is $10 for adults, $8 for seniors, and $5 for children. An all-day pass is $12 for adults, $10 for seniors, and $6 for children. For more specifics on sightseeing and dinner cruises, see "Lake & River Cruises," later in this chapter.

600 E. Grand Ave. (at Lake Michigan). © **800/595-PIER** (outside 312 area code), or 312/595-PIER. www.navypier.com. Free admission. Summer Sun–Thurs 10am–10pm, Fri–Sat 10am–midnight; fall–spring Mon–Sat 10am–10pm, Sun 10am–7pm. Bus: 29, 56, 65, 66, 120, or 121. Parking rates start at $9.50 for the 1st hr. and go up to $17.50 for up to 8 hrs. However, the lots fill quickly. Valet parking is $7 with a restaurant validation. There are also surface lots west of the pier, and free trolley buses make stops on Grand Ave. and Illinois St. from State St. Subway/El: Red Line to Grand/State; transfer to city bus or board a free pier trolley bus.

3 Best Views

Sweeping views of the city from north to south are one of the main attractions of the many **boat tours** that leave from Navy Pier. Hop aboard and get the lay of the land from a watery vantage point. It's the best way to see how the city sweeps from museum campus in the south, to the Loop, across the Chicago River, and up through the Magnificent Mile, then onto the condo buildings that populate the lakefront moving north to the suburbs. See "Kid-Friendly Tours," later in this chapter for a full listing of boat tour options.

The Hancock Observatory ★★   **All ages.** Kids can play "count the rooftop pools" from the 1,000-foot high observation deck as they look down (way down) on the residential neighborhoods below. For my money, the Hancock Center offers the best views in town. Why? You're located right on the Magnificent Mile, offering a close view of the city from the observatory on the 94th floor. (Most people don't agree with me, however, because over 1.5 million people go up the Sears Tower each year.) While not as famous as the Sears, for many local residents the Hancock remains the archetypal Chicago skyscraper, with its bold, tapered shape and exterior steel cross-bracing design. The building rises to a total height of 1,107 ft. above Michigan Avenue—1,456 ft. if you count its twin 349-ft. antennas. The view from the top of Chicago's third-tallest building is enough to satisfy, but a $2.5 million renovation in 1997 of the 94th floor has added a bunch of new bells and whistles to the experience, including "talking telescopes" with sound effects and narration in four languages, history walls illustrating the growth of the city, and the Skywalk open-air viewing deck—a "screened porch" that allows visitors to feel the rush of the wind at 1,000 ft. Kids can check out the building's infrastructure on computers and locate 80 Chicago attractions on virtual reality television screens.

The Hancock Observatory delivers an excellent panorama of the city and an intimate view over nearby Lake Michigan and the various shoreline residential areas. On a clear day you can see portions of the three states surrounding this corner of Illinois (Michigan, Indiana, and Wisconsin), for a radius of 40 to 50 miles. The view up the North Side is particularly dramatic, stretching from the nearby Oak Street and North Avenue beaches, along the green strip of Lincoln Park, to the line of high rises you can trace up the shoreline until they suddenly halt just below the boundary of the northern suburbs. A high-speed elevator carries passengers to the observatory in 40 seconds, and the entrance and observatory are accessible for people with disabilities.

"Big John," as it's referred to by some locals, also has a sleek restaurant, **The Signature Room at the 95th,** with an adjoining lounge. During the day, plenty of tourists make the place kid-friendly; at night, it's more adult-oriented.

94th floor of the John Hancock Center, 875 N. Michigan Ave. (enter on Delaware St.). © **888/887-9596** or 312/751-3681. Fax 312/751-3675. www.hancock-observatory.com. Admission $9 adults, $7 seniors, $6 children 5–12, free for children under 4 and military personnel in uniform or with active-duty cards. Daily 9am–midnight. Bus: 125, 145, 146, 147, or 151. Subway/El: Red Line to Chicago/State.

Navy Pier   All ages. Because Navy Pier juts 3,000 feet into Lake Michigan, the view from the end of the pier looking toward the city is fabulous—the next best thing to seeing the Chicago skyline by boat. And, if you like heights, hop aboard the Ferris wheel and get a 15-story-high vantage point. Go early in the morning to see the sun rise, the rays gleaming off the glass Mies Van Der Rohe buildings lining Lake Shore Drive. Surrounded by Lake Michigan, lush gardens, and

---

Tips Walker's Warning

While Chicago is a great city to explore on foot, I must warn people against trying to cross Lake Shore Drive on foot. People have been seriously injured and even killed attempting to dodge the traffic on the Drive. Look for the pedestrian underpasses at Chicago Avenue, Oak Street, and North Avenue, among other locations.

Fun Fact Did You Know?

The "Sky Chapel" atop the Chicago Temple skyscraper at 77 W. Washington St. (at Clark St.) is listed in the *Guinness Book of World Records* as the loftiest house of worship on earth. The tiny chapel, which belongs to the city's oldest congregation, the First United Methodist Church of Chicago, is located some 400 ft. above street level. (Guinness apparently didn't bother to query any Tibetan monks.) Tours of the chapel are given daily at 2pm and on Sundays after the 8:30am and 11am church services. For information, call ℂ **312/236-4548.**

---

sculpture, the view from the Navy Pier is one of the best in the city. See p. 135 for more details about the other attractions at Navy Pier.

600 E. Grand Ave. (at Lake Michigan). ℂ **800/595-PIER** (outside 312 area code), or 312/595-PIER. www. navypier.com.

North Avenue Beach   All ages. One of the most famous views of Chicago (and one that you'll find in many guidebooks as a featured photo) is taken on the lakefront bike path, looking south to the John Hancock Center. To get a photo of your family in this picture-perfect scene, walk north on Lake Shore Drive to the tunnel at North Avenue that leads under Lake Shore Drive to North Avenue Beach. Once on the lakefront path, turn south toward the city, and you will have your photo opportunity. (Just watch out for cyclists, skaters, runners, and dog walkers if it's a nice summer day!) See "Enjoying the 'Third Coast': Chicago's Beaches," in chapter 8 for more information.

Lake Shore Dr. at North Ave. ℂ 312/742-PLAY for Chicago Park District and beach information.

Sears Tower Skydeck ⭐ *Overrated* **All ages.** When you stand on a perch this high and view the trains, river traffic, and expressways streaming with cars, you can teach your kids the meaning of the term "transportation hub." Sears Tower is one of Chicago's most popular attractions. Since its debut in 1973, the Sears Tower's lock on the crown of "world's tallest building" has been a source of civic pride for the city. Sadly, the building's namesake, Sears, sold the building and moved to cheaper suburban offices in 1992. Another blow to morale came when Petronas Towers in Kuala Lumpur, Malaysia, went up and laid claim to the title of world's tallest buildings. The Sears Tower has since put up a 22-foot antenna in an attempt to win back the title. Tallest-building posturing aside, this is still a great place to orient your family to the city.

The view from the 103rd-floor Skydeck is everything you'd expect it to be— once you get there. Unfortunately, you're usually stuck in a very long, very noisy line, so by the time you make it to the top, your patience could be as thin as the atmosphere up there. One suggestion: I once went up the tower at night on a weeknight, a couple of hours before closing (it stays open until 11pm). We had the observation deck practically to ourselves. On a clear day, visibility extends up to 50 miles, and you can catch glimpses of the surrounding states. The 70-second high-speed elevator trip will feel like a thrill ride for some, but it's a nightmare for anyone with even mild claustrophobia. Recent upgrades to the Skydeck include multimedia exhibits on Chicago history and *Knee High Chicago,* an exhibit for kids.

> **Moments   Photo Op**
>
> For a great photo op, walk on Randolph Street toward the lake in the morning. That's when the sun, rising in the east over the lake, hits the string of high-rises that line South Michigan Avenue—giving you the perfect backdrop for an only-in-Chicago picture.

233 S. Wacker Dr. (enter on Jackson Blvd.). © 312/875-9696. Admission $9.50 adults, $7.75 seniors, $6.75 children 3–12, free for children under 3 and military with active-duty ID. Daily 9am–11pm. Subway/El: Brown, Purple, or Orange lines to Quincy, or Red or Blue lines to Jackson; then walk a few blocks west. Bus: 1, 7, 126, 146, 151, or 156.

4 More Chicago Museums

Chicago has plenty of museums that make every effort to turn a bored child into a stimulated one. Many of the city's museums are leaders in the "please touch me" school of interactive exhibitions, with buttons and lights and levers and sounds and bright colors, and activities for kids at special exhibitions.

Art Institute of Chicago ★★★   **All ages.** Chicago's pride and joy is a warm, welcoming museum—one that's never too stuffy to embrace kids. You know this is a museum with a winning sense of whimsy when at the holidays, the famous lion sculptures that guard its entrance sport Santa hats.

The Art Institute goes the extra mile to help kids get through a few hours here without boredom. The Kraft Education Center on the lower level features interactive exhibits for children and has a list of "gallery games" that encourage kids to "seek and find" to make visiting the museum more fun. Special exhibitions are designed for kids with accompanying hands-on programs. Kids might be taught by a visiting children's book illustrator, for example, and then learn how to make their own books. A highlight tour for kids runs on Saturday. The center is open during regular museum hours and family programs are free with museum admission.

In other parts of the museum, kids will be entranced by the **Thorne Miniature Rooms,** filled with tiny reproductions of furnished interiors from European and American history (heaven for a dollhouse fanatic). Another popular attraction is the original **Trading Room of the old Chicago Stock Exchange,** salvaged when the Adler and Sullivan Stock Exchange building was demolished in 1972. One parent says her boys love the great hall of European arms and armor dating from the 15th to 19th centuries. Composed of more than 1,500 objects, including armor, horse equipment, swords, daggers, polearms, and maces, it's one of the most important assemblages of its kind in the country. (If you do head down here, don't miss Marc Chagall's stunning stained-glass windows at the end of the gallery.)

If you have older kids, you'll find an array of works to satiate any interest: Japanese *ukiyo-e* prints, ancient Egyptian bronzes and Greek vases, 19th-century British photography, masterpieces by most of the greatest names in 20th-century sculpture, or modern American textiles. No matter how many times you visit, there are always new works to be seen and special shows that draw in even more crowds.

For those with limited time, you'll want to head straight to the museum's renowned collection of Impressionist art (including one of the world's largest collections of Monet paintings), one of the more highly trafficked areas of the museum. Among the treasures here you'll find Seurat's pointillist masterpiece *Sunday Afternoon on the Island of La Grande Jatte.* Your second must-see area is the galleries of European and American contemporary art, ranging from paintings, sculptures, and mixed-media works from Pablo Picasso, Henri Matisse, and Salvador Dalí through Willem de Kooning, Jackson Pollock, and Andy Warhol. Visitors are sometimes surprised when they discover many of the icons that hang here. (Grant Wood's *American Gothic* and Edward Hopper's *Nighthawks* are two that bring double-takes from many visitors.) If you want to steer clear of the crowds, you'll find more breathing room in the galleries of Indian, Himalayan, and Southeast Asian art. Other recommended exhibits are the collection of delicate mid-19th-century glass paperweights in the museum's famous Arthur Rubloff collection. The museum also has a cafeteria and an elegant full-service restaurant, a picturesque courtyard cafe with a jazz quintet on Tuesday evenings in the summer, and a large shop. There is a busy schedule of lectures, films, and other special presentations, as well as guided tours, to enhance your viewing of the art. The museum also has a research library, and the School of the Art Institute offers exhibits and—until construction of its successor in the North Loop is finished—a film center.

111 S. Michigan Ave. (at Adams St.). © **312/443-3600.** www.artic.edu. Suggested admission $10 adults; $5 seniors, children, and students with ID. Additional cost for special exhibitions. Free admission Tues. Mon, Wed–Fri, and holidays 10:30am–4:30pm; Tues 10:30am–8pm; Sat–Sun 10am–5pm. Closed Thanksgiving and Dec 25. Subway/El: Green, Brown, Purple, or Orange lines to Adams, or Red Line to Monroe or Jackson. Bus: 3, 4, 60, 145, 147, or 151.

Chicago Cultural Center ★ *Finds*   **Ages 3 & up.** Free family programs are the main attraction of this landmark building, built in 1897 as the city's public library, and transformed into a showplace for visual and performing arts in 1991. Its basic beaux arts exterior conceals a sumptuous interior of rare marble, fine hardwood, stained glass, polished brass, and mosaics of Favrile glass, colored stone, and mother-of-pearl inlaid in white marble. The crowning centerpiece is Preston Bradley Hall's majestic Tiffany dome, said to be the largest of its kind in the world.

The building also houses one of the Chicago Office of Tourism's visitor centers, which makes it a good place to kick-start your visit, and the highly enjoyable **Museum of Broadcast Communications** (p. 154). If you stop in to pick up tourist information and take a quick look around, your visit won't take longer than half an hour. But the Cultural Center also hosts an array of art exhibitions, concerts, films, lectures, and other special events (many free), which might convince you to extend your time here. Programs might include African

---

⟨Tips⟩ Touring the Art Institute

Keeping track of your kids in the crowds that flood the Art Institute during its peak days might reduce your enjoyment of your favorite masterpieces.

Your best bet is to avoid the craziest times: Many people don't realize the museum is open on Mondays, so the galleries are relatively subdued. Wednesdays are a close second. Tuesdays tend to draw the masses because the Art Institute is free and open late (until 8pm). Try to arrive when the doors open in the morning or else during the lunchtime lull. Another tip: If the Michigan Avenue entrance is crowded, head around to the entrance on the Columbus Drive side, which is usually less congested and is more convenient to the Grant Park underground parking garage. There's a small gift shop near the Columbus Drive entrance, too, if the main shop is too bustling.

drumming, a recital by a mezzo-soprano from the Lyric Opera, or readings by Chicago playwrights. A long-standing tradition is the 12:15pm Dame Myra Hess Memorial classical concert every Wednesday in the Preston Bradley Hall. Other ongoing programs include a monthly cultural festival—which highlights a different city or country over a weekend with art, theater, and film.

Guided architectural tours of the Cultural Center are offered Tuesday to Saturday at 1:15pm. For information, call ℂ 312/744-8032.

78 E. Washington St. ℂ **312/744-6630**, or 312/FINE-ART for weekly events. Fax 312/744-2089. www.ci.chi.il.us/Tour/CulturalCenter. Free admission. Mon–Wed 10am–7pm; Thurs 10am–9pm; Fri 10am–6pm; Sat 10am–5pm; Sun 11am–5pm. Closed holidays. Subway/El: Brown, Green, Orange, or Purple lines to Randolph, or Red Line to Washington/State. Bus: 3, 4, 20, 56, 60, 127, 131, 145, 146, 147, 151, or 157.

Chicago Historical Society ⭐ **Ages 3 & up.** Located at the southwestern tip of Lincoln Park, the Historical Society is one of Chicago's oldest cultural institutions (founded in 1856), but one that has successfully brought its exhibits into the 21st century. Inside the Historical Society's lovely red-brick and glass-walled building, you'll find a fascinating display of objects, artifacts, artworks, and other items in galleries that are both beautifully executed and easy to navigate. (It's also just a Frisbee toss from North Avenue Beach, the best beach in the city, and across the street from the Gold Coast's most elite addresses.) Kids can climb aboard the 160-year-old Pioneer, Chicago's first locomotive, and visit the Hands-On Gallery, where they can step into an early fur trader's cabin. An Illinois Pioneer Life gallery features daily craft demonstrations.

Casual visitors can get a good overview of the highlights in about an hour; history buffs will need more time. The must-see permanent exhibit is *A House Divided: America in the Age of Lincoln,* which explores the institution of slavery in America and the devastation of the Civil War. (Items on display include the bed that Lincoln died in and an original copy of the 13th amendment abolishing slavery, signed by Honest Abe himself.) Another highlight is the CHS's costume collection, which includes suits worn by George Washington and John Adams, articles of clothing belonging to Abraham and Mary Todd Lincoln, and, of more current vintage, one of Michael Jordan's uniforms and numerous gowns by contemporary fashion designers. Other worthy stops are the Charles F. Murphy architectural study center, featuring one of the nation's largest collections of architectural working drawings; the decorative and industrial-arts collection, including stained-glass designs by Frank Lloyd Wright and Louis Sullivan; and *We the People,* a permanent exhibit on the founding of the United States. (Objects on display include an original copy of the *Ephrata Cloister Hymnal,* a memento of a little-known early communal religious group in colonial Pennsylvania, and the "Boweles' New Pocket Map" from 1784, which depicts Mount Desert Island and Penobscot Bay along the coast of Maine in reverse order.)

The Historical Society also sponsors lectures, symposia, and seminars; film screenings; family programs; historical reenactments and performances by local theater companies; and music concerts on the beautiful plaza overlooking Lincoln Park. On the ground floor of the museum, past the gift shop, is Big Shoulders Cafe, entered through a flora- and fauna-decorated terra-cotta arch removed from the old Stockyard Bank and reassembled here. The museum's website is worth checking out before your visit, especially the impressive online "exhibit" on the Great Chicago Fire.

1601 N. Clark St. (at North Ave.). ℂ **312/642-4600.** www.chicagohistory.org. Admission $5 adults, $3 seniors and students, $1 children 6–12, free for children under 6. Free admission on Mon. Mon–Sat 9:30am–4:30pm; Sun noon–5pm. Research center Tues–Sat 10am–4:30pm. Bus: 11, 22, 36, 72, 151, or 156.

Chicago Public Library/Harold Washington Library Center   **Ages 2 & up.** The Harold Washington Library Center is named in memory of Chicago's first and only African-American mayor, who died of a heart attack in 1987 at the beginning of his second term in office. The largest public library in the world, this massive red-brick neoclassical edifice—occupying an entire city block at State Street and Congress Parkway—announced the city's revitalization of State Street in a big way in 1991. There's a stunning 52-foot glass-domed winter garden on the top floor. On the second floor is another treasure: the vast **Thomas Hughes Children's Library,** housing more than 100,000 volumes. The library offers an interesting array of events and art exhibitions worth checking out. A 385-seat auditorium is the setting for a unique mix of dance and music performances, author talks, and children's programs, including "Playtime on the Prairie," featuring librarians reading stories about life in old Illinois; puppet shows; and visits from book characters are frequent. (Recently, kids could meet "Angelina Ballerina" and make crowns with her.) The library also has a cafe adjacent to the ninth-floor winter garden, and a coffeehouse and used bookstore on the ground floor.

400 S. State St. ℂ 312/747-4300. www.chipublib.org. Free admission. Mon 9am–7pm; Tues and Thurs 11am–7pm; Wed and Fri–Sat 9am–5pm; Sun 1–5pm. Closed holidays. Subway/El: Red Line to Jackson/State, or Brown Line to Van Buren/Library. Bus: 2, 6, 11, 29, 36, 62, 145, 146, 147, or 151.

DuSable Museum of African-American History   **Ages 5 & up.** The DuSable Museum is a repository of the history, art, and artifacts pertaining to the African-American experience and culture. Named for Chicago's first permanent settler, Jean Baptiste Point du Sable, a French-Canadian of Haitian descent, it is admirable not so much for its collections and exhibits as for the inspiring story behind its existence. Founded in 1961 with a $10 charter and minimal capital, the museum began in the home of Dr. Margaret Burroughs, an art teacher at the city's Du Sable High School. In 1973, as a result of a community-based campaign, the museum took up residence in its present building (a former parks administration facility and police lockup) on the eastern edge of Washington Park. With no major endowment to speak of, the DuSable Museum has managed to accumulate a respectable collection of more than 13,000 artifacts, books, photographs, art objects, and memorabilia. Its collection of paintings, drawings, and sculpture by African-American and African artists is excellent.

Still, this remains a work in progress to some degree. The exhibits that the museum offers are very worthwhile, but, unfortunately, the bulk of the collection dates only from the WPA period in the late 1930s and the black arts movement of the 1960s, with only sketchy exhibits tracing the earlier stages of the African-American experience in this country. In 1993, the DuSable Museum added a 25,000-square-foot wing named in honor of the city's first and only African-American mayor, Harold Washington. The permanent exhibit on

---

Moments Summer Solstice

If you're here in mid-June, don't miss the Museum of Contemporary Art's annual **Summer Solstice** celebration (ℂ 312/280-2660), a 24-hour festival of contemporary art and music. It's a mind-blowing mix of cutting-edge entertainment and family-focused fun (with plenty of hands-on activities for kids). The event is free, and it takes place every June 21.

Washington contains memorabilia and personal effects, and surveys important episodes in his political career. More recent is a permanent exhibit called ***Blacks in Aviation,*** which celebrates the achievements of the legendary Tuskegee Airmen and features such items as the flight jacket of Major Robert H. Lawrence, the nation's first African-American astronaut.

Youth programming and workshops are scheduled year-round, including jazz and blues series and children's film series. The Arts and Craft Festival is held in mid-July; call or visit the website for details.

740 E. 56th Place. ℂ **773/947-0600**, TDD 773/947-7203. www.dusablemuseum.org. Admission $3 adults, $2 students and seniors, $1 children 6–12, free for children under 6. Free admission Sun. Daily 10am–5pm. Closed Easter, Thanksgiving, Dec 25, and Jan 1. Subway/El: Red Line to 55th or 63rd in Washington Park. Bus: 3, 4, or 55.

ECHO ⭐⭐ **Ages 8 & up.** The centerpiece of Symphony Center's ambitious music education program is ECHO, an interactive hands-on learning space that lets children explore the world of music through themes relevant to their daily lives. ("ECHO" draws its name from letters in its official title, the Eloise W. Martin Center of the Chicago Symphony Orchestra.) Part of ECHO is dedicated to music labs for groups that book them in advance for teaching sessions led by resident artists. But visitors can drop by anytime to use the **A-Musing Room,** which teaches participants different music concepts—such as timing, pitch, and rhythm—while they create and record their own piece of music. The method is a novel one: You're handed an "instrument box" upon entering the room, which you then connect to a computer terminal in five different activity stations resembling giant London telephone booths. A colorful touch screen and interactive software guide you through a variety of activities. Afterward, you plug the box into ECHO's **Orchestra Wall,** which plays back your finished composition, and those of other visitors, as part of a group piece. To avoid running into school-group spillover from the Music Labs, it's best to phone first to check availability.

67 E. Adams St. ℂ **312/294-3000**. www.chicagosymphony.org. Admission $5.50 adults, $2.50 students 8–17 and seniors. Tues–Sat 10am–5pm; Sun 11am–5pm. Subway/El: Red Line to Adams/State. Bus: 29, 36, 146, or 151.

Museum of Contemporary Art **Ages 5 & up.** The MCA is the largest contemporary art museum in the country, emphasizing experimentation in a variety of media—painting, sculpture, photography, video and film, dance, music, and performance. To be honest, some of the works are challenging enough for adults, much less kids, but kids might get into some of the recent touring shows, which have included Roy Lichtenstein, Cindy Sherman, and Chuck Close.

Sitting on a front-row piece of property between the lake and the historic Water Tower, the classically styled building, clad in aluminum panels, is a subdued, almost-somber presence, and the steep rise of stairs leading to the entrance is monumental yet a bit daunting. But don't let the gloomy exterior get you down; the interior spaces are more vibrant, with a sun-drenched two-story central corridor, elliptical staircases, and three floors of exhibition space.

You can see the MCA's highlights in about an hour, although art lovers will want more time to wander (especially if a high-profile exhibit is in town). Your first stop should be the handsome barrel-vaulted galleries on the top floor, dedicated to pieces from the permanent collection. For visitors who'd like a little guidance for making sense of the rather challenging works found at a contemporary art museum, there is a free daily tour, as well as an audio tour for rent. In addition to a range of special activities and educational programming, including films, performances, and a lecture series in a 300-seat theater, the museum features Puck's at the MCA, a cafe operated by Wolfgang Puck of Spago restaurant fame, with seating that overlooks a 1-acre terraced sculpture garden. There's also a store, Culturecounter, with one-of-a-kind gift items, that's worth a stop even if you don't make it into the museum.

220 E. Chicago Ave. (1 block east of Michigan Ave.). © 312/280-2660. Fax 312/397-4095. www.mcachicago.org. Admission $8 adults, $5 seniors and students with ID, free for children under 12. Free admission on Tues. Wed–Sun 10am–5pm; Tues 10am–8pm. Subway/El: Red Line to Chicago/State. Bus: 3, 10, 11, 66, 125, 145, 146, or 151.

Museum of Contemporary Photography   **Ages 8 & up.** Columbia College's photography museum sometimes has shows that kids find appealing (a recent show featured fairy-tale based photography aimed at pre-teens)—so call or check out the website for current shows. Ensconced in a ground-floor space at the college, a progressive arts- and media-oriented institution that boasts the country's largest undergraduate film department and a highly respected photojournalism-slanted photography department, the Museum of Contemporary Photography is the only museum in the Midwest of its ilk. As the name indicates, it exhibits, collects, and promotes modern photography, with a special focus on American works from 1959 to present. Rotating exhibitions showcase images by both nationally recognized and "undiscovered" regional artists. Related lectures and special programs are scheduled during the year.

600 S. Michigan Ave. © 312/663-5554. Fax 312/344-8067. www.mocp.org. Free admission. Mon–Wed and Fri 10am–5pm; Thurs 10am–8pm; Sat noon–5pm. Subway/El: Red Line to Harrison. Bus: 6, 146, or 151.

Newberry Library   **Ages 16 & up.** The Newberry Library is a bibliophile's dream. Established in 1887 at the bequest of the Chicago merchant and financier Walter Loomis Newberry, the noncirculating research library today contains many rare books and manuscripts (such as Shakespeare's first folio and Jefferson's copy of *The Federalist Papers*). While most of the library is off-limits to kids under 16, the library does hold children's story hours throughout the year. It also houses a vast depository of published resources for those who are seriously delving into American and European history and literature, as well as other aspects of the humanities from the late Middle Ages onward. The library is also a major destination for genealogists digging at their roots, and—thanks to a recent $20 million philanthropic campaign—its holdings are now open for the use of the public free (over the age of 16 with a photo ID). The collections, many items of which are displayed during an ongoing series of public exhibitions, include more than 1.5 million volumes and 75,000 maps, housed in a comely five-story granite building, designed in the Spanish-Romanesque style by Henry Ives Cobb and built in 1893. The library also operates a fine bookstore. One popular annual event that older kids might enjoy is the "Bughouse Square" debates. Held across the street in Washington Square Park, the debates re-create the fiery soapbox orations of the left-wing agitators in the 1930s and 1940s. Chicago favorite son Studs Terkel, the Pulitzer Prize–winning oral historian, often emcees the hullabaloo.

60 W. Walton St. (at Dearborn Pkwy.). © 312/943-9090 or 312/255-3700 for programs. www.newberry.org. Reading room Tues–Thurs 10am–6pm; Fri–Sat 9am–5pm. Gallery Mon and Fri–Sat 8:15am–5:30pm; Tues–Thurs 8:15am–7:30pm. Bookstore Tues–Thurs 10am–6pm; Fri–Sat 9am–5pm. Free 1-hr. tours Thurs at 3pm and Sat at 10:30am. Validated parking available at Clark and Chestnut sts. Subway/El: Red Line to Chicago/State. Bus: 22, 36, 125, 145, 146, 147, or 151.

Oriental Institute Museum ★ *Finds*   **Ages 5 & up.** Don't skip this museum because the name sounds intimidating: Kids love its Egyptian artifacts (including toys and clothes from ancient Egyptian children). Located near the midpoint of the University of Chicago campus, just north of the Memorial Chapel, the Oriental Institute houses one of the world's major collections of Near Eastern art, dating from 9000 B.C. to the 10th century A.D. Founded in 1931, the institute is beginning to see the fruits of a $10 million renovation and expansion that closed the museum to the public for 3 years. Installing a climate-control system and adding a storage wing were the main objectives, but the renovation has given the curators a rare opportunity to totally redesign the museum's five galleries.

The first to reopen was the Egyptian Gallery, which debuted in 1999. It is endlessly fascinating, showcasing the finest objects among the 35,000 artifacts from the Nile Valley held by the museum. At the center of the new gallery stands a monumental 17-foot solid-quartzite **statue of King Tutankhamen,** the boy king who ruled Egypt from about 1335 to 1324 B.C. The largest Egyptian sculpture in the Western Hemisphere (tipping the scales at 6 tons), it was excavated by the Oriental Institute in 1930. The surrounding exhibits, which document the life and beliefs of Egyptians from 5000 B.C. to the 8th century A.D., have replaced the esoteric design of the old displays with a wonderfully accessible approach that emphasizes themes, not chronology. Among them: mummification (there are 14 mummies on display—5 people and 9 animals, including hawks, an ibis, a shrew, and a baby crocodile), kingship, society, writing (including a deed for the sale of a house, a copy of the *Book of the Dead,* and a schoolboy's homework), family, art, tools and technology, occupations, popular religion, medicine, the gods, food, games, clothing, and jewelry. The new climate-control system also makes it possible to exhibit many fragile objects never before on display, such as papyrus documents and a child's linen tunic from 1550 B.C.

The museum's Persian Gallery opened last fall. The Oriental Institute houses the nation's premier archaeological collection of artifacts from civilizations that once flourished in what is now Iran. The gallery displays approximately 1,000 objects dating from the Archaic Susiana period (ca. 6800 B.C.) to the Islamic period (ca. A.D. 1000), including early forms of seals, glazed ceramics from the early Islamic period, and sculptures from the ruins of Persepolis, which thrived from approximately 520 B.C. until Alexander the Great and his troops destroyed it in 331 B.C.

Currently, only the Egyptian and Persian galleries are open. The Mesopotamian Gallery, featuring a re-creation of a royal courtyard of Assyrian King Sargon II, opens in September 2003. New galleries filled with artifacts from Sumer, ancient Palestine, Israel, Anatolia and Nubia will be opened over the next year or two.

The gift shop at the Oriental Institute, called the Suq, is also terrific and remains open during construction.

1155 E. 58th St. (at University Ave.). **(℃ 773/702-9514** for information, 773/702-9507 for special tours. www.oi.uchicago.edu. Free admission. Tues and Thurs–Sat 10am–4pm; Wed 10am–7pm; Sun noon–4pm. Bus: 6.

The Smart Museum of Art 🛝 **Ages 5 & up.** The Smart Museum of Art is named for David and Alfred Smart, two of the founders of *Esquire* magazine, whose family foundation created the University of Chicago's fine arts museum. Like the Oriental Institute Museum, the Smart Museum also has recently undergone a $2 million renovation to install a climate-control system, improve lighting, add storage space, and reconfigure its exhibition galleries. Unlike the Oriental Institute, it is a relatively contemporary addition to the university's campus, built in 1974 and designed with big concrete blocks. Inside, though, the Smart is only partially modern.

Its permanent collection of more than 7,500 works spans Western and Eastern civilizations and ranges from classical antiquity to the present day. Though modest in scope, the museum's paintings, sculptures, and objets d'art include some bona fide treasures, including ancient Greek vases, Chinese bronzes, and Old Master paintings; Frank Lloyd Wright furniture; Tiffany glass; sculptures by Degas, Matisse, and Rodin; and 20th-century paintings and sculptures by Mark Rothko, Arthur Dove, Mexican muralist Diego Rivera, Henry Moore, and Chicago sculptor Richard Hunt. The museum is reaching out to families through Art Wednesdays, when families can try a hands-on art activity, and Art Sundays, designed for families to explore techniques related to current exhibits. Both are available for a small fee. In the museum's outdoor sculpture garden, families can picnic on the lawn. The museum also has a gift shop, a cafe, and an adjacent sculpture garden where you can enjoy an alfresco nibble, if you so desire.

5550 S. Greenwood Ave. (at E. 55th St.). ✆ 773/702-0200. www.smartmuseum.uchicago.edu. Free admission; donations welcome. Tues–Wed and Fri 10am–4pm; Thurs 10am–9pm; Sat–Sun noon–6pm. Closed holidays. Bus: 6 or 55.

Spertus Museum   **Ages 5 & up.** The Spertus Museum, an extension of the Spertus Institute of Jewish Studies, showcases intricately crafted and historic Jewish ceremonial objects, textiles, coins, paintings, and sculpture, tracing 5,000 years of Jewish heritage. Kids enjoy the Artifact Center, with 12 authentic archaeological dig sites and tools that let future archaeologists discover replicas of artifacts (such as pottery) under the sand. Though small in scale, the **Zell Holocaust Memorial** exhibit is particularly moving, featuring a video montage of Holocaust victims with a Chicago connection and a display of related artifacts and documents. Lunchtime lectures are open to the public, as is the institute's Asher Library, which boasts one of the largest collections of Jewish books, periodicals, videos, and music in the country. The Bariff Shop for Judaica carries a large selection of art, books, music, videos, and contemporary and traditional Jewish ceremonial gifts.

618 S. Michigan Ave. ✆ 312/322-1747. www.spertus.edu. Admission $5 adults; $3 seniors, students, and children; $10 maximum family rate. Free admission Fri. Sun–Wed 10am–5pm; Thurs 10am–8pm; Fri 10am–3pm. Validated parking in nearby lots. Subway/El: Red Line to Harrison, or Brown, Purple, Orange, or Green lines to Adams. Bus: 3, 4, 6, 145, 147, or 151.

Terra Museum of American Art ★ *Finds* **Ages 5 & up.** Sandwiched between high-rises on North Michigan Avenue, in the heart of the city's most prestigious retail district, the Terra's narrow rectangular building is passed without so much as a glance by droves of shoppers making a beeline for Crate & Barrel or Water Tower Place. But this unique art repository is well worth a visit.

The core of the Terra's holdings was originally the private collection of Daniel Terra, a wealthy industrialist and rainmaker for Ronald Reagan who founded his eponymous museum in north-suburban Evanston in 1980. Moved to the present location in 1987, its excellent collection has grown to include some 600 pieces of American art from the late 18th century to the present. (Another 200 works reside at the Terra's sister museum, Musée d'Art Américain, in Giverny, France.) Many of the paintings and prints, and a limited number of sculptures, on display are by American artists whose names will assuredly draw a blank—but that's part of the Terra's appeal. The other part is coming across works by household names such as Mary Cassatt, Winslow Homer, Andrew Wyeth, John

For Train Lovers

Chicago and trains go together like, well, kids and trains. From little red streetcars to thundering steam trains, two area museums are the place to ride the rails—and maybe even learn a bit about history.

At the **Fox River Trolley Museum** in west suburban South Elgin, hop a trolley to ride a real electric railway that first opened on July 4, 1896. The 3-mile ride takes you along the banks of the scenic Fox River. The Aurora, Elgin and Fox River Electric Co. Interurban Line once connected communities along the Fox River, including Carpentersville, Elgin, Aurora, and Yorkville. The railway was abandoned to passenger traffic in 1935, and in 1972, the museum purchased part of the line. At the museum, you can check out antique trolleys from 1891 to 1952. The museum's most popular annual event is the Pumpkin Trolley, run on 2 weekends in October. Ride the trolley to the museum's pumpkin patch, pick your own, and head back to the museum for a picnic lunch and a visit to the museum store.

The museum is located at 361 South LaFox Street (Illinois Rte. 31) in South Elgin, about 40 miles west of Chicago. Fares are $2.50 for adults, $2 for senior citizens, and $1.50 for children 2 to 11. The museum is open Mother's Day through Nov. 4 on Sunday from 11am to 5pm, and June 30 to September 1 on Saturday from 11am to 5pm. To get there, take I-90 or U.S. Rte. 20 west to Elgin, and exit on Illinois Rte. 31 south-bound. To make it an all-train day, take the Metra commuter train to Elgin on the Milwaukee District West Line. Then take Pace bus 801 to State Street, South Elgin, and walk 3 blocks south to the museum (or take a taxi from the Elgin train station).

America's largest railway museum is the **Illinois Railway Museum,** located in Union, about 60 miles northwest of Chicago. With 120 acres

Singer Sargent, James McNeill Whistler, and Edward Hopper. The museum is particularly known for its outstanding American Impressionism collection.

Families should make a point of visiting on the first Sunday of each month, when a free family day, held from 1 to 3pm, combines gallery tours and activities with a hands-on art project. Call 𝒞 312/654-2255 for reservations.

664 N. Michigan Ave. (near Erie St.). 𝒞 **312/664-3939.** Fax 312/664-2052. www.terramuseum.org. Admission $7 adults; $3.50 seniors, students, educators; free for children under 12 and veterans with valid ID. Free admission on Tues and first Sun of each month. Tues 10am–8pm; Wed–Sat 10am–6pm; Sun noon–5pm. Subway/El: Red Line to Grand/State or Chicago/State. Bus: 3, 11, 125, 145, 146, 147, or 151.

SMALL BUT NOTEWORTHY MUSEUMS

Chicago has a slew of smaller museums devoted to all manner of subjects. Many of their collections preserve the stories and heritage of a particular immigrant group that has become inseparable from the history of the city as a whole.

American Police Center & Museum **Ages 8 & up.** Carrying a mandate to help prevent crime by fostering better civilian understanding of law enforcement, the museum displays police equipment and memorabilia. It was opened in 1974, not too many years after Chicago's cops went berserk with blackjacks and tear gas during the city's infamous political protest rallies and race riots of and 400 engines and cars, sprawling rail lines criss-cross the property. (Be sure to look both ways before crossing any tracks!). The museum has a 5-mile rail line, where you'll find steam, diesel, and heavy electric trains chugging along, and a mile-long streetcar loop. On the weekend, you can jump on a steam or diesel train from the museum's East Union depot (built around a station dating from 1851) and take a 40-minute round-trip ride to Kishwaukee Grove, passing prairie and farmland. Whether you get on a steam locomotive with its hissing brakes and billowing steam, diesels dating from the 1950s, or an Electroliner, which ran between Chicago and Milwaukee until 1963 and is powered by overhead wires, you're in for a thrill. Smaller trains depart from the 50th Avenue rapid transit station built in 1910 and removed from Cicero.

A streetcar line encircles the museum grounds so you can hop on and off at different "barns" that house everything from red cabooses to luxurious private passenger cars from the late 1800s. Call ℂ **800/BIG-RAIL** or 815/923-4000 in advance to find out which trains are operating. Diesels operate most weekends and holidays, but steam trains only run about 12 times a season. Electric cars run daily.

The museum is open from April through October. Grounds are open from 9am to 6pm, and trains run on weekends from 10:30am to 5pm, and weekdays from 10 am to 4pm. Rides cost $6 to $10 (depending on the trains running) for adults, and $4 to $8 for children, with family maximums of $20 to $40. To get there, take I-90 to U.S. Rte. 20. Take the Marengo exit and drive northwest on Rte. 20 to Union Road. Go north on Union Road.

the late 1960s. In general, the museum packs more punch as a humorous contrivance, with displays of badges from various police departments and some mannequins that make the department-store variety look positively Madame Tussaud. But it has added a new exhibit on the history of women in law enforcement that's worth a look, and its shrine to Chicago police officers killed in the line of duty is certainly nothing to laugh about.

1717 S. State St. (at 17th St.). ℂ **312/431-0005.** Admission $4 adults, $3 seniors, $2.50 children 3–11, free for children under 3. Tours require reservations and a minimum of 20 people. Mon–Fri 9:30am–4:30pm. Bus: 29, 44, 62, or 164.

Balzekas Museum of Lithuanian Culture   All ages. The Balzekas Museum of Lithuanian Culture gives insight into the history and ancient culture of the tiny Baltic state that was absorbed into the former Soviet Union and achieved independence in August 1991. The museum is located on the Far Southwest Side, home to the largest Lithuanian community outside Lithuania. The collection contains a range of objects, including books, artwork, photographs, arms and armor, maps, and decorative ornaments. In early December, the museum offers a class for making Christmas ornaments; using plastic straws, kids make

Lithuanian-style ornaments. A few weeks before Easter, the museum runs classes in Easter egg decorating, also open to kids. Cost for a 1½-hour class is $12.

6500 S. Pulaski Rd. (at 65th St.). (✆) **773/582-6500**. Admission $4 adults, $3 students and seniors, $1 children. Daily 10am–4pm. Subway/El: Orange Line to Pulaski, transfer to bus 53A south.

City Gallery   All ages. Along with the pumping station across the street, the Chicago Water Tower is one of only a handful of buildings to survive the Great Chicago Fire of 1871. It has long been a revered symbol of the city's resilience and fortitude, although today—more than 130 years after it first rose to a once-mighty height of 154 feet—the Water Tower is dwarfed by the high-rise shopping centers and hotels of North Michigan Avenue. The Gothic-style limestone building now has been reinvented as an art gallery. While this may be a welcome and inventive use of the structure, it's actually an idea that first cropped up in 1948 but was never acted upon. The spiffed-up interior is intimate and sunny, and it's a refreshing pit stop of culture on your way to the Water Tower shopping center or pumping-station tourist information center across the street. Recent exhibits have included works by Chicago-based photographer Victor Skrebneski.

806 N. Michigan Ave. (between Chicago Ave. and Pearson St.). (✆) **312/742-0808**. Free admission. Mon–Sat 10am–6:30pm; Sun 10am–5pm. Bus: 3, 11, 145, 146, 147, or 151.

International Museum of Surgical Science *(Finds)*   **Ages 12 & up.** This museum is not for the faint of stomach. (Although I lived three doors down from this museum for 7 years, I was afraid to set foot inside—maybe it was the real skeletons they put in the windows every Halloween that scared me off?) Run by the International College of Surgeons, the museum is housed in a historic 1917 Gold Coast mansion designed by the noted architect Howard Van Doren Shaw, who modeled it after Le Petit Trianon at Versailles. Displayed throughout its four floors are surgical instruments, paintings, and sculpture depicting the history of surgery and healing practices in Eastern and Western civilizations. You'll look at your doctor in a whole new way after viewing the trepanned skulls excavated from an ancient tomb in Peru. The accompanying trepanning tools were used to bore holes in patients' skulls, a horrific practice thought to release the evil spirits causing their illness. (Some skulls show signs of new bone growth, meaning that some lucky headache-sufferers actually survived this low-tech surgery.) There are also battlefield amputation kits, a working iron-lung machine in the polio exhibit, and oddities such as a stethoscope designed to be transported inside a top hat. Other attractions include an apothecary shop and dentist's office (ca. 1900), re-created in a historic street exhibit, and the hyperbolically christened "Hall of Immortals," a sculpture gallery depicting 12 historic figures in medicine, from Hippocrates to Madame Curie.

1524 N. Lake Shore Dr. (between Burton Place and North Ave.). (✆) **312/642-6502**. www.imss.org. Suggested donation $5 adults, $3 seniors and students. Tues–Sat 10am–4pm. Bus: 151.

Intuit: The Center for Intuitive and Outsider Art   Ages 3 & up. Chicago is home to an active community of collectors of so-called outsider art, a term attached to a group of unknown, unconventional artists who do their own artwork without any formal training or connection to the mainstream art world. Often called folk or self-taught artists, their work is highly personal and idiosyncratic, and they work in a range of media, from bottle caps to immense canvases. Intuit was founded in 1991 to bring attention to these artists through exhibitions and educational lectures. Housed in the warehouse district northwest of the

Loop, with two galleries and a performance area, Intuit is slowly gaining a higher profile on the city's art scene. The museum offers a regular lecture series, and if you time your visit right, you might be here for one of the center's tours of a private local art collection. Guided tours of the museum are available at 1pm on the first Saturday of every month. Intuit doesn't offer special programs for kids, but events like quilt sales featuring quilts of the African-American improvised tradition, or graffiti art, should satisfy them.

756 N. Milwaukee Ave. (at Chicago and Ogden aves.). ℭ 312/243-9088. www.outsider.art.org. Free admission. Wed–Sat noon–5pm. Subway/El: Blue Line to Chicago. Bus: 56 or 66.

Jane Addams' Hull-House Museum   Ages 8 & up.
In 1889, a young woman named Jane Addams bought an old mansion on Halsted Street that had been built in 1856 as a "country home" but was now surrounded by the shanties of the immigrant poor. Here Addams and her co-worker, Ellen Gates Starr, launched the American settlement-house movement with the establishment of Hull House, an institution that endured on this site in Chicago until 1963. (It continues today as a decentralized social-service agency known as Hull House Association.) Orphans found a home here, and immigrants received health care, job training, and English lessons. In 1963, all but two of the settlement's 13 buildings, along with the entire residential neighborhood in its immediate vicinity, were demolished to make room for the new University of Illinois at Chicago campus, which now owns the museum buildings. The story of the opposition to this project is eloquently told in the words of the participants themselves, who appear among the scores of others interviewed by Studs Terkel for his book *Division Street: America.* Of the original settlement, what remains today is the Hull-House Museum, the mansion itself, and the residents' dining hall, snuggled among the ultramodern, poured-concrete buildings of the university campus. Inside are the original furnishings, Jane Addams's office, and numerous settlement maps and photographs. Rotating exhibits re-create the history of the settlement and the work of its residents, showing how Addams was able to help transform the dismal streets around her into stable inner-city environments worth fighting over.

University of Illinois at Chicago, 800 S. Halsted St. (at Polk St.). ℭ 312/413-5353. www.uic.edu/jaddams/hull/hull_house. Free admission. Mon–Fri 10am–4pm; Sun noon–5pm. Subway/El: Blue Line to Halsted/University of Illinois. Bus: 8.

Martin D'Arcy Gallery of Art   Ages 5 & up.
A treasure trove of medieval, Renaissance, and baroque art, the Martin D'Arcy Gallery of Art covers the years A.D. 1100 to 1700. All the rich symbolism of Catholicism through the baroque era is embodied in such works as a gem-encrusted silver and ebony sculpture of Christ's scourging, a head of John the Baptist on a silver platter, golden chalices, rosary beads carved with biblical scenes, and many other highly ornamented ritual objects.

Loyola University, 6525 N. Sheridan Rd. ℭ 773/508-2679. Free admission. Tues–Sat noon–4pm. Closed May–Aug. Subway/El: Red Line to Loyola. Bus: 151.

Mexican Fine Arts Center Museum ✦ All ages.
Chicago's vibrant Pilsen neighborhood, just southwest of the Loop, is home to one of the nation's largest Mexican-American communities. Ethnic pride emanates from every doorstep, *taqueria,* and bakery, and the multitude of colorful murals splashed across building exteriors and alleyways. But the neighborhood's most prized possession could be this vivacious cultural institution, the largest of its kind in the country

and the only Latino museum accredited by the American Association of Museums. That's quite an accomplishment, given that the Mexican Fine Arts Center Museum was founded in 1987 by a passel of public schoolteachers who pooled $900 to get it started.

The museum is very family-oriented, offering a deluge of educational workshops for kids and parents. This is truly a living museum. There are wonderful exhibits to be sure, showcasing Mexican and Mexican-American visual and performing artists, and often drawing on the museum's permanent collection of more than 2,400 works. But it's the visiting artists, festival programming, and community participation where the museum really shines. Its Day of the Dead celebration, which runs for about 8 weeks beginning in September, is one of the most ambitious in the country. The Del Corazon Mexican Performing Arts Festival, held in the spring, features programs by local and international artists here and around town. And the Sor Juana Festival, presented in the fall, honors Mexican writer and pioneering feminist Sor Juana Ines de la Cruz with photography and painting exhibits, music and theater performances, and poetry readings by Latino women.

The museum also has a splendid gift shop, and it stages a holiday market, featuring gift items from Mexico, on the first weekend in December.

1852 W. 19th St. (a few blocks west of Ashland Ave.). © 312/738-1503. www.mfacmchicago.org. Free admission. Tues–Sun 10am–5pm. Subway/El: Blue Line to 18th St. Bus: 9.

Museum of Broadcast Communications ★ **Ages 3 & up.** Housed in the basement of the Chicago Cultural Center, the Museum of Broadcast Communications claims to be one of only two broadcast-oriented museums in the nation. Though relatively small, at just over 15,000 square feet, this is a very fun, nostalgia-soaked destination—easily accommodated during a visit to the Cultural Center. Those among you who fondly recall the golden days of radio will be especially thrilled to explore the Radio Hall of Fame, which the museum assumed control of from the Emerson Radio Corporation in 1991. It features exhibits of Jack Benny's vault (where the lovable penny-pincher claimed to hoard his wealth), Edgar Bergen's Charlie McCarthy, and a replica of Fibber McGee's closet, complete with original crash sound effects used on the show.

The museum's most popular attraction, though, is the **Kraft Television Center,** operated in conjunction with local television superstation WGN-TV. Here, you and your kids can live out your Tom Brokaw and Katie Couric fantasies, reading news from a video prompter as you "anchor" your own newscast. (Souvenir tapes of your performance are available for purchase.) The museum's massive archives—12,000 TV shows, 50,000 hours of radio programming, 9,000 TV commercials, and 3,000 newscasts—are all accessible to the public. A $2 user fee is charged for the A.C. Nielsen Research Center, which features 26 screening suites where visitors can watch or listen to selected programs. In spring 2004, the museum will move to new quarters in River North at State and Kedzie streets, doubling its space to 30,000 square feet.

78 E. Washington St. (at Michigan Ave.). © 312/629-6000. www.mbcnet.org. Free admission. Mon–Sat 10am–4:30pm; Sun noon–5pm. Subway/El: Red Line to Washington/State, or Brown, Green, Orange, or Purple lines to Randolph. Bus: 3, 4, 60, 145, 147, or 151.

National Vietnam Veterans Art Museum *Finds* **Ages 12 & up.** Junior high kids and older can emerge with a better understanding of the war and the lives touched by this experience. This museum houses one of the most stirring art collections anywhere—and the only one of its kind in the world—telling the story of the men who fought in Vietnam. Since the war, many of the veterans made art as personal therapy, never expecting to show it to anyone, but in 1981, a small group of them began showing their works together in Chicago and in touring exhibitions. The collection has grown to more than 700 paintings, drawings, photographs, and sculptures from all over the country and other countries, including Vietnam. Titles such as *We Regret to Inform You, Blood Spots on a Rice Paddy,* and *The Wound* should give you an idea of the power of the images in this unique legacy to the war. Housed in a former warehouse in the Prairie Avenue district south of the Loop, the museum is modern and well organized. A new installation that's suspended from the ceiling, **Above & Beyond** ⭐, comprises more than 58,000 dog tags with the names of the men and women who died in the war—the emotional effect is similar to that of the Wall in Washington, D.C. The complex also houses a small theater, a cafe open for breakfast and lunch, a gift shop, and an outdoor plaza with a flagpole that has deliberately been left leaning because that's how veterans saw them in combat.

1801 S. Indiana Ave. (at 18th St.). ℭ **312/326-0270.** www.nvvam.org. Admission $5 adults, $4 seniors and students with ID. Tues–Fri 11am–6pm; Sat 10am–5pm; Sun noon–5pm. Closed major holidays. Bus: 3 or 4.

Peace Museum **Ages 8 & up.** Perhaps you might want to visit here after spending a couple of hours at the National Vietnam Veterans Art Museum. Founded in 1981 by an artist-activist and a U.S. ambassador to UNICEF, the museum presents four exhibits a year and keeps on permanent display such 20th-century artifacts as manuscripts by Joan Baez, Civil Rights–era photos, and a John Lennon guitar. Here's a little trivia for you: The rock group U2 named one of its albums, *The Unforgettable Fire,* for an exhibition of drawings by survivors of Hiroshima and Nagasaki that Bono and the boys viewed at this museum.

314 W. Institute Place (at Orleans St.). ℭ **312/440-1860.** www.peacemuseum.org. Admission $3.50 adults; $2 seniors, students, and children. Tues–Sat 11am–5pm. Subway/El: Brown Line to Chicago. Bus: 11, 22, or 65.

Polish Museum of America **Ages 6 & up.** This year, the museum celebrates the 65th anniversary of its opening, making it the oldest (and still the largest) ethnic museum in the country. Located in the heart of the first Polish neighborhood in Chicago, this museum has one of the most important collections of Polish art and historical materials outside Poland. The museum's programs include rotating exhibitions, films, lectures, and concerts, and a new permanent exhibit about Pope John Paul II. Parents should request a "seek and find" booklet with questions for kids (and get a free Polish Museum pen, too).

984 N. Milwaukee Ave. (at Augusta Blvd.). ℭ **773/384-3352.** PGSAmerican@aol.com. Suggested donation $2 adults, $1 children. Daily 11am–4pm. Subway/El: Blue Line to Division.

State Street Bridge Gallery **All ages.** Not so much a museum as a novel gesture on the part of Chicago's cultural-affairs and transportation departments, the newly installed State Street Bridge Gallery is located in what has to be the strangest venue for art in the city: the State Street bridge house along the Chicago River. The gallery space shares the building with bridge-raising equipment, including 15-foot gearing and a 3½-million-pound counterweight. The idea for an art gallery came about because Chicago's famous movable bridges are now operated by computer systems, rendering bridge-house attendants obsolete. If you're there at the right moment—such as late spring to early summer, when tall-masted sailboats wend their way to Lake Michigan from river harbors farther inland—you might be able to watch the counterweight drop away as the bridge is lifted (an interesting vantage point, to say the least, of one of Chicago's many trunnion bascule bridges, which work somewhat like a giant seesaw). It's anyone's guess what's coming up, so call for an update.

Riverwalk at State St. and Lower Wacker Dr. ✆ 312/744-6630. Free admission. Open May–Oct Mon–Sat 10am–7pm, Sun 10am–5pm. Subway/El: Red or Brown lines to State/Lake. Bus: 22, 36, or 44.

Swedish-American Museum Center ⋆ **Ages 4 & up.** Chicago parents recommend a visit to this storefront museum, which chronicles the Swedish immigrant contribution to American life. The museum is a hub of activity with cultural lectures, concerts, and classes and folk dancing geared to Swedish Americans, some of whom still live in the surrounding Andersonville neighborhood. A new **Children's Museum of Immigration** recently opened on the third floor, where Swedish craft demonstrations and classes, as well as language classes, are offered. Geared toward kindergarteners through sixth graders, the museum lets kids experience the journey from the old world. They can step inside an authentic Swedish farmhouse, board a steamship for America and begin a new life in a log cabin. A modern-day refugee's raft connects children to today's immigration story.

The permanent exhibits on display draw on a small collection of art and artifacts dating to the mass immigration of Swedes to Chicago 2 centuries ago. Temporary exhibitions (usually Swedish folk art) are mounted four times a year. There's also a nice gift shop that offers Orrefors glassware; books on Swedish folk art, decorating, and cooking; children's toys; and holiday knickknacks. Strolling down this stretch of Clark Street, where Swedish bakeries and gourmet food stores are interspersed with an attractive mix of restaurants, bars, cafes, and theater companies, is the best reason for stopping in here.

5211 N. Clark St. (near Foster Ave.). ✆ 773/728-8111. www.museum@samac.org. Suggested donation $4 adults, $2 seniors and students, $1 children. Tues–Fri 10am–4pm; Sat–Sun 10am–3pm. Subway/El: Red Line to Bryn Mawr, then walk several blocks west to Clark. Bus: 22.

Ukrainian National Museum **All ages.** The Ukrainian National Museum possesses an unmistakably old-world atmosphere; few cultures seem to have changed as little over the ages as that of the Ukrainians. Throughout the museum you will find decorative Easter eggs, fine embroidery, woodcarvings, artwork, crafts, and folk costumes, all of which reflect an incredible continuity in technique over the years. The museum is ideally located for a walk around the neighborhood known as Ukrainian Village, where there are also a couple of beautiful churches and a small retail strip of ethnic businesses.

721 N. Oakley Blvd. (near Chicago Ave.). ✆ 312/421-8020. Suggested donation $2 adults, $1 students. Mon–Wed by appointment; Thurs–Sun 11am–4pm. Bus: 66.

5 Best Rides

The best ride in the city is the "El," with boat tours of the river and lake a close second (see "Kid-Friendly Tours," later in this chapter). Other rides are tucked away in Chicago's top attractions: Don't miss the endangered species merry-go-round at Lincoln Park Zoo and the Ferris wheel and carousel at Navy Pier. Not enough excitement for you? Thrill seekers should head directly to an amusement park.

Six Flags Great America **All ages.** One of the Midwest's biggest theme/amusement parks is located midway between Chicago and Milwaukee on

(C) The (Frank Lloyd) Wright Stuff

Oak Park has the highest concentration of houses or buildings any-where designed and built by Wright, probably the most influential fig-ure in American architectural history. People come here to marvel at the work of a man who saw his life as a twofold mission: to wage a sin-gle-handed battle against the ornamental excesses of architecture, Vic-torian in particular, and to create in its place a new form that would be at the same time functional, appropriate to its natural setting, and stimulating to the imagination.

Not everyone who comes to Oak Park shares Wright's architectural philosophy. But scholars and enthusiasts admire Wright for being con-sistently true to his own vision, out of which emerged a unique and genuinely American architectural statement. The reason for Wright's success could stem from the fact that he himself was a living exemplar of a quintessential American type. In a deep sense, he embodied the ideal of the self-made and self-sufficient individual who had survived, even thrived, in the frontier society—qualities that he expressed in his almost-puritanical insistence that each spatial or structural form in his buildings serve some useful purpose. But he was also an aesthete in Emersonian fashion, deriving his idea of beauty from natural environ-ments, where apparent simplicity often belies a subtle complexity.

The three principal ingredients of a tour of Wright-designed struc-tures in Oak Park are the **Frank Lloyd Wright Home & Studio tour,** the **Unity Temple tour,** and a **walking tour**—guided or self-guided—to view the exteriors of homes throughout the neighborhood that were built by the architect. Oak Park has, in all, 25 homes and buildings by Wright, constructed between the years 1892 and 1913, which consti-tute the core output of his Prairie School period. Visiting another 50 dwellings of architectural interest by Wright's contemporaries, scat-tered throughout this community and neighboring River Forest, is also worthwhile.

I-94 in Gurnee, Illinois. The park has more than 100 rides and attractions and is a favorite of roller-coaster devotees. There are a whopping 10 of them here, including the **Raging Bull,** which makes Robert DeNiro's scowling portrayal of pugilist Jake LaMotta in the film of the same name look cherubic by compari-son. Touted as the world's first "hyper twister" coaster, it begins with a 200-foot plunge at 73 mph down a nearly straight drop into an underground cavern, and features six steep, high-speed turns banked as much as 50 degrees. If that's not enough to dislodge your internal organs or jettison that nacho dip you scarfed 5 minutes earlier, hop aboard the **Giant Drop,** a 227-foot tower from which rid-ers fall back to the ground at 60 mph, or **Shock Wave,** said to be one of the world's fastest and tallest steel-loop roller coasters. Six Flags also has shows, restaurants, and theme areas.

I-94 at Rte. 132 East., Gurnee. (C) **847/249-4636.** www.sixflags.com. Admission (including unlimited rides, shows, and attractions) $39.99 adults, $19.99 seniors and children over 2 and under 48 in. tall, free for chil-dren 2 and under. Open seasonally Apr–Oct 10am–8 or 10pm daily. Parking $8. Take I-94 or I-294 West to Rte. 132 (Grand Ave.). Approximate driving time from Chicago city limits is 45 min.

⸢*Tips*⸣ **The Wright Plus Tour**

Die-hard fans of the architect will want to plan to be in town the third Saturday in May for the annual Wright Plus Tour, during which the public can tour several Frank Lloyd Wright–designed homes and several other notable Oak Park buildings, in both the Prairie School and the Victorian styles, in addition to Wright's home and studio and the Unity Temple. The tour includes 10 buildings in all. Tickets go on sale March 1 and can sell out within 6 weeks. Call ℰ **708/848-1976** for details and ticket information.

6 Historic Houses

An extensive tour of the neighborhood surrounding the Frank Lloyd Wright Home and Studio leaves from the **Ginkgo Tree Bookshop,** 951 Chicago Ave., on weekends from 10:30am to 4pm. This tour lasts 1 hour and costs $9 for adults and $7 for seniors and children 7 to 18, and is free for children under 7. If you can't make it to Oak Park on the weekend, you can follow a self-guided map and audiocassette tour of the historic district (recorded in English, French, Spanish, German, Japanese, and Italian). Available at the Ginkgo Tree Bookshop from 10am to 3:30pm, the self-guided tour costs $9 for adults and $7 for seniors and children. In addition to Wright's work, you will see that of several of his disciples, as well as some very charming examples of the Victorian styling that he so disdained. A more detailed map selling for $4 at the bookshop, "Architectural Guide Map of Oak Park and River Forest," includes text and photos of all 80 sites of interest in Oak Park and neighboring River Forest.

The Frank Lloyd Wright Home & Studio ★★★ **Ages 3 & up.** For the first 20 years of Wright's career, this remarkable complex served first and foremost as the sanctuary from which Wright was to design and execute more than 130 of an extraordinary output of 430 completed buildings. The home began as a simple shingled cottage that Wright built for his bride in 1889 at the age of 22, but it became a work in progress, as Wright remodeled it constantly until 1911 (he left there in 1909). During this highly fertile period, the house was Wright's showcase and laboratory, but it also embraces many idiosyncratic features molded to his own needs rather than those of a client. With many add-ons—including a barrel-vaulted children's playroom and a studio with an octagonal balcony suspended by chains—the place has a certain whimsy that others might have found less livable. This, however, was not an architect's masterpiece, but the master's home, and every room in it can be savored for the view it reflects of the workings of a remarkable mind. The Home and Studio Foundation has restored the residence and studio to its 1909 vintage.

The special guided Youth Architectural Tours present the home through the eyes of the six Wright children who grew up here. (One of those children later invented Lincoln Logs.) Tours, which are for kids age 6 to 14, are led the fourth Saturday of the month, except during December, when the tours take place on a couple of weekdays instead. (Dates change, so call ahead.) Admission is $3.

951 Chicago Ave. ℰ **708/848-1976.** www.wrightplus.org. Admission $9 adults, $7 seniors and children 7–18, free for children under 7. Combined admission for Home & Studio tour and guided or self-guided historic district tour (see below) $15 adults, $11 seniors and children 7–18. Admission to home and studio is by guided tour only; tours depart from the Ginkgo Tree Bookshop Mon–Fri 11am, 1pm, and 3pm; Sat–Sun every 15 min. 11am–3:30pm. Facilities for people with disabilities are limited; please call in advance.

Oak Park Attractions

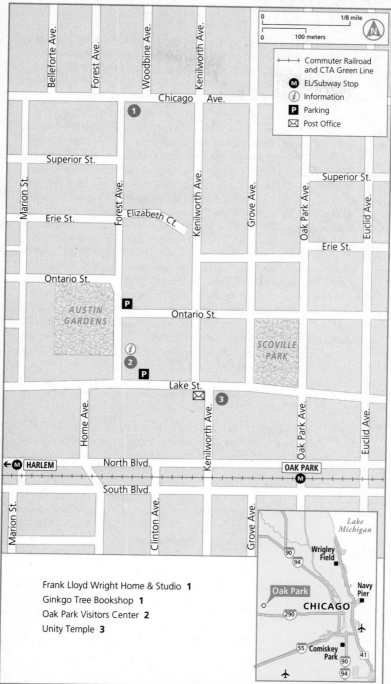

Frank Lloyd Wright Home & Studio **1**
Ginkgo Tree Bookshop **1**
Oak Park Visitors Center **2**
Unity Temple **3**

(*Finds* **More Frank Lloyd Wright Homes**

In addition to Robie House, several of Wright's earlier works, still privately owned, dot the streets of Hyde Park, such as the **Heller House**, 5132 S. Woodlawn Ave. (1897); the **Blossom House**, 1332 E. 49th St. (1882); and the **McArthur House**, 4852 S. Kenwood Ave. (1892).

Robie House ★★ **Ages 7 & up.** One of Frank Lloyd Wright's finest works, the Robie House is considered among the masterpieces of 20th-century American architecture. The open layout, linear geometry of form, and craftsmanship are typical of Wright's Prairie School design. Completed in 1909 for inventor Frederick Robie, a bicycle and motorcycle manufacturer, the home is also notable for its exquisite leaded- and stained-glass doors and windows. It's also among the last of his Prairie School–style homes: During its construction, Wright abandoned both his family and his Oak Park practice to follow other pursuits, most prominently the realization of his Taliesin home and studio in Spring Green, Wisconsin. Docents from Oak Park's Frank Lloyd Wright Home and Studio Foundation, which recently took over management from the University of Chicago and has embarked on a 10-year, $4 million restoration, now give visitors access to areas of the Robie House once occupied by university offices, adding views of the first-level playroom and billiard room to the long-standing tours of the second-level living/dining room. Another new addition is a Wright specialty bookshop in the building's former three-car garage—which was highly unusual for the time in which it was built. Although I've noted that this is for ages 7 and up, older children and teens will appreciate Robie House most.

5757 S. Woodlawn Ave. (at 58th St.). © **773/834-1847.** Admission $9 adults, $7 seniors and children 7–18. Mon–Fri tours at 11am, 1pm, and 3pm; Sat–Sun every ½ hr. 11am–3:30pm. Bookshop open daily 10am–5pm. Bus: 55.

Unity Temple ★ **Ages 5 & up.** After fire destroyed its church around 1900, a Unitarian Universalist congregation asked one of its members, Frank Lloyd Wright, to design an affordable replacement. Using poured concrete with metal reinforcements—a necessity, owing to the small budget of $40,000 allocated for the project—Wright created a building that on the outside seems as forbidding as a mausoleum but that on the inside contains in its detailing the entire architectural alphabet of the Prairie School that has since made Wright's name immortal. Following the example of H. H. Richardson (Glessner House), Wright placed the building's main entrance on the side, behind an enclosure—a feature often employed in his houses as well—to create a sense of privacy and intimacy. Front entrances were too anonymous for these two architects. Wright complained, furthermore, that other architectural conventions of the church idiom, such as the nave in the Gothic-style cathedral across from the future site of Unity Temple, were overpowering. Of that particular church, he commented that he didn't feel a part of it.

Yet his own vision in this regard was somewhat confused and contradictory. He wanted Unity Temple to be "democratic." But perhaps Wright was unable to subdue his own personal hubris and hauteur in the creative process, for the ultimate effect of his chapel, and much of the building's interior, is very grand and imperial. Unity Temple is no simple meetinghouse in the tradition of Calvinist iconoclasm. Instead, its principal chapel looks like the chamber of the Roman

The Pride of Prairie Avenue

Prairie Avenue, south of the Loop, was the city's first "Gold Coast," and its most famous address is **Glessner House**, a must-see for anyone interested in architectural history. The only surviving Chicago building designed by Boston architect Henry Hobson Richardson, it represented a dramatic shift from traditional Victorian architecture when it was built in 1886 (and inspired a young Frank Lloyd Wright).

The imposing granite exterior gives the home a forbidding air. (Railway magnate George Pullman, who lived nearby, complained, "I do not know what I have ever done to have that thing staring me in the face every time I go out my door.") But step inside, and the home turns out to be a welcoming, cozy retreat, filled with Arts and Crafts furniture and decorative arts.

Visits to Glessner House are by guided tour only. Tours are given Wednesday to Sunday at 1, 2, and 3pm year-round (except major holidays). Tours are first-come, first-served, with no advance reservations except for groups of 10 or more. 1800 S. Prairie Ave. © **312/326-1480.** www.glessnerhouse.org. $7 adults, $6 students and seniors, $4 children 5 to 12. Bus: 1, 3, or 4 from Michigan Ave. at Jackson Blvd. (Get off at 18th St.)

Senate. Even so, the interior, with its unpredictable geometric arrangements and its decor reminiscent of Native American art, is no less beautiful.

Wright used color sparingly within Unity Temple, but the pale, natural effects that he achieved are owed in part to his decision to add pigment to the plaster rather than use paint. Wright's use of wood for trim and other decorative touches is still exciting to behold; his sensitivity to grain and tone and placement was akin to that of an exceptionally gifted woodworker. Wright was a true hands-on, can-do person; he knew the materials he chose to use as intimately as the artisans who carried out his plans. And his stunning, almost-minimalist use of form is what still sets him apart as a relevant and brilliant artist. Other details to which the docent guide will call your attention, as you complete a circuit of the temple, are the great fireplace, the pulpit, the skylights, and the clerestory (gallery) windows. Suffice it to say, Unity Temple—only one of Wright's masterpieces—is counted among the 10 greatest American architectural achievements. For small kids, a brief peek into the temple on a walk around the neighborhood (after touring the Frank Lloyd Wright Home & Studio, for example) is best; teens will appreciate the architecture more.

875 Lake St. © **708/383-8873.** Self-guided tours $4 adults; $3 seniors, children, and students with ID. 45-min. guided tours $6 adults; $4 seniors, children, and students with ID. Guided tours Sat–Sun on the hour 1–3pm. Summer daily 10am–5pm; fall–spring Mon–Fri noon–4pm, Sat–Sun 10am–5pm. Church events can alter the schedule; call in advance.

7 Zoos

Brookfield Zoo ✮✮✮   **All ages.** Brookfield is the Chicago area's largest zoo. In contrast to the rather efficient Lincoln Park Zoo, Brookfield is spacious and spreads out over 216 acres with 2,700 animal residents—camels, dolphins, giraffes, baboons, wolves, tigers, green sea turtles, Siberian tigers, snow leopards, and more—living in naturalistic environments that put them side by side with other inhabitants of their regions. These creative indoor and outdoor settings—filled with activities to keep kids interested—are what set Brookfield apart. One of the newest exhibits, *The Living Coast,* explores the western coast of Chile and Peru and includes everything from a tank of plate-size moon jellies to a rocky shore where Humboldt penguins swim and nest as Inca terns and gray gulls fly freely overhead. Other impressive exhibits include *The Swamp,* which re-creates the bioregions of a southern cypress swamp and an Illinois river scene and discusses what people can do to protect wetlands, and *Habitat Africa!,* a multiple ecosystem exhibit-in-progress that eventually will encompass 30 acres—about the size of the entire Lincoln Park Zoo. The thrills here aren't always high concept: Some of my favorite exhibits are the Australia House, where fruit bats flit around your head, and Tropic World, where you wander at tree-top level with monkeys. The dolphins at the **Seven Seas Panorama** put on an amazing show that has been a Brookfield Zoo fixture for years. If you go on a weekend, buy tickets to the dolphin show at least a couple of hours before the one you plan to attend because they tend to sell out quickly.

First Ave. and 31st St., Brookfield. ℭ 708/485-0263. www.brookfieldzoo.org. Regular admission $7 adults, $3.50 seniors and children 3–11, free for children under 3. Free admission Tues and Thurs Oct–Mar. Summer daily 9:30am–5:30pm; fall–spring daily 10am–4:30pm. Take the Stevenson (I-55) and Eisenhower (I-290) expressways 14 miles west of the Loop. Parking $4. Bus: 304 or 311.

Lincoln Park Pritzker Children's Zoo & Farm-in-the-Zoo ★ (Value) **All ages.** The Children's Zoo is a delight for children and adults alike. Kids have the opportunity to touch many of the animals, which are handled by zoo keepers. Hedgehogs, rabbits, and iguanas are common residents. There's also a very popular glass-walled animal nursery, where zoo docents and keepers care for the babies of more exotic species—often, this means gorillas and chimpanzees—who are ill, born weak, or rejected by their mothers. The Children's Zoo also features a relatively new annex called **Conservation Station,** with interactive exhibits and workshop activities focusing on wildlife and environmental preservation. The adjacent outdoor portion of the Children's Zoo, which has patiently awaited a sorely needed renovation while the zoo focuses on more major rebuilding projects, has owls, otters, and other small critters in winding habitats sculpted from concrete.

At the Farm-in-the-Zoo, kids will discover a working reproduction of a Midwestern farm, complete with a white-picket-fenced barnyard, chicken coops, and stalls filled with livestock, including cows, sheep, and pigs. Even the aroma is authentic.

2200 N. Cannon Dr. ℭ 312/742-2000. Free admission. Daily 9am–4:30pm. Bus: 151 or 156.

Lincoln Park Zoo ★★★ (Value) **All ages.** The term "zoological gardens" truly fits here: Lincoln Park Zoo occupies a scant 35 acres, and its landmark Georgian Revival brick buildings and modern structures sit among gently rolling pathways, verdant lawns, and a kaleidoscopic profusion of flower gardens. A tour of the various habitats takes all of 2 or 3 hours—a convenience factor even more enticing when you consider that the nation's oldest zoo (it was founded in 1868) stays open 365 days a year and is one of the last free zoos in the country. Lincoln Park Zoo has held a special place in the hearts of Chicagoans since the days of Bushman, the mighty lowland gorilla who captivated the world in the 1930s and 1940s, and now suffers the ignominious fate of a stuffed exhibit at the Field

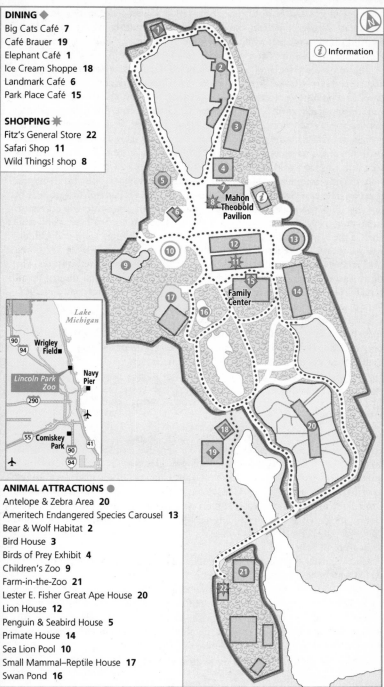

Lincoln Park Zoo

(i) Information

DINING ◆
Big Cats Café **7**
Café Brauer **19**
Elephant Café **1**
Ice Cream Shoppe **18**
Landmark Café **6**
Park Place Café **15**

SHOPPING ☀
Fitz's General Store **22**
Safari Shop **11**
Wild Things! shop **8**

Mahon
Theobold
Pavilion

Family
Center

Lake
Michigan

90
94
Wrigley
Field■

Navy
Pier■

Lincoln Park
Zoo

290

55 Comiskey
Park
90
41
94

ANIMAL ATTRACTIONS ●
Antelope & Zebra Area **20**
Ameritech Endangered Species Carousel **13**
Bear & Wolf Habitat **2**
Bird House **3**
Birds of Prey Exhibit **4**
Children's Zoo **9**
Farm-in-the-Zoo **21**
Lester E. Fisher Great Ape House **20**
Lion House **12**
Penguin & Seabird House **5**
Primate House **14**
Sea Lion Pool **10**
Small Mammal–Reptile House **17**
Swan Pond **16**

Museum of Natural History. The late Marlon Perkins, legendary host of the *Mutual of Omaha's Wild Kingdom* TV series, got his start here as the zoo's director, and filmed a pioneering TV show called *Zoo Parade* (*Wild Kingdom's* predecessor) in the basement of the old Reptile House.

The zoo has a population of approximately 1,200 mammals, birds, reptiles, and amphibians—from the highly endangered Siberian tiger to acrobatic white-cheeked gibbons to graceful Baringo giraffes. For years, the star attraction has been the lowland gorillas at the **Lester E. Fisher Great Ape House** ★. The gorillas are not separated into individual habitats but are kept in large family groups, as would be the case in the wild for these highly social animals. More than 50 gorillas have been born at Lincoln Park Zoo since 1970, an astounding record in the zoo world.

A recently completed $50 million campaign has the zoo looking its best in decades. The new **Small Mammal–Reptile House** is a state-of-the-art facility, housing 200 species and featuring a glass-enclosed walk-through ecosystem simulating river, savanna, and forest habitats. The popular **Sea Lion Pool,** situated in the center of the zoo and home to harbor seals, gray seals, and California sea lions, has been converted to saltwater and features an improved underwater viewing area spanning 70 feet and an updated amphitheater. The north end of the zoo—including the bear and wolf habitat and the big mammals (elephants, rhinos, giraffes, and more)—was completely renovated in 2002. Park Place Café is a food court located in a historic building that originally was Chicago's first aquarium. And the new Mahon Theobold Pavilion features a sprawling indoor gift shop and a unique rooftop eatery called Big Cats Café that opens at 8am (1 hr. before the exhibits do) and serves fresh-baked muffins and scones, focaccia sandwiches, salads, and flatbreads.

2200 N. Cannon Dr. (at Fullerton Pkwy.). ✆ 312/742-2000. www.lpzoo.com. Free admission. Summer Mon–Fri 10am–5pm, Sat–Sun 10am–6:30pm; fall–spring daily 10am–5pm; grounds open at 8am year-round. Bus: 151 or 156. Free trolley service from area CTA stations and parking garages on Sat–Sun and holidays 11am–7pm.

8 Gardens & Conservatories

Garfield Park Conservatory ★ **All ages.** Designed by the great landscape architect Jens Jensen in 1907, Garfield Park Conservatory is one of the largest gardens under glass in the world at 2 acres in size. And, it's open 365 days a year from 9am to 5pm, with free admission. Surprisingly, it took a blockbuster exhibit by glass artist Dave Chihuly in 2001 to 2002 for many Chicagoans to "discover" the conservatory. Whether the crowds will return once the show ends remains to be seen.

Chicago parents give the conservatory a thumbs-up for the special kids' area, which features a slide, climbing equipment, a big pile of dirt (and digging tools), all within an environment that feels downright tropical. Educational displays such as plants, pods and insects, and staff members who work with kids ensure that some learning gets done along with digging. Unfortunately, the conservatory is now surrounded by a rather blighted neighborhood with a high crime rate. I advise driving there and forgoing public transportation.

300 N. Central Park Ave. ✆ 312/746-5100. Free admission. Daily 9am–5pm. Free parking in an adjacent lot.

Lincoln Park Conservatory ★ **All ages.** Just beyond the zoo's northeast border is a lovely botanical garden housed in a soaring glass-domed structure. Inside are four great halls filled with thousands of plants that, unless you're an avid horticulturist, will take you perhaps a half-hour to explore. The Palm House features giant palms and rubber trees (including a 50-ft. fiddle leaf rubber tree dating from 1891), the Fernery nurtures plants that grow close to the forest floor, and the Tropical House is a shiny symphony of flowering trees, vines, and bamboo. The fourth environment is the Show House, where seasonal flower shows are held.

Even better than the plants inside, however, might be what lies outside the front doors. The expansive lawn with its French garden and lovely fountain on the conservatory's south side is one of the best places in town for an informal picnic (especially nice if you're visiting the zoo and want to avoid the congestion at its food concession venues).

Fullerton Ave. (at Stockton Dr.). ℂ **312/742-7736.** Free admission. Daily 9am–5pm. Bus: 73, 151, or 156.

9 Nature Centers

Morton Arboretum   **Ages 5 & up.** Should your visit to Chicago coincide with Arbor Day, here's the place to celebrate: More than 3,000 kinds of trees, shrubs, and vines grow on the 1,700-acre site in west suburban Lisle. Special areas include the Illinois Tree Trails' woodlands, meadows, and marshes; an area with sugar maples (colorful in the fall); a crabapple orchard (splendid when the trees are in full bloom); and a prairie with tall grasses and flowers that blossom in summer and fall. The arboretum also features trees from other countries. Most of the 13 miles of trails are covered with wood chips, so they are not stroller-friendly. If your kids are young, it's best to see the landscape by car along 11 miles of one-way roads or take a bus tour. Tram tours depart at noon and 1:15pm Wednesday, Saturday, and Sunday from May to October. Stop by the visitor center for additional information. Light meals are available in the Ginkgo Restaurant; sandwiches and soups are served in the coffee shop; a picnic area is located near a small lake.

4100 Illinois Hwy. 53 (at Interstate 88, the East-West Tollway), Lisle. ℂ **630/719-2400.** Admission: $7 per car ($3 on Wed). Nov–March daily 7am–5pm; Apr–Oct daily 7am–7pm. Visitor Center daily 9am–5pm; Gingko Tree restaurant daily 11am–3pm; coffee shop daily 9am–5pm. Free parking. Subway/El: Metra train stops at Lisle, 1½ miles away; cabs available.

Peggy Notebaert Nature Museum ★★   **All ages.** Built on an ancient sand dune—once the shoreline of Lake Michigan—Chicago's newest museum bills itself as "an environmental museum for the 21st century." Shaded by huge cottonwoods and maples, the sand-colored exterior with its horizontal lines composed of interlocking trapezoids itself resembles a sand dune. Rooftop-level walkways give strollers a view of birds and other urban wildlife below. Paths wind through gardens planted with native Midwestern wildflowers and grasses, and trace the shore of the newly restored North Pond.

Inside, large windows throughout create a dialogue between the outdoor environment and the indoor exhibits designed to illuminate it. The 73,000-square-foot facility features plenty of exhibits on nature and the interaction between human activities and the environment. Throughout, the focus is on interactivity, done with imagination and intelligence. Don't miss the **Butterfly Haven** ★, a greenhouse habitat where about 25 Midwestern species of butterflies and moths carry on their complex life cycles. (Wander through as a riot of color flutters all around you.) Another top exhibit is **City Science,** a 3,000-square-foot, two-story "house" with functional rooms where visitors can view the pipes and ducts that connect our homes with power sources miles away. Other permanent exhibits include the innovative **Environmental Central,** a computer-simulated "town meeting" in which participants at computer workstations collaborate—or compete—to solve a hypothetical environmental crisis. **Water Lab** is a model river system demonstrating the uses and abuses that a waterway undergoes as it meanders from rural to urban environments. It's probably safe to say that the **Children's Gallery** is the only place in town where kids can clamber in and out of a model ground-squirrel town or explore a beaver lodge from the inside.

The sunny Butterfly Cafe offers fresh, healthful meals cafeteria-style. In summer, get there early to enjoy coffee and a muffin—and the lovely surroundings—with joggers and other locals.

Fullerton Ave. and Cannon Dr. © 773/871-2668. www.chias.org. Admission $6 adults, $4 seniors and students, $3 children ages 3–12, children under 3 free. Free admission Tues. Mon–Fri 9am–4:30pm, Sat–Sun 10am–5pm; snack bar opens 8am. Closed Thanksgiving, Dec 25, and Jan 1. Bus: 151 or 156.

10 Kid-Friendly Tours

If you want someone else to organize your sightseeing, by bus or by boat, Chicago has a number of experienced companies that provide just about any kind of itinerary you can imagine.

ORIENTATION TOURS

Chicago Motor Coach Company **Ages 6 & up.** This company offers 1½-hour narrated double-decker bus tours of the Loop, Michigan Avenue, and the lakefront. Board the buses, which stop every 15 to 25 minutes, at several stops around the city, including the Art Institute, the Museum Campus, the Sears Tower, the Michigan Avenue bridge (at Wacker Drive), Navy Pier, and the Water Tower. Buy your ticket from a seller at any of these locations. You'll be given a brochure describing the day's stops.

© 312/666-1000. All-day hop-on, hop-off pass $13 adults, $7 seniors, $7 children under 11 and military personnel in uniform. Apr–Nov (weather permitting) daily 9:30am–5pm. Usually closed Dec–Mar.

Chicago Trolley Company **All ages.** Chicago Trolley Company offers guided tours on a fleet of rubber-wheeled "San Francisco–style" trolleys that stop at a number of popular spots around the city, including Navy Pier, the Grant Park museums, the Museum of Science and Industry, Lincoln Park Zoo, and the cluster of theme restaurants in River North. You can stay on for the full 1½-hour ride or get on and off at each stop.

© 773/648-5000. www.chicagotrolley.com. All-day hop-on, hop-off pass $18 adults, $15 seniors, $8 children. Summer Mon–Fri 9am–5pm; hours vary the rest of the year and depend on the weather (when the vehicles are enclosed and heated).

Gray Line **Ages 8 & up.** And then there's the company whose name is synonymous with bus tours. Gray Line offers sightseeing by both trolley and motor coach, including 3- to 5-hour guided tours and all-day hop-on, hop-off tours.

27 E. Monroe St., Suite 515. © 800/621-4153 or 312/251-3107. www.grayline.com. Tours cost $27–$45.

CHICAGO ARCHITECTURE FOUNDATION TOURS

Chicago is the first city of architecture, and the **Chicago Architecture Foundation (CAF),** 224 S. Michigan Ave. (© 312/922-3432, or 312/922-TOUR for recorded information; www.architecture.org), offers first-rate guided programs, led by nearly 400 trained and enthusiastic docents. The foundation offers walking, bike, boat, and bus tours to more than 60 architectural sites and environments in and around Chicago. The foundation also has another tour center in the John Hancock Center, 875 N. Michigan Ave. Below is a sampling of the tours the foundation offers.

BY BOAT

Perhaps the CAF's most popular tour is its 1½-hour **"Architecture River Cruise,"** which glides along both the north and the south branches of the Chicago River. Although you can see the same 50 or so buildings that the cruise covers on your own by foot, traveling by water lets you enjoy the buildings from a unique perspective. The excellent docents also provide interesting historical details, as well as some fun facts. (David Letterman once called the busts of the nation's retailing legends that face the Merchandise Mart the "Pez Hall of Fame."). The cruise points out both landmark buildings, such as the Gothic 1925 Tribune Tower, and contemporary ones, including the late-1980s NBC Tower, constructed in wedding-cake style in homage to the city's old zoning codes mandating that sunlight reach down to the street.

The docents generally do a good job of making the cruise enjoyable for visitors with all levels of architectural knowledge. In addition to pointing out famous buildings—Marina City, the Civic Opera House, the Sears Tower, to name a few—they approach the sites thematically, explaining, for example, how Chicagoans' use of and attitudes toward the river have changed in the past 2 centuries.

Tickets are $21 per person for tours Monday through Friday. Although it's expensive, I still highly recommend a tour, especially if you're at all interested in architecture—it's by far the best tour in the city, on land or on water. If your kids are small, and you just want a "fun" cruise on the water, you'd be better off opting for a cruise with Wendella Sightseeing Boats or Mercury Chicago's Skyline Cruiseline (p. 170), where kids' tickets are under $10.

Tours are operated hourly every day from May through October—an increased schedule recently made possible by the CAF's addition of a second boat. The trips are extremely popular, so purchase tickets in advance through **Ticketmaster** (© **312/902-1500;** www.ticketmaster.com), or avoid the service charge and buy your tickets at one of the foundation's tour centers, 224 S. Michigan Ave. or the John Hancock Center, or from the CAF/Mercury boat launch on the southwest corner of the Michigan Avenue bridge. The cruises leave from the southwest side of the Michigan Avenue bridge, on the river level.

BY BUS

Reservations are required for all bus tours, although walk-ins are welcome if there's space.

The **"Chicago Architecture Highlights by Bus"** is a 3½-hour tour offered Saturdays at 9:30am that covers the Loop, Hyde Park, and the Gold Coast, plus several other historic districts. The tour includes a visit to the interior of Frank Lloyd Wright's Robie House. Tickets are $25 per person; tours depart from the CAF tour center on 224 S. Michigan Ave. To keep up with popular demand, the foundation adds Sunday morning tours periodically throughout the year.

The **"Loop and Near North by Bus"** is a 2-hour tour that concentrates on downtown and the ritzy residential neighborhoods north of the Loop. It offers dramatic views of the skyline and includes the site where the Great Chicago Fire started. Tickets are $15 per person; tours depart from the CAF tour center in the John Hancock Center May to October.

The Chicago Historical Society usually offers three or four daylong guided tours, called **"Exploring Chicago,"** May to July that cover unique themes or aspects of the metropolitan area's history. Led by historians and scholars, they take place in the city and surrounding areas. Tours are different every year, so call the Historical Society (© **312/642-4600,** ext. 399) for updates (the tours usually are tied in to exhibits at the museum). Prices vary but are usually about $50

⌒Tips   **Oak Park Bus Tours**

The **Chicago Architecture Foundation** offers a 4-hour bus tour of Wright sights in Oak Park once a month on Saturday from May to October ($25). The tour includes walks through three neighborhoods and commentary on more than 25 houses—but does not take visitors inside Wright's home and studio. A separate 4-hour bus tour takes Wright fans inside the master's home and Oak Park's Unity Temple ($35). Both tours leave from the John Hancock Center, 875 N. Michigan Ave. Reservations are required; call ℂ **312/922-3432,** ext. 240.

---

per person. Due to the price and the tour length, I'd recommend this only for adults and teens with an interest in the subject on offer. Tours depart from the Historical Society's museum at Clark Street and North Avenue, and include lunch and light refreshments.

BY TRAIN

The city's Office of Tourism runs the **"Loop Tour Train"** ★★ a guided way to see and feel the city aboard the CTA's El. Of course, you can always take your own tour with bunches of regular Chicago folks (the Ravenswood Brown Line offers impressive vistas heading south toward downtown), but the weekly (Sat only) 40-minute, docent-led tour details the history of the century-old El and the downtown area, visible as the train circles the "loop" of tracks that give the central business district its name. The 100-year old tracks circle architectural landmarks and outdoor sculpture, with so many to see that the train makes three loops per tour. The train departs from the Randolph and Wabash station every 40 minutes Saturdays from 12:15 to 2:15pm mid-June through mid-October. Tickets are free, but they must be obtained in advance from the Visitor Information Center on the first floor of the **Chicago Cultural Center,** 77 E. Randolph St., a block east of the CTA station (ℂ **312/744-0528**).

ON FOOT

If you prefer exploring on your own two feet, the CAF offers a variety of guided walking tours. Two popular tours in the Loop are **"Historic Skyscrapers,"** which covers buildings built between 1880 and 1940, including the Rookery and the Chicago Board of Trade, and **"Modern Skyscrapers,"** which includes modern masterpieces by Mies van der Rohe and postmodern works by contemporary architects. The 2-hour tours cost $10 each ($15 for both) for adults and $7 each ($10 for both) for seniors and students. The tours are offered daily and depart from the CAF tour center at 224 S. Michigan Ave. Call ℂ **312/922-TOUR** for exact tour times.

The CAF also offers more than 50 **neighborhood tours,** including the Gold Coast, River North, Grant Park, Old Town, the Jackson Boulevard Historic District, and even the Lincoln Park Zoo. Most cost $5 to $10 and last a couple of hours. Call ℂ **312/922-TOUR** for details.

The Chicago Historical Society offers a handful of walking tours every summer of the **Gold Coast, Old Town, and Lincoln Park neighborhoods.** Led by CHS docents, they average about four per month from June through August. Day and evening tours are available, and a few specialty walking tours usually are offered as well. Tours are $6 per tour or $15 for a pre-registered combination of any three tours. Registration is recommended but not required. Tours depart from the CHS museum at Clark Street and North Avenue, and light refreshments are served immediately afterward. Call ℂ **312/642-4600** for updates.

MORE ARCHITECTURE TOURS

For do-it-yourselfers, **audio walking tours** are offered by the Chicago Department of Cultural Affairs. The 90-minute tape, narrated by local broadcast journalist Bill Kurtis, provides visitors with an overview of downtown's skyscrapers, public spaces, and sculptures. The tour package costs $5 (with a $50 returnable deposit, cash or credit card) and includes rental of a tape player and a map and booklet of the downtown area. For more information, call the **Chicago Office of Tourism** at ℂ 312/744-2400.

The cultural affairs department also runs **"Great Chicago Places and Spaces,"** an architecture-focused event that takes place over a weekend in late May and features a variety of walking and lobby tours. Tour guides include some of the city's top urban planners and architecture faculty from local universities. All tours depart from either the Chicago Cultural Center, 78 E. Randolph St., or the Chicago Architecture Center, 224 S. Michigan Ave. Call ℂ **312/744-2400** for information on this year's event.

Architecture junkies also might want to inquire about house tours of the **Charnley-Persky House** (ℂ **312/915-0105** or 312/573-1365), designed by Frank Lloyd Wright and Louis Sullivan in 1891. The house is located in the Gold Coast at 1365 N. Astor St. and would make a nice highlight to an informal walking tour of the area.

LAKE & RIVER CRUISES

Tired of just looking out at the deep blue water from the top of the Hancock, the Shedd Aquarium, Oak Street Beach, and a host of other spots? Reverse your perspective. Take a sightseeing cruise and check out Chicago's incredible skyline from an offshore vantage point.

Buccaneer Pirate Adventure Cruises   Ages 1 & up. Come aboard this 100-foot, pirate-themed passenger cruise vessel for a 1½-hour adventure cruise on the Chicago River and Lake Michigan. Aspiring pirates get all the necessary props, including pirate hats and are welcomed by a crew dressed in ragged clothes, striped shirts and bandannas. (The captain, of course, wears a ruffled white shirt and jacket.) The ship flies the Jolly Roger and has a mermaid figurehead on her bow. Kids get goodie bags with eye patches, gold doubloons (filled with chocolate), and rub-on tattoos or a mini spyglass. Pirate magicians perform tricks and make balloon sculptures. Open to ages 1 to 13, but it's best for the littlest ones.

Board at the Wagner Charter Cruise Co. Dock on the south side of the Chicago River, east of the Columbus Dr. bridge. ℂ 630/653-8690. Tickets $12. Cruises run May to mid-Oct. Sat at 10:30am.

Chicago from the Lake Ltd   All ages. This company runs 90-minute architectural river cruises and lake and river historical cruises. Complimentary coffee (Starbucks, no less), lemonade, cookies, and muffins are served. For tickets, call or stop by the company's ticket office, located on the lower level on the east end of River East Plaza.

Departing from Ogden Slip adjacent to River East Plaza (formerly North Pier) at the end of E. Illinois St. ℂ 312/527-2002. Tickets $18.50 adults, $16.50 seniors, $12 children 7–18, free for children under 7. Cruises run May–Oct daily.

Mercury Chicago's Skyline Cruiseline   All ages. Like Wendella, Mercury offers 1- to 2-hour boat rides that give a good overview of the Chicago River and Lake Michigan. In the summer, a sunset cruise departs nightly at 7:30pm and makes a stop at 9pm to admire the lights of Buckingham Fountain. Another Mercury Line offering is a daylong cruise along the National Heritage Corridor, the river route that links Chicago with the Mississippi River, taking in everything from the cityscape to the prairie lands. The cruise, narrated by a geography expert, runs weekends in September only; call for details. All tickets go on sale 1 hour before departure time.

Departing from Michigan Ave. and Wacker Dr. (on the south side of the river). ✆ 312/332-1353. Tickets $14 adults, $7 children under 12. Cruises run May 1–Oct 1 daily.

Shoreline Sightseeing   All ages. Shoreline schedules 30-minute lake cruises every half-hour from its three dock locations: the Shedd Aquarium, Navy Pier, and Buckingham Fountain in Grant Park. Shoreline has also gotten in on the popularity of architecture tours by offering its own version, narrated by an architectural guide (with higher prices than their regular tours). A water taxi also runs every half-hour from Navy Pier to both the Sears Tower and the Shedd Aquarium. One-way tickets for the water taxi are $6 for adults, $5 for seniors, and $3 for children under 12; all-day passes cost $12 for adults and $6 for children.

Departing from Navy Pier, Shedd Aquarium, and Buckingham Fountain in Grant Park. ✆ 312/222-9328. Tickets $9 adults, $8 seniors, $4 children under 12. Cruises run daily from Memorial Day to Labor Day.

The Spirit of Chicago   **Ages 12 & up.** This luxury yacht offers a variety of wining and dining harbor cruises, from the Big Band Lunch Buffet to the Moonlight Dance Party. Children are allowed, with some restrictions; otherwise, book a sitter and hit one of the cruises. However, this can be a fairly pricey night out if you go for the whole dinner package.

Departing from Navy Pier. ✆ 312/836-7899. www.spiritcruises.com. Lunch cruises $34–$39, Sun brunch $37.35, dinner (seated) $68–$98, cocktails $27–$30; moonlight cruises $29. Ask about children's rates. Cruises run year-round daily.

uglyduck Cruises   All ages. It's hard to overlook the newest boat at Navy Pier, which was built specifically for cruising along the Chicago skyline and, as such, boasts large picture windows. This big, yellow, 500-passenger cruiser operates daily lunch and dinner excursions on the lake, as well as midnight weekend voyages. The "duck" started as a lower-priced alternative to boats such as *The Spirit of Chicago,* and even though prices have been steadily increasing, uglyduck still promotes itself as more of a "fun" ship.

Departing from Navy Pier. ✆ 888/289-8833 or 312/396-9007. www.uglyduckcruises.com. Lunch cruises $26, dinner $42–$53, midday cruise $19, moonlight cruise $24. Cruises run year-round.

Wendella Sightseeing Boats   All ages. Wendella is the granddaddy of all sightseeing operators in Chicago. Started in 1935, it's run by the original owner's son, Bob Borgstrom, whose own two sons serve as captains. You won't find a more authoritative source on the Chicago River than Borgstrom.

Wendella operates 1- to 2-hour water tours late April to early October, taking in a stretch of the Chicago River and the area of the lake off the downtown district. (One of the most dramatic events during the boat tours is passing through the locks that separate the river from the lake.) Sunset is a good time to go, but scheduling for cruises depends on the season and the weather, so call ahead for the current hours.

Departing from Michigan Ave. and Wacker Dr. (on the north side of the river at the Wrigley Building). (C) 312/ 337-1446. www.wendellaboats.com. Tickets $12–$16 adults, $10–$14 seniors, $6–$8 children under 12. Cruises run Apr–Oct daily.

Windy **Ages 8 & up.** One of the more breathtaking scenes on the lake is watching this tall ship approach the docks at Navy Pier. The 148-foot-long, four-masted schooner (and its new sister ship, the *Windy II*) sets sail for 90-minute cruises two to five times a day, both day and evening. Of course, the boats are at the whims of the wind, so every cruise charts a different course. Passengers are welcome to help raise and trim the sails and occasionally take turns at the ship's helm (with the captain standing close by). The boats are not accessible for people with disabilities.

Departing from Navy Pier. (C) 312/595-5555. Tickets $25 adults, $15 seniors and children under 12. Tickets go on sale 1 hr. before the first sail of the day at the boat's ticket office, on the dock at Navy Pier. Reservations (except for groups) are not accepted. Call for sailing times.

CARRIAGE & PEDICAB RIDES

Noble Horse ((C) 312/266-7878) maintains the largest fleet of antique horse carriages, stationed around the old Water Tower Square, at the northwest corner of Chicago and Michigan avenues. Each of the drivers, outfitted in black tie and top hat, has his own variation on the basic Magnificent Mile itinerary (and can also do tours of the lakefront, river, Lincoln Park, and Buckingham Fountain). The charge is $30 for each half-hour. The coaches run year-round, with convertible coaches in the warm months and enclosed carriages furnished with wool blankets on bone-chilling nights. There are several other carriage operators, all of whom pick up riders in the vicinity.

If you want to explore the city by bike but want to leave the pedaling to somebody else, flag down one of the half-dozen guys who operate colorful tricycle **pedicabs,** the self-powered rickshaws so ubiquitous in many Asian capitals. Here in Chicago, they were introduced by veteran local actor Ron Dean, whose hard-boiled mug has appeared in countless made-in-Chicago movies and TV series. You'll find these guys congregating around Wrigley Field on game days, where they ferry lazy Cubs fans to their cars, at many of the summer festivals, and often along Southport and Lincoln avenues in Lincoln Park and Lakeview. Rides generally cost about $10 per mile for two passengers. Remember to wave to the crowd!

SPECIAL-INTEREST TOURS

NEIGHBORHOOD TOURS   It's a bit of a cliché to say that Chicago is a city of neighborhoods, but if you want to see what really makes Chicago special, that's where you have to go. **Chicago Neighborhood Tours** ((C) 312/742-1190; www.chgocitytours.com) are half-day, narrated bus excursions to about a dozen diverse communities throughout the city. Embarking from the Chicago Cultural Center, 77 E. Randolph St., every Saturday (not on major holidays and not during Jan, generally, so call first), the tours visit different neighborhoods, from Chinatown and historic Bronzeville on the South Side to the ethnic enclaves of Devon Avenue and Uptown on the North Side. Neighborhood representatives serve as guides and greeters along the way as tour participants visit area landmarks, murals, museums, and shopping districts. Several specialty tours have recently been added to the mix, including "Gay and Lesbian History"; "Great Chicago Fire"; "Roots of Blues, Gospel, & Jazz"; "Threads of Ireland"; "Jewish Legacy"; and an "Ethnic Cemetery" tour. The tours, organized by the Chicago

Office of Tourism, have sparked some neighborhood organizations to develop gift shops aimed at capitalizing on the arrival of visitors. Tickets (including a light snack) are $25 for adults and $20 for seniors, students, and children 8 to 18. (Some of the longer specialty tours cost more).

Groups can arrange tours of Chicago's **"Black Metropolis,"** the name given to a South Side area of Bronzeville where African Americans created a flourishing business and artistic community after World War II. Contact **Tour Black Chicago** (© 312/332-2323; www.tourblackchicago.com) for more information.

GANGSTER TOURS   Untouchable Tours, or so-called "gangster tours," P.O. Box 43185, Chicago, IL 60643 (© **773/881-1195;** www.gangstertour. com), is the only bus tour that takes you to all of the city's old hoodlum hangouts from the Prohibition era. The focus is definitely more on entertainment (the guides appear in costume and role-play their way through the tour) than a seriously historic take on the era, but the bus trip gives you a pretty thorough overview of the city, in addition to the gangster hot spots. You'll see the site of O'Bannion's flower shop, the site of the St. Valentine's Day massacre, plus much more. The tour is pretty tame, but if you have impressionable young ones, use your discretion; kids over age 8 should be fine. The cost is $22 for adults, $16 for children. Tours, which depart from the **Rock-N-Roll McDonald's** at Clark and Ohio streets (the east side of the restaurant), run Monday to Wednesday at 10am; Thursday at 10am and 1pm; Friday at 10am, 1pm, and 7:30pm; Saturday at 10am, 1pm, and 5pm; and Sunday at 11am and 2pm. The same company also offers Sunday tours of the historic Beverly Hills/Morgan Park neighborhood of stately old homes; call © **773/881-1831** for details.

GHOST TOURS   Another offbeat way to experience the real "spirit" of Chicago is to take a narrated **supernatural bus tour** of cemeteries, murder sites, Indian burial grounds, haunted pubs, and other spooky places. Richard Crowe, who bills himself as a "professional ghost hunter," spins out ghost stories, legends, and lore on the 5-hour trip, held both day and night (afraid of the dark?). I'd only take teens on these tours due to touchy subject matter and the rather expensive price; use your discretion. Tickets are $33 per person, and the tour begins at **Goose Island Restaurant,** 1800 N. Clybourn Ave. (a short walk from the North/Clybourn El station on the Red Line). Two-hour **supernatural boat excursions** are available for $22 per person in July and August through Labor Day weekend, and board at 10:30pm from the Mercury boat dock, at Michigan Avenue and Wacker Drive. Reservations are required for each tour; call © **708/ 499-0300** or visit www.ghosttours.com.

CEMETERY TOURS   Don't wait until it's too late to take a cemetery tour. Cemeteries are fascinating places, whether in New Orleans, where the dearly departed aren't really buried at all but are enclosed in above-ground sarcophagi; or in Boston, where Revolutionary War heroes are crowded together; or here in Chicago, where some of the cemeteries are as pretty as parks.

One of the best area cemeteries is **Graceland,** which stretches along Clark Street in the Swedish neighborhood of Andersonville. The land between Irving Park Road and Montrose Avenue, running for about a mile along Clark Street, is occupied exclusively by cemeteries—primarily Graceland. Here you can view the tombs and monuments of many Chicago notables. When Graceland was laid out in 1860, public parks as such did not exist. The elaborate burial grounds that were constructed in many large American cities around this same time had the dual purpose of relieving the congestion of the municipal cemeteries closer to town and providing pastoral recreational settings for the Sunday outings of the living. Indeed, cemeteries like Graceland were the precursors of such great municipal green spaces as Lincoln Park. Much of Lincoln Park, in fact, had been a public cemetery since Chicago's earliest times. Many who once rested there were reinterred in Graceland when the plans for building Lincoln Park went forward.

The Chicago Architecture Foundation (*Ⓒ* **312/922-3432**) offers walking tours of Graceland on selected Sundays during August, September, and October. The tour costs $5 per person and lasts about 2 hours. Among the points of interest you will discover as you meander the paths of these 121 beautifully landscaped acres are the Ryerson and Getty tombs, famous architectural monuments designed by Louis Sullivan. Sullivan himself rests here in the company of several of his most distinguished colleagues: Daniel Burnham, Ludwig Mies van der Rohe, and Howard Van Doren Shaw, an establishment architect whose summer home in Lake Forest, called Ragdale, now operates as a writers' and artists' colony. Some of Chicago's giants of industry and commerce are also buried at Graceland, including Potter Palmer, Marshall Field, and George Pullman. An ambiguous reference in the *WPA Guide to Illinois* (Pantheon Books, 1983), reprinted without revisions, records that Graceland also contains the grave of Chicago's first white civilian settler, John Kinzie. (The racial adjective is a reminder that Chicago's very first settler was a black man named Jean Baptiste Point du Sable.) The Chicago Architecture Foundation offers tours of some other cemeteries, as well, including the Oak Woods Cemetery, Rosehill Cemetery, and the suburban Lake Forest Cemetery. Call for details. **Oak Woods,** located just south of Hyde Park on the city's South Side, is the final resting place for many of Chicago's most famous African-American figures, including Jesse Owens, Ida B. Wells, and the late Mayor Harold Washington. Also buried here are nuclear physicist Enrico Fermi, who helped give birth to the atomic age while at the University of Chicago, and legendary trial lawyer Clarence Darrow.

7

Neighborhood Strolls

The best way to get a feel for Chicago is to stroll its streets. Every block brings interesting window-shopping, people-watching, or snippets of conversation that are sure to keep you and the wee ones entertained. The orderly configuration of Chicago's streets and the excellent public transportation system make walking a breeze—when you get tired, you can hop on a bus or the El without having to veer too far off your course.

This chapter provides brief walks that will give you a snapshot of the city's most frequented neighborhoods.

1 Near North/Magnificent Mile

North Michigan Avenue is known as the Magnificent Mile, from the bridge spanning the Chicago River on the south end, to Oak Street on the northern tip. Many of the city's best hotels, shops, and restaurants are to be found on and around elegant Michigan Avenue. But never fear—while elegant, Michigan Avenue offers excellent family shopping, too. Scattered among the shops owned by Gucci, Salvatore Ferragamo, and Cartier are more kid-friendly stops such as American Girl Place, Niketown, and FAO Schwarz. You and your kids will feel right at home making your way up this storied avenue. To stroll the entire mile will take you half a day, especially because you'll want to stop frequently. Of course, if you're determined to avoid the shops, you can do it in less than an hour—but who'd want to?

Start at the **riverwalk** that goes along the north side of the Chicago River. Walk down the steps that lead off the Michigan Avenue Bridge. You can walk for a short distance and see the plaza of the NBC Tower, as well as some of the newest condominium and town house developments along the river. Backtrack and continue north on Michigan Avenue. You'll run right into the **Chicago Tribune Tower.** The tower is notable for its signature array of stones jutting out from the exterior. The collection was started shortly after the building's completion in 1925 by the newspaper's notoriously despotic publisher Robert R. McCormick, who gathered them during his world travels. *Tribune* correspondents then began supplying stone souvenirs encountered on assignment. Each one now bears the name of the structure and country whence it came. There are 138 stones in all, including chunks and shards from the Great Wall of China, the Taj Mahal, the White House, the Arc de Triomphe, the Berlin Wall, the Roman Colosseum, London's Houses of Parliament, the Great Pyramid of Cheops in Giza, Egypt, and the original tomb of Abraham Lincoln in Springfield. How many can you find? *Hint:* Inside the *Tribune's* lobby, there's a brochure telling you where they are.

Continue north along Michigan Avenue. When you reach Chicago Avenue, just ahead of you is the **Chicago Water Tower** (not to be confused with a mall of the same name, located kitty-corner from the real tower). Michigan Avenue's best-known landmark is dwarfed by high-rises today, but still gleams like a fairy tale castle. Surrounded by lawns and park benches, the tower is illuminated at night, and street musicians often play here. As one of the few buildings to survive the Great Fire of 1871, Chicagoans are proud of their talisman. (And, it serves a real purpose by covering an ugly, 138-ft.-high standpipe used in connection with pumping water from Lake Michigan!) The gothic-style limestone building now houses an art gallery, and is a refreshing pit stop of culture. Across the street, the pumping station has been transformed into a tourist information center.

To conclude your walk up Michigan Avenue, step across the street to **Ghirardelli's** (located on DeWitt, ½ block west of Michigan Ave.) and grab an ice cream cone. If you walk up one more block north, you can enjoy your ice cream in the shaded, ivy-covered courtyard of **Fourth Presbyterian Church,** located at Chestnut Street and Michigan Avenue—a tranquil spot just steps from the bustle of Michigan Avenue.

2 The Loop

South Michigan Avenue is less congested than its northerly branch, the Magnificent Mile. Down here, you can amble along and take in a couple of Chicago's famous museums and two parks, including Millennium Park, expected to become Chicago's second-largest tourist draw after Navy Pier. The park won't be finished until 2004, but portions of the park are opening as they are completed. South Michigan Avenue can be strolled in an hour or two, but if you stop to check out building lobbies and have lunch, it can be a half-day event. Because this walk focuses on architecture, it's best for older children and teens.

Cross the Chicago River on the Michigan Avenue Bridge and walk south. You are heading into the Loop business district. On this easterly fringe of the Loop lie some of Chicago's top cultural institutions and parks. Continue south, past Lake and Randolph Streets. On your left, you will see a clearing: This is the new **Millennium Park.** Located on the north end of Grant Park along Michigan Avenue, it's still taking shape as this book goes to press (after years of delay). Large public art displays have become common, and although the landscaping is in place, we're still waiting to admire the dramatic new music pavilion designed by Frank Gehry.

At the corner of Michigan and Randolph is a huge beaux arts–style building, called the **Chicago Cultural Center.** Built in 1897 as the city's public library, the cultural center is now your home base for tourist information. Go in, pick up all the information you need, and while you're at it, check out the building's stunning interior. Free tours guide visitors up a sweeping staircase of white Italian marble to admire what is, for my money, the most stunning interior in Chicago. At the top of the staircase is a majestic Tiffany dome, believed to be

---

⌐Tips Sorting Out the Post Office

While you're near the Loop, treat your kids to a look at the inner workings of the **Chicago Main Post Office,** 433 W. Harrison (© **312/983-7550**), and see for yourselves what happens to the letters you send. The 90-minute tour includes the sorting process, a look at the latest automated equipment, and an enormous stamp collection. The tour is suggested for ages 10 and older and reservations are required. Tours are available Monday through Friday from 10am to 12:30pm; free admission.

Walk This Way: Chicago's Underground Pedway

Rainy day? Snowy? So windy you're afraid your kids will blow away? Take a break and cruise around Chicago's Loop through the not-so-secret underground **Pedway.** The city started building tunnels to connect subway stations in the early 1950s, and today, the underground system of tunnels covers 23 blocks that are fun for kids to explore. You'll find stores, restaurants, and other businesses. Don't worry—if you ever get lost, just look for an exit and go up to street level to get your bearings (and you can pick up a map at the Chicago Cultural Center).

A nearby spot to enter the Pedway is the State Street subway station, between Randolph and Washington streets. On the stretch west of State Street, you'll find a newsstand selling snacks and fresh fruits, a barbershop, a Starbucks, a big gift store, and a food court. Beneath the Chicago Cultural Center, your children can look through the window for a radio station, where people are broadcasting books for the blind. Farther along, at the Athletic Club, kids can see a seven-story climbing wall and watch office workers working out at lunchtime. The eastern section is the most elegant—it travels under several hotels and has a shopping concourse.

---

the world's largest. You'll also discover mosaics of Favrile glass, colored stone, and mother-of-pearl inlaid in white marble.

As you stroll south from the Cultural Center, you are seeing "Michigan Avenue Cliff," a particularly impressive great wall of buildings that stretches south to Congress Parkway (location of the Auditorium Building). It's a visual treat for architecture lovers and novices alike.

Abutting the park on the south, starting at Adams Avenue, is the **Art Institute.** Save the tour for another time—for now, climb the steps and visit the stone lions. Watch the other people who are sitting on the steps, people-watching. If you need a break, stop in the outdoor cafe. Mom and Dad can get a glass of wine, while the kids enjoy a lemonade.

Further south on the avenue is the **Fine Arts Building,** constructed in 1885 as a showroom for Studebaker carriages, and converted into an arts center in 1917. The building offers two theaters, offices, shops, and studios for musicians, artists, and writers. Frank Lloyd Wright, sculptor Lorado Taft, and L. Frank Baum, author of *The Wonderful Wizard of Oz,* had offices here. Located throughout the building are a number of interesting studios and musical instrument shops. Take a quick walk through the marble-and-wood lobby, which suggests something monastic and cloister-like, or visit the top floor to see the spectacular murals (and to get there, you'll be fortunate to ride in an old-fashioned elevator manned by a real, live operator!).

Last stop on our south Michigan Avenue tour is the **Auditorium Building.** This wonder of architecture was designed and built in 1889 by Louis Sullivan and Dankmar Adler. At the time, it was the heaviest (110,000 tons) and most massive modern building on earth, the most fireproof building ever constructed, and the tallest building in Chicago. It was also the first large-scale building to be electrically lighted, and its theater was the first in the country to install air-conditioning. The lobby fronting Michigan Avenue has faux ornamental marble columns, molded ceilings, mosaic floors, and Mexican onyx walls. If this inspires you and your kids, take the elevator to the 10th floor library reading room and have a look at what was once the city's first top-floor dining room. Soak in the decorative details and show your kids that they just don't make them like this any more—the barrel-vaulted, muraled ceiling and marvelous views of Grant Park and the lake will make architecture fans out of novices.

3 The Gold Coast

Walking north on **Lake Shore Drive** from North Michigan Avenue, you will enter a neighborhood known as the Gold Coast. The neighborhood runs from about Oak Street on the south to North Avenue on the north and includes some of Chicago's most desired real estate and historic architecture. This is the classic "old money" neighborhood of Chicago, where many of the city's wealthiest citizens built homes after the 1871 fire. Sadly, most of the mansions that once lined Lake Shore Drive have been torn down and high rises put in their stead. (You can see the remnants of that storied past in the 3 mansions still standing near Lake Shore Drive's intersection with Goethe St.) This hour-long stroll is suitable for the whole family and can be combined with a foray into Lincoln Park to make a day's worth of activities.

To get a feel for the neighborhood, walk up Lake Shore Drive to **Schiller Street.** Turn left and walk 1 block to **Astor Place.** Turn right onto Astor and enjoy the amble past stately mansions and beautiful brownstones. (Just a block or two further west, State and Dearborn sts. also feature homes fit for magazine covers.) Once you reach **North Avenue,** you'll see a red brick mansion on your left. This is the home of Cardinal Francis George, Catholic archbishop of Chicago, and is owned by the Catholic archdiocese of Chicago. Ask your kids to count the chimneys—I bet they'll lose track. (My best count was 17.)

You can continue on into **Lincoln Park,** or turn back south. If you go south, walk 1 block west to State Street and follow that to Division Street. From there going south, you will find a thriving zone of restaurants, bars, and nightclubs, many featuring sidewalk seating—all the better to view the beautiful people that frequent the area.

4 Old Town

This residential neighborhood is best known as the home of the Second City comedy troupe for the past 30-plus years. This formerly hippie haven of the 1960s and '70s has gentrified as Cabrini Green (located on the far southern border of Old Town), America's most notorious housing project, has fallen to the wrecking ball. The northern part of Old Town, particularly that located north of North Avenue and west of Wells Street, has a lovely residential neighborhood, and on any given day, you will see plenty of strollers and parents with kids in tow. I'd allow a couple of hours to stroll through the neighborhood, including time to linger in the shops.

To get the flavor of Old Town, start at the intersection of Wells Street and North Avenue. On the northwest corner is **Pipers Alley,** a shopping complex containing a large cinema, Starbucks, restaurants, and shops. Directly to the north is **Second City.** Walk north up Wells Street. Small retail shops, florists, cafes, bread stores, and more line the street. When you reach the intersection with Lincoln Avenue, turn back and head south down the opposite side of the

Chicago & the Great Black Migration

From 1915 to 1960, hundreds of thousands of black Southerners poured into Chicago, trying to escape segregation and seeking economic freedom and opportunity. The so-called "Great Black Migration" radically transformed Chicago, both politically and culturally, from an Irish-run city of recent European immigrants into one in which no group had a majority and in which no politician—white or black—could ever take the black vote for granted. Unfortunately, the sudden change gave rise to many of the social and economic disparities that still plague the city, but it also promoted an environment in which many black men and women could rise from poverty to prominence.

From 1910 to 1920, Chicago's black population almost tripled, from 44,000 to 109,000; from 1920 to 1930, it more than doubled, to 234,000. The Great Depression slowed the migration to a crawl, with 278,000 blacks residing here in 1940. But the boom resumed when World War II revived the economy, causing the black population to skyrocket to 492,000 from 1940 to 1950. The postwar expansion and the decline of Southern sharecropping caused the black population to nearly double again, to 813,000, by 1960.

While jobs in the factories, steel mills, and stockyards paid much better than those in the cotton fields, Chicago was not the paradise that many blacks envisioned. Segregation was almost as bad here as it was down South, and most blacks were confined to a narrow "Black Belt" of overcrowded apartment buildings on the South Side. But the new migrants made the best of their situation, and for a time in the 1930s and 1940s, the Black Belt—dubbed "Bronzeville" or the "Black Metropolis" by the community's boosters—thrived as a cultural, musical, religious, and educational mecca, much as New York's Harlem did in the 1920s. As journalist and Great Migration historian Nicholas Lemann writes in *The Promised Land: The Great Black Migration and How It Changed America,* "Chicago was a city where a black person could be somebody."

Some of the Southern migrants who made names for themselves in Chicago included black separatist and Nation of Islam founder Elijah Muhammed; Robert S. Abbott, publisher of the powerful Chicago Defender newspaper, who launched a "Great Northern Drive" to bring blacks to the city in 1917; Ida B. Wells, the crusading journalist who headed an antilynching campaign; William Dawson, for many years the only black Congressman; New Orleans–born jazz pioneers Jelly Roll Morton, King Oliver, and Louis Armstrong; *Native Son* author Richard Wright; John H. Johnson, publisher of *Ebony* and *Jet* magazines and one of Chicago's wealthiest residents; blues musicians Willie Dixon,

street. Cross North Avenue going south. Your kids will be magnetically attracted to the colorful fish swimming around the front windows of **Old Town Aquarium,** a shop located on the west side of the street at 1538 N. Wells St.

Muddy Waters, and Howlin' Wolf; Thomas A. Dorsey, the "father" of gospel music, and his greatest disciple, singer Mahalia Jackson; Robert Taylor, head of the Chicago Housing Authority, after whom the CHA's most notorious buildings are named; and Ralph Metcalfe, the Olympic gold-medalist sprinter who turned to politics once he got to Chicago, eventually succeeding Dawson in Congress.

When open housing legislation enabled blacks to live in any neighborhood, the flight of many Bronzeville residents to less crowded areas took its toll on the remaining community. Through the 1950s, almost a third of the housing became vacant, and, by the 1960s, the great social experiment of urban renewal through wholesale land clearance and the creation of large tracts of public housing gutted this once thriving neighborhood.

In recent years, however, community and civic leaders appear committed to restoring the neighborhood to a semblance of its former glory. Landmark status has been secured for several historic buildings in Bronzeville, including the **Liberty Life/Supreme Insurance Company**, 3501 South King Dr., the first African American–owned insurance company in the northern United States, and the **Eighth Regiment Armory**, which, when completed in 1915, was the only armory in the United States controlled by an African-American regiment. The former home of the legendary **Chess Records** at 2120 S. Michigan Ave.—where Howlin' Wolf, Chuck Berry, and Bo Diddley gave birth to the blues and helped define rock-and-roll—now houses a museum and music education center, **Blues Heaven Foundation** (✆ **312/808-1286**), set up by Willie Dixon's widow, Marie Dixon, with financial assistance from rock musician John Mellencamp. Entertainer Lou Rawls, who grew up at 45th Street and King Drive (formerly South Pkwy.), is building the **Lou Rawls Theater and Cultural Center** at the famous crossroads of 47th Street and King Drive, where Chicago's fabled Regal Theater once stood, hosting performances by such legends as Count Basie, Duke Ellington, and Ella Fitzgerald. Along Dr. Martin Luther King, Jr., Drive, between 24th and 35th streets, several **public art installations** now celebrate Bronzeville's heritage as well. The most poignant of them is sculptor Alison Saar's **Great Northern Migration bronze monument,** at King and 26th, depicting a suitcase-toting African-American traveler standing atop a mound of worn shoe soles.

For tours of Bronzeville, contact the Chicago Office of Tourism's **Chicago Neighborhood Tours** at ✆ 312/742-1190; **Tour Black Chicago** at ✆ 312/332-2323; or the **Black Metropolis Convention and Tourism Council** at ✆ 773/548-2579.

5 Lincoln Park

Chicago's most popular residential neighborhood is fashionable Lincoln Park. Stretching from North Avenue to Diversey Parkway, it's bordered on the east by the huge park of the same name, which is home to two major museums and one of the nation's oldest zoos (established in 1868). You'll find it easy to spend a whole day and evening in Lincoln Park and the surrounding neighborhood. Thanks to the museums, zoo, and beach, plus shopping and restaurants in the surrounding neighborhood, there's something for all ages.

To explore the park, start at the **Chicago Historical Society,** located at Clark Street and North Avenue. You can pick up a walking path behind the building and pass through a pedestrian tunnel that takes you underneath a busy street and into the heart of the park. You'll have company on the wide gravel path, as joggers, bikers, and dog walkers make good use of this route. Veer right coming out of the tunnel and walk past the baseball fields to the pedestrian bridge. If you cross the bridge going over Lake Shore Drive, you'll wind up on **North Avenue Beach,** Chicago's busiest beach. In the summer, this is beach volleyball central. Take your shoes off, dig your toes in the sand, and check out Lake Michigan's water temperature. (*Warning:* It will be cold, even in August!) Your kids might want to explore the beach house, designed like a real boat, and you can pick up some ice cream and cool drinks inside.

Now that you've seen the park, it's time to check out the neighborhood of the same name. The trapezoid formed by **Clark Street, Armitage Avenue, Halsted Street,** and **Diversey Parkway** contains many of Chicago's most happening bars, restaurants, retail stores, music clubs, and off-Loop theaters. One manageable area to explore on foot is the Armitage Avenue area, which starts at the intersection of Halsted Street and Armitage Avenue. Strolling west on Armitage Avenue, you'll find a string of charming boutiques, featuring shoes and clothing for kids and adults, outdoor outfitters, home decor, and more. Should you choose to go north on Halsted from Armitage Avenue, you'll find more shops, including GapKids and other chain stores. Going south from Halsted on Armitage, you will find restaurants and the nationally acclaimed theater, **Steppenwolf Theatre Company.**

6 Andersonville

This formerly Scandinavian neighborhood stretches several blocks along North Clark Street immediately north of Foster Avenue. Today, a burgeoning community of gays and lesbians make Andersonville their home, and other immigrant groups have moved in. You might want to have lunch at **Ann Sather** (see p. 115 for a full review) and walk the meal off by strolling up and down Clark Street for an hour or two.

Clark Street going north from Foster is a very walkable small stretch that includes the **Swedish-American Museum Center** (p. 156), a pair of Scandinavian delis, a Swedish bakery, and two good Swedish restaurants. Since the wave of Scandinavian immigrants ended over 100 years ago, new immigrants have moved in. You'll find excellent Middle Eastern restaurants, including a northern branch of **Reza's** (p. 102), and delis with barrels of olives, figs, and other Middle Eastern delicacies. Make sure to stop at **Women & Children First** (p. 205), a wonderful bookstore for kids (and women). Stop for a bite at stroller-friendly **Kopi Café,** where you can get a mean mango smoothie, or at Ann Sather, where you can get gooey fresh-baked cinnamon rolls (plus free advice for moms from the very motherly owner).

7 Bucktown/Wicker Park

Home to the third-largest concentration of artists in the country, this neighbor-hood is rapidly gentrifying. Over the past century, the area has hosted waves of German, Polish, and, most recently, Spanish-speaking immigrants (not to men-tion writer Nelson Algren). Heading north on Damen Avenue, you'll pass hot new restaurants, stores featuring the latest in alternative culture, and loft-dwelling yuppies surfing the gentrification wave that's washing over this still-somewhat-gritty neighborhood.

The go-go gentrification of the Wicker Park/Bucktown area has been fol-lowed by not only a rash of restaurants and bars, but also retailers with an artsy bent reflecting the neighborhood's Bohemian spirit. Mixed in with old neigh-borhood businesses, such as discount furniture stores and religious icon purvey-ors, is a proliferation of antique-furniture shops, too-cool-for-school clothing boutiques, and eclectic galleries and gift emporiums. Teenagers will love this walk—in 2001, the neighborhood was the location for MTV's *The Real World: Chicago,* so if your kids have watched the show, they might recognize many of the area's restaurants and bars.

To get a feel for the neighborhood's artsy vibe, stroll up and down Damen Avenue, starting from the intersection with North Avenue. Head south for the best concentration of restaurants and shops. Two notable kids' stores along your path are **Little Folk Art,** for children's clothing (p. 204), and **The Red Balloon Company,** 2060 N. Damen (p. 212). When you're ready for a break, stop at **Sil-ver Cloud Bar & Grill,** 1700 N. Damen, for grilled cheese and tomato soup (p. 117 for a full review), or pop across the street to **Northside Café,** 1635 N. Damen, for a burger or a beverage on the huge outdoor patio (p. 117).

8

For the Active Family

With its wide blue lake and emerald string of parks, Chicago is one big playground for kids. The city's ample green space means it's easy to get out and be active. Whether your kids like water-based sports or activities on solid ground, you'll probably be able to find it here.

A handy resource for those interested in the sporting life is *Windy City Sports* (© 312/421-1551; www.windycitysportsmag.com), a free monthly publication that you'll find at many retail shops, grocery stores, and bars and cafes.

1 Enjoying the "Third Coast": Chicago's Beaches

Public beaches line Lake Michigan all the way up north into the suburbs and Wisconsin, and southeast through Indiana and into Michigan. The most well known is **Oak Street Beach** ⭑, the location of which at the northern tip of the Magnificent Mile creates some interesting sights as sun worshippers sporting swimsuits and carting coolers make their way down Michigan Avenue. The most popular is **North Avenue Beach,** about 6 blocks farther north, which has developed into a volleyball hotspot and recently rebuilt its landmark steamship-shaped beach house and added a Venice Beach–style gym; this is where the Lincoln Park singles come to play, check each other out, and fly by on bikes and in-line skates. While families might be outnumbered by singles, the atmosphere is open and easy, and you won't feel out of place in the least. The beach has a **Bike Chicago** shop for renting bicycles, a chess pavilion, and Stefani's Castaway Restaurant for sandwiches. The beach is the place to be during the annual Air and Water Show, which takes place along the waterfront in August.

For more seclusion, try **Ohio Street Beach,** an intimate sliver of sand in tiny Olive Park, just north of Navy Pier, which, incredibly enough, remains largely ignored despite its central location. If you have a car, head up to **Montrose Beach,** a beautiful unsung treasure about midway between North Avenue Beach and Hollywood–Ardmore Beach (with plenty of free parking). Long popular with the city's Hispanic community, it has an expanse of beach mostly uninterrupted by piers or jetties, and a huge adjacent park with soccer fields and one big hill great for kite flying—even a small bait shop where anglers can go before heading for a nearby long pier designated for fishing. If your kids are teens, they can find a pickup game of volleyball here during the warmer months. **Hollywood–Ardmore Beach** (officially Kathy Osterman Beach), at the northern end of Lake Shore Drive, is a lovely crescent that's less congested and has steadily become more popular with gays who've moved up the lakefront from the Belmont Rocks, a longtime hangout.

If you've brought the family pooch along, you might want to take him for a dip at the **doggie beach** south of Addison Street, at about Hawthorne and Lake Shore Drive—although this minute spot aggravates some dog owners because it's situated in a harbor where the water is somewhat fouled by gas and oil from nearby boats. *Tip:* Try the south end of North Avenue Beach in early morning, before it opens to the public for the day. (Also consider that, in off-season, all beaches are fair game for dogs.)

Beaches are officially open with a full retinue of lifeguards on duty beginning about June 20, but swimmers can wade into the chilly water from Memorial Day to Labor Day. Only the bravest souls venture into the water before July, when the temperature creeps up enough to make swimming an attractive proposition. Please take note that the entire lakefront is not beach, and don't go doing anything stupid such as diving off the rocks—especially because the lake is currently at its lowest level in a decade. Be extremely careful with your kids. The lake has drop-offs at points along the shore, and kids can easily get into deeper water than they bargained for. Lake Michigan can develop large waves too, so exercise the same caution you would at the ocean.

Oak Street, North Avenue, Loyola, Osterman, Montrose, South Shore and Rainbow beaches are wheelchair friendly—they offer specially designed mats that create a path over the sand to the water. For questions about the 29 miles of beaches and parks along Lake Michigan, call the park district's lakefront region office at © **312/747-2474.**

2 Green Chicago: Our Parks

Thanks to architect Daniel Burnham and his coterie of visionary civic planners—who drafted the revolutionary 1909 Plan of Chicago in the aftermath of the Great Chicago Fire of 1871—the city boasts a wide-open lakefront park system unrivaled by most major metropolises. Downtown Chicago has two extensive downtown parks, Grant Park on the southern end of Michigan Avenue, and Lincoln Park, starting at North Avenue.

GRANT PARK ★★★

Modeled after the gardens at Versailles, Grant Park is Chicago's front yard, composed of giant lawns segmented by *allées* of trees, plantings, and paths, and pieced together by major roadways and a network of railroad tracks. Covering the greens is a variety of public recreational and cultural facilities (although these are few in number and nicely spread out, a legacy of mail-order magnate Aaron Montgomery Ward's *fin de siècle* campaign to limit municipal buildings in the park). Incredibly, the entire expanse was created from sandbars, landfill, and Chicago Fire debris; the original shoreline extended all the way to Michigan Avenue. Grant Park is the major venue for festivals in the city; while it's beautiful, it has fewer attractions for families than Lincoln Park (see review below).

The immense **Buckingham Fountain,** accessible along Congress Parkway, is the baroque centerpiece of the park, composed of pink Georgia marble and patterned after—but twice the size of—the Latona Fountain at Versailles, with adjoining esplanades beautified by rose gardens in season. Throughout the late spring and summer, the fountain spurts columns of water up to 165 feet in the air, illuminated after dark by a whirl of

> (*Fun Fact* **Did You Know?**
>
> **Buckingham Fountain's** jets and electric light displays are actually controlled by a computer 700 miles away in Atlanta.

colored lights, and building toward a grand finale before it shuts down for the night at 11pm. New concession areas and bathrooms have also opened on the plaza.

A popular summer series of outdoor classical music concerts is staged at the **Petrillo Music Shell,** at Jackson Boulevard and Columbus Drive, by the Grant Park Symphony Orchestra and Chorus. If construction goes according to plan, the symphony will be performing in the new Millennium Park at the north end of Grant Park, in a band shell designed by superstar architect Frank Gehry. The music festival, which includes performances over a 10-week period every Wednesday through Sunday evening, bills itself as the nation's only remaining free, municipally funded outdoor classical music festival. For a schedule of concert times and dates, contact the **Grant Park Music Festival** (© **312/742-7638**). Other favorite annual events are the free outdoor blues festival (in June) and the jazz festival (Labor Day). **Taste of Chicago** (© **312/744-3315**), purportedly the largest food festival in the world (the city estimates its annual attendance at around 3.5 million), takes place every summer for 10 days around the July 4th holiday. Local restaurants serve up more ribs, pizza, hot dogs, and beer than you'd ever want to see, let alone eat. (See chapter 2 for a comprehensive listing of summer events in Grant Park.)

Scattered about the park are a number of sculptures and monuments, including a heroic sculpture of two Native Americans on horseback entitled *The Spearman and the Bowman* (at Congress Pkwy. and Michigan Ave.), which has become the park's trademark since it was installed in 1928, as well as likenesses of Copernicus, Columbus, and Lincoln (*The Seated Lincoln*), the latter by the great American sculptor Augustus Saint-Gaudens, located on Congress Parkway between Michigan Avenue and Columbus Drive. On the western edge of the park, at Adams Street, is the **Art Institute** (p. 142), and at the southern tip in the newly redesigned Museum Campus are **The Field Museum of Natural History** (p. 128), the **Adler Planetarium** (p. 127), and the **Shedd Aquarium** (p. 131). At the north end of the park, adjacent to the nascent Millennium Park, is Daley Bicentennial Park, featuring an outdoor sports plaza with a dozen lighted tennis courts, a rink for ice skating in the winter and 'blading or rollerskating in the summer, and a field house.

331 E. Randolph St. © **312/742-7648.** Subway/El: Brown Line to the Loop. Bus: 3, 4, 6, 60, 146, or 151.

LAKE SHORE PARK

Located just behind the Museum of Contemporary Art, this park offers a view of the lake and packs some good facilities into a small space. You'll find baseball diamonds, a fitness center, a gym for basketball, an outdoor running track, and tennis courts. Again, although it's tiny, this little green space is a big find for families staying in the heart of the city.

808 N. Lake Shore Dr. (at Chicago Ave., 3 blocks east of Michigan Ave.). © **312/742-PLAY.** Bus: 151.

LINCOLN PARK ★★★

Lincoln Park is the city's largest park, and certainly one of the longest, stretching for six miles. Straight and narrow, Lincoln Park begins at North Avenue and follows the shoreline of Lake Michigan northward as far as Ardmore Avenue (not far from the East Asian enclave radiating from Argyle Ave. and quaint Andersonville). Within its elongated 1,200 acres are a world-class zoo, a half-dozen bathing beaches, a botanical conservatory, two excellent museums, a golf course, and the usual meadows, formal gardens, sporting fields, and tennis courts typical of urban parks. Attractions in the park include the **Chicago Historical Society** (p. 144), **Lincoln Park Zoo** (p. 162), **Lincoln Park Conservatory** (p. 164), and **Peggy Notebaert Nature Museum** (p. 165).

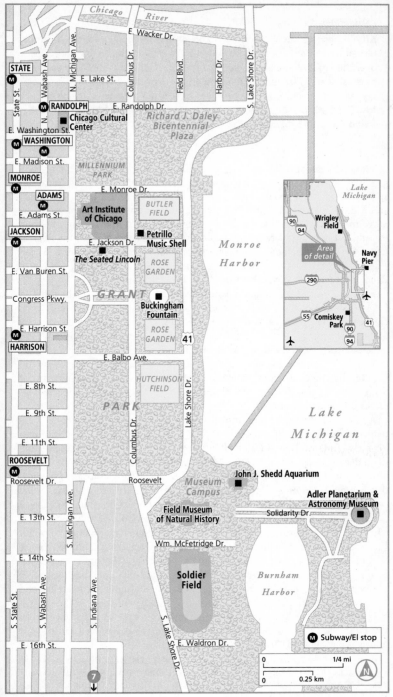

Grant Park

STATE
Ⓜ

N. Michigan Ave.
Wabash Ave.
State St.

E. Wacker Dr.

Chicago   River

E. Lake St.

RANDOLPH Ⓜ

Chicago Cultural Center

E. Washington St.

WASHINGTON Ⓜ
Ⓜ

E. Madison St.

MONROE
Ⓜ

ADAMS
Ⓜ

E. Adams St.

JACKSON
Ⓜ

E. Van Buren St.

Congress Pkwy.

E. Harrison St.

HARRISON
Ⓜ

E. 8th St.

E. 9th St.

E. 11th St.

ROOSEVELT
Ⓜ

Roosevelt Dr.

E. 13th St.

E. 14th St.

E. 16th St.

S. State St.
S. Wabash Ave.
S. Michigan Ave.
S. Indiana Ave.

Columbus Dr.

Field Blvd.
Harbor Dr.
S. Lake Shore Dr.

E. Randolph Dr.

Richard J. Daley Bicentennial Plaza

MILLENNIUM PARK

E. Monroe Dr.

BUTLER FIELD

Art Institute of Chicago

Petrillo Music Shell

E. Jackson Dr.

The Seated Lincoln

ROSE GARDEN

GRANT

Monroe Harbor

Buckingham Fountain

ROSE GARDEN

41

E. Balbo Ave.

HUTCHINSON FIELD

PARK

Lake Shore Dr.

Columbus Dr.

Lake Michigan

Roosevelt

Museum Campus

John J. Shedd Aquarium

Field Museum of Natural History

Adler Planetarium & Astronomy Museum

Solidarity Dr.

Wm. McFetridge Dr.

Soldier Field

Burnham Harbor

S. Lake Shore Dr.

E. Waldron Dr.

Ⓜ Subway/El stop

0   1/4 mi
0   0.25 km

N

7
↓

Area of detail inset

Lake Michigan

90
94

Wrigley Field

Navy Pier

290

55

Comiskey Park

90
94

41

Area of detail

Moments A Great View

After a visit to the Lincoln Park Zoo or the Peggy Notebaert Nature Museum, take a quick stroll on Fullerton Avenue to the bridge that runs over the lagoon (just before you get to Lake Shore Dr.). Standing on the south side of Fullerton Avenue, you'll have a great view of the Chicago skyline and Lincoln Park—an excellent backdrop for family souvenir photos. This path can get very crowded on summer weekends, so I suggest trying this photo op during the week.

The park's lakes, trails, and pathways make it ideal for biking, hiking, picnicking, and enjoying nature. Baseball, softball, and soccer fields, and basketball and tennis courts are concentrated mainly around the South Field, Waveland, and Montrose sections. You'll find archery and a nine-hole golf course in the Waveland area. Mini golf and a driving range are located near Diversey Harbor. Families can rent paddleboats and explore the South Pond from a little dock in front of Café Brauer, located on the northwest side of lovely South Pond ($9 per half-hr., $15 per hr.). You can also rent boats from the boathouse on North Pond. Boat rentals are available from May through September.

Families with small children won't want to miss the **Farm-in-the-Zoo** (p. 162), located on the southern end of South Pond. Five barns house cows, chickens, horses, goats, and other livestock. Kids can get a farmhand's eye view of butter churning, milking, and other farm activities throughout the day.

The **statue of the standing Abraham Lincoln** (just north of the North Ave. and State St. intersection) in the park that bears his name is one of two in Chicago by Augustus Saint-Gaudens. (*The Seated Lincoln* is in Grant Park.) Saint-Gaudens also did the Bates Fountain near the conservatory. The statue marks the southern boundary of the park.

A one-time Chicago dining institution near the zoo, **Café Brauer** (p. 112) reopened its doors to the public in 1990. Operating a cafe and ice cream parlor on the ground floor, and a ballroom called the Great Hall on the second floor that's flanked by two curving loggias, the return of the Brauer restores some of the elegant atmosphere that characterized the park around 1900, when this landmark building was erected. (If you visit on a weekend, chances are good that caterers will be setting up for a wedding in the Great Hall, but they'll usually let you in to sneak a peek.) I've heard from park district employees that, while touring the restoration, the son of the building's late architect, Dwight Perkins, was moved to tears. Perkins was one of the leaders of Chicago's Prairie School architecture movement, and Brauer is undeniably his masterwork. Best of all, though, is the picture-postcard view from the adjacent bridge spanning the pond of the John Hancock Center and neighboring skyscrapers beyond Lincoln Park's treetops.

If you're looking for an evening's entertainment, check out the **Theater on the Lake,** Fullerton Avenue, for open-air theater with a relaxed setting. For information, call © **312/742-7994.**

Bounded by Lake Shore Dr. from North Ave. to Bryn Mawr Ave. © **312/742-7726.** The park's visitor center is located in the Lincoln Park Cultural Center, 2045 N. Lincoln Park West. Park open daily from dawn until dusk. Visitor center open year-round Mon–Thurs 9am–9pm; Fri 11am–7pm; Sat 8am–4pm; and Sun 11am–5pm. Bus: 22, 145, 146, 147, 151, or 156.

Lincoln Park

■ Bird Sanctuary

N. Pine Grove Ave.
N. Broadway
Harbor Dr.
Belmont Lake Shore Dr.

Hawthorne

St.
Buckingham Pl.
Aldine   Ave.
Melrose   St.
Ave.

Broadway

Briar   Pl.
Barry   Ave.
Wellington   Ave.
Oakdale   Ave.
Surf   St.   Rd.

N. Sheridan

Belmont Harbor

■ Yacht Club

U.S. Military Reservation

LINCOLN PARK

41

Pkwy.

Wrightwood   Pl.

N. Orchard St.
N. Burling St.

Deming

N.

Arlington Pl.

Ave.

North

North Pond

Diversey Harbor

Lake Shore Dr.

Lake Michigan

Peggy Notebaert ■ Nature Museum

■ Theater on the Lake

Belden   Ave.

Clark

Webster

Lincoln

OZ PARK

Ave.

Ave.

Lincoln Park ■ Conservatory

■ Lincoln Park Zoo

Stockton

N. Lincoln

South Pond

Park Dr.

John Cannon Dr.

Fullerton Beach

Armitage   Ave.

N. Burling
N. Orchard
N. Larrabee
N. Mohawk
N. Cleveland
Sedgwick St.

Wisconsin St.   N.

Menomonee

N. Park Ave.

St.

Lincoln Park ■ Cultural Center

■ Café Brauer

■ Farm-in-the-Zoo

LINCOLN PARK

41

Eugenie   St.

Halsted St.

Avenue

Ⓜ NORTH/CLYBOURN

Ⓜ SEDGWICK   64

■ Chicago Historical Society

Lincoln Statue ■

N. State St.

North Ave. Beach

0   1/4 mi
0   0.25 km

Ⓜ Subway/El stop

Lake Michigan

90
94

Wrigley Field ■

Area of detail

Navy Pier ■

290

55   Comiskey Park

41

90
94

PING TOM MEMORIAL PARK

Families touring Chinatown should make a point of stopping at this wonderfully themed playground and park. Brightly colored swing sets, rubberized surfacing, and signs in Mandarin and English are surrounded by grounds landscaped with plants indigenous to China, such as bamboo. The park shelter is of Chinese design. It's all part of the Chicago Park District's new efforts to make parks attractive to both kids and adults, and appropriate to their neighborhood.

300 W. 19th St. ℂ **312/742-PLAY.** Subway/El: Orange Line to Cermak.

WASHINGTON SQUARE PARK

This little park, built on 3 acres, was possibly named after Washington Square Park, located in a similarly elegant New York neighborhood. Although small in size, its location is wonderful, just west of the Magnificent Mile. If you need a place for your kids to run free after a day of shopping or touring, this park will give them some open space and let you get into a "neighborhood" area not far from busy Michigan Avenue.

The park has had its ups and downs, following the fortunes of the neighborhood. Surrounded by fine residences and churches in the late 1800s, the neighborhood fell upon harder times in the 1910s and many mansions were converted into flophouses. The park earned the nickname "Bughouse Square." Like Speakers' Corner in London's Hyde Park, Washington Square became a popular spot for soapbox orators. Artists, writers, political radicals, and hobos pontificated, read poetry, and ranted and raved.

In the late 1990s, the park district, city, and neighborhood organizations restored the park by reconstructing a historic Victorian fountain and installing period lighting, fencing, and new plantings. Today, the park is surrounded by historic mansions, new condo buildings, and **Newberry Library** (p. 147).

901 N. Clark St. (at Delaware St.). ℂ **312/742-PLAY.** Bus: 11.

3 Playgrounds in the City Center

Chicago has a network of 552 city parks—most of which have playgrounds. To find information on a neighborhood park, go to **www.chicagoparkdistrict.com** or call ℂ **312/742-PLAY** for a list of parks and their facilities.

One of the most centrally located children's playgrounds is located at **Daley Bicentennial Plaza in Grant Park,** at 337 E. Randolph St. The recently refurbished playground (to the tune of $500,000) is set in the shadow of downtown skyscrapers at Randolph Street and Lake Shore Drive, which has fine views of the skyline and the lake. Kids will find all-new equipment for climbing, playing, and interacting, including swing sets and more, on a safe, rubberized surface. In addition to the play area, the plaza also offers a fitness center, locker rooms, and tennis courts, plus ice-skating in the winter. (For more on the skating rink, see "Sports & Games," below.)

Another heavily used playground is **Seneca Playlot Park,** 228 E. Chicago Ave., located just west of Chicago's venerable pumping station on Michigan Avenue. Seneca Park features both a lawn with shaded walkways and a playlot with a standard swing set, slide, and more. While it's small, and could use a little updating, Seneca provides a quiet oasis near the bustling Magnificent Mile. On the lawn sit two recent sculptures by nationally-recognized artists: *Ben,* a bronze horse by sculptor Debra Butterfield, and *Farmer's Dream,* an abstract piece by sculptor Richard Hunt. The heavily used playlot is named for Eli

Schulman (1910–88), a well-known restaurateur who founded Eli's, The Place For Steak, and who was active in promoting recreational activities for children. The park itself takes its name from adjacent Seneca Street, named for the Iroquois tribe of upstate New York.

4 Sports & Games

BASEBALL

Chicago's Park District offers baseball in many of its 552 parks; one diamond that's easily accessible and in a central location is **Lincoln Park.** The baseball fields are located on the southern tip, just north of the Chicago Historical Society. Even if a game is under way, you'll find some room to throw a ball back and forth with your child. For more information on baseball in city parks, visit www.chicagoparkdistrict.com.

Chicago parents who want to get kids involved in baseball should contact **Little League.** Kids ages 5 to 12 can participate. Teams change every year, so the best way to find one near you is to visit www.littleleague.org. Click on the "League Finder" link to start your search for a team for your child.

Comiskey Park, 333 W. 35th St. (© **312/674-1000;** www.whitesox.mlb.com), does a great job getting kids excited about baseball. Before every Chicago White Sox home game, White Sox Training Center coaches conduct a baseball clinic. Kids can practice in the batting cages, at the base running drill, and in the practice pitching areas. It's all free of charge. Enter Comiskey Park at Gate 3 or ask a Guest Services Representative how to get there. FUNdamentals, as the program is called, opens the gates about 1½ hours before game time and stays open for 1½ hours after the game starts. (If you're worn out after your pre-game workout, a Pepsi Kids Corner near Section 100 offers kids' concessions, with peanut butter and jelly sandwiches and other kid favorites. Near Section 101, you'll find a kids' gift shop, featuring kids' souvenirs and apparel.)

If it's a little batting practice you're seeking, head for the batting cages at **Novelty Golf,** 3640 W. Devon Ave., Lincolnwood (© **708/679-9434**). Choose from a slow, medium, or fast cage or softball cages. For those in the family who may not be baseball-crazy, a miniature golf course is open from April to October. In the city, you can practice at **Sluggers,** located near Wrigley Field at 3540 N. Clark St. (© **773/248-0055**). This neighborhood sports bar offers dozens of TV screens bringing in games via satellite, a fitting backdrop for you to test your skill in the batting cages. The upstairs batting cages approximate both softball and baseball pitches; there's also Pop-a-Shot and high-ball (a basketball-type game played on a trampoline).

BASKETBALL

One of Chicago's better public parks to catch (or watch) a game of hoops is **Blackhawk Park,** located at 2318 N. Lavergne Ave. in the Irving Park neighborhood (© **773/746-5014**). A basketball court (plus baseball and softball fields) dot the grounds of this family-friendly park. Basketball programs are offered for ages 5 and up. You'll also find an outdoor playground and spray pool and an indoor swimming pool. Park hours are Monday through Friday from 8am to 9pm and Saturday and Sunday from 9am to 5pm. Also recommended for their excellent kids' basketball programs are **Oz Park,** at 2021 N. Burling in the Lincoln Park neighborhood; **Portage Park,** 4100 N. Long Ave. on the northwest side; and **Independence Park,** at 3945 Springfield Ave. in the Irving Park neighborhood.

You can walk in to any **YMCA of Metropolitan Chicago** and use the gym to play basketball for a small fee. The most centrally located YMCA in the downtown area is New City YMCA, located at 1515 N. Halsted at Clybourn (© **312/440-7272**). For more information, see www.ymcachgo.org.

BIKING

Biking is a great way to see the city, particularly the lakefront, along which there's a bike path that extends for more than 18 miles. To rent bikes, try **Bike Chicago** (© **800/915-BIKE**), which is located at Navy Pier. Open from 8am to 11pm April through October (weather permitting), Bike Chicago stocks mountain and touring bikes, kids' bikes, strollers, and—most fun of all—quadcycles, which are four-wheeled contraptions equipped with a steering wheel and canopy that can accommodate four or five people. Rates for adult bikes are $8.75 an hour, $34 a day, with helmets, pads, and locks included; kids' bikes are $6 an hour, $24 a day. On weekdays, special rates of $10 a day are available. Quadcycles rent for $20 per hour. Once a day, the company leads a 1-hour bike tour from Navy Pier designed for all fitness levels.

Both the park district (© **312/747-2474**) and the **Chicagoland Bicycle Federation** (© **312/42-PEDAL;** www.chibikefed.org) offer free maps that detail popular biking routes. The latter, which is the preeminent organization for cyclists in Chicago, also sells a much larger, more extensive map for $6.95 that shows routes within a seven-county area. They sponsor a number of bike rides throughout the year, including the highly enjoyable **Boulevard Lakefront Tour,** held in late June, which follows the historic circle of boulevards that had their genesis in the Chicago Plan of 1909. It starts in Hyde Park at the University of Chicago campus.

A word of caution: Locking your bike anywhere you go is a no-brainer. More important, though, is never heading anywhere on the city's streets without first strapping on a helmet. Chicago Mayor Richard M. Daley is an avid cyclist himself and has tirelessly promoted the addition of designated bike lanes along many main thoroughfares. But, that said, most cabbies and drivers tend to ignore them. On a more positive note, last summer saw the debut of a pilot program allowing cyclists to haul their bikes onto CTA trains during weekends. If all goes well, the program will be continued.

BOWLING

What better way to bond as a family than an evening of gutter-dusting? Two popular hangouts mix teens, serious league bowlers, and families in an irresistible recipe for fun. At **Diversey River Bowl,** 2211 W. Diversey Ave. (© **773/227-5800**), tunes spun by a DJ (from an eclectic 300-CD collection) will get your feet tapping as you lace your bowling shoes. Now in its 10th year, you'll find plenty of 20-somethings here on weekends, many of whom play in leagues. Prepare for a wait: It can be an hour. The festive atmosphere is complemented by a collection of bowling pins signed by "bowling greats" such as Dolly Parton and Eddie Vedder. Lanes are open Monday through Friday from noon to 2am; call for hours on Saturday and Sunday, as leagues are usually scheduled. Cost is $19 per hour per lane Sunday through Thursday, and $26 per hour per lane on Friday and Saturday. Shoe rental is $3.

Another option is **Waveland Bowl,** 3700 N. Western Ave. (© **773/472-5900**). Open 24/7, Waveland has 40 lanes and gets pretty loud when busy. Even though the place is huge, expect to wait your turn.

When in the suburbs, **Brunswick Zone** is your best bet and birthday-party central. One plus for families is the video games. The company has lanes in suburban Algonquin, Carol Stream, Deerfield, Deer Park, Glendale Heights, Kankakee, Mount Prospect Naperville, Niles, Oak Lawn, Palatine, Roselle, Waukegan/Lakehurst, and Woodridge. For phone numbers or to make online reservations, visit **www.brunswickbowling.com**.

CLIMBING

Sorry to point out the obvious, but Chicago has no hills, much less mountains. (When I was in a training group for the Chicago Marathon, we did our hill training by running up the corkscrew ramp in the John Hancock Center parking garage—that's how serious Chicago's hill shortage is!) Your best option for climbing in the city is "Mount Chicago," located at the **Lakeshore Athletic Club** (© 312/616-9000). Billed as "the world's highest indoor climbing wall," the man-made wall rises 110 feet. Kids ages 5 and up can climb on Saturdays after 2pm and all day Sunday. You don't have to be a member to use the wall. Cost for kids is $12.50 for an orientation class plus a $10 fee, for a total of $22.50. Kids' classes and private lessons are available; classes take place Sunday mornings from 9 to 10am and require pre-registration. Even if you don't have previous experience, adults too can venture onto the wall through an orientation and safety class (all while wearing a protective harness, of course). The club is private, but is open to guests of any hotel for $18 a day and to guests at the nearby Fairmont Hotel and Hyatt Regency Chicago for $15 a day. It's located at 211 N. Stetson, 1 block east of North Michigan Avenue at Lake Street. To get there, take any bus that serves Michigan Avenue.

Chicago residents who want to enroll their kids in classes might investigate the indoor rock climbing at **Lakeshore Academy,** located at 937 W. Chestnut, near the intersection of Halsted and Chicago (© 312/563-9400; www.lakeshoreacademy.com). Membership is $100 per year and lasts until the same term 1 year later, and classes are organized by age group for kids from age 5 to 16. "Hidden Peak," as the climbing area is called, is a great way to discover the challenge of indoor rock climbing. Staffed with experienced and friendly people, Hidden Peak offers tons of user-friendly programs for kids (and adults). *Tip:* A fun option for a birthday party is climbing parties, held for kids age 6 and up, that cost $40 per instructor and $10 per child. Lakeshore Academy gives these parties over a 2-hour period on Saturday and Sunday evenings, or Sunday mornings. Check out the website for more information.

FISHING

The Chicago Park District runs fishing programs for kids; for the latest details, check out **www.chicagoparkdistrict.com**. One program, "Fish N Kids," offers rods, reels, bait, and instruction for four daily 45-minute sessions at all Chicago Park District lagoons and at four lakefront locations. The Sam Romano Youth Fishing Derby (named for a charter boat captain who loved fishing and kids) that runs all summer is open to kids ages 8 to 15. Kids enter their catches in a category: rock bass, panfish, catfish, and carp. Twenty kids in each category win prizes of new fishing equipment.

Want to do battle with the scrappy coho salmon, or tie into a tackle-testing, arm-aching 20-pound chinook? Salmon fishing has been popular on Lake Michigan since Pacific species were introduced in the 1970s. Gather a group of six (to split the cost of $395 for 5 hr. of fishing) and be prepared to start at dawn.

You can find a charter boat through the **Chicago Sportfishing Association** (© **312/922-1100**).

Lake perch are another popular Lake Michigan fish—they won't give you the fight that salmon do, but they are fun to catch and good to eat. (Pan-fried is the way to go.) They are plentiful from May to August. Jumbo perch weigh in at 1 pound and are caught with ultralight spinning tackle or hand lines rigged with multiple hooks. Check sporting goods stores for equipment and bait. The local anglers' favorite spot is Montrose Harbor Pier, east of Lake Shore Drive at Wilson Avenue. Harbor fishing is allowed in designated areas of Belmont, Montrose, Diversey, DuSable, Monroe, Burnham, 59th Street, and Jackson Inner and Jackson Outer harbors. To find out more, call **Chicago Park District** harbor information at © **312/747-7527.**

GOLF

The Chicago Park District offers 6 courses, 3 driving ranges, and 3 learning centers. Don't let a little cold weather stop you: As further evidence of the hardiness of Chicagoans, the golf courses closed only 1 day in 2001, when there was a blizzard. (Yes, you can golf in Chicago year-round, even on Christmas Day!) For tee times and information, call © **312/245-0909.** Most recommended for kids is the **Diversey Driving Range,** located in Lincoln Park at Diversey Street; it's a fun way to get outside after dinner on a summer evening.

In the northern suburbs, **Skokie Sports Park,** 3459 Oakton (© **847/674-1500**), offers an 18-hole around the world-themed miniature golf course, a 9-hole miniature golf course for the smallest tots, a two-tiered driving range, and junior golf lessons. The Traveler's Quest miniature golf course, geared toward older kids and adults, lets you putt around the Eiffel Tower and over the waterfall near Easter Island. Check out the African water hole (in which you putt into the hippo's mouth), the Japanese garden with lanterns offering sizable hazards, and the Great Wall of China. The park is open April through October Monday through Friday from 8am to 10pm, Saturday and Sunday until 11pm; November through March Monday through Friday from 10am to 7pm, Saturday and Sunday from 9am.

In nearby Lincolnwood, **Bunny Hutch Novelty Golf and Games,** 3550 W. Devon Ave. (© **847/679-9434**), offers miniature golf, batting cages, a video arcade, and an ice cream parlor. It's a 50-year-old operation that's open daily from 10am to midnight from early March through late October.

HORSEBACK RIDING

Let me be frank: Horseback riding in downtown Chicago is impossible. About the closest you can get is a horse-and-buggy ride. Carriages depart from the southwest corner of Michigan Avenue and Pearson Street (next to the Water Tower). For $30 for a half-hour ride (for up to four people), it's a picturesque way to take in the city's sights. The rides are operated by The Noble Horse, which owns the only remaining stable in downtown Chicago from a 1917 brick building at 1410 N. Orleans Ave. For group tours or other information, call **The Noble Horse** at © **312/266-7878.**

To hit the happy trails, your best bet is the suburbs. Our top pick is **Dragons Lair Stables,** 26011 Rand Rd. in northwest suburban Wauconda (© **847/526-0055**). Located directly west of Lake Forest, near Highway 12, the stables are a short ride from the trails of Lake County's Lakewood Forest Preserve. Kids must be 10 and older to ride. Stables are open daily from 10am to 6pm and the cost is $26 per hour. Reservations are required.

ICE SKATING

Whether you and your kids are executing graceful toe loops or merely stumbling across the ice, you can hit the ice in the heart of Chicago's Loop. A downturn in the real-estate market was a blessing for Chicagoans who love to skate outside in the chilly winter air. A proposed downtown office project went unbuilt in the late 1980s and left a huge gaping hole in the heart of the Loop; some creative thinking led to the creation of **Skate on State** (✆ 312/744-3315). The seasonal rink is installed November through March across from Marshall Field's, along State Street between Washington and Madison streets. It operates daily until 7:30pm. Skating is free if you bring your own skates, or $2 to $3 if you rent a pair. Concessions and a warming hut are available. It's fun, but developers are again eyeing the block, so it's impossible to know whether the rink will be back next year.

The park district runs dozens of other skating surfaces throughout the city, both along the lakefront and in neighborhood parks. Call ✆ 312/742-PLAY for locations. The newest is the **McCormick Tribune Ice Rink** in Millennium Park, located at the intersection of Michigan Avenue and Monroe Street. Another place to find ice is **Daley Bicentennial Plaza** (✆ 312/742-7650), located in the shadow of downtown skyscrapers at Randolph Street and Lake Shore Drive, which has fine views of the skyline and the lake. Try going on a weeknight when the city lights sparkle over you, and grab a hot chocolate from a vending machine to warm up before hitting the ice. Another smallish rink exists at **Navy Pier,** 600 E. Grand Ave. (✆ 312/595-PIER).

Year-round skating and ice-skating lessons are available at **McFetridge Sports Complex,** located in the Lakeview neighborhood at 3845 N. California Ave. at Irving Park Road (✆ 773/742-7585). Open skating sessions in the indoor rink are held Wednesday and Friday afternoons from 3:30 to 5pm, and Saturday and Sunday from 4:30 to 6pm. Skates can be rented for $2.50 a pair; the rink fee is $3 for adults, $2.75 for teens 14 to 17, and $2.25 for kids 13 and under. The rink is huge and can be very crowded on weekends. You might want to take advantage of the free skating lessons, available on Mondays from 5:15 to 5:55pm.

IN-LINE SKATING

Wheeled ones have been taking over Chicago's sidewalks, streets, and bike paths since the early 1990s. Numerous rental places have popped up, and several sporting goods shops that sell in-line skates also rent them. The rentals generally include helmets and pads. **Bike Chicago** (✆ 800/915-BIKE) rents in-line skates at Navy Pier. Bike Chicago charges adults $8 an hour or $30 a day, kids ages 5 and up $6 an hour, $24 a day; pick them up Saturday morning and keep them until closing on Sunday at 7pm. They also offer free delivery to downtown locations for day rentals. If your kids are big enough to wear adult sizes (starting with men's and women's size 5), a second spot is **Londo Mondo,** 1100 N. Dearborn St. (✆ 312/751-2794), on the Gold Coast, renting blades for $7 an hour or $20 a day. Every Wednesday from about April to Labor Day at 6:30pm, Londo Mondo is the starting point for a free skate-through-the-city party open to all. It ends at Melvin B's, a Gold Coast cafe where the first drink is on the house. A second, beginner-oriented roll-about hits the streets on Tuesdays.

The best route to skate, of course, is the lakefront trail that leads from Lincoln Park down to Oak Street Beach. Beware, though, that those same miles of trail are claimed by avid cyclists—and I've seen plenty of collisions between 'bladers and bikers. Approach Chicago lakefront traffic as carefully as you would a major expressway!

At the **Rainbo Roller Rink,** 4836 N. Clark St. (© **312/271-6200**), you and your kids can skate to a pulsing light show and great music. There's pizza and soda for breaks. During afternoon family sessions, you can roller-dance with the dino-on-wheels master of ceremonies named Skateasaurus. A smaller, separate rink for beginners makes this a family-oriented rink.

SAILING

It seems a shame just to sit on the beach and watch all those beautiful sailboats gliding across the lake. Go on, get out there. The **Chicago Sailing Club,** in Belmont Harbor (© **773/871-SAIL**), rents J-22 and J-30 boats from 9am to sunset, weather permitting, May through October. A J-22 holds four or five people. Rates for a J-22 range from $30 to $45 an hour ($10 extra for a skipper). A J-30 accommodates up to 10 people and can sail at night. Rates are $60 to $80 per hour, plus $20 per hour for a skipper. If you want to take the boat out without a skipper, you need to demonstrate your skills first (for an additional $10 checkout fee). Reservations are recommended. Charters are also available.

SWIMMING

The Chicago Park District maintains about 30 indoor pools for lap swimming and general splashing around. If you are a resident, you should check out your local park (to find out where parks are located, see www.chicagopark district.com). Some neighborhoods have incredible facilities that are safe and clean. **Portage Park,** for example, located on Chicago's northwest side, has a stunning outdoor Olympic-sized pool, a diving board with three levels and its own dive pool, and a kids' pool with a water playhouse, waterfalls, and more. It's absolutely wonderful, and it's free. The neighborhood is populated by Hispanic and Eastern European immigrants and tons of kids jam the pool every summer weekend. Another great park for swimming is **Blackhawk Park,** located at 2318 N. Lavergne Ave. in the Irving Park neighborhood (© **773/746-5014**). You'll find an outdoor spray pool and an indoor swimming pool. Pool hours vary according to age: Youth swim is at 3pm, teen swim at 5pm, and family swim at 7pm.

Still, my advice to visitors would be to skip the park district pools, because many are located in off-the-beaten-track neighborhoods. As a visitor, your best bet for summer swimming is **Lake Michigan,** where beaches are open for swimmers Memorial Day through Labor Day from 9am to 9:30pm in areas watched over by lifeguards (no swimming off the rocks, please). Not only can you be sure of feeling safe here, it's a uniquely "Chicago" experience. How often do you and your kids get the chance to take a dip in a great lake? Watch the news for beach closings, which happen occasionally, as the water is tested daily for bacteria.

The Chicago Park District manages 31 beaches along 24 miles of lakefront. Amenities vary, but most have a comfort station or a beach house and food vendors selling hot dogs, burgers, and soda. The two beaches I can recommend without hesitation are **Oak Street Beach** and **North Avenue Beach.** Both also feature a broader menu for dining: The Oak Street Beachstro (p. 94) offers gourmet salads, beef tenderloin, grilled salmon, and Key lime pie; the restaurant in the beach house at North Avenue Beach offers Jamaican jerk chicken and specialty ice cream. For adults and older kids intent on doing some serious swimming, a good place is the water along the wall beginning at Ohio Street Beach, located slightly south of Oak Street Beach and just northwest of Navy Pier. The Chicago Triathlon Club marks a course here each summer with a buoy at both the quarter- and the half-mile distance. It's a popular swimming route because it follows the shoreline in a straight line, and the water is fairly shallow.

For more information, call the park district's beach and pool office at ✆ 312/747-0832.

TENNIS

The best—and cheapest—tennis in the city is found at **Waveland Courts,** located on Lake Shore Drive at Addison. For $4 per hour, you can play on these public courts. It's first-come, first-served, so get there early in the morning—the park is open from 6am to 11pm. Pay before you play at the trailer located close to the Addison entrance. Tennis buffs report that the availability of courts is pretty good in the morning. League play takes place in the evenings, and it's difficult to get a court. (*Note to non-tennis players in a tennis-playing family:* Golf is also available here.)

If it's lessons you're seeking, head for **McFetridge Sports Complex,** 3845 N. California Ave. (✆ 773/742-7585). Students here report that the tennis pros are great, lessons are good, and the price is right: An 8-week-long group lesson ranges from $35 for 4-year-olds to $41 for teens (no single lessons are available). The complex offers lessons and tournaments for kids. You can also pay for court time here just to play on your own, but book ahead, especially in winter. In the summer, you'll have no problem booking an indoor court.

5 Indoor Playgrounds

The only city-run indoor playground is free, highly recommended, and located in **Garfield Park Conservatory;** see p. 164 for a full description.

The national chain, **Gymboree,** offers a series of classes for kids from newborn to age 4 in a playscape with slides, inflatable logs, colorful mats, and all kinds of things to jump on and crawl inside. A Gymboree teacher leads the way with activities and songs. Visitors can call ahead to request space in one of the classes, although most parents sign up for a full series. The cost is $179 for 12 weeks, or about $15 per class. In Chicago, the sole location is at 3158 N. Lincoln Ave. (✆ 773/296-4550; www.gymboree.com). You'll also find branches in suburban Wilmette, Northbrook, and Wheaton.

Odyssey Fun World (www.odysseyfunworld.com), in west suburban Naperville and Tinley Park, features 250 video games and rides, plus a Little Tykes playground, a four-level soft playland (for kids 12 and under), a rollercoaster simulator, a cafe, a rock climbing wall thrill ride, and some outdoor attractions, including 36 holes of adventure golf, go-cart tracks, and batting cages. Each activity has a fee, and games require tokens (usually 25¢ each, less if bought in quantity); admission to the soft playground is $6.95. Other rides vary from $2 to $5. Locations are at 19111 S. Oak Park Ave., Tinley Park (✆ 708/429-3800), and 3440 Odyssey Court, Naperville (✆ 630/416-2222).

6 Classes & Workshops

Chicago Children's Museum   A plethora of wonderful classes is available at the museum. The array might include wintertime decorating of fleece scarves that kids can wear, making glitzy bookmarks, designing quilt squares of kids' favorite books, or dancing out storybook classics such as *The Gingerbread Man.* Classes are available for all ages. They change often, so see the "Activities" section of the website, www.chichildrensmuseum.org.

700 E. Grand Ave. ✆ **312/527-1000**. www.chichildrensmuseum.org. Class fee included in museum admission fee ($6.50 adults and children, $5.50 seniors). Subway/El: Red Line to Grand/State; transfer to city bus or Navy Pier's free trolley bus. Bus: 29, 56, 65, or 66.

The Field Museum of Natural History "The Two of Us" is an 8-week program designed for kids ages 3 to 6 and an adult companion. Each week, stories, songs, fun facts, an art project, and snack help introduce kids to the wonder of the Field Museum. The program costs $95 for a child and parent. For more information, see the "Education" section of www.fmnh.org, or call ✆ 312/665-7400.

Roosevelt Rd. and Lake Shore Dr. ✆ **312/922-9410** or 312/341-9299 TDD (for hearing-impaired callers). www.fmnh.org. Bus: 6, 10, 12, 130, or 146.

Lill Street Art Center This center for working artists offers a huge array of classes for kids from 2 years old and up, involving pottery, watercolors, singing, and more. If you want to drop in, you can browse the studios, where the kids can see the artists at work.

1021 W. Lill, 3 blocks north of Fullerton St. in the DePaul University area. ✆ **773/477-6185**. www.lillstreet.com. 10-week-long kids' courses cost $140–$185 (single lessons not available). Gallery hours Tues–Sat 11am–6pm and Sun noon–5pm. Subway/El: Red Line to Fullerton.

Museum of Science and Industry Who knows how many current chemists, biologists, and real-life rocket scientists were once inspired by this museum? Get your little Einstein involved in the wonders of science with "Taste of Science" workshops, offered between April and August. Past workshops have explored aerospace through building and flying kites and gliders (with a visit from a real United Airlines pilot!); papermaking; and the underwater world of the *Titanic*, where kids learned how scientists care for the ship and artifacts. Workshops are for kids grades 1 to 6. (Some have suggested age ranges.) The cost is $15 per child for a 3-hour workshop; the adult who accompanies the child can attend for no charge. For current offerings, see the "Education" section of the website, www.msichicago.org, or call ✆ 773/684-7844, ext. 2687.

57th St. and Lake Shore Dr. ✆ **800/468-6674** outside the Chicago area, 773/684-1414, or TTY 773/684-3323. www.msichicago.org. Bus: 6, 10, 55, 151, or 156.

Old Town School of Folk Music Chicago's premier music education center offers kids' classes in music, dance, art, and theater as well as private lessons. Children's courses last 8 or 16 weeks, and are 45 minutes to 1 hour in length. Visitors, however, can get a taste of the fun by trying out a class. You can show up the day of the class and pay $13 to attend that day. (Art classes are excluded.) Drop-in opportunities include the Wiggle Worms class, a music and movement class that Chicago parents say is the absolute most fun class in the city for small children.

Teen classes are just for students ages 11 to 18, and are offered during after-school and weekend hours. All classes meet once a week, and most are 80 minutes in length, in a relaxed group atmosphere of 8 to 12 students. Most teen music classes cost $90 for 8 weeks of classes; theater classes run 16 weeks. Starlight: Teen Open Mic at the Old Town School takes the stage from 7 to 10pm on the second Friday of every month. Call for information or to be added to the Teen Open Mic mailing list. This new monthly event is a showcase for musicians, actors, and audience members at the 909 W. Armitage Ave. location.

4544 N. Lincoln Ave. ✆ **773/728-6000**. www.oldtownschool.org. Subway/El: Brown Line to Western.

9

Shopping with Your Kids

When I talked to other Chicago parents about shopping with their kids, they often joked, "The best shopping experience is *no* shopping experience!" True, shopping with kids can be a strain, and maybe this chapter is better titled "Shopping *for* Your Kids." To keep kids interested during your shopping expeditions, I've included some stores that wouldn't necessarily be considered children's stores, but which kids find fascinat-ing—stores that sell thousands of different buttons, for example.

For more on shopping for adults in Chicago, pick up a copy of *Frommer's Chicago*. This chapter concentrates on the Magnificent Mile, State Street, and several trendy neighborhoods, where you'll find one-of-a-kind shops and boutiques that make shopping such an adventure. It also includes a sampling of retailers organized by merchandise category.

1 The Shopping Scene

SHOPPING HOURS & SALES TAXES

As a general rule, stores are open Monday through Saturday from 10am to 6 or 7pm, and Sunday from noon to 5pm. Neighborhood stores tend to keep later hours, with some remaining open until 8pm Monday through Saturday and until 6pm on Sunday. Many stores are open later on Thursday, and almost all have extended hours during the holiday season. Nearly all the stores in the Loop are open for daytime shopping only, generally Monday through Saturday from 9 or 10am to no later than 6pm. (The few remaining big downtown department stores have some evening hours; see below.) Many Loop stores not on State Street are closed Saturday; on Sunday, the Loop—except for a few restaurants, theaters, and cultural attractions—is shut down pretty tight.

You might do a double take after checking the total on your purchase: At 8.75%, the state and local sales taxes on nonfood items is one of the steepest in the country.

SHOPPING DISTRICTS
THE MAGNIFICENT MILE

The Magnificent Mile, Chicago's top shopping destination, is magnificent not because of the sightseeing or the architecture. On the Magnificent Mile, the stores are the thing. The density of first-rate shopping is, quite simply, unmatched anywhere. Even jaded shoppers from other worldly capitals are delighted at the ease and convenience of the stores concentrated here. Taking into account that tony Oak Street is just around a corner (again, if you want to hit Hermès and Prada, I must refer you to *Frommer's Chicago!*), the overall area is a little like New York's Fifth Avenue and Beverly Hills's Rodeo Drive rolled into one. Whether your passion is Bulgari jewelry, Prada suits, or Ferragamo footwear, you'll find it on this stretch of concrete. Window-shoppers and peo-ple-watchers also will find plenty to amuse themselves. This is the city's liveliest corridor: The sidewalks are packed in the summer and on weekends with hordes of shoppers strolling up and down the avenue and pausing to enjoy the many street performers who enliven this strip. Holidays on Michigan Avenue are a magical time, as the city knocks itself out with lights and music and a spectacular Christmas tree in the John Hancock Center plaza.

The face of one of Chicago's most prestigious addresses has been dramatically transformed over the past quarter-century since the first mall—Water Tower Place—went up on the north end of the street. Several more malls and large-scale, hotel-retail projects have followed. As the rush for square footage escalated beginning in the late 1980s, many city residents lamented the metamorphosis of the street from a rather intimate and graceful promenade of 1920s buildings to a glitzy canyon of retail theater. Eager to get in on the action, national and international retailers—from middle-brow discounters to high-brow couture purveyors—have continued to look for front-row locations to squeeze into.

For the ultimate Mag Mile shopping adventure, start at one end of North Michigan Avenue and try to work your way to the other. (The "Mile" runs from Oak Street on the north end to the Chicago River on the south end.) In this section are listed some of the best-known kid-related shops on the avenue and on nearby side streets.

NORTH MICHIGAN AVENUE & THE MAGNIFICENT MALLS

North Michigan Avenue is lined with shops and includes four vertical malls—each a major shopping destination in its own right. These indoor malls offer shopping on multiple levels.

WATER TOWER PLACE   Chicago's first—and still busiest—vertical mall is Water Tower Place, a block-size, marble-sheathed building at 835 N. Michigan Ave. (© 312/440-3165; www.shopWaterTower.com), between East Pearson and East Chestnut streets. The mall, which received a facelift this year to bring it out of the 1980s and into the new millennium, has seven floors that contain about 100 stores. (The mall reportedly accounts for roughly half of all the retail trade transacted along the Magnificent Mile.) The mall also houses a dozen different cafes and restaurants. It's open Monday through Saturday from 10am to 7pm and Sunday from noon to 6 pm.

For all its fame as both a movie backdrop and a retail temple, Water Tower is the most accessible of the developments on the street. It houses the Mag Mile outpost of the Loop's famed **Marshall Field's** (© 312/335-7700; p. 206) and a **Lord & Taylor** (© 312/787-7400; p. 206). You'll find a few surprises, but you'll also see many of the same stores from your mall back home—as well as the same packs of teenagers roaming from floor to floor. The innovative **foodlife** food court contains more than a dozen stations, from burgers and pizza to Mexican and Moroccan, plus the Mity Nice Grill, a faux-1940s diner (see p. 99 for a full review). Two movie complexes contain eight screens. Of note to kids are the **Warner Bros. Studio Store** (© 312/664-9440), offering Bugs Bunny and friends merchandise; **Michael Jordan Golf** (© 312/944-4545), with clothing, clubs, balls, and anything else you can dream up for hitting the links; **Accent Chicago** (© 312/944-1354) for T-shirts, pizza pans, logo sports gear, and other souvenirs that say "Chicago"; and **WTTW Store of Knowledge** (© 312/642-6826) for educational games, videos, and other intellectually stimulating merchandise. The mall is home to **Abercrombie Kids** (p. 207), **GapKids** (p. 208), **Limited Too, Claire's Boutique, Jacadi** (p. 208) and **Gymboree** (p. 208). Chicago's famous **Fanny May Candies**, on the ground level behind Marshall Field's, is also sure to please the kids.

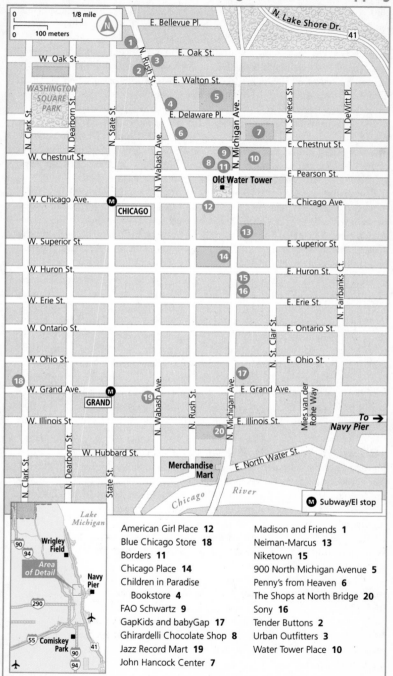

Magnificent Mile Shopping

E. Bellevue Pl.
N. Lake Shore Dr.
41
W. Oak St.
E. Oak St.
N. Rush St.
E. Walton St.
WASHINGTON SQUARE PARK
E. Delaware Pl.
N. State St.
N. Wabash Ave.
E. Chestnut St.
N. Michigan Ave.
N. Seneca St.
N. DeWitt Pl.
W. Chestnut St.
E. Pearson St.
Old Water Tower
W. Chicago Ave.
M CHICAGO
E. Chicago Ave.
W. Superior St.
E. Superior St.
W. Huron St.
E. Huron St.
W. Erie St.
E. Erie St.
N. St. Clair St.
N. Fairbanks Ct.
W. Ontario St.
E. Ontario St.
W. Ohio St.
E. Ohio St.
W. Grand Ave.
M GRAND
E. Grand Ave.
Mies van der Rohe Way
To → Navy Pier
W. Illinois St.
E. Illinois St.
N. Clark St.
N. Dearborn St.
N. Rush St.
N. Michigan Ave.
State St.
W. Hubbard St.
Merchandise Mart
E. North Water St.
Chicago River
M Subway/El stop

0   1/8 mile
0   100 meters

Lake Michigan
90 94
Wrigley Field
Area of Detail
Navy Pier
290
55 Comiskey Park
90 94
41

American Girl Place **12**
Blue Chicago Store **18**
Borders **11**
Chicago Place **14**
Children in Paradise Bookstore **4**
FAO Schwartz **9**
GapKids and babyGap **17**
Ghirardelli Chocolate Shop **8**
Jazz Record Mart **19**
John Hancock Center **7**

Madison and Friends **1**
Neiman-Marcus **13**
Niketown **15**
900 North Michigan Avenue **5**
Penny's from Heaven **6**
The Shops at North Bridge **20**
Sony **16**
Tender Buttons **2**
Urban Outfitters **3**
Water Tower Place **10**

900 NORTH MICHIGAN AVENUE The most upscale of the Magnificent Mile's three vertical malls, 900 North Michigan (© 312/915-3917; www.shop900.com) is often called the "Bloomingdale's building," for its most prominent tenant. The mall avoids the tumult of Water Tower Place while still generating the vitality essential to a satisfying shopping spree. In addition to about 70 stores are a few good restaurants and a nice movie multiplex on the lower level. The mall is open Monday through Saturday from 10am to 7pm and Sunday from noon to 7 pm.

Young teens will make a beeline for **Club Monaco** (© 312/787-8757), with minimalist casual-chic clothes at affordable prices. **J. Crew** (© 312/751-2739) offers sweaters, slacks, hats, belts, and other clothing featuring the scrubbed-clean look, popular with young teens. You'll also want to check out **Galt Toys** (p. 216), and **Mini Me** (p. 208) features great kids' clothing.

The mall's bathrooms are large, clean, and well equipped with infant changing areas; you'll find them on the second and fifth levels. An added treat: Shoppers are serenaded by live piano music on weekends from noon to 5pm on the second level. You'll also find kid-friendly restaurants, including **Tucci Benucch,** a casual Italian restaurant that has a kids' menu, coloring sheets and crayons; and **Boudin Bakery & Café,** a reliable place for a quick sandwich.

CHICAGO PLACE Inaugurated in 1991 at 700 N. Michigan Ave., Chicago Place (© 312/266-7710) has been looking for an identity ever since. The mall is mainly notable as the home of **Saks Fifth Avenue** (© 312/944-6500; p. 207). You won't find much for kids here, except a **Talbots Kids** (p. 209) for those seeking out the preppy look, and a food court on the eighth floor that features cheap eats. You'll find the usual mall favorites (Subway, Taco Bell, Wendy's), but healthier dishes are available at **Pattie's Quick and Lite** (salads, wraps, pasta) and **Pita Pavilion** (Mediterranean). Kids love the crispy french fries at the **Great Steak & Potato Company.** Grab one of the tables behind Pita Pavilion for a great Michigan Avenue view. The mall is open Monday through Friday from 10am to 7pm, Saturday from 10am to 6pm, and Sunday from noon to 5pm.

THE SHOPS AT NORTH BRIDGE The best concentration of kids' stores on the Mag Mile is located in this new mall at 520 N. Michigan Ave. (© 312/327-2300; www.northbridgechicago.com). The third floor is devoted to children's shops, the best of which is **The Lego Store** (© 312/494-0760). Look for the replicas of Chicago landmarks built out of those distinctive colored-plastic blocks, and be prepared to stay awhile: Kids can easily spend an hour here. Other stores of interest to kids are **Benetton** (p. 204), **Chicago Harley-Davidson, The Children's Place, Hoohobbers** (p. 214), **Jordan Marie, Oilily Children** (p. 209), and **Sanrio.**

The anchor of the mall is a four-story **Nordstrom** (© 312/464-1515). The mall includes the first Chicago locations for **A/X Armani Exchange** (© 312/467-5702), Giorgio Armani's younger and more affordable line, and a big hit with young teens. Eating options at North Bridge include **Big Bowl** (p. 97), **ESPN Zone** (p. 96), **California Pizza Kitchen** (p. 98), and a host of fast-food outlets on the fourth floor. The mall is open Monday through Saturday from 10am to 8pm, and Sunday from 11am to 6pm.

STATE STREET & THE LOOP

This shopping district got its start when Potter Palmer moved his dry-goods business to the thoroughfare in 1852. By World War I, seven of the largest and

Wicker Park/Bucktown Shopping

M Subway/El stop

Homer St.
Cortland St.
Moffat St.
Churchill St.
Willow St.
W. St. Paul
W. Wabansia Ave.
Concord Pl.
W. North Ave.
W. Pierce Ave.
W. Le Moyne St.
W. Schiller St.
Evergreen Ave.
Potomac Ave.
W. Crystal St.
W. Division St.
W. Haddon St.

Cortland St.
Bloomingdale St.

Wilmot Ave.
N. Milwaukee Ave.
N. Hoyne Ave.
N. Damen Ave.
N. Winchester Ave.
N. Wolcott Ave.
N. Honore St.
N. Wood St.
N. Hermitage Ave.

Oakley Blvd.
N. Bell Ave.
N. Leavitt St.

W. Wabansia Ave.
W. Le Moyne St.
Hirsch St.

WICKER PARK
Evergreen Ave.
N. Milwaukee Ave.
Ellen Ct.

Flat Iron Building

Lake Michigan
Wrigley Field
Area of detail
Navy Pier
Comiskey Park

94 90
290
55 90 41
94

Little Folk Art 2
The Red Balloon Company 1
Sweet Thang 3

most lavish department stores in the world were competing for shoppers' loyalties along a half-mile stretch between Randolph Street and Congress Parkway. Two of the grand old stores remain: **Marshall Field & Co.,** 111 N. State St., at Randolph Street (© 312/781-1000; p. 206); and **Carson Pirie Scott & Co.,** a few blocks south, at 1 S. State St., at the corner of Madison Street (© 312/641-7000; p. 206). Both buildings are city landmarks and attractions in themselves. Architecturally speaking, the Louis Sullivan–designed Carson's is the more celebrated of the two; however, Field's State Street store remains one of the world's largest, occupying an entire city block and featuring the largest Tiffany glass mosaic dome in the United States. If you're in Chicago between Thanksgiving and New Year's, a visit to Marshall Field's to see the holiday windows and to have lunch under the Great Tree in the Walnut Room is in keeping with local tradition.

Tips Point Zero

If the quick change from north to south in the Loop confuses you, keep in mind that in Chicago, point zero for the purpose of address numbering is the intersection of State and Madison streets.

By the early 1970s, the Magnificent Mile had begun to supplant State Street. Many of the Loop's old department stores—Sears, Roebuck and Co.; Montgomery Ward; Goldblatts; and Wieboldt—closed their doors in favor of greener pastures in the suburbs. Marshall Field's and Carson Pirie Scott hung on, keeping State Street alive until the city took notice in the 1980s and began to revive it.

Although State Street has not recaptured the glamour of decades past, it manages to draw crowds of loyal customers from the Loop's office towers and Chicagoans turned off by Michigan Avenue's snob factor. There's no better example of the street's revival than the recent opening of a new **Sears** store (© 312/373-6000) at the corner of State and Madison streets. A large **Old Navy** store at Washington and State streets (© 312/551-0522; p. 209) also brings in the crowds—check out the kids' wares, which are cheap and hip. A **Lord & Taylor** (p. 206) has been tentatively slated as part of a mixed-use development planned for the long-vacant block west of State and between Washington and Randolph streets.

Just off State Street, heading east on Randolph Street, is the **Gallery 37 Store,** 66 E. Randolph St. (© 312/251-0371; www.gallery37.org). The store sells goods made by Chicago youth ages 14 to 21 who are participants in the Gallery 37 arts training program. The not-for-profit pairs young artists with experienced artists. Proceeds from the sales of the paintings, jewelry, ceramics, decorated furniture, textiles, and sculptures benefit the program.

RIVER NORTH

River North, the area west of the Magnificent Mile and north of the Chicago River, is Chicago's primary art gallery district. Other interesting shops, concentrated on Wells Street from Kinzie Street to Chicago Avenue, include home furnishings and collectibles, and are probably of most interest to adults. The neighborhood even has a mall of its own—**The Shops at the Mart** (© 312/527-7990)—in the Merchandise Mart, at Wells and Kinzie streets, with a standard collection of chain stores. The area doesn't have many shops to interest kids, unless they have a mature understanding of art, so check out *Frommer's Chicago* if you have an interest in that area.

LINCOLN PARK

I highly recommend shopping in Lincoln Park for kids. Sidewalks are crowded with parents and strollers on a weekend afternoon. This North Side neighborhood has a variety of unique specialty shops that make it easy to browse through this leafy, picturesque community. While many of the shops on Michigan Avenue are branches of national chains and offer few surprises, the shops and boutiques in Lincoln Park tend to be locally owned and offer unique and interesting wares. Shops are located on the primary commercial arteries running through the area, including Armitage Avenue, Webster Avenue, Halsted Street, Clark Street, and Lincoln Avenue. For kids, the highest concentration of stores is found on Armitage Avenue and Halsted Street.

ARMITAGE AVENUE   Armitage Avenue has emerged as a shopping destination in its own right, with a variety of shops and boutiques selling everything from artisan-made apparel to interesting, offbeat gifts. Most of the shops are concentrated between Halsted Street and Clybourn Avenue.

To give you a sampling of the number of children's boutiques in this area, clothing stores alone include **Bercot, The Second Child, Active Kids, Alcala's, Benetton Kids, GapKids,** and **LMNOP.** All are covered in detail under "Baby & Pre-Schooler Clothes" and "Fashion," later in this chapter.

LAKEVIEW

Shoppers will find elements of both prosperous Lincoln Park and alternative-ish Wicker Park when they're wandering along Lakeview's principal commercial avenues. One strip worth a stroll—and one that's popular with the stroller set—is the gentrifying retail row along Southport Avenue, a few blocks west of Wrigley Field. With the **Music Box Theater** at 3733 N. Southport Ave., north of Addison Street, as its anchor, the area has an interesting mix of quirky and artsy merchants and restaurateurs. Start at Southport and Roscoe streets and walk north to find a string of hip kids' clothing and toy boutiques, including **Sweet Pea,** 3447 N. Southport (© **773/281-4426**); **Elizabeth Marie,** 3453 N. Southport (© **773/525-4100**); and **Wear Me Out,** 3724 N. Southport (© **773/868-6781;** p. 205). Nearby, on Ashland Avenue, you'll find **Bebe Elegante,** 3338 N. Ashland (© **773/477-2323**), and on Lincoln Avenue, **Building Blocks Toy Store,** 3306 N. Lincoln (© **773/525-6200**).

BELMONT AVENUE & CLARK STREET   Radiating from the intersection of Belmont Avenue and Clark Street is a string of shops catering to rebellious kids on tour from their homes in the 'burbs. (The Dunkin' Donuts on the corner is often referred to as "Punkin' Donuts" in their honor.). If you have preteens or young teens, they will be fascinated by the youth culture, the street life—and the shops.

Alley, 858 W. Belmont Ave., at Clark Street (© **773/525-3180**), is an "alternative shopping complex" selling everything from plaster gargoyles to racks of leather jackets. It has separate shops specializing in condoms, cigars, and bondage wear.

All the latest men's (and some women's) fashion—from names such as Fresh Jive, Fuct, and Diesel—can be found under the same roof at the multiroom scene housing the **Aero** and **Untitled** shops, 2707 N. Clark St. (© **773/404-9225**). Whether you're into tight, fitted fashion or the layered, droopy-pants look, it's here. **Tragically Hip,** a storefront women's boutique at 931 W. Belmont Ave. (© **773/549-1500**), next to the Belmont El train stop, has outlasted many other similar purveyors of cutting-edge women's apparel.

Or, you can get plugged into what the kids are reading at **Chicago Comics,** 3244 N. Clark St. (✆ **773/528-1983**), the industry's 1998 pick for best comics shop in the country. Besides the usual superhero titles, the shop stocks the Midwest's largest selection of alternative comics. You'll also find lots of back stock and European and Japanese comics, along with underground books and 'zines.

WICKER PARK/BUCKTOWN

The go-go gentrification of the Wicker Park/Bucktown area has been followed by not only a rash of restaurants and bars, but also retailers with an artsy bent reflecting the neighborhood's Bohemian spirit. Mixed in with old neighborhood businesses, such as discount furniture stores and religious icon purveyors, is a proliferation of antique-furniture shops, too-cool-for-school clothing boutiques, and eclectic galleries and gift emporiums. While the neighborhood focus is art, collectibles, and hip adult clothing, you'll find a few kids' stores, including **Little Folk Art,** 1659 N. Damen Ave. (✆ **773/235-7619**), for children's clothing; and **The Red Balloon Company,** 2060 N. Damen (✆ **773/489-9800;** see p. 212 for a detailed listing).

2 Shopping A to Z

As you might expect, Chicago has shops selling just about anything your kids could want or need, be it functional or ornamental, whimsical or exotic. The following list only scratches the surface, but it will give you an idea of the range of merchandise available.

ARTS & CRAFTS

Pearl Art and Craft Supplies   Graphic designers, artists, and arts and crafts aficionados flock to Pearl for every art supply known on earth. If you need to pick up supplies for a rainy-day project, you'll love Pearl. 255 West Chicago Ave. (at Franklin St.). ✆ 312/915-0200. www.pearlpaint.com. Subway/El: Brown Line to Chicago.

Tender Buttons *Finds*   Here's a perfect little break while shopping on the Magnificent Mile—a store filled floor to ceiling with thousands of buttons. From simple white buttons selling for 50¢ to antique gold buttons selling for hundreds of dollars, your kids will marvel over the colors and styles. If you're looking to replace missing buttons, no matter how unusual, or are trying to find just the perfect accent to update an existing jacket, this little store is just the place. 946 N. Rush (at Oak St.). ✆ 312/337-7033. Subway/El: Red Line to Chicago/State.

BABY & PRE-SCHOOLER CLOTHES

Benetton   Pricey but prone to frequent sales, Benetton's children's collection is colorful and fun, with great knits—just like the grown-up version of the store. The design is sporty rather than frilly and streamlined rather than fussy, for kids from infant through school age. The Shops at North Bridge, 520 N. Michigan Ave. ✆ 312/494-9161. Subway/El: Red Line to Grand/State.

Bercot *Finds*   Classic, well-made clothing in unique fabrics with attention to perfect fitting are the hallmark of designer Kristine Bercot, who has sold her wares in the likes of Macy's and Nordstrom's. Now with her own boutique, you'll get attentive service along with the clothing for boys and girls, newborn through size 6/7. (Looking for matching sibling outfits and coordinating accessories? This is the place). 2009 N. Fremont St., (at W. Armitage Ave.). ✆ 773/348-7933. www.bercot childrenswear.com. Subway/El: Red Line to Sheffield.

Penny's from Heaven *(Finds)*   Here's the perfect spot to find a unique gift for children, from infant to size 8. Clothing and accessories, as well as furniture, toys, books, and shoes are all here, and you can be sure none of it will ever be found in a department store. Hand-knit layette items and hand-painted furniture are two specialties. You'll also find some special occasion clothing here. 838 N. Rush (at E. Chestnut St.). © 312/266-2700. Subway/El: Red Line to Chicago/State.

Wear Me Out *(Finds)*   Nothing "been there, done that" about this shop—everything you'll find here looks fresh and cool. In fact, the shop's tagline is COOL CLOTHES FOR URBAN CRITTERS. For children from newborn through size 8. 3724 N. Southport Ave. (at W. Grace St.). © 773/868-6781. Subway/El: Brown Line to Southport.

BOOKS

Barbara's Bookstore   This haven for small, independent press titles also has extensive selections of everything current. In addition, it has a well-stocked children's section, with sitting areas for the tots to peruse the books. If you enjoy author readings, call the store to see if your visit coincides with that of one of your favorite writers. Two other branches include a small tourist-targeted shop at Navy Pier, 700 E. Grand Ave. (© 312/222-0890), and a shop in Oak Park at 1100 Lake St. (© 708/848-9140). 1350 N. Wells St. (between Division St. and North Ave.). © 312/642-5044. Subway/El: Brown Line to Sedgwick.

Barnes & Noble   Barnes & Noble opened its first downtown store in the heart of the Gold Coast a few years ago. The two-level store comes complete with a cafe, in case you get the munchies while perusing the miles of books. Check out postings for readings, book groups, and other special events. The children's section offers easy access to picture books, first readers and young adult books, plus cozy reading nooks. There's another store in Lincoln Park, at 659 W. Diversey Ave., 1 block west of Clark Street (© 773/871-9004), and one at 1441 W. Webster Ave., at Clybourn Avenue (© 773/871-3610). 1130 N. State St. (at Elm St.). © 312/280-8155. Subway/El: Red Line to Clark/Division.

Borders   You couldn't ask for a better location, right across from Water Tower Place. Head to the lower level for the kids' section, which features a particularly impressive collection of picture books. There are carpeted platforms for sitting and perusing. This place is like a mini department store, with books, magazines, CDs, and computer software spread over four floors, and a cafe with a view overlooking the Mag Mile. There are also author readings, book signings, and other special events. There's also a new Borders in the Loop at 150 N. State St., at Randolph Street (© 312/606-0750), and one in Lincoln Park at 2817 N. Clark St., at Diversey Avenue (© 773/935-3909). 830 N. Michigan Ave. (at Pearson St.). © 312/573-0564. Subway/El: Red Line to Chicago.

Children in Paradise Bookstore *(Finds)*   Chicago's largest children's bookstore is a must-see for parents with young readers. For little ones, storytelling hours are Tuesday and Wednesday at 10:30am. On Saturday, you'll find special events, including sidewalk chalk drawing and visits from book characters and authors. Highly qualified staff makes this store a joy to visit. 909 N. Rush St. (between Delaware Place and Walton St.). © 312/951-5437. www.chicagochildrensbooks.com. Subway/El: Red Line to Chicago.

Women & Children First   This feminist and children's bookstore holds the best selection in the city of titles for, by, and about women. Co-owner Linda

Bubon holds a children's storybook hour every Wednesday at 10:30am; several book groups meet regularly as well, including one for mothers and daughters. The store also hosts frequent readings by the likes of Gloria Steinem, Amy Tan, Alice Walker, and Naomi Wolf. 5233 N. Clark St. (between Foster and Bryn Mawr aves.). © 773/769-9299. wcfbooks@aol.com. Subway/El: Red Line to Berwyn.

DEPARTMENT STORES

Bloomingdale's   The first Midwestern branch of the famed New York department store, Bloomingdale's is on par in terms of size and selection with Marshall Field's Water Tower store. The fifth floor features kids' clothing. 900 N. Michigan Ave. (at Walton St.). © 312/440-4460. Subway/El: Red Line to Chicago.

Carson Pirie Scott & Co.   Carson's still appeals primarily to working- and middle-class shoppers. But this venerable Chicago institution that was almost wiped out by the Chicago Fire has made a recent bid to capture the corporate, if not the carriage, trade. Carson's has added a number of more upscale apparel lines, plus a trendy housewares department, to appeal to the moneyed crowd that works in the Loop. On the seventh floor, you'll find children's clothing and stuffed animals. 1 S. State St. (at Madison St.). © 312/641-7000. Subway/El: Red Line to Monroe.

Lord & Taylor   Lord & Taylor, one of two large department stores in Water Tower Place (see also Marshall Field's, below), carries about what you'd expect: cosmetics, accessories, and women's, men's, and children's clothing. Head for the second floor for children's apparel. The layout is cramped and somewhat disorganized, so don't venture in if you're easily frustrated (or tired). Its star department is most definitely shoes; the selection is fairly broad, and something's usually on sale. Water Tower Place, 835 N. Michigan Ave. © 312/787-7400. Subway/El: Red Line to Chicago.

Marshall Field's   Although it's now owned by the Minneapolis-based Target Corporation, Chicagoans still consider Marshall Field's their "hometown" department store. The flagship store, which covers an entire block on State Street, is second in size only to Macy's in New York City. Within this overwhelming space, shoppers will find areas unusual for today's homogeneous department stores, such as the Victorian antique-jewelry department and a gallery of antique-furniture reproductions. Store craftspeople are still on hand to fix antique clocks, repair jewelry, and restore old paintings. A basement marketplace offers gourmet goodies, including a bakery and upscale cafeteria. For children's wear, head to the fifth floor for toys and clothing.

The breadth is what makes this store impressive; shoppers can find a rainbow of shirts for under $20, a floor or so away from the 28 Shop, the Field's homage to designer fashion. For a sophisticated take on the latest trends at a more affordable price, look for clothes from Field's own label, 111 State. The recently expanded shoe department is huge, with everything from killer high heels (at killer prices) to slippers and casual sandals.

The Water Tower store—the Water Tower Place mall's primary anchor—is a scaled-down but respectable version of the State Street store. Its eight floors are actually much more manageable than the enormous flagship, and its merchandise selection is still vast (although this branch tends to focus on the more expensive brands). Look for children's wear on the eighth floor. The mall location is at 835 N. Michigan Ave., at Pearson St. (© 312/335-7700); take the Red Line to Chicago. 111 N. State St. (at Randolph St.). © 312/781-1000. www.marshall fields.com. Subway/El: Red Line to Washington.

Neiman Marcus   Yes, you'll pay top dollar for designer names here—the store does, after all, need to live up to its "Needless Mark-ups" moniker—but Neiman's has a broader price range than many of its critics care to admit. It also has some mighty good sales. The four-story store, a beautiful environment in its own right, also sells cosmetics, shoes, furs, fine and fashion jewelry, and menswear and children's wear. On the top floor is the children's department, plus a fun gourmet food department and a pretty home-accessories area. Neiman's has two restaurants: one relaxed, the other a little more formal. 737 N. Michigan Ave. (between Superior St. and Chicago Ave.). ℃ **312/642-5900.** Subway/El: Red Line to Chicago.

Nordstrom   The newest arrival on the Chicago department store scene, Nordstrom has upped the stakes with its spacious, airy design and trendy touches (wheatgrass growing by the escalators, funky music playing on the stereo system). Kids' clothing is found on the third floor, with a nice selection of clothing and gifts for infants through teens. The selection of children's shoes is extensive. In keeping with the store's famed focus on service, a concierge can check your coat, call a cab, or make restaurant reservations. If you need a lift, Cafe Nordstrom offers a shopping break, with salads and sandwiches. Set up cafeteria-style, the restaurant also features a Kid's Cafe. The bathrooms, one on each level, contain an infant changing area and a women's lounge equipped with upholstered chairs where you can comfortably and semi-privately nurse an infant. The Shops at North Bridge, 55 E. Grand Ave. (at Rush St.). ℃ **312/464-1515.**. Subway/El: Red Line to Grand.

Saks Fifth Avenue   Saks Fifth Avenue might be best known for its designer collections—Valentino, Chloe, and Giorgio Armani, to name a few—but the store also does a swell job of buying more casual and less-expensive merchandise. Check out, for example, Saks's own Real Clothes or The Works women's lines. Plus, the store has very good large-size and petite women's apparel departments. The children's department has a variety of casual and dress clothes, as well as a few stuffed animals. An expanded men's department recently opened in a separate building across Michigan Avenue. Don't forget to visit the cosmetics department, where Saks is known, in particular, for its varied fragrance selection. Chicago Place, 700 N. Michigan Ave. (at Superior St.). ℃ **312/944-6500.** Subway/El: Red Line to Chicago/State.

DOLLS & DOLLHOUSES

Think Small   If your child dreams of building (in other words, dreams of having mom and dad build) a dollhouse, you'll find everything you need here. Sometimes the path of least resistance is best: In that case, check out the readymade dollhouses that are available for purchase. You can also buy the dolls and furniture that will reside in the house. For those ambitious enough to build their child's dream house themselves, the store offers workshops on Wednesdays, Thursdays, Saturdays, and Sundays. You can drop in, but it might be a good idea to call ahead before you go. The fee is $75, and includes the use of tools and paintbrushes, paper goods, wood glue and cleaning materials. 3209 N. Clark St. (at W. Belmont St.). ℃ **773/477-1920.** Subway/El: Red Line to Belmont.

FASHION

Abercrombie Kids   The cool "uniform" of preference for middle school kids is anything Abercrombie. Clothes here are pricey but well made, and if you break down and buy a t-shirt or more, it shouldn't break your budget. Water Tower Place, 849 Michigan Ave. ℃ **312/274-9859.** www.abercrombiekids.com. Subway/El: Red Line to Chicago/State.

Active Kids *(Finds)*   This offshoot of the popular outdoor and sporting goods store Active Endeavors (p. 212) specializes in clothes for kids living the outdoorsy life—or who just look like they are. Patagonia and other big-name outdoor outfitters are featured among the clothing for infants through size 16. 838 W. Armitage Ave. (at North Dayton St.). 🕾 **773/281-2002.** www.activeendeavors.com. Subway/El: Red Line to Sheffield.

Alcala's   Do your kids dream of the open range? Here's just the spot to help them look the part. Cowboy hats, boots, shirts, jeans, and chaps for miniature cowpokes are the focus at Alcala's. And to prove that you're never too young to start appreciating the Wild West, soft leather booties get even the littlest cowpokes off to the right start. 1733 W. Chicago Ave. (at Wood St.). 🕾 **312/226-0152.** www.alcalas.com. Subway/El: Red Line to Sheffield.

Anthropologie   Eclectic and funky clothes that appeal to the young teen set (sorry, females only) and a mix of new and vintage home furnishings and accessories that appeal to Mom make this store a delight to browse. 1120 N. State St. 🕾 **312/255-1848.** www.anthropologie.com. Subway/El: Red Line to Clark/Division.

GapKids and babyGap   Classic and fun, although definitely not avant-garde, Gap produces reliable clothes and accessories for kids. Inventory turns quickly here, so it's easy to pick up a few things on sale. The store has five locations in Chicago. The largest store is located at 555 N. Michigan Ave., where you'll find a large kids' and baby section on the lower level. (1) 555 N. Michigan Ave. (at E. Ohio St.). 🕾 **312/335-1896.** Subway/El: Red Line to Grand/State. (2) Water Tower Place, 835 N. Michigan Ave. 🕾 **312/255-8883.** Subway/El: Red Line to Chicago/State. (3) 2108 North Halsted (at W. Webster St.). 🕾 **773/549-2065.** Subway/El: Red Line to Sheffield. (4) 3033 N. Broadway Ave. (at W. Wellington St.). 🕾 **773/929-4085.** Subway/El: Brown Line to Diversey. (5) 3155 N. Lincoln Ave. (at W. Barry St.). 🕾 **773/883-9050.** Subway/El: Brown Line to Wellington.

Gymboree   Bright primary colors and strong patterns are the trademark of Gymboree clothing. You'll find items here for infants up to age seven. The chain also runs play centers (see "Indoor Playgrounds," in chapter 8). Water Tower Place, 835 N. Michigan Ave. 🕾 **312/649-9074.** www.gymboree.com. Subway/El: Red Line to Chicago/State.

Jacadi   An upscale Parisian clothing company with beautiful (and pricey) clothing for infants through age 12. Rich colors and pastels in cottons and knits are the focus here. Water Tower Place, 835 N. Michigan Ave. 🕾 **312/337-9600.** www.jacadi usa.com. Subway/El: Red Line to Chicago/State.

LMNOP   Nothing ordinary about the children's clothing you'll find here, for ages newborn to 6. 2574 North Lincoln Ave. (at Sheffield Ave.). 🕾 **773/975-4055.** Subway/El: Red or Brown lines to Fullerton.

Madison and Friends   When Chicago parents with a money's-no-object attitude go shopping for special occasion clothing for kids, they make a beeline for Madison and Friends. The selection is top-of-the-line, the inventory large and unique. Don't be confused by the two locations, across the street from each other: One focuses on babies, the other on older kids. Together, you can find clothing for kids from newborn through size 16. (1) 11 East Oak St. (between State and Rush sts.; includes the complete baby collection); (2) 1003 N. Rush (at E. Oak St.; includes toddlers through size 16). 940 N. Rush St. 🕾 **888/332-8610** or 312/642-6403. www.madisonand friends.com. Subway/El: Red Line to Chicago/State.

Mini Me   This store specializes in European-style clothing for girls from infant through age 10 and boys up to size 4. In the mall at 900 N. Michigan Ave. 🕾 **312/988-4011.** Subway/El: Red Line to Chicago/State.

Oilily   Even if you don't mix plaids and florals on a daily basis (a trademark of this designer), just one of Oilily's distinctive and colorful items can perk up a wardrobe from infant to size 12. Clothes are the focus, but some accessories like quilts and backpacks are also offered. To keep kids happy while you shop, rolling wooden chairs and blocks are on hand. The Shops at North Bridge, 520 N. Michigan Ave. ℓ 312/527-5747. Subway/El: Red Line to State/Grand.

Old Navy *Value*   The lower-priced relative of the Gap carries an extensive collection of kids' clothes, from infants and up. Sales here are fantastic—and frequent. Clothes are trendy and stylish. The collection for boys is great, a refreshing change for moms who are frustrated with the ho-hum choices available at most stores. The store has three Chicago locations. The biggest and best is the State Street location. (1) 35 N. State St. (at E. Washington St.). ℓ 312/551-0523. Subway: Brown, Purple, Green and Orange lines to Randolph/Wabash and walk 1 block south and 1 block west; or Red Line to Washington/State. (2) 1596 W. Kingsbury (at North Ave.). ℓ 312/397-0624. Subway/El: Red Line to Clybourn. (3) 1730 W. Fullerton Ave. (at N. Clybourn Ave.). ℓ 773/871-0613. Subway/El: Red Line to Fullerton.

The Second Child *Value*   This consignment store offers children's clothing for infants through size 14, plus toys, furniture, and equipment for kids (and maternity clothes if you've got another on the way). Yes, the merchandise is second-hand, but thanks to the store's location in a tony Lincoln Park neighborhood, it's *upscale* second-hand. You'll find name brands and excellent quality. The store ensures that its collection of furniture and equipment meets current safety standards. Lock your stroller just outside the building and take the stairs up. 954 W. Armitage (just east of N. Sheffield Ave.). ℓ 773/883-0880. www.2ndchild.com. Subway/El: Red Line to Sheffield.

Talbots Kids   Just what you'd expect from Talbots—well made, classic clothes for kids with a decidedly preppy flair. You'll find everything from basics to party clothes here, all with that neatly pressed look. Chicago Place, 700 N. Michigan Ave. ℓ 312/943-0255. www.talbots.com. Subway/El: Red Line to Chicago/State.

Urban Outfitters   Fun, funky and offbeat clothing and accessories, from beanbag chairs to trendy clothing and glittery nail polish, sure to please young teens. 933 N. Rush St. (at Walton St.). ℓ 312/640-1919. www.urbanoutfitters.com. Subway/El: Red Line to Chicago/State.

GAMES & HOBBY SHOPS

Ash's Magic   Mr. Ash, a real-life magician with a love of his craft, stocks his shop with tricks, jokes, books, and videos that will make you believe in magic, too. 4955 N. Western Ave. (at West Argyle). ℓ 773/271-4030. Subway/El: Brown Line to Western.

Fantasy Headquarters   Although this store is meant for adults (if you need a Halloween costume to end all Halloween costumes, this is the place), I dare you not to have fun with your kids here. This sprawling costume shop covers an entire city block and is devoted to make-believe. The store stocks more than a million items, including 800 styles of masks (priced from $1–$200) and all the accessories and makeup needed to complete your costume. (Make sure to check out the full-service wig salon.) 4065 N. Milwaukee Ave. (west of Cicero Ave.). ℓ 773/777-0222. Subway/El: Blue Line to Irving Park.

Magic Inc.   The inventory of tricks is huge here, and if you call ahead, you can make sure your visit coincides with a demonstration by a real live magician. 5082 North Lincoln Ave. (at W. Carmen Ave.). ℓ 773/334-2855. Subway/El: Brown Line to Western.

Tips From Chicago with Love

Need to bring some Chicago gifts home for friends and family? With more national chain stores hitting town, it's getting harder to find distinctive, only-in-Chicago souvenirs. Here are some unique ideas:

- The **Chicago Architecture Foundation** runs gift shops at two locations, the Chicago Architecture Center at 224 S. Michigan Ave. (© **312/922-3432**), and the John Hancock Center at 875 N. Michigan Ave. (© **312/751-1380**). Look for the Frank Lloyd Wright building blocks, stained-glass lamps, Christmas tree ornaments of famous Chicago buildings, and an extensive selection of beautiful coffee-table books.
- The **Chicago Tribune** store, at 435 N. Michigan Ave. (© **312/222-3232**), has your standard tourist selection ("Chicago" emblazoned on everything from shirts to shot glasses). But this is also a good place to pick up Cubs memorabilia (the Tribune Company owns the team), along with books from some of the city's top journalists.
- **Sportmart,** at 620 N. LaSalle St. (© **312/337-6151**), is where you'll find jerseys and hats from Chicago's other pro sports teams. The victorious Jordan years might be behind us, but his shirts still sell well here.
- The ultimate Chicago tasty treats are Frango Mints from **Marshall Field's.** Although they now come in a variety of flavors, stick with the original: melt-in-your-mouth chocolate mixed with mint. Once you're hooked, you might find yourself returning to Chicago more often to stock up.

Uncle Fun *Finds*   Uncle Fun and his staff travel the world to bring home bobbing head figurines, accordions, and stink bombs from all corners of the earth—for the sole purpose of tickling your fancy. Bins and cubbyholes are stuffed full of the standard joke toys (rubber-chicken key chains and chattering wind-up teeth), but you'll also find every conceivable modern pop-culture artifact, from Jackson Five buttons to demon-on-wheels *Speed Racer*'s Mach-Five model car. 1338 W. Belmont Ave. (near Southport Ave.). © **773/477-8223**. www.unclefunchicago.com. Subway/El: Red or Brown lines to Belmont.

MUSIC

Beat Parlor   If the idea of hanging out with local DJs appeals to your kids, then Beat Parlor is your place. In the city where house music was born, Howard Bailey's Bucktown shop sells lots of it, plus plenty of hip-hop and local DJs' mix tapes, on CD and vinyl. The store's two turntables are always in use by cutters checking out new merchandise. 1653 N. Damen Ave. © **773/395-CUTS**. Subway/El: Blue Line to Damen.

Blue Chicago Store *Finds*   Here's one that's near and dear to my blues-loving heart—a store that's dedicated to teaching kids about the blues. America's original contribution to the world of music, and the basis for jazz and rock 'n' roll, is alive and thriving in Chicago. Treat your kids to a stop here, pick up some books, and maybe even plan to attend the Saturday night dance-a-thons that are open to all ages. 534 N. Clark (at W. Grand Ave.). ✆ 312/661-1003. www.bluechicago.com. Subway/El: Red Line to State/Grand.

Clubhouse   Young teens will love a visit to Clubhouse, opened in 1993 by Alyse Matlak, and located next door to Chicago's premier rock venue, Metro. Today, the store sells T-shirts, pins, and patches, plus a sophisticated inventory of ska and punk records, CDs, and tapes. To keep the store fresh, almost the entire inventory is new music, much of it of the underground variety. 3728 N. Clark St. ✆ 773/549-2325. www.go-town.com. Subway/El: Red Line to Addison.

Dusty Groove America   In April 1996, using a rickety old PC, Rick Wojcik and John Schauer founded an online record store, Dusty Groove America. Since then, the operation has expanded in both cyberspace and the real world. Dusty Groove covers a lot of ground, selling soul, funk, jazz, Brazilian, lounge, Latin, and hip-hop music on new and used vinyl and all new CDs. For the most part, all selections are either rare or imported, or both. 1180 N. Milwaukee Ave., 2nd floor. ✆ 773/645-1200. www.dustygroove.com. Subway/El: Blue Line to Damen.

Guitar Center   When your kids are oh, somewhere around age 12, and decide it's time to start their own garage band, you'll need to find the one store that can satisfy their needs. Guitar Center is it: Your kids can check out the keyboards, music software, recording equipment, dance music gear, drums, amplifiers, basses, acoustic guitars, accessories, and vintage instruments. Good luck! 2633 North Halsted (at Diversey). ✆ 773/248-2808. www.guitarcenter.com. Subway/El: Brown Line to Wellington.

Jazz Record Mart *(Finds)*   This is possibly the best jazz record store in the country. It's so cool, even your disenchanted teenager will love it, despite himself. The first of four rooms houses the "Killer Rack," a display of albums that the store's owners consider essential to any jazz collection. Besides jazz, there are bins filled with blues, Latin, and "New Music"; the albums in the record rooms are filed alphabetically and by category (vocals, big band, and so on), and there are a couple of turntables to help you spend wisely. Jazz Record Mart also features a stage, with seating for 50, where local and national artists coming through town entertain with in-store performances. 444 N. Wabash Ave. (at Grand Ave.). ✆ 312/222-1467. www.jazzmart.com. Subway/El: Red Line to Grand.

New Sound Gospel   Chicago is the birthplace of gospel music, but when Lee Johnson opened New Sound Gospel 20 years ago, few people were selling it. That has all changed, thanks to the recent resurgence in gospel led by Kirk Franklin, whose platinum albums have crossed over into mainstream success. All the major labels now have gospel music divisions, and the rising tide has helped store owners like Johnson, who has since opened a second location at 10723 S. Halsted St. (✆ 773/785-8001). Both brim with records, CDs, and tapes, from gospel's greatest legend, Mahalia Jackson, to groups with names such as Gospel Gangstaz. 5958 W. Lake St. ✆ 773/261-1115. Subway/El: Green Line to Austin.

SHOES

Carrara Children's Shoes   Hard-to-fit foot? Head to Carrara, where sizes span a huge range, as does the inventory of styles. The focus is on Italian footwear for kids, from infant to size 9 (yes, that's size 9 in men's and women's terms). Anything from slippers to snow boots to sneakers is fair game here. Pick up some socks and tights on your way to the register. 2506 N. Clark St. (at W. Deming Place). ✆ 773/529-9955. Subway/El: Red or Brown lines to Fullerton; Bus: 22, 36.

Fleet Feet Sports *Finds*   This store, owned by a former banker who decided to follow his love of running to create a new business, is a wonderful place to buy shoes for little athletes. While running is the forte here, you can buy all types of athletic shoes. The staff is made up of athletes who can relate when you complain about your sore Achilles—and better yet, they can find a pair of shoes that will help. You'll even get a chance to hop on a treadmill to get your running gait videotaped. The staff will assess your style and bring you a variety of shoes to try. (*Note:* Don't ask to try on a pair of shoes simply because you like the color. That request is sure to get you a disapproving look!) 210 W. North Ave. (at Wells St., in the Pipers Alley complex). © 312/587-3338. www.fleetfeetchicago.com. Subway/El: Brown Line to Sedgwick.

Piggy Toes   European makers are featured in this boutique's selection of shoes, sandals and boots, plus hats, socks, tights, and other accessories. Shoe sizes for infants through children's size 6. 2205 N. Halsted (at W. Belden Ave.). © 773/281-5583. www.ptoes.com. Subway: Brown Line to Armitage.

Steve Madden *Value*   Funky and inexpensive, Steve Madden specializes in the platform, chunky-heel style shoe. Your teenaged daughter probably covets Steve Maddens already. Boys' styles are appearing in the store as well, although it's still female-dominated territory. Most styles start at size 5. When a sale is on, you can sometimes pick up a pair for as little as $15. Water Tower Place, 845 N. Michigan Ave. © 312/440-1590. www.stevemadden.com. Subway/El: Red Line to Chicago/State.

Wesley Shoes   All the major brands are represented here, and if your kids are aspiring dancers, you'll also find toe and tap shoes, leotards, and tights. Sizes run from infant to children's size 5. 2120 N. Halsted St. (at W. Webster St.). © 773/755-0904. Subway/El: Red Line to Sheffield.

SHOWER & BABY GIFTS

Cradles of Distinction   Don't let the name of this shop fool you: It offers much more than cradles. You'll be the star of the baby shower when you pick up the much sought-after Petit Bateau onesies sold here, or a set of cushiony fabric hangars to keep baby's finery in good condition. Check out the fountain, created to adhere to feng shui standards (and an effort by the store to make shopping with kids a soothing experience). 2100 N. Southport Ave. © 773/472-1001. www.cradlesofdistinction.com. Subway/El: Brown Line to Armitage.

The Red Balloon Company *Finds*   This creative little shop in the trendy Wicker Park neighborhood offers casual clothes for infants through size 6, hand-painted furniture, linens, and books. It's a great place to find a special gift. Children's classic books such as *The Red Balloon, The Lonely Doll,* and *Mike Mulligan and His Steam Shovel* are displayed atop decoupaged bedroom furnishings. There are lots of vintage-inspired items, too, including Pinecone Hill reversible blankets, caps and burp cloths. The store features antiques and one-of-a-kind pieces. If there's a furniture item you want made, just ask the staff—some items can be custom-made. 2060 N. Damen Ave. (at W. Armitage Ave.). © 773/489-9800. www.thered balloon.com. Subway/El: Blue Line to Damen.

SPORTS STUFF

Active Endeavors *Finds*   Everything you need for the outdoor life can be found right here, from camping gear to running shoes, plus everyday sporty apparel. For the low-down on the kids' version of this store, which features outdoor clothing, see the review of Active Kids on p. 208. 935 W. Armitage Ave. (between Sheffield Ave. and Halsted St.). © 773/281-8100. Subway/El: Brown Line to Armitage.

Kozy's Cyclery   A Chicago favorite, this third-generation, family-owned business has been selling and servicing bikes for 56 years. You'll find name brands, a vast collection of accessories, and store personnel with opinions you can trust. If you're a Chicago resident, you can count on complete servicing for your bikes, and the staff will connect you with all kinds of cycling resources. Check out Kozy's online catalog (www.kozy.com), complete with photos, to get an idea of what the shop carries. (For out-of-towners, shipping is available.) The store has three locations. (1) 601 S. LaSalle (at W. Harrison St.). ☎ 312/360-0020. Subway/El: Blue Line to LaSalle. (2) 1451 W. Webster (at N. Clybourn Ave.). ☎ 773/528-2700. Subway/El: Brown Line to Armitage. (3) 3712 N. Halsted (at W. Waveland Ave.). ☎ 773/281-2263. Subway/El: Red Line to Addison.

Niketown *Overrated*   When Niketown opened almost 10 years ago, it was truly something new: A store that felt more like a funky sports museum than a place hawking running shoes. In the days when Michael Jordan was the city's reigning deity, Niketown was the place to bask in his glory. These days, Niketown is no longer unique to Chicago (it's sprung up in cities from Atlanta to Honolulu), and the store's celebration of athletes can't cover up the fact that the ultimate goal is to sell expensive shoes. But the crowds keep streaming in—and snatching up products pitched by Niketown's new patron saint, Tiger Woods. 669 N. Michigan Ave. ☎ 312/642-6363. Subway/El: Red Line to Grand.

> **Tips Pop On In**
>
> Across the street from Niketown, you'll probably see a line of people trailing out from the **Garrett Popcorn Shop**, 670 N. Michigan Ave. (☎ 312/944-2630), a 50-year-old landmark. Join the locals in line and pick up some caramel corn for a quick sugar rush.

Sportmart   The largest sporting-goods store in the city, the flagship store of this chain offers seven floors of merchandise, from running apparel to camping gear. Sports fans will be in heaven in the first- and fifth-floor team merchandise departments, where Cubs, Bulls, and Sox jerseys abound. Cement handprints of local sports celebs dot the outside of the building; step inside to check out the prints from Michael Jordan and White Sox slugger Frank Thomas. 620 N. LaSalle St. (at Ontario St.). ☎ 312/337-6151. Subway/El: Red Line to Grand.

Vertel's   Here's a store that takes running seriously. Shoe shoppers are advised to bring in their old shoes and invest at least half an hour while the salespeople help fit you for a new pair, including letting you do a lap on the sidewalk out front. The store also stocks running apparel and accessories, as well as swimwear. 2001 N. Clybourn Ave. (between North and Fullerton aves.). ☎ 773/248-7400. www.vertels.net. Subway/El: Brown Line to Armitage.

STROLLERS, CRIBS & FURNITURE

Bellini   Outfitting your dream nursery? Head to this high-end boutique for furniture with Italian design and a distinctly contemporary flair. (And even if some prices are a bit out of your budget stratosphere, you'll at least find inspiration.) Cribs, changing tables, armoires, and rocking chairs are on offer, plus items to achieve just the right decor. Clothing and accessories for baby top off the selection here. 2001 N. Halsted (at W. Dickens). ☎ 312/943-6696. www.bellini.com. Subway/El: Red Line to Sheffield.

Cella for Baby   When you're outfitting your first nursery and find yourself overwhelmed by stores, brands, and friends' recommendations, here's a place to find a little clarity. Cella's buyers have sorted through all of the baby paraphernalia on the market and stocks what they have decided are "the best" items available in the market. The large showroom is packed with nursery furniture, cribs, strollers, carseats, lamps, books, toys, bedding, feeding and personal care items, and clothing (from preemie to 4-toddler). Anything from all-terrain baby joggers to handmade layette items are covered here. 2310-12 N. Lincoln Ave. (at N. Belden Ave.). ℂ **773/472-9380.** www.cellaforbaby.com. Subway/El: Red or Brown lines to Fullerton.

Hoohobbers   For more than 20 years, Hoohobbers has manufactured its own line of tables, chairs, easels, bedding, diaper bags, back packs, and towels. Most products can be personalized while you wait. You'll also find just about everything to complete the decor for your child's room, including wallpaper borders and paints, and music CDs. Hoohobbers carries asthma and allergy friendly products that are 100% environmentally safe. The Shops at North Bridge, 520 N. Michigan Ave. ℂ **312/494-0278.** www.hoohobbers.com. Subway/El: Red Line to Grand/State.

The Right Start   Gadgets for babies and toddlers and sanity-saving devices such as bouncers, swings, and exersaucers are the focus here. If Junior is suddenly up and walking and you need to baby-proof your home, this store is your source for gates, electrical outlet covers, and cabinet locks. While it's a chain, you can't beat the convenience of being able to buy so many gadgets in one location. 2121 N. Clybourn Ave. (at N. Wayne St. in the Market Square Shopping Center). ℂ **773/296-4420.** www.therightstart.com. Subway/El: Brown Line to Armitage.

SWEETS FOR THE SWEET

Ghirardelli Chocolate Shop & Soda Fountain   This Midwest outpost of the famed San Francisco chocolatier, just a half block off the Mag Mile, gets swamped in the summer, but they've got their soda fountain assembly line down to a science. Besides the incredible hot fudge sundaes, there's a veritable mudslide of chocolate bars, hot-cocoa drink mixes, and chocolate-covered espresso beans to tempt your sweet tooth. 830 N. Michigan Ave. ℂ **312/337-9330.** Subway/El: Red Line to Chicago.

Margie's Candies (Value)   This family-run candy and ice cream shop hasn't changed much since it opened in 1921. It still offers some of the city's finest handmade fudge, whether it comes in a box or melted over a banana split served in a clamshell dish. The store is known for its turtles—chocolate-covered pecan and caramel clusters—and may be the only place in the city still selling rock candy on wooden sticks. 1960 N. Western Ave. (just north of Armitage Ave.). ℂ **773/384-1035.** Subway/El: Blue Line to Western.

Sweet Thang   When bopping around Wicker Park's boutiques and quirky shops, don't miss Bernard Runo's Euro-style cafe for a tasty treat to tide you over. Runo, a classically trained pastry chef who has worked in the kitchens of the city's best hotels and learned his trade in France, imports most of the ingredients for his croissants, cookies, tarts, and other pastries from across the pond. The cafe has a laid-back atmosphere, with red distressed walls covered with abstract art and Parisian-style tables and chairs that are set outside in warm weather. 1921 W. North Ave. ℂ **773/772-4166.** Subway/El: Blue Line to Damen.

Vosges Haut-Chocolat (Finds)   Some of the works of chocolatier Katrina Markoff might be a reach for kids (such as wasabi-flavored truffles), but chocolate bars and the best toffee I've ever tasted are a hit no matter what the age range. Markoff studied at Le Cordon Bleu in Paris and honed her skills throughout Europe and Asia. Her exotic gourmet truffles—with fabulous names such as absinthe, mint julep, wink of the rabbit, woolloomooloo, and ambrosia—are made from premium Belgian chocolate and infused with rare spices, seasonings, and flowers from around the world. The store—which looks more like a modern art gallery than a chocolatier—includes a gourmet hot chocolate bar, where you're welcome to sit and sip. The Shops at North Bridge, 520 N. Michigan Ave. © 312/ 644-9450. Subway/El: Red Line to Grand.

THEME STORES

American Girl Place   One of Chicago's hottest family destinations, this three-story doll emporium attracts hordes of young girls (and parents with credit cards at the ready) hooked on the popular mail-order doll company's line of historic character dolls. A stage show brings stories from the American Girl books to life, and the store's cafe is a nice spot for a special mother-daughter lunch or afternoon tea. All of the American Girl dolls from different eras of U.S. history, plus their many accessories, are for sale here. Dioramas for each doll change with the seasons. A cafe serves food mentioned in the books—and your doll can dine with you. Lunch, tea, and dinner seatings are available 7 days a week. *The American Girl Revue* at the in-store theater is a musical revue ($25) for ages 6 and up. Reservations are needed for the theater and cafe. American Girl also does parties. For $25 per person, you get a two-course meal, cake, and goody bags. The store also hosts special events, such as "play alongs" for kids ages 3 to 5, usually on Wednesday mornings; reservations are required. Bathrooms are spacious and clean, and one has a changing table. You'll need 1 to 2 hours to explore the store. If you include the cafe and theater, this can be a full-day activity. (For a review of the American Girl Place Cafe, see p. 93.) 111 E. Chicago Ave. © 877/AG-PLACE or 312/943-9400. Subway/El: Red Line to Chicago/State.

Sony Gallery of Consumer Electronics   The latest high-tech gadgets are displayed in a museum-like setting at this multi-level store. Kids will want to head up to the second floor to try out the newest PlayStation games. 663 N. Michigan Ave. © 312/943-3334. Subway/El: Red Line to State/Grand.

TOYS

Dorby Magoo & Co. *(Finds*   What's not to love about a toy store that's laid out like your own home? Kids feel an immediate welcome as they look for toys in the bedroom or books in the library. There's even a living room, den, kitchen, and bathroom. Birthday parties can be scheduled for the dining room and back yard area (complete with Astroturf "grass" and a ceiling painted to look like the sky). 2744 N. Lincoln Ave. (at W. Diversey St.). © 773/935-2663. Subway/El: Brown Line to Diversey.

FAO Schwarz   You'll know you're in the right place when you spot the life-size toy soldier holding the door open for giddy kids. Boxing kangaroos, a life-sized gorilla, a perpetual-motion machine, and thousands of toys make this three-level store irresistible. This branch of the famous New York toy store is an all-you-can-eat buffet of name-brand toys, from Barbie to Barney. The store is often the first to get the hot new toys, so beware the frenzy. You'll usually find a line of kids waiting to try out the huge piano keyboard that runs across the floor (made famous in the Tom Hanks movie *Big*). Another cool feature: a photo booth that turns photos into stickers. You'll be lured inside by friendly employees dressed as toy soldiers, trying out new toys on passers-by. 840 N. Michigan Ave. (at E. Chestnut St.). © 312/587-5000. www.faoschwarz.com. Subway/El: Red Line to Chicago.

Galt Toys   This shop offers its own brand of toys, which are known for their craftsmanship, quality and design. In the mall at 900 N. Michigan Ave. ✆ **312/440-9550.** www.galttoys.com. Subway/El: Red Line to Chicago/State.

Kite Harbor   On breezy days when the wind is just right off of Lake Michigan, stop in to Kite Harbor to pick up a colorful kite. (There are the standard kid-size kites, all the way up to spectacular jumbo kites for the ambitious—or experienced.) The shop stocks all sorts of flying objects, from boomerangs to whirligigs, and even juggling sets. 435 E. Illinois St. ✆ **312/321-5483.** Subway/El: Brown Line to Merchandise Mart.

LEGO Store   You'll marvel at replicas of Chicago landmarks, made entirely of LEGOs. Special edition sets for young builders who want to create huge animals and people are often featured, too. A LEGO Construction Zone just outside of the store lets kids design and build in their own play area with a life-size racecar built from LEGO bricks; LEGO walls; and tables. The play zone is open daily from 11am to 5:30pm. The Shops at North Bridge, 520 N. Michigan Ave. ✆ **312/494-0760.** www.lego.com. Subway: Red Line to Grand/State.

Saturday's Child   The clever toys here range from rubber snakes and frogs to sidewalk chalk and kids' large-face wristwatches. Cooperative and creative play is the focus here—not a high-tech gadget or computer game in sight. Real old-fashioned toys and picture books, Folkmanis puppets, arts and crafts supplies, and puzzles and games are stocked here. 2146 N. Halsted St. (south of Webster Ave.). ✆ **773/525-8697.** www.childtoystore.com. Subway/El: Brown Line to Armitage.

Toys and Treasures   Tired of mass-market toys? Check out this boutique for children that offers toys for infants up to kids age 10, baby and kids clothes up to size 6, plus books, art supplies, and stuffed animals. Many of the toys are handmade and have an educational and developmental bent. The store stocks a few lines of infant clothes that are made by local women. The owner, Bea, has a talent for matching the kid to the toy, so be sure to ask her advice! 5311 N. Clark St. (at Berwyn Ave.). ✆ **773/769-5311.** Subway/El: Red Line to Berwyn.

Toyscape   Don't walk in here expecting to buy a G.I. Joe or a Sony PlayStation. This shrine to anti-commercialism sells only old-fashioned toys that let kids exercise their imagination. Wooden toys, musical instruments, and puppets are all in stock. The environment is friendly, and the store hosts special events during the year. One perennial favorite is "Bunnies on Parade," held in April, when kids are invited to put on some ears or bunny suits and parade around and in front of the store. 2911 N. Broadway (between Diversey Pkwy. and Belmont Ave.). ✆ **773/665-7400.** www.toyscapecatalog.com. Subway/El: Brown Line to Diversey.

Toys et cetera   Next time you're visiting the Museum of Science and Industry, make the short trek into Hyde Park to visit this special toy store. While it's known for its excellent website, you'll have more fun at the real store. The space is small, but packed with educational puzzles and games, and toys, toys, toys. (Check out the wide assortment of dolls.) Dress-up clothes and an arts and crafts area round out the store. 5211-A S. Harper (in Harper Court Shopping Center) in Hyde Park. ✆ **773/324-6039.** www.toysetcetera.com. Bus: 4.

Zany Brainy   A mind-boggling array of toys, plus trains, building materials, video games, software, books, videos, and music await you. The focus is on educational toys. 2163 N. Clybourn. ✆ **773/281-2371.** www.zanybrainy.com. Subway/El: Brown Line to Armitage.

10

Entertainment for the Whole Family

For most families, show-biz central in Chicago is the North Loop theater district. Until a couple of years ago, the district had a down-on-its-luck, brother-can-you-spare-a-dime atmosphere—not the kind of place you wanted to be after dark with tots in tow. Happily, the district has undergone something of a renaissance, particularly along State and Randolph streets. Many of the city's major theater venues have been restored to their former glory. This is good news for parents, as many of those glorious old theaters host traveling Broadway productions that attract families.

Chicago is a regular stop on the big-name entertainment circuit, whether it's the national tour of Broadway shows such as *Rent* and *Cabaret* or pop music acts such as U2 or the Dave Matthews Band (both of whom sell out multiple nights at stadiums when they come to town). High-profile shows such as Disney's *Aida* and Mel Brooks's stage version of *The Producers* had their first runs here before moving on to New York.

While Chicago's off-Loop theaters, such as Steppenwolf Theatre, have built their reputations on a gritty style of acting (and a repertoire geared to adults), Chicago has plenty of theater companies that are less avant-garde and more attuned to the younger set. Even the city's blues community sees the wisdom of bringing the next generation into the fold, with special nights that are smoke- and alcohol-free. In the classical realm, the Chicago Symphony has invested in education with ECHO, a music learning center (for more on that, see p. 146) and supports a youth symphony. Even Chicago's opera companies make an effort to reach out to kids—so don't limit yourself!

FINDING OUT WHAT'S ON Check out *Chicago Parent Magazine* (© 708/386-5555; www.chicago parent.com) for calendars of upcoming cultural events targeted to kids. You can usually pick up free copies of the magazine at public libraries, bookstores, toy stores, and kids' clothing stores. The City of Chicago has cultural listings on its website at **www.cityofchicago.org/tourism**. For theater, you can't beat **www.chicago plays.com**, the website for the League of Chicago Theatres. The site links you to more than 130 Chicago-area theaters, and provides an online database of all current and upcoming productions, updated weekly. (They are also categorized so you can look up "children's theater.") The league's Hot Tix website (**www.hottix.org**) has twice-daily posts offering half-price tickets at the seven Chicago-area Hot Tix locations.

Chicago Dance and Music Alliance's website, **www.chicago performances.org**, provides listings on performances in these categories: Cultural Center, Ravinia, Grant Park, Dame Myra Hess Memorial Concerts, Jazz, Children's, and Dance. The website also provides a calendar where you can search for events by date.

The Loop & Magnificent Mile Entertainment

The Theatre at American
  Girl Place **1**
Arie Crown Theater **19**
Art Institute of Chicago **16**
Auditorium Theatre **17**
Chicago Cultural Center **11**
Chicago Music Mart **14**
Chicago Shakespeare
  Theater **3**
Chicago Theatre **8**
The Dance Center–Columbia
  College Chicago **18**
Goodman Theatre **5**
House of Blues **4**
Jazz Showcase **2**
Lyric Opera **12**
Noble Fool Theatre
  Company **7**
Oriental Theatre and
  Palace Theatre **6**
Schubert Theatre **13**
Storefront Theater **9**
Studio Theater **10**
Symphony Center **15**

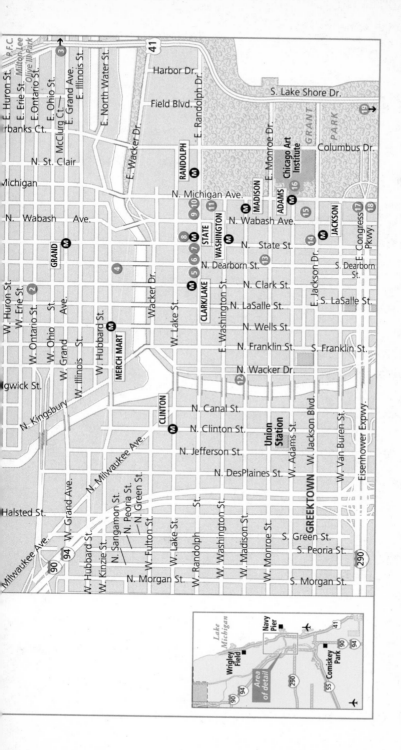

E. Huron St.
E. Erie St.
E. Ontario St.
E. Ohio St.
E. Grand Ave.
E. Illinois St.
E. North Water St.

P.F.C.
Milton Lee
Olive III Park

3

41

Harbor Dr.

Field Blvd.

S. Lake Shore Dr.

rbanks Ct.
McClurg Ct.
N. St. Clair

E. Wacker Dr.
E. Randolph Dr.

GRANT
PARK

Columbus Dr.

9

Michigan

N. Wabash Ave.

RANDOLPH
M

N. Michigan Ave.

MADISON
M

E. Monroe Dr.

Chicago Art
Institute
16
M

9 10
11

N. Wabash Ave.

ADAMS
M

15

W. Huron St.
W. Erie St.
2

GRAND
M

8
6 7

STATE
WASHINGTON
M

N. State St.

JACKSON

17
18

W. Ontario St.
St.

W. Ohio St.
Ave.

W. Grand

5

N. Dearborn St.

13

14

E. Congress Pkwy.

4

CLARK/LAKE
M

N. Clark St.

S. Dearborn
St.

W. Illinois St.

Wacker Dr.

E. Washington St.

N. LaSalle St.

E. Jackson Dr.

S. LaSalle St.

W. Hubbard St.
M

N. Wells St.

MERCH MART

W. Lake St.

N. Franklin St.

S. Franklin St.

gwick St.

N. Wacker Dr.

N. Kingsbury

12

N. Milwaukee Ave.

CLINTON
M

N. Canal St.

N. Clinton St.

Union
Station

W. Grand Ave.

W. Hubbard St.

W. Grand

N. Jefferson St.

W. Adams St.

W. Van Buren St.

N. DesPlaines St.

W. Jackson Blvd.

Eisenhower Expwy.

Halsted St.

94

N. Sangamon St.
N. Peoria St.
N. Green St.

St.

GREEKTOWN

Milwaukee Ave.

90

W. Hubbard St.
W. Kinzie St.

N. Fulton St.

W. Lake St.

W. Randolph St.

W. Washington St.

W. Madison St.

W. Monroe St.

S. Green St.

S. Peoria St.

290

N. Morgan St.

W. Fulton St.

S. Morgan St.

Lake
Michigan

Navy
Pier

41

Wrigley
Field

90
94

Area
of detail

290

Comiskey
Park

55

90
94

Lincoln Park & Wrigleyville Entertainment

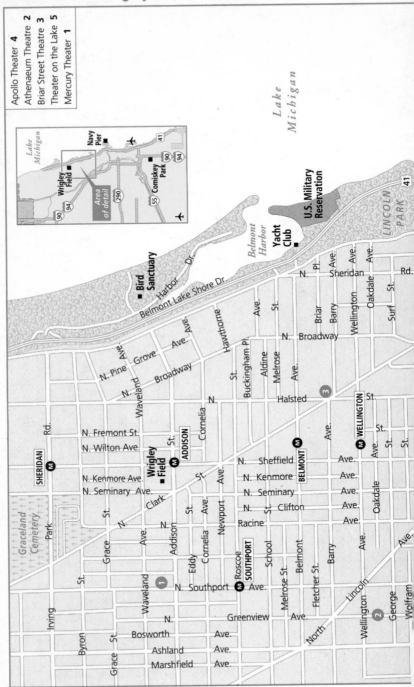

Apollo Theater **4**
Athenaeum Theatre **2**
Briar Street Theatre **3**
Theater on the Lake **5**
Mercury Theater **1**

Lake
Michigan

Fullerton
Beach

N. State St.

N. Dearborn St.

N. Clark St.

N. La Salle St.

Chicago
Historical
Society

Burton Pl.

St.

LINCOLN

PARK

Shore   Dr.

Dr.

5

John Cannon

sey Harbor

Lincoln
Park
Zoo

South
Pond

N. Park   Ave.

Eugenie

Stockton

Dr.

N.   Lincoln   Park   West

St.

64

SEDGWICK

M

St.

Schiller

North
Pond

Clark

N.   Sedgwick   St.

Menomonee

Wisconsin St.

N.   Cleveland   Ave.

Pl.

Deming

Arlington Pl.

N.

Lincoln

Ave.

Ave.

N.   Mohawk   St.

N.   Larrabee   St.

Orchard   St.

N. Burling St.

OZ
PARK

Armitage

N.   Orchard   St.

Avenue

NORTH/CLYBOURN

M

Ave.

North

Ave.

N.   Burling   St.

N.   Halsted   St.

4

on   Ave.

St.

DePaul
University

N.   Dayton St.

Freemont

Willow

North   St.

Weed   St.

M

FULLERTON

Wrightwood

Montana

St.

N.   Freemont St.

N.   Bissell   St.

N.   Sheffield   Ave.

Wisconsin St.

Ave.

M

ARMITAGE

Belden

TREBES
PARK

Webster

Dickens

Clybourn

Kingsbury

Turning
Basin

N. Racine   Ave.

Fullerton

St.

North

64

Lakewood

Wayne

Branch

Ave.

Noble

N.   Southport   Ave.

Elston

Expressway

N. Greenview

Greenview

Altgeld

North

North

Cortland

90

94

N. Bosworth

N.   Ashland

Kennedy

N.

West

N.   Ashland

N.   Wood

St.

41

M Subway/El stop

N

0   0.25 mi

0   0.25 km

For up-to-date entertainment listings, check the local newspapers and magazines, particularly the "Friday" and "Weekend Plus" sections of the two dailies, the *Chicago Tribune* and the *Chicago Sun-Times;* the *Chicago Reader* and *New City*, two free weekly tabloids with extensive listings; and the monthly *Chicago* magazine. The *Tribune*'s entertainment-oriented website, **www.metromix.com**, is an excellent source for reviews of cultural events, and the *Reader*'s website, **www.chireader.com**, is known for having one of the most complete weekly listings of cultural happenings. The local Citysearch website, **www.chicago.citysearch.com**, is also an excellent source of information, with lots of opinionated reviews.

GETTING TICKETS Why pay full price? **Hot Tix** (www.hottix.org) offers half-price tickets to more than 125 theaters throughout the Chicago area. Tickets are sold Sunday through Thursday for the day of performance.

On Friday, half-price tickets for many weekend shows are available. You must buy the tickets in person at a Hot Tix outlet; the main Hot Tix box office is located at 78 W. Randolph St., in the Cultural Center. If the show you've got your heart set on doesn't have half-price tickets available, never fear: Hot Tix is also a Ticketmaster outlet selling full-price tickets to all Ticketmaster events. A second, smaller Hot Tix outlet is located in the heart of the city's shopping district, in the old pumping station at Michigan and Chicago avenues. Recently renamed the **Chicago Water Works Visitor Center,** its entrance is on Pearson Street, across from the Water Tower Place mall. It's open daily from 7:30am to 7pm. (Maybe you'll want to stay right there for a show, as part of the Visitor Center has been converted into a theater, including a small cabaret space for tourist-oriented shows and a larger playhouse for the acclaimed Lookingglass Theatre.)

1 The Big Venues

Arie Crown Theater   Musicals and pop acts are the focus here; a renovation has improved what were terrible acoustics (Elton John once interrupted a performance to complain about the sound), but this is still a massive, somewhat impersonal hall. 2301 S. Lake Shore Dr., in the McCormick Place convention center at 23rd St. and Lake Shore Dr. ☎ 312/791-6190. Bus: 3, 4.

Auditorium Theatre   This beautiful theater is a certified national landmark, too. Built in 1889 by Louis Sullivan and Dankmar Adler, the grand hall hosts mostly musicals and dance performances. Even if you don't catch a show here, stop by for a tour. The occasional show will appeal to kids, from *Riverdance* to The Joffrey Ballet of Chicago's *The Nutcracker.* 50 E. Congress Pkwy., between Michigan and Wabash aves. ☎ 312/922-2110. www.auditoriumtheatre.org. Subway/El: Brown, Green, Orange, or Purple lines to Library/Van Buren, or Red Line to Jackson. Bus: 145, 147, or 151.

Briar Street Theatre   The Briar Street Theatre has been turned into the "Blue Man Theater" since fall 1997. I dare you to find a kid who doesn't get a kick out of seeing the Blue Men stuff their faces (literally) with marshmallows. The New York City performance phenomenon known as **Blue Man Group** has transformed the 625-seat theater, beginning with the lobby, which is now a jumble of tubes and wires and things approximating computer innards. The show—which mixes percussion, performance art, mime, and rock 'n' roll—has become an immensely popular permanent fixture on the Chicago theater scene. The three strangely endearing performers, whose faces and heads are covered in latex and blue paint, know how to get the audience involved. Your first decision: Do

---

Tips   **Scoring the Elusive Ticket**

Will Junior be crushed if you miss the traveling Broadway show he's been dreaming about seeing? Here are some tips for coming out a hero in your kids' eyes by getting tickets when demand is high.

- Hard-core Chicago theatergoers say the best way to score tickets is to **head right for the box office,** even for a hot show. (This is how I got tickets to *The Producers*—on the day of the show—when it was previewed in Chicago!) Don't phone. This way, you avoid those additional fees—and you will probably get better seats than you would by phone.
- **Use Hot Tix.** In New York, plentiful half-price tickets usually means the show is a loser. In Chicago, the League of Chicago Theatres expects all its members to offer tickets to its Hot Tix program, whether the show is a hit or flop.
- **Catch shows while they're still in previews.** Tickets are less expensive and more plentiful. If you want to see the cast in ideal form, get tickets for the final preview, which might coincide with the press opening.

---

you want the "splatter" or the "nonsplatter" seats? (The former necessitates the donning of a plastic sheet.) This show is often a sellout, so call for tickets in advance. 3133 N. Halsted St. (at Briar St.). © **773/348-4000.** Tickets $43–$53. Subway/El: Red or Brown Line to Belmont.

Chicago Cultural Center *Value*   Built in 1897, the Cultural Center's mandate has always been to provide the people of Chicago with access to the arts. Fortunately for families, children's shows are a major thrust of their programming, especially on Saturdays and sometimes Sundays. The center puts on workshops and performances for children several times a month, and major festivals four times a year. Concerts featuring Thai music or dance programs depicting the history and architecture of Chicago are just a few of types of programs you might find. Your children can become familiar with many performing arts genres and with the artists themselves. Best of all, it's free. 78 E. Washington St. © **312/346-3278.** Free tickets. www.ci.chi.il.us/tourism/culturalcenter. Subway: Red or Brown Line to Randolph and State.

Chicago Shakespeare Theater on Navy Pier   Normally I wouldn't recommend that parents take kids to Shakespeare, especially with audiences as dedicated as those who attend this theater. However, this company also produces the occasional family-friendly musical. Opened in October 1999 as the final piece in the redevelopment of Navy Pier, the new home of Chicago's third-largest nonprofit producing theater is a visually stunning, state-of-the-art jewel. The centerpiece of the glass-box complex, which rises seven stories and was built at a cost of $24 million, is a 525-seat courtyard-style theater patterned loosely after the Swan Theater in Stratford-upon-Avon. The complex also houses a 180-seat studio theater, an English-style pub, and lobbies with commanding views of Lake Michigan and the Chicago skyline. In 2002, *The Wizard of Oz* was the family musical. "Short Shakespeare" is an annual spring offering that runs for about a month in April and May. This 75-minute abridgement of the Shakespearean play is a great introduction to the Bard for kids. 800 E. Grand Ave. © **312/642-2273.**

Tips **Finding a Better Seat**

Most of Chicago's grand old theaters have balconies that go way, way up toward the ceiling—and if you're stuck in the cheap seats, you'll be straining to see what's happening on stage. While theaters are very strict about checking tickets when you arrive, the ushers relax during intermission. So scope out empty seats during the first act, and then move down to better (and much pricier) spots for the rest of the show.

Tickets $10–$38. Guaranteed parking in attached garage at 40% discount. Subway/El: Red Line to Grand, then bus 29 to Navy Pier.

Chicago Theatre   This 1920s music palace has been reborn as an all-purpose entertainment venue, hosting everything from pop acts and magicians to stand-up comedy. The theater also hosted a long run of *Joseph and the Technicolor Dreamcoat,* starring Donny Osmond. 175 N. State St., (at Lake St.). © 312/443-1130. Subway/El: Red Line to Lake/State; Brown or Orange Line to Clark/Lake.

Goodman Theatre   Chicago kids (and their parents) come back year after year for the Goodman's annual production of *A Christmas Carol,* a Chicago holiday tradition. The show runs from mid-November to the end of December. Book well in advance; the run always sells out. It's a great way for families to experience the Goodman's new $46 million state-of-the-art theater complex in the heart of Chicago's revitalized downtown theater district. Long planned but beset by delays over the years, the new Goodman—a quantum leap from the theater's old digs in an unrestored, pre–World War II building hidden behind the Art Institute of Chicago—is the final jewel in the crown of restored and new theaters that the city has put its considerable energy behind during the past decade.

During the season, the Goodman presents a Family Theatre Series, written and performed for children, so call or check online for this season's offerings. 170 N. Dearborn St. © 312/443-3800. www.goodman-theatre.org. Tickets $34–$45 main stage, $23–$37 studio. Subway/El: Red Line to Washington/State or Lake/State; Brown or Orange Line to Clark/Lake.

Noble Fool Theater Company   Kids over 12 will enjoy the newest addition to the downtown theater scene. This comedy-focused company was started in 1994 and features seasoned performers who've done time with Second City, Steppenwolf, and other well-known Chicago performing arts groups. The company moved into a new home at State and Randolph streets in spring 2001, and it has taken advantage of the extra space to offer an expanded, eclectic selection of entertainment, including its signature show, *Flanagan's Wake,* an "interactive" Irish wake that encourages audience participation. Other recent shows have included an original musical comedy based on the Vikings, the Renee Taylor and Joe Bologna–penned *Lovers and Other Strangers,* and *The Complete History of America (Abridged).* Noble Fool also runs a regular improv show, the signature element being live music and unscripted songs. 16 W. Randolph St. (at State St.). © 773/202-8843. Tickets $10–$25. Subway/El: Brown Line to Randolph, or Red Line to Washington.

North Shore Center for the Performing Arts in Skokie   Home to the well-respected Northlight Theater, the Skokie Valley Symphony Orchestra, and a series of touring acts, including comics, dance troupes, and children's programs. 9501 Skokie Blvd., Skokie. (© 847/673-6300). To reach the theater, take the Edens Expressway and exit at Old Orchard Rd.; go right onto Old Orchard; make a right onto Skokie Blvd. The theater is at the intersection of Skokie Blvd. and Golf Rd.

Oriental Theatre and Palace Theatre   Late 1990s renovations of these opulent theaters inevitably required corporate sponsorship—in this case, from car companies—transforming them into the Cadillac Palace and the awkwardly named Ford Center for the Performing Arts/Oriental Theatre. Both book major touring shows and are well worth a visit for arts buffs. The Oriental's fantastical Asian look includes elaborate carvings almost everywhere you look; dragons, elephants, and griffins peer down at the audience from the gilded ceiling. The Palace features a profusion of Italian marble surfaces and columns, gold-leaf accents a la Versailles, huge decorative mirrors, and crystal chandeliers. Oriental Theatre: 24 W. Randolph St. © 312/782-2004. Palace Theatre: 151 W. Randolph St. © 312/384-1510. Subway/El: Brown Line to Randolph.

Rosemont Theatre   This is a top suburban stop for musicals and concerts. *Radio City Christmas Spectacular Starring the Rockettes* and *Bear and the Big Blue House* are recent offerings that have appealed to kids of a wide age range. 5400 River Rd. in Rosemont, near O'Hare Airport. © 847/671-5100.

Shubert Theatre   Built in 1906 as a home for vaudeville, today the Schubert books mostly big-name musicals and sometimes comedy performers. A lot of the musicals are great family fare, so you may well find yourself here. If you get balcony seats, be aware that you are going to be way, way up. The view is still good, but if you have any fear of heights (or want to see expressions on the performers' faces), you might want to try for tickets on the main floor. 22 W. Monroe St. © 312/977-1700. Subway/El: Red Line to Washington.

Storefront Theater   Every kind of lively art, from theater, dance, performance art, chamber opera, puppetry, and cabaret to staged readings, finds a home here. Located in the Gallery 37 Center for the Arts, in the heart of the Loop's revitalized theater district, this state-of-the-art black box theater is providing a forum for Chicago's best artists to show off their accomplishments. 66 E. Randolph St. © 312/742-8497. Subway/El: Brown Line to Randolph.

Studio Theater *Value*   When you pop in to the Chicago Cultural Center, you might find yourself seeing a show here, at an intimate stage. The theater is used as an incubator space, giving Chicago's best off-Loop theater companies the opportunity to share their work with downtown audiences. The Department of Cultural Affairs provides the space for free to encourage the growth of new creative talent. Ticket prices are kept low or admission is free for select events to allow everyone the chance to enjoy some of Chicago's best theater. 77 E. Randolph St. © 312/744-6630. Subway/El: Brown, Green, Orange, or Purple Line to Randolph, or Red Line to Washington/State. Bus: 3, 4, 20, 56, 60, 127, 131, 145, 146, 147, 151, or 157.

Symphony Center   Symphony Center is the building that encompasses Orchestra Hall, home of the Chicago Symphony Orchestra. Expanded and renovated a few years back, the building now includes a six-story skylit arcade, recital spaces, an education center (for more on ECHO, see p. 146), and the fine-dining restaurant Rhapsody. While the CSO is the main attraction (and it's off-limits to kids under 12), the Symphony Center hosts a family matinee series, plus a series of piano recitals, classical and chamber music concerts, and the occasional jazz or pop artist. 220 S. Michigan Ave., between Adams St. and Jackson Blvd. ☎ **312/294-3000.** Subway/El: Red Line to Washington/State. Bus: 3, 4, 20, 56, 60, 127, 145, 146, 147, 151 or 157.

The Theatre at American Girl Place *Circle of Friends: An American Girl Musical* has an open run Thursday through Sunday for $26 per ticket at this theater inside the American Girl store. Inspired by the American Girls stories, the musical features young girls in the roles of seven brave characters who teach girls about believing in your strengths and following your heart. At the heart of American Girls is a popular series of books about living in different places and eras of American history, from Colonial Williamsburg to World War II. Besides providing a history lesson, young readers can discover similarities between their own lives and the lives of these girls. 111 E. Chicago Ave. ☎ **877/247-5223.** www. americangirl.com. Subway/El: Red Line to Chicago/State.

2 Seasonal Events

Chicago Human Rhythm Project *(Finds* **Ages 6 & up.** This group performs an annual tap-dance festival that was created in 1990 and brings together tap and percussive dancers from all over the world. It's an impressive sight (and sound). Dancers spend a month in Chicago, taking a series of workshops and outreach programs. It all culminates in a stirring week of performances in late July at the Athenaeum Theatre, 2936 N. Southport Ave. (at Lincoln Ave.). Office: 1920 Lincoln Ave. ☎ **312/587-8370.** www.chicagotap.com. Tickets $20. Subway/El: Brown Line to Wellington.

A Christmas Carol **Ages 6 & up.** This beloved Chicago holiday tradition took on a new look in 2001 when the Goodman Theater moved into its new home and unveiled a completely redesigned set. The new production of *A Christmas Carol,* with expenses of more than $1 million, was darker and more operatic—along the lines of a Tim Burton take on the old classic. Kids love it, parents love it, and theater buffs loved the fact that the Goodman didn't turn the show, admittedly one of the darker Christmas stories ever penned, into a sugarcoated Broadway event. In fact, the show is even better for being more of a serious play and ghost story—it makes the ending even more uplifting. The show runs every year from the third weekend in November until just before Christmas. 170 N. Dearborn St. ☎ **312/443-3800.** www.goodman-theatre.org. Tickets $30–$50. Subway/El: Red Line to Washington/State or Lake/State; Brown or Orange Line to Clark/Lake.

Dance Chicago *(Value* **Ages 5 & up.** The Athenaeum also hosts the annual Dance Chicago, a highly engaging month-long festival showcasing the talents of up-and-coming contemporary dance companies and choreographers. It usually takes place in October or November. In 2002, the programs included jazz, hiphop, tap, ballroom, tango, salsa, swing, and more. A kids' show ran every Saturday afternoon, called *Dance for Kids, Too!* at a cost of $12 for adults and $5 for kids ages 4 and up. (To attend the evening programs, kids need to be age 5 and up.) The kids' program featured 15 dance companies, both youth and professional, whose work is geared to families. At the Athenaeum Theatre, 2936 N. Southport Ave. (at Lincoln Ave.). ☎ **773/935-6860.** www.dancechicago.com. Tickets $5–$25. Subway/El: Brown Line to Wellington.

Grant Park Music Festival **All ages.** Grant Park Symphony and Chorus performs annually during the Grant Park Music Festival, begun in 1931 by Mayor A.J. Cermak, who suggested free concerts to lift Chicagoans' spirits. Now

---

Tips A Do-It-Yourself *Messiah*

Fancy yourself an ecclesiastical crooner? Should you be in town over the holidays, don't skip the LaSalle Talman **Do-It-Yourself** *Messiah,* an extraordinarily popular and rousing rendition of the Handel classic. Now staged at the opulent Civic Opera House (although, for years, Orchestra Hall provided the setting), the program enlists audience members as part of a 3,500-voice chorus, who are accompanied by a volunteer orchestra and four professional soloists. Even if you and your kids don't join in the singing, just sitting in the audience and absorbing the roof-raising aural power that fills the theater guarantees goose bumps. This is a hot, hot, hot ticket, so call early for reservations at (773/776-4300.

---

held from late June through August, the series of free outdoor classical music concerts given by the summer orchestra and a number of visiting artists is performed in Grant Park just a block from Lake Michigan. Concerts are held Wednesday through Sunday, with most performances beginning at 7:30pm. Bring a blanket if you plan to sit on the lawn; seats in the band shell are reserved for subscribers, but unclaimed seats are offered to the public about 15 minutes before the concert begins. It's a great way for families to enjoy music together. Selections might include Broadway favorites, Bernstein, Mozart, Brahms, Cole Porter, and Gershwin. In 2003, the Grant Park Symphony moves to a stunning new pavilion designed by Frank Gehry. Petrillo Music Shell, in Grant Park at the corner of Jackson Blvd. and Columbus Dr. (312/742-4763. www.grantparkmusicfestival.com. Subway/El: Red Line to Jackson.

The Nutcracker **Ages 8 & up.** When the Joffrey Ballet of Chicago moved here several years ago, it brought along a new holiday tradition: its annual production of *The Nutcracker.* The ballet is performed at the beautiful Auditorium Theater for 3 weeks in December. It's simply the best version in town, with a live orchestra helping to bring Tchaikovsky's holiday tale to life. Office: 70 E. Lake St. (312/739-0120. www.joffrey.com. Tickets $34–$74. Auditorium Theater, 50 E. Congress Parkway. Bus: 145, 147, or 151. Subway/El: Brown, Green, Orange, or Purple lines to Library/Van Buren, or Red Line to Jackson.

Ravinia Festival *(Finds)* **All ages.** Ravinia, summer home of the Chicago Symphony Orchestra in suburban Highland Park, is a Chicago summer tradition. The festival strives to be family-friendly by maintaining low ticket prices and inviting patrons to pack their own picnics. There's even a series of **Kraft Kids Concerts** that reach out to the next generation of music lovers. In 2002, the series featured the Ravinia Festival Jazz Mentors with the Muntu Dance Theatre of Chicago, Ravinia Festival Orchestra, Chicago Human Rhythm Project, The Apollo Chorus, River North Dance Chicago, and more. Held about eight times each summer, the kids' concerts usually begin at 11am on Saturdays and have a discounted price of $5 to $8 for reserved seats (in the Pavillion) and $3 for lawn tickets. My advice? Bring a picnic lunch and stake out a spot on the lawn (with the added bonus that your kids can run and burn off excess energy).

If your kids are a bit older, they would enjoy hanging on the lawn during the regular season, which runs from mid-June to Labor Day and includes far more than classical concerts: You can also catch pop acts, dance performances, operatic arias, and blues concerts. Tickets are sold to both the covered pavilion, where you get a reserved seat and a view of the stage, and the lawn, which is the real joy of Ravinia: sitting under the stars and a canopy of leafy branches while listening to music and indulging in an elaborate picnic. (It's a local tradition to try to outdo everyone else by bringing candelabras and fine china.) Whether it's Mozart or Lyle Lovett, the setting is magical every time. The wide lawn to the left of the stage is a popular place for families to spread out.

Dining options available at the park range from the fine-dining restaurant **Mirabelle** (© 847/432-7550 for reservations) to pre-packed picnic spreads from the **Gatehouse,** featuring gourmet items to go. Lawn catering is also available for parties of 20 or more. But what most cognoscenti do is pack a picnic of delectables and eat on the lawn. Do arrive early if you're coming for a pop act because the lawn can get packed. For $8, you can rent a pair of lawn chairs and a table. In case you're wondering about the weather conditions at concert time, dial Ravinia's Weather Line (© 847/433-5010). Green Bay and Lake-Cook rds., Highland Park. © 847/266-5100 or 312/RAVINIA. www.ravinia.org. Tickets pavilion $15–$50; lawn $10. Most concerts are held in the evening. Catch the Ravinia bus at the following locations: Marshall Field's (State and Randolph sts.); the Palmer House Hilton (Monroe St. entrance); Westin River North, 320 N. Dearborn St. (the Clark St. side); The Drake hotel (Walton St. and Michigan Ave.); Harbor House (3200 N. Lake Shore Dr.); Sheridan and Hollywood; Sheridan and Devon; or the Davis St. Station in Evanston. Round-trip tickets are $12. Many of the major hotels also charter buses during the season. You can also catch the 5:50pm commuter train, which leaves from the North Western Station near the Loop at Madison and Canal sts. The train stops in Highland Park directly at the festival; the "Ravinia Special" round-trip fare is $4.

Ringling Bros. and Barnum & Bailey Circus   **Ages 6 & up.** Come one, come all to this massive circus, which stops in Chicago every fall for several weeks beginning in November. As promised, three rings of glitzy, over-the-top entertainment are in store, from trapeze artists to the horses, tigers, elephants, and crocodiles who make up some of the 200 human and animal performers. Nothing subtle about this show—in fact, smaller kids might be overwhelmed by the sheer size of the United Center, plus the flashing lights and eardrum-blasting music. Still, at least once in your life, it's worth it to see this darn impressive "greatest show on earth." United Center, 1901 W. Madison St. © 312/455-4500. www.ringling.com. Tickets $10.50–$50. Bus: 9, 20.

SummerDance   **Ages 5 & up.** Now entering its sixth year, the annual Chicago SummerDance Festival usually runs from late June to early September in the Spirit of Music Garden in Grant Park. Presented by the Chicago Department of Cultural Affairs, the festival features 1-hour dance lessons to taped music, followed by dancing to live orchestras, every Thursday, Friday, and Saturday evening from 6 to 9:30pm and Sunday afternoons from 2 to 5pm, weather permitting. The festival also presents folk dance from Scandinavia, Israel, Ireland, Scotland, Wales and more at various venues throughout the city. Grant Park, 601 S. Michigan (between Harrison and Balbo, across from Columbia College). For complete information on what's scheduled, call the Chicago Department of Cultural Affairs at © 312/744-6630. Free admission. Subway/El: Red Line to Jackson.

3 Theater

Chicago Playworks for Families and Young Audiences (Value   **Ages 3 & up.** How can the 35,000 kids and adults who flock to see this company's performances each year be wrong? Founded in 1925 as Goodman Children's Theatre, Chicago Playworks later became part of DePaul University, and is one of the first important children's theaters in the United States. The company presents three shows per season, which runs from October through April. Located in the historic Merle Reskin Theatre, built in 1910 as the Blackstone Theater, kids can cozy up in plush red seats and marvel at the sparkling chandeliers and grand scale of the surroundings. If you're a Chicago resident, you might want to try the season tickets, which entitle you to two free admission tickets to the Chicago Children's Museum at Navy Pier. Ask about the Ice Cream Social package, offered three times a year, which gets you into an after-show ice-cream bar, discussion and autograph session with the cast at the nearby Hilton Chicago. Shows run from October to May, usually Tuesday and Thursday at 10am and Saturdays at 2pm. Merle Reskin Theatre, 60 E. Balbo Dr. ✆ **312/922-1999.** http://theatre school.depaul.edu. Tickets $8 and up. Subway/El: Red Line to Jackson.

The Children's Theater Fantasy Orchard   **Ages 3 & up.** Performing in the Mercury Theater, a small, modern theater in Lakeview's hot Southport Avenue area, Children's Theater Fantasy Orchard presents fairy and folk tales from around the world. Founded in 1990, the company now performs for 30,000 kids annually. Some 30 actors and technicians come up with new productions each year. In doing so, the company tries to depict universal struggles and truths as they stoke kids' imaginations. In 2003, the schedule included *Three Cinderella Stories,* featuring an African, Asian, and Spanish Cinderella. At Mercury Theater, 3745 N. Southport. ✆ 773/ 539-4211. www.kidtheatre.com. Tickets $10 for adults, $5 for kids. Subway/El: Brown Line to Southport.

Emerald City Theatre Company   **Ages 2 & up.** From Tarzan and Jane to Dr. Seuss classics, this relative newcomer to the kids' theater scene produces shows for kids aged 2 and up. The company is currently performing at the Apollo Theater, a modern theater with 400 seats—although that has changed from time to time throughout the years. Emerald City Theatre Company was founded in 1996, and recent shows have included musicals like *Once Upon a Mattress, Charlie and the Chocolate Factory,* and *Frosty,* which is an annual holiday treat. Each season, Emerald City produces five shows, some of which are original works written for the company. Many Chicago kids had their first theater experience with Emerald City (named in honor of *The Wonderful Wizard of Oz,* written by Frank L. Baum while he lived in Chicago). At the Apollo Theater, 2540 N. Lincoln. Office: 2936 N. Southport. ✆ 773/935-6100. www.emeraldcitytheatre.com. Tickets $8 for children 2–12, $10 for ages 13 and up. Subway/El: Red or Brown Line to Fullerton.

Lifeline Theatre KidSeries   **Ages 2 & up.** Lifeline Theatre—the grown-up version—has a faithful following who anticipates its creative stage adaptations of literary classics such as *Jane Eyre.* Its KidSeries plays are original adaptations of favorite children's books, and often include music written especially for them. These shows, which are presented on Saturday and Sunday afternoons, are great for even the youngest kids. Recent performances include *Click Clack Moo,* a world premiere musical in which a farmer receives demands from his livestock after they find an antique typewriter in their drafty barn, and *Mike Mulligan and his Steam Shovel,* a musical. After each performance, actors come out to the lobby to meet kids, give autographs, and answer questions. The theater is small—100 seats—and in a slightly run-down neighborhood. Look for metered parking on Morse Avenue or free parking 3 blocks north of the theater at the corner of Glenwood and Estes avenues in the Trilogy, Inc. lot. 6912 N. Glenwood Ave. ✆ 773/761-4477. www.lifelinetheatre.com. Tickets $8. Subway/El: Bus 147 to Sheridan and Arthur; transfer to Bus 155 to Glenwood.

Medieval Times   Ages 6 & up. Does jousting count as "theater"? This dinner and tournament show features knights competing in games, swordplay, jousting, and pyrotechnics. Sound familiar? You may have caught the act in the Jim Carrey film, *The Cable Guy*. (Naturally, Jim Carrey got a bit too involved in the show, but in real life, kids shouldn't expect to find themselves wearing armor and riding horses.) It's pure kitsch, but if you can get off your high horse (so to speak) you might find yourself sucked in to the "drama." Besides, kids dig it. Guests dine on a four course "medieval" banquet served by staff posing as "serving wenches." Performances take place Wednesday through Sunday. 2001 Roselle Rd. at I-90, Schaumburg. ✆ 847/843-3900. Tickets $46 for adults, $32 for children 12 and under. Matinee rates might be available, so call for show times and ticket prices.

4 Concerts

Blue Chicago *(Finds)* **Ages 8 & up.** A blues club for families? Yes, it's true— from 8pm to midnight on Saturdays, the basement of the Blue Chicago store becomes a venue geared to families, featuring the music of the Gloria Shannon Blues Band. In fact, "Down in the Basement" is the only venue in Chicago that offers a regular live blues show for all ages. No alcohol is served and no smoking is allowed.

Blue Chicago pays homage to female blues belters with a strong lineup of the best women vocalists around. The 1940s-style brick-walled room, decorated with original artwork of Chicago blues vignettes, is open Monday through Saturday, with music beginning at 9pm. Admission allows you to club-hop between this venue and a second location, open Tuesday through Sunday, down the street at 536 N. Clark St. Next door, at 534 N. Clark, is the Blue Chicago Store, which sells blues-related clothing, merchandise, and artwork. 736 N. Clark St. (between Chicago Ave. and Superior St.) ✆ 312/642-6261. www.bluechicago.com. Tickets $5 for adults, free for children 12 and under. Subway/El: Red or Brown Line to Chicago.

Chicago Children's Choir   Ages 6 & up. Two self-produced concerts are performed each year, in May and December, by this multiracial, multicultural choral music education program. Venues change, so call for information. This is not just any kids' choir: In December 2002, the choir performed with Bobby McFerrin at the Chicago Theatre. Founded in 1956, the choir trains nearly 3,000 young singers a year. The choir runs 61 in-school choruses in 40 Chicago elementary schools and five after-school Neighborhood Choirs. The showpiece is the 125-voice Concert Choir, which includes Treble and Chamber ensembles, Madrigals, and a Show Choir. Office: Chicago Cultural Center, 78 E. Washington, 5th floor. ✆ 312/849-8300. www.ccchoir.org. Tickets $27–$47.

Chicago Music Mart at DePaul Center   All ages. Spark the interest of the budding musician in your family at the "Mart," where instrument stores abound, and kids are welcome to test out the instruments. At lunchtime, "Tunes at Noon" presents free concerts on weekdays, indoors in winter and outdoor in summer, featuring high school bands, choral groups, or young performers playing everything from classical to jazz. 333 S. State St. ✆ 312/362-6700. Subway/El: Red Line to Jackson.

Chicago Opera Theater   Ages 8 & up. As the "other" opera company in town, Chicago Opera Theater doesn't get all the big names, but it does make opera accessible to a wider audience with an emphasis on American composers and performers who sing in English. The opera has a wonderful educational outreach program that features one opera per season (a short one, usually!) that is performed by and for children. Call well in advance for tickets to the next performance, as they always sell out. In 2002, the performance was *Brundibár*, a 30-minute opera first performed in 1942 at the Jewish boys' orphanage in Prague for which it was written. By the time of the premiere, the composer, conductor, and director had all been sent to Terezin, a Nazi concentration camp. The opera is a story of good triumphing over evil, and each performance was followed by a discussion with performers. The production was designed by famed author and artist Maurice Sendak. At the Athenaeum Theatre, 2936 N. Southport Ave. (at Lincoln Ave.). *©* 312/704-8414. www.chicagooperatheater.org. Tickets $27–$56 adults, $13–$28 children. Subway/El: Brown Line to Wellington.

Chicago Symphony Orchestra   **Ages 6 & up.** CSO Kraft Family Matinee series exposes kids to the storytelling of music through classics. This season, performances include "special guests" such as Woofgang and Meowzart, who appear at performances of "Stomp Your Foot!," and Underground Railway Theater puppeteers at performances of "The Firebird." The series runs on select Saturdays at 11am and 12:30pm. Concerts are performed by members of the Chicago Symphony Orchestra and guest artists.

Another option for kids is the Chicago Youth Symphony Orchestra, which performs at Orchestra Hall (*©* **312/939-2207;** www.cyso.org). Founded in 1946, the orchestra is comprised of a senior-level group of 105 top high school musicians in the Chicagoland area. Recognized as one of the nation's best youth orchestras, the CYSO performs in November and May.

If your children are over age 12, they are welcome to attend a performance of the CSO, now led by music director Daniel Barenboim, and among the best in the world—a legacy of the late maestro Sir Georg Solti, who captured a record-breaking 31 Grammy awards for his CSO recordings and showcased the orchestra at other major musical capitals during frequent international tours. In addition to classical music, the "Symphony Center Presents" series has included some of the top jazz, world beat, Latin, and cabaret artists in the world in recent years. Although they're in high demand, good seats often become available on concert day.

Summertime visitors have an opportunity to hear a CSO performance at the delightful **Ravinia Festival** (p. 227) in suburban Highland Park, led by music director Christoph Eschenbach. Orchestra Hall, in Symphony Center, 220 S. Michigan Ave. *©* 312/294-3000. www.chicagosymphony.org. Tickets $10–$90; box seats $165. Subway/El: Red Line to Jackson.

House of Blues   **Ages 8 & up.** Gospel as well as blues originated in Chicago, and the House of Blues' popular Sunday gospel brunch, offering a Southern-style buffet, brings a different Chicago gospel choir to the stage each week; the three weekly "services" often sell out, so get tickets in advance. Kids will delight in the funky decor at the club, part of a nightclub, restaurant, and hotel complex that has breathed new life into Marina City. The largest outpost in the growing House of Blues chain, this 55,000-square-foot complex, extravagantly decorated with 600 pieces from owner Isaac Tigrett's collection of Mississippi Delta folk art, isn't really a blues club as much as a showcase for rock, R&B, zydeco, reggae, and everything else. 329 N. Dearborn St. (at Kinzie St.). *©* 312/923-2000 for general information, 312/923-2020 for concert information. www.hob.com. Ticket prices vary depending on the act. Subway/El: Red Line to Grand.

Jazz Showcase   **Ages 8 & up.** The Segals make an effort to cultivate new generations of jazz lovers: The club admits all ages (children under 12 are free), has a nonsmoking policy, and offers a Sunday 4pm matinee show that won't keep the kids up late. Spanning more than 50 years and several locations, founder Joe Segal has become synonymous with jazz in Chicago. His son, Wayne, recently took over the business, but this latest venue in the River North restaurant and entertainment district is the spiffiest yet, a spacious and handsome room with sharp black-and-white photographs of jazz greats, many of whom have passed through Segal's clubs. There are two shows a night, and reservations are recommended when a big-name headliner is featured. Such well-regarded musicians as McCoy Tyner, Clark Terry, Maynard Ferguson, and Ahmad Jamal have made appearances in recent years.

The Segals's latest outpost is the new **Joe's Be-bop Cafe and Jazz Emporium** at Navy Pier, 600 E. Grand Ave. (© **312/595-5299**), a Southern-style BBQ restaurant with live music nightly. 59 W. Grand St. (at Clark St.). © **312/670-2473**. Tickets $15–$20. Subway/El: Red Line to Grand.

Lyric Opera of Chicago   **Ages 12 & up.** A major American opera company, the Lyric attracts top-notch singers from all over the world. Naturally, this is not the place for toddlers, but if you have kids in seventh grade or older, you might want to expose them to opera through the company's student matinees. Kids should be prepared for performances to run approximately 3 hours, including one 30-minute intermission. Just soaking in the ambience at the glamorous and opulent opera house is quite an experience. Add to that the magnificence of the Lyric Opera Orchestra and chorus, the amazing sets and costumes, and the beautiful voices, and it's an experience your kids won't soon forget. Kids are encouraged to dress up for the occasion, and proper etiquette is expected. Ticket prices are $5 for the upper balcony; $10 for the first balcony; $13 for the 2nd section of the main floor; and $15 for box seats and the front section of the main floor.

If you can't snag tickets or if you visit during the opera's off-season, you can still check out the theater by taking a tour (© 312/827-5685). Civic Opera House, at Madison St. and Wacker Dr. © **312/332-2244**. Fax 312/332-8120. www.lyricopera.org. Tickets $26–$125. Subway/El: Brown Line to Washington.

Old Town School of Folk Music *(Finds)*   **All ages.** Country, folk, bluegrass, Latin, Celtic—the Old Town School of Folk Music covers a spectrum of indigenous musical forms. A full schedule of classes, concerts, and special events are geared to children ages 6 months to teen years. (For more on dropping in for a class, see chapter 8.) The school hosts an annual Chicago Folk and Roots Festival in July in Wells Park at Lincoln and Montrose, with stage performances and

---

Tips **Facets' Film Festival**

Facets Multi-Media, 1517 W. Fullerton Ave. (© **773/281-4114**; www. facets.org; Subway/El: Red or Brown Line to Fullerton), is for the die-hard cinematic thrill-seeker, a nonprofit group that screens independent film and video from around the world. The group also hosts the **Chicago International Children's Film Festival** (Oct–Nov), the largest in the U.S. In 2002, the festival screened 220 children's films from 40 countries—many of which you'll never see in mainstream theaters. For more information about the film festival or to check out Facets' kids' programs, including Young Chicago Critics and Take One! Workshops, log on to **www.cicff.org**.

Chicago as Backdrop

Get your teen warmed up for your trip to Chicago by renting one of these Chicago-based flicks (all of which are rated PG-13):

- *Ferris Bueller's Day Off* (1986)
- *The Fugitive* (1993)
- *My Best Friend's Wedding* (1997)
- *Prelude to a Kiss* (1992)
- *Save the Last Dance* (2001)

an activity and craft tent for kids. Headliners are name-brand performers such as Patti Smith. The school, celebrating its 45th anniversary this year, is best known as a training center offering a slate of music classes, but it also hosts everyone from the legendary Pete Seeger to bluegrass phenom Alison Krauss. The school's home, in a former 1930s library, is the world's largest facility dedicated to the preservation and presentation of traditional and contemporary folk music. Don't believe it? Try this on for size: Folk-rock legend Joni Mitchell came out of retirement to make a rare concert appearance inaugurating the music center 4 years ago. The Old Town School also houses an art gallery showcasing exhibitions of works by local, national, and international artists; a music store offering an exquisite selection of instruments, sheet music, and hard-to-find recordings; and a cafe. The school maintains another retail store and a schedule of children's classes at its first location, 909 W. Armitage Ave. 4544 N. Lincoln Ave. (between Wilson and Montrose aves.). (©) 773/728-6000. www.oldtownschool.org. Tickets $10–$30. Subway/El: Blue Line to Western.

5 Movies

Chicago has its share of multiplex theaters that feature kid fare. In fact, Chicago's first real multiplex, a 21-screen theater, opened in November 2002. The **AMC River East,** located at 322 E. Illinois, east of Columbus Drive (© **312/596-0333**), features stadium seating and digital sound in all auditoriums. The opening of the theater doubled the number of first-run movie screens downtown. Other major downtown cinemas include: **McClurg Court,** 330 E. Ohio St. (© **312/642-0723**), **600 N. Michigan Theaters,** at that address (© **312/255-9340**), **Esquire 6,** 58 E. Oak (© **312/280-0101**), and **Pipers Alley 4,** 1608 N. Wells (© **312/642-7500**).

One IMAX and one Omnimax theater surround you with sights and sounds. Cineplex Odeon's **IMAX Theater on Navy Pier** (© **312/595-0060**), shows not only traditional IMAX films on its six-story, 80-foot-wide screen, but also 3D movies. The **Omnimax Theater** at the Museum of Science and Industry, 57th Street and Lake Shore Drive (© **773/684-1414;** www.msichicago.org), usually presents movies in conjunction with exhibits. The theater also has an Omnilaser Fantasy light show featuring rock music and costs the same as a movie. To ensure tickets, reserve in advance—even if you have a ticket, get there early, as the line for seats begins forming about 20 minutes in advance.

6 Dance

Ballet Chicago   **Ages 10 & up.** Under artistic director Daniel Duell, a former New York City Ballet dancer, the group is notable for its specialty, the ballets of Balanchine. The ballet performs one full-length story ballet a year, usually in April during the Spring Festival of Dance. Because the ballet has no permanent home, call for venue information. © 312/251-8838. www.balletchicago.org. Tickets $10–$15.

The Dance Center–Columbia College Chicago   **Ages 10 & up.** Columbia College, a liberal-arts institution specializing in the arts and media, has been growing by leaps and bounds in recent years. One of the college's most recent and exciting purchases is a 33,000-square-foot Art Deco–style building, located on its South Loop campus, that now accommodates the school's Dance Center and resident professional troupe, Mordine & Company Dance Theatre. Why exciting? Because for years the Dance Center—the hub of Chicago's modern dance milieu—was located in the gritty Uptown neighborhood on the city's far–North Side. Not only is the new spot more accessible and safe, but its intimate "black box" 275-seat performance space also provides stadium seating with marvelous sight lines. The Dance Center will continue to host at least a dozen performances a year by both international and national touring groups and homegrown choreographers. Its annual DanceAfrica festival of dance and music, held in October, is a colorful crowd-pleaser. 1306 S. Michigan Ave. © 312/344-8300. www.dancecenter.org. Tickets $20. Subway/El: Red Line to Roosevelt. Bus: 151.

Hubbard Street Dance Chicago   **Ages 12 & up.** Hubbard Street is Chicago's best-known dance troupe whose mix of jazz, modern, ballet, and theater dance has won many devoted local fans. Sometimes whimsical, sometimes romantic, the crowd-pleasing 22-member ensemble incorporates a range of dance traditions, from Kevin O'Day to Twyla Tharp, who has choreographed pieces exclusively for Hubbard Street. Recently, the troupe has been performing at the Cadillac Palace Theatre for 2- to 3-week engagements in the fall and spring. But the really good news is that as of 2003, the group is the flagship resident company of the new music and dance theater at Lakefront Millennium Park in Grant Park. In the summer, the dancers often perform at Ravinia Festival (p. 227). Office: 1147 W. Jackson Blvd. © 312/850-9744. www.hubbardstreetdance.com. Tickets $15–$50.

Joffrey Ballet of Chicago   **Ages 10 & up.** This major classical company, which recently celebrated its 45th anniversary, was welcomed warmly when it relocated to Chicago from New York 7 years ago. Although the company concentrates on touring, the Joffrey schedules about 6 weeks of performances a year in its adopted hometown. Led by cofounder and artistic director Gerald Arpino, the company is committed to the classic works of the 20th century. Its repertoire extends from the ballets of Arpino, Robert Joffrey, Balanchine, and Jerome Robbins to the cutting-edge works of Alonzo King and Chicago choreographer Randy Duncan. The Joffrey continues to draw crowds to its popular rock ballet, *Billboards,* which is set to the music of Prince, and continues to tour internationally. When the company is in town, it divides its time between the Auditorium Theatre—performing in March, October, and December, when it stages its rendition of the holiday favorite *The Nutcracker*—and in the summer at the open-air Ravinia Festival in north-suburban Highland Park. Office: 70 E. Lake St. © 312/739-0120. www.joffrey.com. Tickets $15–$50.

Muntu Dance Theatre of Chicago   **Ages 8 & up.** The tribal costumes, drumming, and energetic moves of this widely touring group, which focuses on both traditional and contemporary African and African–American dance, are always a hit with audiences. The company performs in town several times a year, including a run during the Spring Festival of Dance, at the Dance Center of Columbia College's DanceAfrica festival in October, and in early December. Office: 6800 S. Wentworth Ave. © 773/602-1135. www.muntu.com. Tickets $15–$25.

River North Dance Company   **Ages 10 & up.** Chicago can be a brutal testing ground for start-up dance companies, who have to struggle to find performance space and grab publicity. But the odds didn't buckle the well-oiled knees of the River North Dance Company. This terrifically talented jazz dance ensemble performs programs of short, Broadway-style numbers by established and emerging choreographers. You never know where they'll pop up next, though, so call for information on upcoming shows. Office: 1016 N. Dearborn St. © 312/944-2888. www.rivernorthchicago.com. Tickets $20–$35.

7 Puppet Shows

Puppet Parlor Theatre   **Ages 4 & up.** Don't be fooled by the converted grocery store venue: Puppet Parlor's repertoire includes 50 different productions, including classics such as *Hansel and Gretel* and *Pinocchio* in an intimate theater that holds about 60 people. The well-staged, European-style marionette shows take place every Saturday and Sunday at 2pm. Call ahead for reservations. 1922 W. Montrose. © 773/989-0308. Tickets $8. Subway/El: Brown Line to Montrose.

Redmoon Theater *Finds*   **Ages 10 & up.** Redmoon Theater might well be the most intriguing and visionary theater company in Chicago. Founded a little more than 10 years ago in the West Side neighborhood of Logan Square, the company produces "spectacle theater" comprising masks, objects, and an international range of puppetry styles in indoor and outdoor venues around town— including, at least once a year lately, in Steppenwolf Theatre's studio space. Utterly hypnotic, highly acrobatic and visceral, and using minimal narration, their adaptations of Melville's *Moby-Dick,* Mary Shelley's *Frankenstein,* Victor Hugo's *The Hunchback of Notre Dame,* and *Rachel's Love,* an original work based on Jewish folktales, were revelations that have earned the company an ardent and burgeoning following. If you're here in late October, don't miss Redmoon's annual "All Hallows' Eve Ritual Celebration" in Logan Square—a guaranteed spine-chilling experience. © 773/388-9031. www.redmoon.org. Ticket prices vary.

8 Spectator Sports

Chicago Bears   **Ages 8 & up.** Bears fans still reminisce about the 1985 Mike Ditka–led team's NFL championship like it happened yesterday. There is still something quintessentially Chicago about bravely freezing your derriere off in the historic open-air coliseum that is Soldier Field, or, for that matter, grilling up ribs and brats in the parking lot before the Bears go to battle against our arch enemy, the Green Bay Packers. True story: I once sat through a Bears-Packers game late in the season in which it rained, then sleeted, then snowed! Just make sure you bring a thermos of hot chocolate for the kids and a flask of something warming for the adults before you experience "Bear Weather" for the first time. At Soldier Field, Lake Shore Dr. and 16th St. © 847/615-2327. www.chicagobears.com. Tickets $40–$65. Bus: 12, 127, 130, 146.

Chicago Blackhawks   Ages 8 & up. The 'Hawks have a devoted, impassioned following of fans who work themselves into a frenzy with the first note of the "Star Spangled Banner." But don't expect any heroics on ice along the lines of past 'Hawks legends such as Bobby Hull and Tony Esposito. Any player that turns into a star and, hence, earns the right to restructure his contract for a higher salary is immediately traded by penny-pinching owner Bill Wirtz—derided by fans and local sportswriters as "Dollar Bill." Blackhawks practices at "The Edge," the ice facility in west suburban Bensonville (near O'Hare Airport), are open to the public; for information, call ✆ 312/455-7000. (Practices at the United Center are not open to the public.) At the United Center, 1901 W. Madison St. ✆ 312/455-4500. www.chicagoblackhawks.com. Tickets $15–$250. Bus: 9, 20.

Chicago Bulls   Ages 8 & up. Woe is us. After dismantling the world-famous six-time NBA championship Chicago Bulls following the 1998 season, the Bulls losing 5, 10, or 15 games in a row, year after year is so dismal, I almost can't write about it. Still, in late 2002, the young team was being touted as a possible comeback story—who knows? Maybe basketball in Chicago will become fun again. Back in the glory days, the planet's most celebrated athlete, Michael Jordan, pulled off the impossible: Replacing the world's perception of Chicago as gangster Al Capone's playground with an image of his royal Airness executing a signature tomahawk dunk. We started to take for granted the frenzied celebrations in the street that inevitably occurred each June in the wake of the latest championship crown. It was a wonderful boost for a perennially pessimistic sports-loving metropolis, and a rare, indelible moment when the city's white and black populations seemed to embrace in simple camaraderie and festivity. United Center, where the Bulls play, feels like an airplane hangar–size funeral parlor these days, and for the time being, tickets are worth about as much as the paper they're printed on. So grab yourself a courtside seat—there are plenty to go around. At the United Center, 1901 W. Madison St. ✆ 312/455-4000. www.nba.com/bulls. Tickets $10–$90. Bus: 9, 20.

Chicago Cubs   Ages 4 & up. The Cubbies haven't made a World Series appearance since 1945 and haven't been World Champs since 1908, but don't let the team's less-than-stellar track record stop you. You must, absolutely must, take your kids here. Attend a day game. Buy a hot dog and box of Crackerjacks, and join in the chorus of "Take Me Out to the Ballgame" during the seventh-inning stretch. (Since the death of long-time announcer Harry Caray, the crowd is led by a guest singer, often a visiting celebrity.) Because Wrigley Field is small, just about every seat is decent. Families might want to avoid the bleacher seats, because fans there can get a little overzealous in their routing for the home team (and drinking). The ivy-covered outfield walls, hand-operated scoreboard, view of the shimmering lake from the upper deck, and "W" or "L" flag announcing the outcome of the game to the unfortunates who couldn't attend make Wrigley a pure slice of Americana. About a dozen tours of the ballpark are led each season; tickets are $10 and are sold through the Wrigley Field ticket office or Ticketmaster. Known as Wrigleyville, the entire area around the stadium is surrounded by souvenir shops, sports bars, and restaurants. One sandwich shop, the **Friendly Confines,** is actually located within the stadium itself, just off the sidewalk. **Sluggers,** a sports bar with real batting cages, is right around the corner from Wrigley at 3540 N. Clark St. (✆ 773/248-0055). At Wrigley Field, 1060 W. Addison St. ✆ 773/404-CUBS. www.cubs.mlb.com. Tickets $10–$30; games do sell out (especially against long-time rivals such as the Mets), so it pays to call ahead. To order tickets in person, stop by the ticket windows at Wrigley Field Mon–Fri 9am–6pm, Sat 9am–4pm, and on game days. Or, call ✆ 312/831-CUBS for tickets through Ticketmaster (✆ 800/347-CUBS outside IL). Subway/El: Red Line to Addison. Bus: 22.

Chicago Fire   Ages 4 & up. The city's Major League Soccer team launched in 1998 and quickly became a hit with families. The team usually plays at Soldier Field; until the $632 million renovation going on there is complete in September 2003, you can catch the Fire at Cardinal Stadium, located at North Central College in Naperville. Bringing your kids to a game is highly recommended— tickets are cheaper than for other professional sporting events, you can walk right up to the box office before a game and buy them, and kids understand soccer, because many of them play it. During the summer, games usually take place in late afternoon or early evening. Regular fans of the Fire make the games fun, with organized stadium cheers and a band. The team reaches out to kids 12 and under with Sparky's Kids Club (Sparky the Dalmatian is the team's mascot), and to moms with the occasional Soccer Mom Saturday, with half-time games and prizes for moms. The occasional Kids' Fest features music, games, and clowns, so check the website for upcoming events. ✆ 312/705-7200. www.chicago-fire.com. Tickets $20–$40; to order, call ✆ 888/MLS-FIRE. To get to Cardinal Stadium, take I-290 West to I-88 West. Exit Naperville Rd. Turn right at the bottom of the ramp. Take Naper Blvd. south to Chicago Ave. Turn right on Chicago Ave. to Brainard St. Turn left on Brainard St.

Chicago White Sox   Ages 4 & up. Located in the South Side neighborhood of Bridgeport, Comiskey Park has made a real effort to be family-friendly, although the sterile stadium and the blighted neighborhood that surrounds it remain deterrents. When the owners replaced the admittedly dilapidated former stadium with a concrete behemoth that lacks the yesteryear charm of its predecessor, they did improve sightlines and added every conceivable amenity—from above-average ballpark food concessions to shops to plentiful restrooms. The endearing quality about the White Sox is their blue-collar, working-class aura with which so many Cubs-loathing South Siders identify. Comiskey has the added bonus of pre-game batting practice for kids (see "Sports & Games," in chapter 8) At Comiskey Park, 333 W. 35th St. ✆ 312/674-1000. www.whitesox.mlb.com. Tickets $12–$26, half-price on Mon (kids get in for $1 on certain Sun games). To get Sox tickets, call Ticketmaster at ✆ 312/831-1769 or visit the ticket office at Comiskey, open Mon–Fri 10am–6pm, Sat–Sun 10am–4pm (from 9am on game days). Subway/El: Red Line to Sox/35th St.

DePaul Blue Demons   Ages 8 & up. The local college basketball team, the Blue Demons, have a loyal following and are a good bet for an entertaining game at a reasonable price. The season begins at the end of November. At the Allstate Arena, 6920 N. Mannheim Rd., Rosemont. Tickets $9–$40; call ✆ 773/325-7526. (Some of their games are at the United Center.)

Northwestern Wildcats   Ages 8 & up. The smallest of the Big Ten colleges plays ball here. While the team has occasionally surprised everyone by winning that coveted spot in the Rose Bowl, more often, Northwestern crowds like to remind themselves why they attend Northwestern and not Michigan or Wisconsin or Ohio, with cheers of, "Someday, we'll be your boss" to opposing teams. At Ryan Field, 1501 Central St., in north suburban Evanston. ✆ 847/491-CATS. Tickets $25. Subway/El: Purple Line to Central.

Thoroughbred Racing   Ages 6 & up. Arlington International Racecourse, with its gleaming-white, palatial, six-story grandstand and lush gardens, is one of the most beautiful showcases for thoroughbred horse racing in the world. Arlington likes to say that it caters to families, and it must be said that the ambience here is more Disney than den-of-iniquity. It has a storied history stretching back to 1927, and its track has been graced by such equine stars as Citation, Secretariat, and Cigar. The track's annual Arlington Million (the sport's first million-dollar race) has attracted the top jockeys, trainers, and horses in past years and recently became part of the new World Series Racing Championship, which includes the Breeders Cup races. Arlington's race days are thrilling to behold, with all of racing's time-honored pageantry on display—from the bugler in traditional dress to the parade of jockeys. Sunday is Family Day, with special activities for kids 12 and under. In 2002, kids could see a blacksmith shoe a horse, learn about horse care from a groomer and the track veterinarian, and get goggles signed by jockeys. Chicago parents should ask about the Junior Jockey Club, which keeps kids informed of these activities. You can sign up through the website. At Arlington International Racecourse, 2200 W. Euclid Ave., Arlington Heights. ☎ 847/255-4300. www.arlingtonpark.com. Seating $3–$6. Gates open Wed–Sun at 11am; post times are 1:05 and 3:05pm. Season runs June 13–Oct 28. Take the Kennedy (I-94W) expwy. to the I-90 tollway and exit north on Rte. 53. Follow 53 north until you reach the Euclid exit. Or, take the Metra train line to its Arlington Heights stop, which is within walking distance of the racecourse. General parking $4, valet parking $8.

9 Story Hours

Feel like you've read *The Cat in the Hat* about 10,000 times? Take your kids to one of these story hours, and they can get their story fix while you get a rest—and you'll be inspiring a love of reading in your children.

Borders Books & Music   Ages 2 to 8. Kids can hear stories, with special visits from costumed characters at this story hour, held at 11am on Tuesdays. 830 N. Michigan Ave. ☎ 312/573-0564. Free admission. Subway/El: Red Line to Chicago/State.

Children in Paradise *Finds*   **Ages 2 to 8.** Storytelling and monthly events makes this a hotspot for storytelling. Preschoolers are welcome at the story hour, 10:30am on Tuesday and Wednesday. 909 N. Rush. ☎ 312/951-KIDS. Free admission. Subway/El: Red Line to Chicago/State.

The Field Museum of Natural History   Ages 2 to 4. Designed for preschoolers, "Story Time: Fact, Fables, and Fiction" is a daily event in July and August, and a weekend afternoon event from September to June. Held in the Living Together exhibit area, stories and projects tie in with current exhibits. Roosevelt Rd. at Lake Shore Dr. ☎ 312/665-7400. Free with museum admission of $8 for adults, $4 for children. Bus: 146.

Thomas Hughes Children's Library at Harold Washington Library Center   Ages 3 to 8. Twice a month puppets act out stories, and Saturdays are packed with programs, including puppet shows, videos, crafts, author readings, and book signings. Toddler story times are offered for kids 2 years and up and include storytelling, puppetry, music, movement, and a craft. One-hour Storytime Extravaganzas for ages 3 to 5 and 6 to 8 are scheduled each month. Most Saturday programs start at 2pm, but morning story hours vary, so call or log on for updates. 400 S. State St. ☎ 312/747-4200. www.chicagopubliclibrary.org. Subway/El: Red Line to Jackson/State, Brown Line to Van Buren/Library.

Women and Children First   Ages 2 to 5. Wednesday mornings are story hour for preschoolers, featuring books and poems. 5233 N. Clark St. ☎ 773/769-9299. Free admission. Subway/El: Red Line to Bryn Mawr, then walk several blocks west to Clark. Bus: 22.

10 Arcades

ESPN Zone **Ages 7 & up.** This 35,000-square-foot sports shrine provides arcade fans with sports-inspired video games plus the Sports Arena, where everyone can try out their skills. Future quarterbacks can try to throw the ball through moving cutouts. A simulated rock-climbing wall moves up and down like a vertical treadmill so you can never reach the top. You and your kids can dribble and shoot baskets on a half court, scoring points based on the difficulty of the shots you make. The basket can even be lowered so younger kids get a fair shot. And, you can check your scores against those of the NBA players who showed off their stuff here. If hockey's your sport, you and your kids can pretend to be NHL players, with one of you taking shots on simulated ice while the other plays goalie. The Screening Room is a fan's nirvana, with a 16-foot screen surrounded by skybox viewing suites, along with another 37 monitors to cover everything from the Super Bowl to the Madacascar Knee Volleyball Championships. 43 E. Ohio St. ✆ **312/644-ESPN.** www.espnzone.com. Free admission; cost is $5 for 15-point card, $100 for 600-point card. Games "cost" 3–20 points each. Mon–Thurs 11:30am–midnight, Fri–Sat 11:30am–12:30am; Sun 11:30am–11:30pm. Subway/El: Red Line to State/Grand.

Side Trips from Chicago

Even with all that the city proper has to offer, if you're in town for more than a few days (or if you're staying with friends or relatives in the suburbs), you might want to venture beyond the city limits and check out some of the sights in the surrounding areas.

1 Indiana Dunes State Park

53 miles SE of Chicago (in Indiana)

This all-ages destination is my favorite for escaping to the great outdoors. Not only is running up, down, and around the dunes a great way to burn off some energy, but many dunes front Lake Michigan, making for some beautiful scenery. The dunes are the Midwest's answer to Cape Cod.

ESSENTIALS

To get to the dunes, you'll need to drive. Take I-94 East to Ind. 49 North (east of Porter). Follow Ind. 49 north to Route 12. Travel east on Route 12 for 3 miles to the Dorothy Buell Memorial Visitor Center. There are restrooms and a gift shop with postcards, posters, and slides available.

SEEING THE DUNES

The words "Midwest" and "sand dunes" aren't normally associated, but a trip to Indiana Dunes State Park will change your mind. At the base of Lake Michigan, near Chesterton, Indiana, you'll find 15 miles of dunes—3 miles of which line sandy beaches. In fact, the dunes are so big, you can't see over them! You can visit maple and oak forests, miles of sand piles covered with vegetation, marshes, and bogs, all in one state park. Plenty of well-marked trails help you explore.

Stop at the visitor center for a free map and a 10-minute slide show that will orient you. You might check out Cowles Bog, filled with ponds, wetlands, and marshes, plus delicate vegetation such as orchids, and not-so-delicate vegetation, including Venus Fly Traps. West Beach offers a 3-mile trail that passes through a prairie zone, a conifer zone, and an oak forest-deciduous zone, and ends at a beach. If it's beachgoing that you're focused on, check out Kemil Beach, a long stretch of beautiful white sand. Finally, Mt. Baldy is the largest "living" sand dune in the park, so named for the mounds of sand that are active in the wind.

1600 North 25E, Chesterton, Indiana. ✆ 219/926-1952. Free admission. Visitor center summer daily 8am–6pm, winter daily until 5pm; beaches summer daily 6am–11pm. To park, you'll find some free lots, but some summer lots require payment.

WHERE TO EAT

There are no restaurants here, so bring a picnic. You'll find plenty of picnic areas in the park, some with barbecue pits. If you're staying in downtown Chicago, good places to pick up sandwiches and drinks are Corner Bakery (p. 98) or Potbelly Sandwich Works (p. 91).

2 Kohl Children's Museum

17 miles N of Chicago

Children as young as 1 year can enjoy this top-notch museum. (There's even an infants area, but I'd advise waiting until your child is a year old to really appreciate the museum.) In fact, many Chicago parents prefer Kohl to the Chicago Children's Museum on Navy Pier for its ease of access—you'll find much less of a crowd here than at Navy Pier.

ESSENTIALS

Wilmette is located on the North Shore, a swath of suburbia between Chicago and the state border of Wisconsin that is one of the nation's most affluent residential areas.

BY CAR   Take Lake Shore Drive and proceed northward to **Sheridan Road,** and follow it as it winds through the campus of Northwestern University in Evanston and into Wilmette. To reach the museum, turn left onto Central Street (at Evanston Hospital). Go west to Green Bay Road. Turn right on Green Bay Road and drive ¼-mile to the museum, which is on your left.

BY TRAIN   Catch the **Metra** train (℡ **312/322-6777;** www.metrarail.com) from the Ogilvie Transportation Center at Madison and Canal streets in Chicago to Wilmette. As you exit the train, the museum will be an easy walk of a couple of blocks to the west.

SEEING THE MUSEUM

The Kohl Children's Museum packs a lot into its small square footage: The 200,000 visitors it hosts annually make it the most heavily visited museum per square foot in metropolitan Chicago. Opened in 1985, this museum is a hands-on, dress-up-and-pretend, blow-bubbles sort of place where your kids will amuse themselves for hours. They can shop at a simulated supermarket, take a voyage on a Phoenician sailing ship, and join in puppet shows and sing-alongs.

Permanent exhibits include **The Great Kohl Sailing Ship,** which provides a stage for imaginary play as kids journey to new worlds. The vessel is part sailing ship, part fishing vessel, and part cargo ship. Kids wear real life vests while raising and lowering the sail, using nets or rod and reel to catch schools of colorful fish, steering the ship in the wheel house, ringing the ship's bell, peeking through the portholes or loading cargo into the hold, and talking through the speaking tubes to the ship's captain.

Jewel-Osco, a recently renovated grocery store exhibit, gives children a chance to run the shop. Kids can role-play by pretending to be shoppers or the cashier. They're responsible for the workings of the store, from shopping to restocking to checking out. New additions include a cafe, a fish market, and a nutritional center. Other permanent exhibits include the **StarMax Technology Center,** a computer center that features creative learning software; **Construction Zone,** where you can be a home builder; **H20,** where kids can explore the wonders of water play; **People,** a multicultural exhibit aimed at prejudice prevention and the celebration of Chicago's diversity; and **Things That Go!,** a CTA train that entertains riders on a trip through Chicago.

165 Green Bay Rd., Wilmette. ℡ **847/251-7781.** www.kohlchildrensmuseum.org. Admission $5 per person, $4 for seniors, free for children under age 1. Mon–Sat 9am–5pm and Sun noon–5pm.

AN ADDITIONAL ATTRACTION

Baha'i House of Worship   While you're in the neighborhood, continue your drive up Sheridan Road in Wilmette to the most visited of all the sights in the northern suburbs, the Baha'i House of Worship, an ethereal edifice that seems not of this earth. The gleaming white stone temple, designed by the French Canadian Louis Bourgeois and completed in 1953, is essentially a soaring nine-sided 135-foot dome, draped in a delicate lacelike facade, that strongly reveals the Eastern influence of the Baha'i faith's native Iran. Surrounded by formal gardens, it is one of seven Baha'i temples in the world, and the only one in the Western Hemisphere. The dome's latticework is even more beautiful as you gaze upward from the floor of the sanctuary, which, during the day, is flooded with light. Temple members offer informal tours of the building to anyone who inquires; older children and adults with an interest in architecture will get the most out of a tour of the interior. Not only is the temple itself really a sight, but the drive on Sheridan Road is also one of the most beautiful in the Chicago area.

A word of caution if you're driving: The temple seems to appear out of nowhere as you round a particularly tight curve on Sheridan Road, and it can distract even the most focused of drivers. Take it slow and wait until you're safely parked before gazing skyward.

100 Linden Ave. (at Sheridan Rd.), Wilmette. © 847/853-2300. www.us.bahai.org/how. Free admission. Visitor center daily May–Sept 10am–10pm and Oct–Apr 10am–5pm. Temple daily from 7am. Devotional services are held Mon–Sat at 12:15pm and Sun at 1:15pm (with choral accompaniment). To get there from Chicago, take the Red Line of the El north to Howard St. Change trains for the Evanston train and go to the end of the line, Linden Ave. (Or take the Purple/Evanston Express and stay on the same train all the way.) Turn right on Linden and walk 2 blocks east. If you're driving, take the Outer Dr. (Lake Shore Dr.) north, which feeds into Sheridan Rd.

WHERE TO EAT

From the lines outside the restaurant, it appears that anyone who visits the museum is also required to stop at **Walker Bros. Original Pancake House,** located next door at 153 Green Bay Rd. (© **847/251-6000**). The place is decorated with colorful Tiffany-style lamps, warm woodwork, deep booths, and extraordinary stained-glass art windows. Expect a wait on weekends. Top choices are apple pancakes, which arrive bubbling hot and glazed with cinnamon and German pancakes, which are fluffy, dusted with powdered sugar and served with fruit. Kids often go for the silver-dollar pancakes in chocolate chip, blueberry, or plain varieties. Oven-baked omelets are another favorite. The restaurant also serves lunch and dinner, and offers chicken teriyaki, roast beef, chicken Dijon, Reuben sandwiches, and salads. All menu items are served throughout the day; it's open daily from 7am to 10pm.

Moments   A Suburban Respite

If you've made it up to the Baha'i Temple, take a stroll across Sheridan Road to **Gilson Park** for a taste of north suburban life. Check out the sailors prepping their boats for a lake tour, families picnicking and playing Frisbee, and kids frolicking on the sandy beach. Access to the beach is restricted in the summer (the locals like to keep the Chicago riff-raff out), but in the fall and spring you're welcome to wander (just don't expect to take a dip in the frigid water).

3 Chicago Botanic Garden

About 25 miles N of Chicago

The Botanic Garden is a favorite of Chicago families because it's only a short drive from the city but it offers a welcome change of scenery. Even young children will enjoy a ride on the tram at the gardens. Older kids can explore the fruit and vegetable garden (so this is where bananas come from!) and gardens of animal-shaped topiaries.

ESSENTIALS

BY CAR   Take I-90 (Kennedy Expressway) to the Edens Expressway (I-94). Go north 20 miles and continue north on Rte. 41 and exit on Lake Cook Road. Turn right and go a half-mile to the garden.

BY TRAIN   You can take the **Metra** North Line (✆ **312/322-6777;** www.metra rail.com) from Ogilvie Transportation Center at Madison and Canal streets in Chicago to Glencoe. Connect to the 213 Pace Bus to reach the Botanic Garden.

TOURING THE GARDEN

Owned by the Forest Preserve District of Cook County and managed by the 110-year-old Chicago Horticultural Society, this living preserve includes eight large lagoons and a variety of distinct botanical environments—from the Illinois prairie to an English walled garden to a three-island Japanese garden. To keep the visit manageable for kids, call ahead to find out what's blooming and grab a map from the information desk when you arrive to pick the gardens your family most wants to see. A tram tour lets kids cover more ground without getting tired, which is a real possibility in this 385-acre garden.

Also on the grounds are a large fruit and vegetable garden, an Enabling Garden (which shows how gardening can be adapted for people with disabilities), and a 100-acre old-growth oak woodland. The living collections are composed of more than 1.2 million plants, representing 7,000 plant types. If you're here in the summer, don't miss the extensive rose gardens (just follow the bridal parties who flock here to get their pictures taken). The Botanic Garden also is home to an exhibit hall, an auditorium, a museum, a library, education greenhouses, an outdoor pavilion, a carillon, a cafe, a designated bike path, and a garden shop. Carillon concerts are given on Monday evenings at 7pm from June 21 through August 23, with a preliminary hour-long tour.

Every summer, the Botanic Garden stages a special outdoor exhibition; one year, giant animal-shaped topiaries were placed in unexpected locations throughout the grounds, while in another year, model railroads wound through miniature versions of American national parks. In winter, the greenhouses are nice and warm, and your kids can look for a Venus Fly Trap, animal-shaped topiaries, and food trees such as banana and coffee plants. Check the website or call to learn about upcoming events.

1000 Lake–Cook Rd. (just east of Edens Expressway/I-94), Glencoe. ✆ **847/835-5440.** www.chicago-botanic.org. Free admission. Apr–Oct tram tours $4 adults, $2 children 3–15. Daily 8am–sunset. Closed Dec 25. Parking $8.75.

WHERE TO EAT

The **Garden Café,** located within the Chicago Botanic Garden, serves soup, sandwiches, and salads as well as kid favorites, in a cafeteria-style setting. In the summer, you can sit on a patio overlooking water, and more outdoor tables sit adjacent to the Rose Garden. It's open November through March daily from 8am to 4pm, April through October until 5pm on weekdays and until 5:30pm on weekends.

4 DuPage Children's Museum

About 30 miles W of Chicago

Chicago's western suburbs are rapidly expanding. Naperville, a farming area not so long ago, is now one of Illinois' largest cities. Home to the DuPage Children's Museum, Naperville also has a historic downtown. The two make for a perfect day's outing. The museum is geared to all ages, but toddlers and up will enjoy it most.

ESSENTIALS

BY CAR   Take the Eisenhower Expressway (I-290) West from Chicago. Take the I-294/I-88 West exit toward Indiana/Aurora. Merge onto I-88W, the East–West Tollway. Take the Naperville Road exit and turn right on Naperville Road. Turn right on East Ogden Avenue/US 34. Turn left onto North Washington Street.

BY TRAIN   Catch the **Metra** Burlington Northern Santa Fe Line (*©* **312/ 322-6777;** www.metrarail.com) from Union Station on Canal Street (between Adams and Jackson Blvd.) in Chicago to Naperville.

EXPLORING THE MUSEUM

DuPage Children's Museum is located in Naperville, a historic, formerly rural community with a Main Street U.S.A. downtown district worthy of Norman Rockwell. (Naperville maintains a collection of 19th-century buildings in an outdoor museum setting known as Naper Settlement, with a lovely river walk.) At the museum, visit six "neighborhoods," where kids can learn about everything from construction to art. It's a great layout that eliminates walls, so you can keep an eye on your kids even if they are in different exhibits. **Creativity Connections** brings art, math, and science together; wee ones can enjoy black, white, and red patterns to stimulate their brains, look at themselves in mirrors, and change the color of a light's filter to see themselves in a new perspective, while older kids can play with shadows and light. **Build It** puts kid-size saws, hammers, and other real tools in kids' hands and lets them build a chair for a Beanie Baby, or saw wood. (Never fear, staff members are on hand to make sure everyone stays safe.) The littlest ones get to participate by hammering golf tees into Styrofoam and building with soft blocks. **Make It Move** turns kids into scientists experimenting with gravity. **Air-Works** lets kids walk through a wind tunnel, and with the wave of a special wand, fill up an air sock. **WaterWays** shows kids how the power of water can be harnessed, and how to use sandbags to stop the rush of a waterfall. (Waterproof aprons are on hand to keep clothes dry.) Families with very young children should plan to spend about an hour here (or longer, if attention spans allow). Older children will be happy here for 2 to 3 hours.

301 N. Washington, Naperville. *©* **630/637-8000.** www.dupagechildrensmuseum.org. Admission $6.50 adults and children over age 1, $5.50 seniors. Tues, Wed, Fri and Sat 9am–5pm; Thurs noon–5pm. Members only are admitted Mon 9am–1pm.

WHERE TO EAT

The museum has an eating area with vending machines and a microwave, and nearby, you'll find plenty of fast-food restaurants. For a change of pace, try pizza at **Lou Malnati's,** 131 W. Jefferson St. (*©* **630/717-0700**).

5 Wonder Works

10 miles W of downtown Chicago.

WonderWorks is Chicago's newest children's museum, located in Oak Park, which is one of Chicago's most historic and scenic suburbs, with a wonderful downtown full of shops and restaurants. If your kids are over age 8, I'd recommend spending a day in Oak Park, visiting the museum and taking a tour of the Frank Lloyd Wright Home & Studio. With younger children, I'd limit the visit to just the museum.

ESSENTIALS

BY CAR   Oak Park is about 30 minutes due west of downtown Chicago. Take North Avenue west. You will travel about 9 miles straight on North Avenue to the museum, which is located at Elmwood and North avenues, just west of Ridgeland.

BY BUS   Take the no. 72 (North Avenue) bus from the corner of Clark Street and North Avenue. It's about a 45-minute bus ride straight to the museum.

EXPLORING THE MUSEUM

Originally founded in 1991, Wonder Works lost its lease in 1995 and searched for a new home until 2001, when it purchased a building. At press time, Wonder Works was scheduled for a spring 2003 opening, featuring four permanent exhibits and several temporary exhibits. The 6,500-square-foot museum is designed for kids up to age 10. The museum is funded by contributions from the likes of The Oprah Winfrey Foundation, McDonald's, and the village of Oak Park.

One permanent exhibit is **Lights, Camera, Action!,** a performance area that allows kids to be stars with a low-rise stage, costumes, and backdrops. Kids can sing a song, entertain the audience, and record it all on videotape. Professional puppeteers and storytellers use the stage too during special events throughout the year.

The **Great Outdoors** exhibit lets kids experience the wonders of the natural nighttime world. Sounds and lighting set the mood and a canopy creates a beautiful night sky; tents are set up near a glowing "camp fire." Kids can also climb a ladder into a tree house. A nature trail lets kids wander through the "outdoors," with surprises around every corner.

The **Farm to Market** exhibit is inspired by the Farmer's Market in Oak Park, and gives kids an opportunity to "shop" for fruits and vegetables, pick apples and corn, and milk a cow. Kids can also "make" donuts just as it is done at the real Oak Park Farmer's Market.

6445 W. North Ave., Oak Park. ✆ 708/383-4815. www.wonder-works.org. Admission prices and hours were not available at press time; call or check the website for details.

WHERE TO EAT

An Oak Park tradition, **Peterson's,** located at 715 W. Lake St. (✆ 708/848-5020), is an ice cream shop that also serves up soup and sandwiches for adults, and kiddie treats such as dinosaur-shaped chicken nuggets. Save room for dessert: The specialty is the Merry-Go-Round, a chocolate sundae topped with animal cookies and a parasol.

6 Cuneo Museum & Gardens

About 30 miles from downtown Chicago

Best for kids over 8, this historic mansion and grounds provide a glimpse into how people lived 100 years ago. I wouldn't recommend this museum for very young children.

ESSENTIALS

The museum is not easily accessible by public transportation. To reach the museum **by car,** take the Kennedy (I-94W) expressway north to Rte. 60. Go west on Rte. 60 and then, at the Hawthorn Mall, turn north on Milwaukee Ave. (Rte. 21).

VISITING THE MUSEUM

This is a wonderful place for older kids to see how people lived in the early 20th century. The Cuneo Museum & Gardens was designed in 1914 by architect Benjamin Marshall for Samuel Insull, founder of the powerful Commonwealth Edison electric company and a partner of Thomas Edison. Its present-day name, however, comes from John F. Cuneo, a Chicago printing magnate, philanthropist, and gentleman farmer whose family lived at this vast, luxuriant estate from 1937 to 1990.

If you want to see how the other half lives, here's your chance. The palatial mansion is designed in an opulent Italianate style, with accents such as bold ironwork decor that are reminiscent of a Venetian palazzo. Eighteen of its 32 rooms are on exhibit to the public. The centerpiece is the **Great Hall,** featuring a 30-foot ceiling with skylights over a central courtyard surrounded by marble columns and arcaded balconies. You'll also "ooh" and "ahh" over the fanciful ceiling frescoes in the unusual double dining rooms and exquisite private chapel.

Cuneo was a connoisseur of art treasures, and the core of his collection is on display here, from Old Master paintings and 17th-century tapestries to a custom-made gilt-wood piano and fine Capo di Monte porcelain. The estate's grounds, which at one time spanned 3,000 acres, are now a relatively modest 75 acres. They're quite lovely, with lakes, fountains, formal gardens, antique classical statuary, and even a few peacocks and swans. There's also a conservatory housing exotic plants, and Deer Park, a wooded enclosure that's about the only vestigial reminder of Hawthorn-Mellody Farms, a former farm and dairy operation that for years attracted families with its "Wild West Town," country store, and petting zoo.

1350 N. Milwaukee Ave., Vernon Hills. *(C)* 847/362-3042. Admission $10 adults, $9 seniors, $5 children. Tues–Sun 10am–5pm. Guided tours presented Tues–Sat at 11am, 12:30, 2, and 3:30pm. Grounds fee is $5 (no fee for parking).

WHERE TO EAT

Hawthorne Center Mall is adjacent to the museum and features the usual array of fast-food and chain restaurants. For a more true-to-Chicago experience, head into Vernon Hills to the **Pizzeria Uno** at 545 Lakeview Pkwy. (*(C)* **847/ 918-8667**).

Appendix A:
For International Visitors

Whether it's your first visit or your tenth, a trip to the United States may require an additional degree of planning. This chapter will provide you with essential information, helpful tips, and advice for the more common problems that some visitors encounter.

1 Preparing for Your Trip
ENTRY REQUIREMENTS
Check at any U.S. embassy or consulate for current information and requirements. You can also obtain a visa application and other information online at the **U.S. State Department**'s website at **www.travel.state.gov.**

VISAS The U.S. State Department has a **Visa Waiver Program** allowing citizens of certain countries to enter the United States without a visa for stays of up to 90 days. At press time these included Andorra, Australia, Austria, Belgium, Brunei, Denmark, Finland, France, Germany, Iceland, Ireland, Italy, Japan, Liechtenstein, Luxembourg, Monaco, the Netherlands, New Zealand, Norway, Portugal, San Marino, Singapore, Slovenia, Spain, Sweden, Switzerland, the United Kingdom, and Uruguay. Citizens of these countries need only a valid passport and a round-trip air or cruise ticket in their possession upon arrival. If they first enter the United States, they may also visit Mexico, Canada, Bermuda, and/or the Caribbean islands and return to the United States without a visa. Further information is available from any U.S. embassy or consulate. Canadian citizens may enter the United States without visas; they need only proof of residence.

Citizens of all other countries must have (1) a valid passport that expires at least 6 months later than the scheduled end of their visit to the United States, and (2) a tourist visa, which may be obtained without charge from any U.S. consulate.

To obtain a visa, the traveler must submit a completed application form (either in person or by mail) with a 1½-inch-square photo, and must demonstrate binding ties to a residence abroad. Usually you can obtain a visa at once or within 24 hours, but it may take longer during the summer rush from June through August. If you cannot go in person, contact the nearest U.S. embassy or consulate for directions on applying by mail. Your travel agent or airline office may also be able to provide you with visa applications and instructions. The U.S. consulate or embassy that issues your visa will determine whether you will be issued a multiple- or single-entry visa and any restrictions regarding the length of your stay.

British subjects can obtain up-to-date passport and visa information by calling the **U.S. Embassy Visa Information Line** at ℂ **0891/200-290.** You can also call the **United Kingdom Passport Service** at ℂ **0870/521-0410,** or search the agency's website at www.ukpa.gov.uk.

Irish citizens can obtain up-to-date passport and visa information through the **Embassy of USA Dublin,** 42 Elgin Rd., Dublin 4, Ireland (ℂ **353/1-668-8777**), or by checking the visa page on the website at www.usembassy.ie.

Australian citizens can obtain up-to-date passport and visa information by contacting the **U.S. Embassy Canberra,** Moonah Place, Yarralumla, ACT 2600 (℗ **02/6214-5600**), or check the website's visa page at www.usis-australia.gov.

Citizens of **New Zealand** can obtain up-to-date passport and visa information by contacting the **U.S. Embassy New Zealand,** 29 Fitzherbert Terr., Thorndon, Wellington, New Zealand (℗ **644/472-2068**), or get the information directly from the website at www.usembassy.org.nz.

MEDICAL REQUIREMENTS   Unless you're arriving from an area known to be suffering from an epidemic (particularly cholera or yellow fever), inoculations or vaccinations are not required for entry into the United States. If you have a medical condition that requires **syringe-administered medications,** carry a valid signed prescription from your physician—the Federal Aviation Administration (FAA) no longer allows airline passengers to pack syringes in their carry-on baggage without documented proof of medical need. If you have a disease that requires treatment with **narcotics,** you should also carry documented proof with you—smuggling narcotics aboard a plane is a serious offense that carries severe penalties in the U.S.

For **HIV-positive visitors,** requirements for entering the United States are somewhat vague and change frequently. According to the latest publication of *HIV and Immigrants: A Manual for AIDS Service Providers,* the Immigration and Naturalization Service (INS) doesn't require a medical exam for entry into the United States, but INS officials may stop individuals because they look sick or because they are carrying AIDS/HIV medicine.

If an HIV-positive noncitizen applies for a non-immigrant visa, the question on the application regarding communicable diseases is tricky no matter which way it's answered. If the applicant checks "no," INS may deny the visa on the grounds that the applicant committed fraud. If the applicant checks "yes" or if INS suspects the person is HIV-positive, it will deny the visa unless the applicant asks for a special waiver for visitors. This waiver is for people visiting the United States for a short time, to attend a conference, for instance, to visit close relatives, or to receive medical treatment. It can be a confusing situation. For further up-to-the-minute information, contact the Centers for Disease Control's **National Center for HIV** (℗ **404/332-4559;** www.hivatis.org) or the **Gay Men's Health Crisis** (℗ **212/367-1000;** www.gmhc.org).

DRIVER'S LICENSES   Foreign driver's licenses are mostly recognized in the U.S., although you may want to get an international driver's license if your home license is not written in English.

PASSPORT INFORMATION

Safeguard your passport in an inconspicuous, inaccessible place like a money belt. Make a copy of the critical pages, including the passport number, and store it in a safe place, separate from the passport itself. If you lose your passport, visit the nearest consulate of your native country as soon as possible for a replacement. Passport applications are downloadable from the Internet sites listed below.

Note that the International Civil Aviation Organization (ICAO) has recommended a policy requiring that *every* individual who travels by air have his or her own passport. In response, many countries are now requiring that children must be issued their own passport to travel internationally, where before those under 16 or so may have been allowed to travel on a parent or guardian's passport.

FOR RESIDENTS OF CANADA

You can pick up a passport application at one of 28 regional passport offices or most travel agencies. Since December 2001, Canadian children who travel must have their own passport. However, if you hold a valid Canadian passport issued before December 11, 2001, that bears the name of your child, the passport remains valid for you and your child until it expires. Passports cost C$85 for those 16 years and older (valid 5 years), C$35 children 3 to 15 (valid 5 years), and C$20, children under 3 (valid 3 years). Applications, which must be accompanied by two identical passport-sized photographs and proof of Canadian citizenship, are available at travel agencies throughout Canada or from the central **Passport Office,** Department of Foreign Affairs and International Trade, Ottawa, ON K1A 0G3 (*©* **800/567-6868;** www.dfait-maeci.gc.ca/passport). Processing takes 5 to 10 days if you apply in person, or about 3 weeks by mail.

FOR RESIDENTS OF THE UNITED KINGDOM

To pick up an application for a standard 10-year passport (5-year passport for children under 16), visit your nearest passport office, major post office, or travel agency. You can also contact the **United Kingdom Passport Service** at *©* **0870/ 521-0410** or search its website at www.ukpa.gov.uk. Passports are £30 for adults and £16 for children under 16. Processing takes about 2 weeks.

FOR RESIDENTS OF IRELAND

You can apply for a 10-year passport, costing €57, at the **Passport Office,** Setanta Centre, Molesworth Street, Dublin 2 (*©* **01/671-1633;** www.irlgov.ie/ iveagh). Those under age 18 and over 65 must apply for a €12 3-year passport. You can also apply at 1A South Mall, Cork (*©* **021/272-525**) or over the counter at most main post offices.

FOR RESIDENTS OF AUSTRALIA

You can pick up an application from your local post office or any branch of Passports Australia, but you must schedule an interview at the passport office to present your application materials. Call the **Australian Passport Information Service** at *©* **131-232,** or visit the government website at www.passports. gov.au. Passports for adults are A$144 and for those under 18 are A$72.

FOR RESIDENTS OF NEW ZEALAND

You can pick up a passport application at any New Zealand Passports Office or download it from their website. Contact the **Passports Office** at *©* **0800/ 225-050** in New Zealand or 04/474-8100, or log on to www.passports.govt.nz. Passports for adults are NZ$80 and for children under 16 NZ$40.

CUSTOMS
WHAT YOU CAN BRING IN

Every visitor more than 21 years of age may bring in, free of duty, the following: (1) 1 liter of wine or hard liquor; (2) 200 cigarettes, 100 cigars (but not from Cuba), or 3 pounds of smoking tobacco; and (3) $100 worth of gifts. These exemptions are offered to travelers who spend at least 72 hours in the United States and who have not claimed them within the preceding 6 months. It is altogether forbidden to bring into the country foodstuffs (particularly fruit, cooked meats, and canned goods) and plants (vegetables, seeds, tropical plants, and the like). Foreign tourists may bring in or take out up to $10,000 in U.S. or foreign currency with no formalities; larger sums must be declared to U.S.

Customs on entering or leaving, which includes filing form CM 4790. For more specific information regarding U.S. Customs, contact your nearest U.S. embassy or consulate, or the **U.S. Customs** office (℡ **202/927-1770** or www.customs. ustreas.gov).

WHAT YOU CAN TAKE HOME

U.K. citizens returning from a non-EU country have a customs allowance of: 200 cigarettes; 50 cigars; 250g of smoking tobacco; 2 liters of still table wine; 1 liter of spirits or strong liqueurs (over 22% volume); 2 liters of fortified wine, sparkling wine or other liqueurs; 60cc (ml) perfume; 250cc (ml) of toilet water; and £145 worth of all other goods, including gifts and souvenirs. People under 17 cannot have the tobacco or alcohol allowance. For more information, contact HM Customs & Excise at ℡ **0845/010-9000** (from outside the U.K., 020/8929-0152), or consult its website at www.hmce.gov.uk.

For a clear summary of **Canadian** rules, request the booklet *I Declare,* issued by the **Canada Customs and Revenue Agency** (℡ **800/461-9999** in Canada, or 204/983-3500; www.ccra-adrc.gc.ca). Canada allows its citizens a C$750 exemption, and you're allowed to bring back duty-free one carton of cigarettes, 1 can of tobacco, 40 imperial ounces of liquor, and 50 cigars (if you meet the age requirement of the province where you enter). In addition, you're allowed to mail gifts to Canada valued at less than C$60 a day, provided they're unsolicited and don't contain alcohol or tobacco (write on the package "Unsolicited gift, under $60 value"). All valuables should be declared on the Y-38 form before departure from Canada, including serial numbers of valuables you already own, such as expensive foreign cameras. *Note:* The $750 exemption can only be used once a year and only after an absence of 7 days.

The duty-free allowance in **Australia** is A$400 or, for those under 18, A$200. Citizens age 18 and over can bring in 250 cigarettes or 250 grams of loose tobacco, and 1,125 milliliters of alcohol. If you're returning with valuables you already own, such as foreign-made cameras, you should file form B263. For more information, call the **Australian Customs Service** at ℡ **1300/363-263,** or log on to www.customs.gov.au.

The duty-free allowance for **New Zealand** is NZ$700. Citizens over 17 can bring in 200 cigarettes, 50 cigars, or 250 grams of tobacco (or a mixture of all 3 if their combined weight doesn't exceed 250g); plus 4.5 liters of wine and beer, or 1.125 liters of liquor. New Zealand currency does not carry import or export restrictions. Fill out a certificate of export, listing the valuables you are taking out of the country; that way, you can bring them back without paying duty. Most questions are answered in a free pamphlet available at New Zealand consulates and Customs offices: *New Zealand Customs Guide for Travellers, Notice no. 4.* For more information, contact **New Zealand Customs,** The Customhouse, 17–21 Whitmore St., Box 2218, Wellington (℡ **0800/428-786** or 04/473-6099; www.customs.govt.nz).

HEALTH INSURANCE

Although it's not required of travelers, health insurance is highly recommended. Unlike many European countries, the United States does not usually offer free or low-cost medical care to its citizens or visitors. Doctors and hospitals are expensive, and in most cases will require advance payment or proof of coverage before they render their services. Policies can cover everything from the loss or theft of your baggage and trip cancellation to the guarantee of bail in case you're arrested. Good policies will also cover the costs of an accident, repatriation, or death. See section 5, "Insurance & Health," in chapter 2 for more information. Packages such as **Europ Assistance's "Worldwide Healthcare Plan"** are sold by European automobile clubs and travel agencies at attractive rates. **Worldwide Assistance Services, Inc.** (℃ 800/821-2828; www.worldwideassistance.com) is the agent for Europ Assistance in the United States.

Though lack of health insurance may prevent you from being admitted to a hospital in nonemergencies, don't worry about being left on a street corner to die: The American way is to fix you now and bill the living daylights out of you later.

INSURANCE FOR BRITISH TRAVELERS   Most big travel agents offer their own insurance and will probably try to sell you their package when you book a holiday. Think before you sign. **Britain's Consumers' Association** recommends that you insist on seeing the policy and reading the fine print before buying travel insurance. **The Association of British Insurers** (℃ 020/7600-3333; www.abi.org.uk) gives advice by phone and publishes *Holiday Insurance,* a free guide to policy provisions and prices. You might also shop around for better deals: Try **Columbus Direct** (℃ 020/7375-0011; www.columbusdirect.net).

INSURANCE FOR CANADIAN TRAVELERS   Canadians should check with their provincial health plan offices or call **Health Canada** (℃ 613/957-2991; www.hc-sc.gc.ca) to find out the extent of their coverage and what documentation and receipts they must take home in case they are treated in the United States.

MONEY

CURRENCY   The U.S. monetary system is very simple: The most common **bills** are the $1 (colloquially, a "buck"), $5, $10, and $20 denominations. There are also $2 bills (seldom encountered), $50 bills, and $100 bills. (The last two are usually not welcome as payment for small purchases.) All the paper money was recently redesigned, making the famous faces adorning them disproportionately large. The old-style bills are still legal tender.

There are seven denominations of coins: 1¢ (1 cent, or a penny); 5¢ (5 cents, or a nickel); 10¢ (10 cents, or a dime); 25¢ (25 cents, or a quarter); 50¢ (50 cents, or a half-dollar); the new gold "Sacagawea" coin worth $1; and, prized by collectors, the rare, older silver dollar.

Note: The "foreign-exchange bureaus" so common in Europe are rare even at airports in the United States, and nonexistent outside major cities. It's best not to change foreign money (or traveler's checks denominated in a currency other than U.S. dollars) at a small-town bank, or even a branch in a big city; in fact, leave any currency other than U.S. dollars at home—it may prove a greater nuisance to you than it's worth.

Tips Currency Exchange

If you find yourself in need of a foreign-exchange service while in Chicago, the Chicago consumer Yellow Pages lists names and numbers of foreign-exchange services under the heading "Foreign Exchange Brokers." In the Loop, try **World's Money Exchange, Inc.,** 203 N. LaSalle St. (℃ 312/641-2151).

TRAVELER'S CHECKS   Though traveler's checks are widely accepted, make sure that they're denominated in U.S. dollars, as foreign-currency checks are often difficult to exchange. The three traveler's checks that are most widely recognized—and least likely to be denied—are **Visa, American Express,** and **Thomas Cook.** Be sure to record the numbers of the checks, and keep that information in a separate place in case they get lost or stolen. Most businesses are pretty good about taking traveler's checks, but you're better off cashing them in at a bank (in small amounts, of course) and paying in cash. Remember: you'll need identification, such as a driver's license or passport, to change a traveler's check.

CREDIT CARDS & ATMS   Credit cards are the most widely used form of payment in the United States: **Visa** (Barclaycard in Britain), **MasterCard** (EuroCard in Europe, Access in Britain, Chargex in Canada), **American Express, Diners Club,** and **Discover.** There are, however, a handful of stores and restaurants that do not take credit cards, so be sure to ask in advance. Most businesses display a sticker near their entrance to let you know which cards they accept. (**Note:** Businesses may require a minimum purchase, usually around $10, to use a credit card.)

It is strongly recommended that you bring at least one major credit card. You must have a credit or charge card to rent a car. Hotels and airlines usually require a credit card imprint as a deposit against expenses, and in an emergency a credit card can be priceless.

You'll find **automated teller machines (ATMs)** on just about every block—at least in almost every town—across the country. Some ATMs will allow you to draw U.S. currency against your bank and credit cards. Check with your bank before leaving home, and remember that you will need your personal identification number (PIN) to do so. Most accept Visa, MasterCard, and American Express, as well as ATM cards from other U.S. banks. Expect to be charged up to $3 per transaction, however, if you're not using your own bank's ATM.

One way around these fees is to ask for cash back at grocery stores that accept ATM cards and don't charge usage fees. Of course, you'll have to purchase something first.

ATM cards with major credit card backing, known as "debit cards," are now a commonly acceptable form of payment in most stores and restaurants. Debit cards draw money directly from your checking account. Some stores enable you to receive "cash back" on your debit card purchases as well.

SAFETY
GENERAL SUGGESTIONS   Although tourist areas are generally safe, U.S. urban areas tend to be less safe than those in Europe or Japan. You should always stay alert. This is particularly true of large American cities. If you're in doubt about which neighborhoods are safe, don't hesitate to make inquiries with the hotel front desk staff or the local tourist office.

Avoid deserted areas, especially at night, and don't go into public parks after dark unless there's a concert or similar occasion that will attract a crowd. Avoid carrying valuables with you on the street, and keep expensive cameras or electronic equipment bagged up or covered when not in use. If you're using a map, try to consult it inconspicuously—or better yet, study it before you leave your room. Hold onto your pocketbook, and place your billfold in an inside pocket. In theaters, restaurants, and other public places, keep your possessions in sight. Once you're back at your hotel, always lock your room door—don't assume that once you're inside the hotel you are automatically safe and no longer need to be aware of your surroundings.

> **Tips   In Case of Emergency**
>
> Be sure to keep a copy of all your travel papers separate from your wallet or purse, and leave a copy with someone at home should you need it faxed in an emergency.

For more about personal safety in Chicago, see "Safety" under "Fast Facts: Chicago," in chapter 3.

DRIVING SAFETY   Driving safety is important too, and carjacking is not unprecedented. Question your rental agency about personal safety and ask for a traveler-safety brochure when you pick up your car. Obtain written directions— or a map with the route clearly marked—from the agency showing how to get to your destination. (Many agencies now offer the option of renting a cellular phone for the duration of your car rental; check with the rental agent when you pick up the car.) And, if possible, arrive and depart during daylight hours.

If you drive off a highway and end up in a dodgy-looking neighborhood, leave the area as quickly as possible. If you have an accident, even on the highway, stay in your car with the doors locked until you assess the situation or until the police arrive. If you're bumped from behind on the street or are involved in a minor accident with no injuries, and the situation appears to be suspicious, motion to the other driver to follow you. Never get out of your car in such situations. Go directly to the nearest police precinct, well-lit service station, or 24-hour store. You may want to look into renting a cellphone on a short-term basis. One recommended wireless rental company is **InTouch USA** (© **800/872-7626;** www.intouchusa.com).

Park in well-lit and well-traveled areas whenever possible. Always keep your car doors locked, whether the vehicle is attended or unattended. Never leave any packages or valuables in sight. If someone attempts to rob you or steal your car, don't try to resist the thief/carjacker. Report the incident to the police department immediately by calling © **911.**

2 Getting to the U.S.

British Airways (© **0845/773-3377** in the U.K., or 800/247-9297 in the U.S.) offers direct flights from London's Heathrow Airport to Chicago. Some of the other major international carriers that service Chicago are **Aer Lingus** (© **0818/ 365-000** in Ireland, 0845/084-4444 in the U.K., or 800/424-7424 in the U.S.), **Air Canada** (© **888/247-2262** in Canada and the U.S.), **Qantas** (© **13-13-13** in Australia, or 800/227-4500 in the U.S.), and **Air New Zealand** (© **0800/ 737-767** in New Zealand, or 800/262-1234 in the U.S.). Visitors arriving by air, no matter what the port of entry, should cultivate patience and resignation before setting foot on U.S. soil. Getting through immigration control might take as long as 2 hours on some days, especially on summer weekends, so be sure to have this guidebook or something else to read. Add the time that it takes to clear Customs, and you'll see that you should make a 2- to 3-hour allowance for delays when you plan your connections between international and domestic flights.

In contrast, for the traveler arriving by car or rail from Canada, the border-crossing formalities have been streamlined to the vanishing point. People traveling by air from Canada, Bermuda, and some places in the Caribbean can sometimes clear Customs and Immigration at the point of departure, which is much quicker. For further information about travel to and arriving in Chicago, see the section "Getting There," in chapter 2.

3 Getting Around the U.S.

BY PLANE

Some large airlines (for example, Northwest and Delta) offer travelers on their transatlantic or transpacific flights special discount tickets under the name **Visit USA,** allowing mostly one-way travel from one U.S. destination to another at very low prices. These discount tickets are not on sale in the United States and must be purchased abroad in conjunction with your international ticket. This system is the best, easiest, and fastest way to see the United States at low cost. You should obtain information well in advance from your travel agent or the office of the airline concerned, because the conditions attached to these discount tickets can be changed without advance notice.

BY TRAIN

International visitors (excluding Canada) can also buy a **USA Rail Pass,** good for 15 or 30 days of unlimited travel on Amtrak (© **800/USA-RAIL;** www.amtrak.com). The pass is available through many foreign travel agents. With a foreign passport, you can also buy passes at some Amtrak offices in the United States, including locations in San Francisco, Los Angeles, Chicago, New York, Miami, Boston, and Washington, D.C. Reservations are generally required and should be made for each part of your trip as early as possible. Regional rail passes are also available.

BY BUS

Although bus travel is often the most economical form of public transit for short hops between U.S. cities, it can also be slow and uncomfortable—certainly not an option for everyone (particularly when Amtrak, which is far more luxurious, offers similar rates). **Greyhound/Trailways** (© **800/231-2222;** www.greyhound.com), the sole nationwide bus line, offers an **International Ameripass** that must be purchased before coming to the United States, or by phone through the Greyhound International Office at the Port Authority Bus Terminal in New York City (© **212/971-0492**). The pass can be obtained from foreign travel agents or through Greyhound's website (order at least 21 days before your departure to the U.S.) and costs less than the domestic version. 2003 passes cost as follows: 4 days ($155), 7 days ($204), 10 days ($254), 15 days ($314), 21 days ($364), 30 days ($424), 45 days ($464), or 60 days ($574). You can get more info on the pass at the website, or by calling © **402/330-8552.** In addition, special rates are available for seniors and students.

BY CAR

Unless you plan to spend the bulk of your vacation time in cities where walking is the best and easiest way to get around, the most cost-effective, convenient, and comfortable way to travel around the United States is by car. The interstate highway system connects cities and towns all over the country; in addition to these high-speed, limited-access roadways, there's an extensive network of federal, state, and local highways and roads. Some of the national car rental companies include **Alamo** (© 800/327-9633; www.goalamo.com), **Avis** (© 800/331-1212; www.avis.com), **Budget** (© 800/527-0700; www.budget.com),

Dollar (☎ 800/800-4000; www.dollar.com), **Hertz** (☎ 800/654-3131; www.hertz.com), **National** (☎ 800/227-7368; www.nationalcar.com), and **Thrifty** (☎ 800/367-2277; www.thrifty.com).

If you plan to rent a car in the United States, you probably won't need the services of an additional automobile organization. If you're planning to buy or borrow a car, automobile-association membership is recommended. **AAA, the American Automobile Association** (☎ 800/222-4357), is the country's largest auto club and supplies its members with maps, insurance, and, most important, emergency road service. The cost of joining runs from $63 for singles to $87 for two members, but if you're a member of a foreign auto club with reciprocal arrangements, you can enjoy free AAA service in America.

✐ *FAST FACTS:* **For the International Traveler**

Automobile Organizations Auto clubs will supply maps, suggested routes, guidebooks, accident and bail-bond insurance, and emergency road service. The **American Automobile Association (AAA)** is the major auto club in the United States. If you belong to an auto club in your home country, inquire about AAA reciprocity before you leave. You may be able to join AAA even if you're not a member of a reciprocal club; to inquire, call AAA (☎ **800/222-4357**). AAA is actually an organization of regional auto clubs; so look under "AAA Automobile Club" in the White Pages of the telephone directory. AAA has a nationwide emergency road service telephone number (☎ 800/AAA-HELP).

Business Hours Offices are usually open weekdays from 9am to 5pm. Banks are open weekdays from 9am to 3pm or later and sometimes Saturday mornings. Stores typically open between 9 and 10am and close between 5 and 6pm from Monday through Saturday. Stores in shopping complexes or malls tend to stay open late: until about 9pm on weekdays and Saturday, and many malls and larger department stores are open on Sundays.

Currency & Currency Exchange See "Money" under "Preparing for Your Trip," earlier in this chapter.

Drinking Laws The legal age for purchase and consumption of alcoholic beverages is 21; proof of age is required and often requested at bars, nightclubs, and restaurants, so it's always a good idea to bring ID when you go out. In Chicago, bars may remain open until any time from 2 to 5am, depending on the nature of their license and the day of the week. Beer and wine can often be purchased in supermarkets, but liquor laws vary from state to state.

Do not carry open containers of alcohol in your car or any public area that isn't zoned for alcohol consumption. The police can fine you on the spot. And nothing will ruin your trip faster than getting a citation for DUI ("driving under the influence"), so don't even think about driving while intoxicated.

Electricity Like Canada, the United States uses 110 to 120 volts AC (60 cycles), compared to 220 to 240 volts AC (50 cycles) in most of Europe, Australia, and New Zealand. If your small appliances use 220 to 240 volts, you'll need a 110-volt transformer and a plug adapter with two flat parallel pins to operate them here. Downward converters that change 220 to 240 volts to 110 to 120 volts are difficult to find in the United States, so bring one with you. You can find converters and plug adapters at **Radio Shack,** which has locations throughout the city, including 310 N. Michigan Ave., 1 block south of the river (✆ **312/236-1485**), and in the Merchandise Mart (✆ **312/527-5505**).

Embassies & Consulates   All embassies are located in the nation's capital, Washington, D.C. Some consulates are located in Chicago, and most nations have a mission to the United Nations in New York City. Listed here are the embassies and the Chicago consulates of the major English-speaking countries. If your country isn't listed below, call directory information in Washington, D.C. (✆ **202/555-1212**), or Chicago (✆ **312/555-1212**) for the number of your national embassy or consulate.

The embassy of **Australia** is at 1601 Massachusetts Ave. NW, Washington, DC 20036 (✆ **202/797-3000;** www.austemb.org). There is no consulate in Chicago.

The embassy of **Canada** is at 501 Pennsylvania Ave. NW, Washington, DC 20001 (✆ **202/682-1740;** www.cdnemb-washdc.org). The consulate in Chicago is located at 180 N. Stetson Ave., Suite 2400, Chicago, IL 60601 (✆ **312/616-1860**).

The embassy of **Ireland** is at 2234 Massachusetts Ave. NW, Washington, DC 20008 (✆ **202/462-3939**). The consulate in Chicago is located at 400 N. Michigan Ave., Suite 911, Chicago, IL 60611 (✆ **312/337-1868**).

The embassy of **New Zealand** is at 37 Observatory Circle NW, Washington, DC 20008 (✆ **202/328-4800;** www.emb.com/nzemb). There is no consulate in Chicago.

The embassy of the **United Kingdom** is at 3100 Massachusetts Ave. NW, Washington, DC 20008 (✆ **202/462-1340**). The consulate in Chicago is located in the Wrigley Building, 400 N. Michigan Ave., Suite 1300, Chicago, IL 60611 (✆ **312/346-1810**).

Emergencies   Call ✆ **911** to report a fire, call the police, or get an ambulance anywhere in the United States. This is a toll-free call. (No coins are required at public telephones.)

If you encounter serious problems, contact the **Traveler's Aid Society International** (✆ **773/894-2427;** www.travelersaid.org). This nationwide, nonprofit, social-service organization geared to helping travelers in difficult straits offers services that might include reuniting families separated while traveling, providing food and/or shelter to people stranded without cash, or even emotional counseling. If you're in trouble, seek them out. The office, located in Terminal 3 at O'Hare International Airport, is open Monday to Friday 8:30am to 9pm, and Saturday and Sunday 9am to 9pm.

Gasoline (Petrol)   Petrol is known as gasoline (or simply "gas") in the United States, and petrol stations are known as both gas stations and service stations. Gasoline costs about half as much here as it does in Europe (about $1.80 per gal. in Chicago at press time), and taxes are already included in the printed price. One U.S. gallon equals 3.8 liters or .85 imperial gallons.

Holidays Banks, government offices, post offices, and many stores, restaurants, and museums are closed on the following legal national holidays: January 1 (New Year's Day), the third Monday in January (Martin Luther King, Jr. Day), the third Monday in February (Presidents' Day, Washington's Birthday), the last Monday in May (Memorial Day), July 4 (Independence Day), the first Monday in September (Labor Day), the second Monday in October (Columbus Day), November 11 (Veterans' Day/Armistice Day), the fourth Thursday in November (Thanksgiving Day), and December 25 (Christmas). In addition, many city offices are closed in Chicago for Casimir Pulaski Day, marking the birthday of a Polish-born Revolutionary War hero, which is observed on the first Monday in March. Also, the Tuesday following the first Monday in November is Election Day and is a federal government holiday in presidential-election years (held every 4 years, and next in 2004).

Information There are multilingual information desks in all of the terminals at O'Hare Airport, including two at the international terminal. The Chicago Office of Tourism distributes a brochure titled *Chicago Map and Guide* in five languages—English, Spanish, French, German, and Japanese.

Legal Aid If you are "pulled over" for a minor infraction (such as speeding), never attempt to pay the fine directly to a police officer; this could be construed as attempted bribery, a much more serious crime. Pay fines by mail, or directly into the hands of the clerk of the court. If accused of a more serious offense, say and do nothing before consulting a lawyer. Here the burden is on the state to prove a person's guilt beyond a reasonable doubt, and everyone has the right to remain silent, whether he or she is suspected of a crime or actually arrested. Once arrested, a person can make one telephone call to a party of his or her choice. Call your embassy or consulate.

Mail If you aren't sure what your address will be in the United States, mail can be sent to you, in your name, c/o General Delivery at the main post office of the city or region where you expect to be. (Call ✆ **800/275-8777** for information on the nearest post office.) The addressee must pick up mail in person and must produce proof of identity (driver's license, passport, etc.). Most post offices will hold your mail for up to one month, and are open Monday to Friday from 8am to 6pm, and Saturday from 9am to 3pm. Chicago's main post office is at 433 W. Van Buren St. (✆ **312/654-3895**).

Generally found at intersections, mailboxes are blue with a red-and-white stripe and carry the inscription U.S. MAIL. If your mail is addressed to a U.S. destination, don't forget to add the five-digit postal code (or ZIP code), after the two-letter abbreviation of the state to which the mail is addressed. This is essential to prompt delivery.

At press time, domestic postage rates were 23¢ for a postcard and 37¢ for a letter. For international mail, a first-class letter of up to one-half ounce costs 80¢ (60¢ to Canada and Mexico); a first-class postcard costs 70¢ (50¢ to Canada and Mexico); and a preprinted postal aerogramme costs 70¢.

Measurements See the chart on the inside front cover of this book for details on converting metric measurements to U.S. equivalents.

Medical Emergencies If you become ill, consult your hotel concierge or desk staff for a physician recommendation. The best hospital emergency room in Chicago is, by consensus, at **Northwestern Memorial Hospital,** which opened its new state-of-the-art medical center right off North Michigan Avenue in spring 1999. The emergency department (© **312/ 926-5188,** or 312/944-2358 for TDD access) is located at 250 E. Erie St. near Fairbanks Court. For an ambulance, dial © **911.**

Taxes The United States has no value-added tax (VAT) or other indirect tax at the national level. Every state, county, and city has the right to levy its own local tax on all purchases, including hotel and restaurant checks, airline tickets, and so on. Chicago sales tax is 8.75%. Restaurants in the central part of the city, roughly the 312 area code, are taxed an additional 1%, for a total of 9.75%. The hotel room tax is 3%.

Telephone, Telegraph, Telex & Fax The telephone system in the United States is run by private corporations, so rates, especially for long-distance service and operator-assisted calls, can vary widely. Generally, hotel surcharges on long-distance and local calls are astronomical, so you're usually better off using a **public pay telephone,** which you'll find clearly marked in most public buildings and private establishments as well as on the street. Convenience grocery stores and gas stations always have them. Many convenience groceries and packaging services sell **prepaid calling cards** in denominations up to $50; these can be the least expensive way to call home. Many public phones at airports now accept American Express, MasterCard, and Visa credit cards. **Local calls** made from public pay phones in most locales cost either 25¢ or 35¢. Pay phones do not accept pennies, and few will take anything larger than a quarter.

You may want to look into leasing a cellphone for the duration of your trip.

Most long-distance and international calls can be dialed directly from any phone. **For calls within the United States and to Canada,** dial 1 followed by the area code and the seven-digit number. **For other international calls,** dial 011 followed by the country code, city code, and the telephone number of the person you are calling.

Calls to area codes **800, 888, 866,** and **877** are toll free. However, calls to numbers in area codes **700** and **900** (chat lines, bulletin boards, "dating" services, and so on) can be very expensive—usually a charge of 95¢ to $3 or more per minute, and they sometimes have minimum charges that can run as high as $15 or more.

For **reversed-charge or collect calls,** and for person-to-person calls, dial 0 (zero, not the letter O) followed by the area code and number you want; an operator will then come on the line, and you should specify that you are calling collect, or person-to-person, or both. If your operator-assisted call is international, ask for the overseas operator.

For **local directory assistance** ("information"), dial 411; for long-distance information, dial 1, and then the appropriate area code and 555-1212.

Telegraph and telex services are provided primarily by Western Union. You can bring your telegram into the nearest Western Union office (there are hundreds across the country) or dictate it over the phone (© **800/ 325-6000**). You can also telegraph money, or have it telegraphed to you, very quickly over the Western Union system, but this service can cost as much as 15 to 20 percent of the amount sent.

Most hotels have **fax machines** available for guest use. (Be sure to ask about the charge to use it.) Many hotel rooms are even wired for guests' fax machines. A less expensive way to send and receive faxes may be at stores such as Mail Boxes Etc., a national chain of packing service shops. (Look in the Yellow Pages directory under "Packing Services.")

There are two kinds of telephone directories in the United States. The so-called **White Pages** list private households and business subscribers in alphabetical order. The inside front cover lists emergency numbers for police, fire, ambulance, the Coast Guard, poison-control center, crime-victims hotline, and so on. The first few pages will tell you how to make long-distance and international calls, complete with country codes and area codes. Government numbers are usually printed on blue paper within the White Pages. Printed on yellow paper, the so-called **Yellow Pages** list local services, businesses, industries, and houses of worship according to activity with an index at the front or back. (Drugstores/pharmacies and restaurants are also listed by geographic location.) The Yellow Pages also include city plans or detailed area maps, postal ZIP codes, and public transportation routes.

Time The continental United States is divided into **four time zones:** eastern standard time (EST), central standard time (CST), mountain standard time (MST), and Pacific standard time (PST). Alaska and Hawaii have their own zones. For example, noon in New York City (EST) is 11am in Chicago (CST), 10am in Denver (MST), 9am in Los Angeles (PST), 8am in Anchorage (AST), and 7am in Honolulu (HST).

Daylight saving time is in effect from 1am on the first Sunday in April through 1am on the last Sunday in October, except in Arizona, Hawaii, part of Indiana, and Puerto Rico. Daylight saving time moves the clock 1 hour ahead of standard time.

Tipping Tips are a very important part of certain workers' salaries, so it's necessary to leave appropriate gratuities. In hotels, tip **bellhops** at least $1 per bag ($2–$3 if you have a lot of luggage) and tip the **chamber staff** $1 to $2 per day (more if you've left a disaster area for him or her to clean up). Tip the **doorman** or **concierge** only if he or she has provided you with some specific service (for example, calling a cab for you or obtaining difficult-to-get theater tickets). Tip the **valet-parking attendant** $1 every time you get your car.

In restaurants, bars, and nightclubs, tip **service staff** 15% to 20% of the check, tip **bartenders** 10% to 15%, tip **checkroom attendants** $1 per garment, and tip **valet-parking attendants** $1 per vehicle. Tip the **doorman** only if he has provided you with some specific service (such as calling a cab for you).

As for other service personnel, tip **cab drivers** 15% of the fare; tip **skycaps** at airports at least $1 per bag ($2–$3 if you have a lot of luggage); and tip **hairdressers** and **barbers** 15% to 20%.

Toilets Often euphemistically referred to as "restrooms," public toilets are nonexistent on the streets of Chicago, but they can be found in hotel lobbies, bars, restaurants, museums, department stores, railway and bus stations, or service stations. Large hotels and fast-food restaurants are probably the best bet for good, clean facilities. If possible, avoid the toilets at parks and beaches, which tend to be dirty; some may be unsafe. Restaurants and bars in resorts or heavily visited areas may reserve their restrooms for patrons. Some establishments display a notice indicating this. You can ignore this sign or, better yet, avoid arguments by paying for a cup of coffee or a soft drink, which will qualify you as a patron.

Tour Guides There are two respected multilingual tour guide services in Chicago: **Chicago Tour Guides Institute** (© 773/276-6683; fax 773/252-3729; www.chicagoguide.net) and **Inlingua International Tours** (© 312/641-0488; fax 312/641-1724).

Appendix B:
Useful Toll-Free Numbers & Websites

AIRLINES

Aer Lingus
✆ 800/474-7424 in the U.S.
✆ 0818/365-000 in Ireland
www.aerlingus.com

Air Canada
✆ 888/247-2262
www.aircanada.ca

Air New Zealand
✆ 800/262-1234 in the U.S.
✆ 0800/737-767 in New Zealand
www.airnewzealand.com

Alaska Airlines
✆ 800/252-7522
www.alaskaair.com

American Airlines
✆ 800/433-7300
www.aa.com

American Trans Air
✆ 800/I-FLY-ATA
www.ata.com

America West Airlines
✆ 800/235-9292
www.americawest.com

British Airways
✆ 800/247-9297
✆ 0845/773-3377 in the U.K.
www.britishairways.com

Continental Airlines
✆ 800/525-0280
www.continental.com

Delta Air Lines
✆ 800/221-1212
www.delta.com

Frontier Airlines
✆ 800/432-1359
www.frontierairlines.com

Hawaiian Airlines
✆ 800/367-5320 in the continental
 U.S. and Canada
✆ 800/882-8811 in Hawaii
www.hawaiianair.com

jetBlue Airlines
✆ 800/538-2583
www.jetblue.com

Midwest Express
✆ 800/452-2022
www.midwestexpress.com

Northwest Airlines
✆ 800/225-2525
www.nwa.com

Qantas
✆ 800/227-4500 in the U.S.
✆ 13-13-13 in Australia
www.qantas.com

Southwest Airlines
✆ 800/435-9792
www.southwest.com

United Airlines
✆ 800/241-6522
www.united.com

US Airways
✆ 800/428-4322
www.usairways.com

Virgin Atlantic Airways
✆ 800/862-8621 in continental U.S.
✆ 0293/747-747 in the U.K.
www.virgin-atlantic.com

CAR-RENTAL AGENCIES

Advantage
© 800/777-5500
www.advantagerentacar.com

Alamo
© 800/327-9633
www.goalamo.com

Avis
© 800/331-1212
www.avis.com

Budget
© 800/527-0700
www.budget.com

Dollar
© 800/800-4000
www.dollarcar.com

Enterprise
© 800/325-8007
www.enterprise.com

Hertz
© 800/654-3131
www.hertz.com

National
© 800/CAR-RENT
www.nationalcar.com

Payless
© 800/PAYLESS
www.paylesscar.com

Rent-A-Wreck
© 800/944-7501
www.rentawreck.com

Thrifty
© 800/367-2277
www.thrifty.com

MAJOR HOTEL & MOTEL CHAINS

Best Western International
© 800/780-7234
www.bestwestern.com

Clarion Hotels
© 800/CLARION
www.hotelchoice.com

Comfort Inns
© 800/228-5150
www.hotelchoice.com

Courtyard by Marriott
© 800/321-2211
www.courtyard.com

Days Inn
© 800/325-2525
www.daysinn.com

Doubletree Hotels
© 800/222-TREE
www.doubletree.com

Econo Lodges
© 800/55-ECONO
www.hotelchoice.com

Embassy Suites
© 800/EMBASSY
www.embassy-suites.com

Fairfield Inn by Marriott
© 800/228-2800
www.fairfieldinn.com

Hampton Inns
© 800/HAMPTON
www.hampton-inn.com

Hilton Hotels
© 800/HILTONS
www.hilton.com

Holiday Inn
© 800/HOLIDAY
www.holiday-inn.com

Howard Johnson
© 800/I-GO-HOJO
www.hojo.com

Hyatt Hotels & Resorts
© 888/591-1234
www.hyatt.com

InterContinental Hotels & Resorts
© 888/567-8725
www.intercontinental.com

La Quinta Motor Inns
© 800/531-5900
www.laquinta.com

Marriott Hotels
© 888/236-2427
www.marriott.com

Motel 6
© 800/4-MOTEL6
www.motel6.com

Omni Hotels
© 800/THE-OMNI
www.omnihotels.com

Quality Inns
© 800/228-5151
www.hotelchoice.com

Radisson Hotels
© 888/201-1717
www.radisson.com

Ramada Inns
© 888/298-2054
www.ramada.com

Red Roof Inns
© 800/RED-ROOF
www.redroof.com

Residence Inn by Marriott
© 800/331-3131
www.residenceinn.com

Rodeway Inns
© 800/228-2000
www.hotelchoice.com

Sheraton Hotels & Resorts
© 888/625-5144
www.sheraton.com

Super 8 Motels
© 800/800-8000
www.super8.com

Travelodge
© 800/578-7878
www.travelodge.com

Vagabond Inns
© 800/522-1555
www.vagabondinn.com

Westin Hotels & Resorts
© 800/937-8461
www.westin.com

Wyndham Hotels and Resorts
© 800/WYNDHAM
www.wyndham.com

Index

See also Accommodations and Restaurant indexes, below.

FROMMER'S® COMPLETE TRAVEL GUIDES

Alaska
Alaska Cruises & Ports of Call
Amsterdam
Argentina & Chile
Arizona
Atlanta
Australia
Austria
Bahamas
Barcelona, Madrid & Seville
Beijing
Belgium, Holland & Luxembourg
Bermuda
Boston
Brazil
British Columbia & the Canadian Rockies
Budapest & the Best of Hungary
California
Canada
Cancún, Cozumel & the Yucatán
Cape Cod, Nantucket & Martha's Vineyard
Caribbean
Caribbean Cruises & Ports of Call
Caribbean Ports of Call
Carolinas & Georgia
Chicago
China
Colorado
Costa Rica
Denmark
Denver, Boulder & Colorado Springs
England
Europe
European Cruises & Ports of Call
Florida

France
Germany
Great Britain
Greece
Greek Islands
Hawaii
Hong Kong
Honolulu, Waikiki & Oahu
Ireland
Israel
Italy
Jamaica
Japan
Las Vegas
London
Los Angeles
Maryland & Delaware
Maui
Mexico
Montana & Wyoming
Montréal & Québec City
Munich & the Bavarian Alps
Nashville & Memphis
Nepal
New England
New Mexico
New Orleans
New York City
New Zealand
Northern Italy
Nova Scotia, New Brunswick & Prince Edward Island
Oregon
Paris
Philadelphia & the Amish Country
Portugal
Prague & the Best of the Czech Republic

Provence & the Riviera
Puerto Rico
Rome
San Antonio & Austin
San Diego
San Francisco
Santa Fe, Taos & Albuquerque
Scandinavia
Scotland
Seattle & Portland
Shanghai
Singapore & Malaysia
South Africa
South America
South Florida
South Pacific
Southeast Asia
Spain
Sweden
Switzerland
Texas
Thailand
Tokyo
Toronto
Tuscany & Umbria
USA
Utah
Vancouver & Victoria
Vermont, New Hampshire & Maine
Vienna & the Danube Valley
Virgin Islands
Virginia
Walt Disney World® & Orlando
Washington, D.C.
Washington State

FROMMER'S® DOLLAR-A-DAY GUIDES

Australia from $50 a Day
California from $70 a Day
Caribbean from $70 a Day
England from $75 a Day
Europe from $70 a Day

Florida from $70 a Day
Hawaii from $80 a Day
Ireland from $60 a Day
Italy from $70 a Day
London from $85 a Day

New York from $90 a Day
Paris from $80 a Day
San Francisco from $70 a Day
Washington, D.C. from $80 a Day

FROMMER'S® PORTABLE GUIDES

Acapulco, Ixtapa & Zihuatanejo
Amsterdam
Aruba
Australia's Great Barrier Reef
Bahamas
Berlin
Big Island of Hawaii
Boston
California Wine Country
Cancún
Charleston & Savannah
Chicago
Disneyland®
Dublin
Florence

Frankfurt
Hong Kong
Houston
Las Vegas
London
Los Angeles
Los Cabos & Baja
Maine Coast
Maui
Miami
New Orleans
New York City
Paris
Phoenix & Scottsdale

Portland
Puerto Rico
Puerto Vallarta, Manzanillo & Guadalajara
Rio de Janeiro
San Diego
San Francisco
Seattle
Sydney
Tampa & St. Petersburg
Vancouver
Venice
Virgin Islands
Washington, D.C.

FROMMER'S® NATIONAL PARK GUIDES

Banff & Jasper
Family Vacations in the National Parks
Grand Canyon

National Parks of the American West
Rocky Mountain

Yellowstone & Grand Teton
Yosemite & Sequoia/ Kings Canyon
Zion & Bryce Canyon

FROMMER'S® MEMORABLE WALKS

Chicago	New York	San Francisco
London	Paris	Washington, D.C.

FROMMER'S® GREAT OUTDOOR GUIDES

Arizona & New Mexico	Northern California	Vermont & New Hampshire
New England	Southern New England	

SUZY GERSHMAN'S BORN TO SHOP GUIDES

Born to Shop: France	Born to Shop: Italy	Born to Shop: New York
Born to Shop: Hong Kong, Shanghai & Beijing	Born to Shop: London	Born to Shop: Paris

FROMMER'S® IRREVERENT GUIDES

Amsterdam	Los Angeles	San Francisco
Boston	Manhattan	Seattle & Portland
Chicago	New Orleans	Vancouver
Las Vegas	Paris	Walt Disney World®
London	Rome	Washington, D.C.

FROMMER'S® BEST-LOVED DRIVING TOURS

Britain	Germany	Northern Italy
California	Ireland	Scotland
Florida	Italy	Spain
France	New England	Tuscany & Umbria

HANGING OUT™ GUIDES

Hanging Out in England	Hanging Out in France	Hanging Out in Italy
Hanging Out in Europe	Hanging Out in Ireland	Hanging Out in Spain

THE UNOFFICIAL GUIDES®

Bed & Breakfasts and Country Inns in:
California
Great Lakes States
Mid-Atlantic
New England
Northwest
Rockies
Southeast
Southwest
Best RV & Tent Campgrounds in:
California & the West
Florida & the Southeast
Great Lakes States
Mid-Atlantic
Northeast
Northwest & Central Plains

Southwest & South Central Plains
U.S.A.
Beyond Disney
Branson, Missouri
California with Kids
Chicago
Cruises
Disneyland®
Florida with Kids
Golf Vacations in the Eastern U.S.
Great Smoky & Blue Ridge Region
Inside Disney
Hawaii
Las Vegas
London

Mid-Atlantic with Kids
Mini Las Vegas
Mini-Mickey
New England and New York with Kids
New Orleans
New York City
Paris
San Francisco
Skiing in the West
Southeast with Kids
Walt Disney World®
Walt Disney World® for Grown-up
Walt Disney World® with Kids
Washington, D.C.
World's Best Diving Vacations

SPECIAL-INTEREST TITLES

Frommer's Adventure Guide to Australia & New Zealand
Frommer's Adventure Guide to Central America
Frommer's Adventure Guide to India & Pakistan
Frommer's Adventure Guide to South America
Frommer's Adventure Guide to Southeast Asia
Frommer's Adventure Guide to Southern Africa
Frommer's Britain's Best Bed & Breakfasts and Country Inns
Frommer's Caribbean Hideaways
Frommer's Exploring America by RV
Frommer's Fly Safe, Fly Smart
Frommer's France's Best Bed & Breakfasts and Country Inns
Frommer's Gay & Lesbian Europe

Frommer's Italy's Best Bed & Breakfasts and Country Inns
Frommer's New York City with Kids
Frommer's Ottawa with Kids
Frommer's Road Atlas Britain
Frommer's Road Atlas Europe
Frommer's Road Atlas France
Frommer's Toronto with Kids
Frommer's Vancouver with Kids
Frommer's Washington, D.C., with Kids
Israel Past & Present
The New York Times' Guide to Unforgettable Weekends
Places Rated Almanac
Retirement Places Rated

Booked seat 6A, open return.

Rented red 4-wheel drive.

Reserved cabin, no running water.

Discovered space.

over 700 airlines, 50,000 hotels, 50 rental car companies and
) cruise and vacation packages, you can create the perfect get-
/ for you. Choose the car, the room, even the ground you walk on.

Travelocity.com
A Sabre Company
Go Virtually Anywhere.